KELSEN REVISITED

Forty years after his death, Hans Kelsen (1881–1973) remains one of the most discussed and influential legal philosophers of our time. This collection of new essays takes Kelsen's Pure Theory of Law as a stimulus, aiming to move forward the debate on several central issues in contemporary jurisprudence. The essays in Part I address legal validity, the normativity of law and Kelsen's famous but puzzling idea of a legal system's 'basic norm'. Part II engages with the difficult issues raised by the social realities of law and the actual practices of legal officials. Part III focuses on conceptual features of legal systems and the logical structure of legal norms. All the essays were written for this volume by internationally renowned scholars from seven countries. Also included, in English translation, is an important polemical essay by Kelsen himself.

Kelsen Revisited

New Essays on the Pure Theory of Law

Edited by
Luís Duarte d'Almeida
John Gardner
and
Leslie Green

·HART·
PUBLISHING

OXFORD AND PORTLAND, OREGON
2013

Published in the United Kingdom by Hart Publishing Ltd
16C Worcester Place, Oxford, OX1 2JW
Telephone: +44 (0)1865 517530
Fax: +44 (0)1865 510710
E-mail: mail@hartpub.co.uk
Website: http://www.hartpub.co.uk

Published in North America (US and Canada) by
Hart Publishing
c/o International Specialized Book Services
920 NE 58th Avenue, Suite 300
Portland, OR 97213-3786
USA
Tel: +1 503 287 3093 or toll-free: (1) 800 944 6190
Fax: +1 503 280 8832
E-mail: orders@isbs.com
Website: http://www.isbs.com

British Library Cataloguing in Publication Data
Data Available

ISBN: 978-1-84946-456-7

Typeset by Hope Services, Abingdon
Printed and bound by CPI Group (UK) Ltd, Croydon, CR0 4YY

Acknowledgments

In the preparation of this volume we incurred more debts than we can here discharge.

First, and most important, thanks to the many speakers and attendees who made the 2010 *Legal Science and Legal Theory* conference a place where real progress was made in grappling with the ideas of one of the most important and original jurists of our time.

Second, that gathering of distinguished scholars could not have been possible but for the cooperation and funding provided by Austrian Science Fund Project 'Bibliographical Research on Hans Kelsen' at the University of Vienna (P19287, www.hanskelsen.eu); the support of the Oxford Law Faculty, the Oxford Centre for Ethics & Philosophy of Law and the University of Buenos Aires; and the generosity of Juan Pablo Alonso, Carole Angier, Jürgen Busch, Andrea Dolcetti, Tony Honoré and Thomas Olechowski with their time.

Third, we thank the Hans Kelsen-Institut in Vienna for generous permission to translate and reprint Kelsen's essay 'A "Realistic" Theory of Law and the Pure Theory of Law'.

Fourth, we thank James Lowe for very good research assistance.

Finally, we thank Richard Hart and the referees and editors at Hart Publishing for their encouragement and support of this project.

L.D.A.
J.G.
L.G.

Contents

Contributors

Uta Bindreiter is Associate Professor of Jurisprudence at Lund University.

Jes Bjarup is Professor of Law Emeritus at Stockholm University.

Eugenio Bulygin is Professor of Jurisprudence Emeritus at the University of Buenos Aires.

Pierluigi Chiassoni is Professor of Jurisprudence at the University of Genoa.

Luís Duarte d'Almeida is Chancellor's Fellow in Law at the University of Edinburgh.

John Gardner is Professor of Jurisprudence at the University of Oxford.

Leslie Green is Professor of the Philosophy of Law at the University of Oxford.

Riccardo Guastini is Professor of Jurisprudence and Director of the Department of Legal Culture 'Giovanni Tarello' at the University of Genoa.

Pablo E Navarro is Professor of Legal Philosophy at the Universidad Nacional del Sur, and researcher of the Argentinean National Council for Research in Science and Technology (CONICET).

Stanley L Paulson is sometime Mercator Professor and continuing guest professor at the University of Kiel.

Richard HS Tur is Emeritus Fellow of Oriel College, Oxford.

Bert van Roermund is Professor of Philosophy and senior researcher in the Centre for Transboundary Legal Development at Tilburg University, and annual guest professor at KU Leuven.

1

Introduction

LUÍS DUARTE D'ALMEIDA, JOHN GARDNER and LESLIE GREEN

I have little doubt that Bentham was the greatest analytical jurist of the 19th century and Kelsen of the 20th.

HLA Hart[1]

I. KELSEN IN OXFORD

HANS KELSEN (1881–1973) is universally regarded as the twentieth century's foremost jurist and legal philosopher, and remains, 40 years after his death, one of the most discussed. Not many topics in general jurisprudence exist on which he did not have important things to say. His Pure Theory of Law, developed over the course of many decades, is arguably the single most important intellectual achievement of contemporary jurisprudence. And many leading legal philosophers working in the past six or seven decades – including Oxford's HLA Hart, who regarded Kelsen as a 'writer of genius',[2] albeit one 'both fascinating and puzzling'[3] – have developed their views in dialogue with the Pure Theory. It is no wonder that jurisprudence syllabi in many universities still assign a central place to Kelsen's views, or that the Pure Theory forms the object of an impressive and ever-growing body of scholarship.

This volume is a selection of 10 original essays that refine and develop ideas first presented at the conference, *Legal Science and Legal Theory*, held at the University of Oxford in September 2010 to mark the 50th anniversary of the publication of the enormously influential second edition of Kelsen's *Pure*

[1] See HLA Hart, 'Answers to Eight Questions', a 1988 interview (previously unpublished) forthcoming in L Duarte d'Almeida, J Edwards and A Dolcetti (eds), *Reading HLA Hart's 'The Concept of Law'* (Oxford, Hart Publishing, 2013).

[2] ibid.

[3] HLA Hart, 'Introduction' in his *Essays in Jurisprudence and Philosophy* (Oxford, Clarendon Press, 1983) 18.

Theory of Law.[4] It was a lively and fruitful event that brought together scholars from Argentina, Austria, Brazil, Canada, Chile, Croatia, Denmark, France, Germany, Italy, Japan, Mexico, The Netherlands, Poland, Portugal, Romania, Russia, Slovenia, Spain, Sweden, the UK and the USA. Oxford might strike some as an odd venue for a conference on Kelsen. But the 'Oxford school' of jurisprudence owes as much to the influence of Kelsen as it does to that of its founder, HLA Hart. Kelsen's influence can be seen in the work of Julie Dickson, John Gardner, Leslie Green, Jim Harris, Tony Honoré, Joseph Raz and Richard Tur and, in the backhanded compliment of strenuous criticism, also in the work of John Finnis.

II. VALIDITY AND BINDINGNESS

The collection is divided into three parts. The essays in Part I address and seek to clarify the meaning of the legal 'ought' while engaging with Kelsen's bewildering idea of a legal system's 'basic norm'. The first idea is often known in English under the somewhat equivocal name of the 'normativity' of law: the fact that at least some legal statements are, or can be presented as, statements of what someone *ought* to do. The second idea is part of Kelsen's discussion of the first. Since all law is positive, a matter of fact, it can at the same time be a matter of norm only if there is, in some sense or in some way, a further, different, norm, directing us to comply with positive law. But how could that possibly be?

Bert van Roermund's contribution opens with a critical overview – which those less familiar with the Pure Theory may find especially helpful – of Kelsen's account of legal norms and 'empowerment model' of legal validity. This model, van Roermund argues, has considerable advantages, but it also gives rise to a serious dilemma concerning the status of so-called 'unlawful' law-making decisions. Kelsen tried to tackle this issue with his doctrine of the 'alternative character'[5] of the legal norm – an idea that both Pablo Navarro and Richard Tur (the latter more sympathetically than the former) also discuss in their contributions. Van Roermund proposes to avoid Kelsen's dilemma by enriching the empowerment model with a distinction between two different normative statuses that any candidate authoritative law-making act may have. Such acts are typically recognised as authoritative acts of conflict-settlement, and to say this, van Roermund argues, is to ascribe to the norm that the authority claims to be creating a specific normative status – 'bindingness', as he proposes to call it – that is independent from (though

[4] H Kelsen, *Reine Rechtslehre*, 2nd edn (Vienna, Franz Deuticke, 1960), translated into English as *The Pure Theory of Law*, 2nd edn, M Knight transl (Berkeley, University of California Press, 1967).
[5] ibid 267ff, 273f.

compatible with) its 'validity'. He then connects this proposal to a critical discussion of some aspects of Kelsen's basic norm – a topic which Stanley Paulson's and Riccardo Guastini's essays take up at greater length, also very critically.

The idea of a 'basic norm' was introduced in 1914, Paulson notes, as an attempt to answer a particular sort of 'why'-question. This marked a change in Kelsen's thought. In his 1911 *Hauptprobleme der Staatsrechtslehre*, Kelsen had steered clear of 'why'-questions, and particularly of what Paulson calls the 'overriding "why"-question': the substantive, 'justificatory' question of 'why the law ought to be obeyed' (p 48).[6] From the legal standpoint, thought Kelsen, this moral question cannot intelligibly be raised, for one already *assumes* that 'the legal norm *ought* to be complied with and applied' (p 47). What happens in 1914? 'Too astute', says Paulson, not to work this through, Kelsen comes to think that there is indeed room, from the legal point of view, to engage with that question. His own 'purity' postulate prevents him from offering moral answers, but he now believes that a different kind of answer is available: a 'transcendental' answer, in Kantian vein. Paulson has an interesting argument why this answer must be wrong. But he also believes that Kelsen did not really have to tackle that 'overriding' question. This is because Paulson thinks that Kelsen's question is after all not quite equivalent to the classical question of why law is to be complied with. It was rather, Paulson contends, a question concerning the 'nomological character' of legal science: that is, a question about legal science's 'lawfulness (*Gesetzlichkeit*) running parallel to the law of nature'.[7] This is a bold and controversial claim. Many influential readings of the Pure Theory suppose that for Kelsen the legal 'ought' is essentially a sort of 'moral ought';[8] it is what contemporary legal philosophers call a matter of 'justified normativity'. Paulson denies this,[9] and the matter remains hotly debated.

Among the unconvinced we would probably find Riccardo Guastini, who offers a more orthodox, though no less stringent, assessment of Kelsen's basic norm. Unlike Paulson, Guastini believes that the claim that 'validity is (or entails) binding force' is 'one of the central theses of the Pure Theory of Law' (p 68). He also thinks that Kelsen was genuinely ambivalent, or in any case genuinely confused, about the nature of the basic norm. Is it a power-conferring norm authorising the framers of the historically first constitution?

[6] Page references to the essays in this collection are given in brackets in the text.

[7] *cf* SL Paulson, 'A "Justified Normativity" Thesis in Hans Kelsen's Pure Theory of Law? Rejoinders to Robert Alexy and Joseph Raz' in M Klatt (ed), *Institutionalized Reason. The Jurisprudence of Robert Alexy* (Oxford, Oxford University Press, 2012) 88. For more on the topic, see the last essay in the present volume.

[8] See eg A Ross, 'Validity and the Conflict Between Legal Positivism and Natural Law' (1961) *Revista Jurídica de Buenos Aires* 46ff; or J Raz, 'Kelsen's Theory of the Basic Norm' in *The Authority of Law*, 2nd edn (Oxford, Oxford University Press, 2009).

[9] Most recently in 'A "Justified Normativity" Thesis in Hans Kelsen's Pure Theory of Law?' (n 7).

Is it a duty-imposing norm? If the latter, is it addressed to legal officials, or does it impose duties on legal subjects as well? There are passages in Kelsen's work to support each of these readings. Yet the various readings seem not to cohere. Or does the basic norm have a 'mixed' nature? One possibility is that Kelsen holds the view that the power-conferring and the duty-imposing formulations of the basic norm are somehow equivalent. But can the attribution of a power to an organ *A* be said to be in any sense equivalent to the issuance of a prescription to some individual *B*? Guastini thinks not. However, he does agree with Paulson, if for different reasons, that Kelsen might well have dispensed with any foundational quest for a basic norm – if only he had not unwarrantedly run together the 'validity' and the 'binding force' of law.

III. EFFICACY AND THE 'REAL' EXISTENCE OF LAW

With Pablo Navarro's essay we come to Part II, which focuses on issues raised by the 'real' or social-factual existence of legal systems and the relation between various forms of legal realism and the Pure Theory. Navarro explores the relations between legal validity and legal efficacy, particularly with regard to constitutional norms. Pursuing an argumentative strategy somewhat like Guastini's, Navarro finds that on the subject of efficacy, too, Kelsen seems never to have settled on a clear, definite view. Various remarks point towards accounts of efficacy that are not only strikingly different, but also seemingly inconsistent – and not always very clear. Lack of clarity on such pivotal questions is one of the frustrating features of Kelsen's style that have no doubt contributed to the fact that, at least in the English-speaking world, his work is less well-known than that of other, lesser, legal theorists.[10] But it usually pays to persevere, as Navarro does, reconstructing and articulating the various claims suggested by Kelsen's writings. Not because such claims, once brought out, are always correct, but because they press consistently original views, discussion of which often casts light on the topic at hand. This is what Navarro achieves with his distinction, and subsequent assessment, of an 'internal' and two possible 'external' criteria of constitutional efficacy – even if his concluding verdict is that 'the Pure Theory of Law fails to offer a satisfactory account of the relations between validity, efficacy, and legal dynamics'. (p 98).

This very charge of mischaracterising the relation between the validity and efficacy of law was, paradoxically, one that Kelsen himself pressed against the legal realists (and especially against Alf Ross), whom he accused of conflating the two notions. In his terrific 'A "Realistic" Theory of Law and the Pure

[10] As Joseph Raz remarks, Kelsen's theory has often been dismissed 'for its obscurity rather than its wrongness': *cf* J Raz, 'Kelsen's General Theory of Norms' (1976) 6 *Philosophia* 499.

Theory of Law' – an English translation of which is included at the end of Part II – this criticism is very forcefully presented. Here Kelsen takes Ross to task for inconsistently attempting to set forth a 'realistic' theory – understood as a theory claiming to account for law solely in terms of empirical facts – while simultaneously insisting that the 'specifically legal' element of the concept of law is a 'normative' one. Uta Bindreiter's contribution to this volume focuses on this spirited 1959 essay, which she describes as 'the climax of Kelsen's preoccupation with what are commonly called "realistic" theories'. In a thorough assessment of the points under debate, Bindreiter provocatively proclaims Kelsen the 'undisputed conqueror on the field of battle' (p 103). But she very helpfully begins by introducing Alf Ross's brand of legal realism, his understanding of what 'empirical' cognition amounts to, and his 'predictive' reinterpretation of legal validity.

Though she observes that Kelsen often 'used the adjectives "positivistic" and "realistic" in the same breath' (p 129), Bindreiter's project did not involve a comprehensive examination of the relation between Kelsenian positivism and legal realism more generally. But Pierluigi Chiassoni takes up this cue, and boldly offers a fully-fledged reconstruction of the Pure Theory. His thesis – defended in great detail at both the 'wholesale' and the 'retail' levels – is that Kelsen *always* 'strove to develop and promote a realistic jurisprudence', and indeed that this is the 'one deep, enduring, idea present in Kelsen's work for more than six decades, which can be said to lie at the very core of the Pure Theory of Law' (p 131f). Here, too, Kelsen's 1959 essay on Ross is an important source. But it is by no means the only one. Chiassoni finds evidence for this 'radically realistic' interpretation throughout the Kelsenian corpus, from the early work of the 1910s to the posthumously published *General Theory of Norms*.

Jes Bjarup approaches the relationship between the Pure Theory and legal realism from yet another angle: by reconstituting the debate that might have taken place between Kelsen and Axel Hägerström, the founder of Scandinavian Legal Realism, when the two met in Uppsala in 1933. The actual meeting was apparently a failure. In the recollection of one who was present, 'neither Kelsen nor Hägerström were able to understand each other' (p 165). Yet Bjarup – who examines, contrasts and critically assesses the works of both authors, with special attention to Hägerström's writings on The Pure Theory of Law – comes to the conclusion that it is Hägerström who is more often to blame for misrepresenting his opponent. Misguided as it may have been, however, Hägerström's reading of the Pure Theory proved influential, at least in the Nordic countries. (Alf Ross's objection that Kelsen's is a 'metaphysical' theory of law – an objection that Kelsen tries vigorously to refute in his 1959 essay – can in fact be traced back to Hägerström's early rejoinders.) And yet it also emerges from Bjarup's essay (which thus nicely ties in with both Bindreiter's and Chiassoni's) that on a fair number of issues Kelsen's and Hägerström's views were not that significantly apart.

IV. LEGAL NORMS AND LEGAL PROPOSITIONS

All the essays in Part III are concerned, in some way or other, with the distinction between legal norms and propositions *about* legal norms – a distinction that Kelsen came progressively to adopt in the course of his writings. Eugenio Bulygin's contribution deals with conceptual features of legal systems, leading us through a discussion of two related claims of Kelsen's. One is the claim that legal systems are necessarily complete. The other is the claim that legal systems are necessarily consistent. In fact neither thesis is distinctive of the Pure Theory of Law. Other philosophers, as Bulygin notes, have held similar views. But Bulygin thinks those theses are both wrong. Against Kelsen's version of the consistency thesis, he argues that it is rooted in the Pure Theory's Kantian strand; but this strand is itself inconsistent with Kelsen's theory's other, stronger strand: the positivistic one. This means that Kelsen can only endorse the consistency thesis at the cost of his own project's overall inconsistency. The completeness thesis, in turn, is less directly connected to Kelsen's deeper philosophical allegiances. It is often endorsed – and not only by Kelsen – on the basis of the thought that when a legal system does not contain any norm 'positively regulating' some action, that system permits (and therefore 'negatively' regulates) that action (p 233f). Bulygin's rejoinder – that this equivocates between two senses in which an action may be said to be legally 'permitted' – crucially depends on the distinction between '*norms*, which are prescriptive, and therefore neither true nor false, and *norm-propositions*, which are truth-apt descriptions of (the existence of) norms' (p 226).

Richard Tur's essay seeks to 'enlist Kelsen's aid', as he puts it, 'in the cause of defeasibilism' (p 246). 'Defeasibilism' is the view – which Tur has been propounding and carefully developing over at least two decades – that 'law is best represented, understood and theorised as a body of defeasible, open-ended normative conditional propositions of the form "If A is, then B ought to be, unless . . ."' (p 245). At the core of this view, then, is a concern with the form of legal propositions. Now although Kelsen was not, as Tur acknowledges, 'a fully paid-up, card-carrying, self-styled "defeasibilist"' (p 254), Tur believes that Kelsen's doctrine of the 'alternative character'[11] of the legal norm gives the Pure Theory a surprising flexibility. This doctrine has generally been met with strong criticism, and in this collection both van Roermund and Navarro remind us of its costs. But Tur takes a different approach. Putting the doctrine of the 'alternative character' in its broader theoretical context, he argues that

[11] See text to n 5.

it enables Kelsen to account (in a way that many theories of law cannot) for the very real possibility that legal officials be authorised to disregard, disapply or 'defeat' (weighing justice against certainty) general rules which they would otherwise apply.

The volume closes with a critical assessment of a thesis of Kelsen's that is probably better known in HLA Hart's description of it. This is the thesis that

> what is ordinarily thought of as the content of law, designed to guide the conduct of ordinary citizens, is merely the antecedent or 'if-clause' in a rule which is directed not to them but to officials, and orders them to apply certain sanctions if certain conditions are satisfied. . . . By greater and greater elaboration of the antecedent or if-clauses, legal rules of every type, including the rules defining the manner and exercise of private or public powers, can be restated in this conditional form.[12]

Hart objected that this 'formidable and interesting' theory distorted the 'different social functions which different types of legal rules perform'.[13] If you are among those who find Hart's criticism unpersuasive or off point, then you may be surprised to see that Kelsen's doctrine of the 'complete' legal norm may nonetheless be vulnerable to other, and perhaps more fundamental, objections.

[12] HLA Hart, *The Concept of Law*, 3rd edn (Oxford, Oxford University Press, 2012 [1961]) 36.
[13] ibid 37ff.

Part I

Legal Validity and the Basic Norm

2

Norm-claims, Validity and Self-reference

BERT VAN ROERMUND*

THIS ESSAY ADDRESSES two related issues. Section I is an enquiry into the relation between authoritative and epistemic (in particular scholarly or 'scientific') claims that some given norm 'exists'. To phrase the question in Kelsenian idiolect, what is the relation between 'authentic' and 'inauthentic' interpretation? In order to answer this question satisfactorily, we need, I argue, to differentiate – deviating from Kelsen's views – between two modes of acknowledging the existence of a norm. These two modes, which I refer to as 'validity' and 'bindingness', are interdefinable: bindingness is authoritatively pre-empted validity; validity, cognitively reconfirmed bindingness. Section II turns to the reflexive, self-referential character of a legal system's 'basic norm', and discusses how such a basic norm relates to the pursuit of legal knowledge as a scholarly discipline. Here I argue that Kelsen's own account of the basic norm commits him to the kind of 'recognition' theory of normativity which – mainly because he misunderstood its core tenets – he professed to reject. Section III, in conclusion, makes the connections between these two issues explicit.

I. IS IT AUTHORITY'S TASK, OR IS IT SCHOLARSHIP'S, TO DETERMINE WHICH NORMS ARE LEGALLY VALID?

A. Kelsen on Norms and Empowerment

Kelsen's definition of a norm is well-known.[1] '"Norm",' he writes in chapter one of *The Pure Theory of Law*, is the 'specific meaning' of acts of a certain kind,

* For comments on an earlier version I am indebted to my Tilburg colleague Hans Lindahl and to participants in the Legal Science and Legal Theory conference held in Oxford in September 2010. I am also grateful to Mrs Phyllis Lewis for text corrections.

[1] One should be aware of the fact that Kelsen's views underwent considerable shifts over his many active decades: see SL Paulson, 'Toward a Periodization of the Pure Theory of Law' in L Gianformaggio (ed), *Hans Kelsen's Legal Theory. A Diachronic Point of View* (Turin, Giappichelli, 1990); SL Paulson, 'Introduction' in SL Paulson and BL Paulson (eds), *Normativity and Norms. Critical*

viz. 'acts of will' by which 'a certain behavior is commanded, permitted, or authorized':

> By 'norm' we mean that something *ought* to be or *ought* to happen, especially that a human being ought to behave in a certain way. This is the meaning of certain human acts directed toward the behavior of others. They are so directed, if they, according to their content, command such behavior, but also if they permit it, and – particularly – if they authorize it.[2]

Kelsen's terminology may be idiosyncratic, but the underlying idea is not difficult to unpack. There are acts whose 'specific meaning' (as Kelsen puts it) is 'that something *is*'.[3] The making of a statement ('John closes the door') is a paradigmatic example. But there are also acts whose specific meaning is 'not that something is, but that something ought to be'.[4] The act of issuing an order – 'John, close the door!' – would be an example. The meaning of such an act, Kelsen says, is that the addressee *ought* to close the door. A norm is predicated, in any case, on the meaning of such an act, which is not to say that it coincides with either this meaning or this act, as we shall see below.

The specific 'ought-to-do' meaning does not turn on the linguistic formulation which the agent or speaker may happen to employ. Someone may give an order without resorting to the imperative form; for instance, by using a formulation which may linguistically resemble that of a statement ('I order you to be quiet').[5] Strictly speaking, this meaning does not even hinge on the specific (speech) act performed, since not only ordering but also advising, requesting etc express that someone ought to do something. Kelsen's point, rather, is that the meaning of acts such as the giving of an order is different *in kind* from the meaning of acts such as the making of a statement. The meaning of acts of the former kind is that the addressee *ought* to behave in some given way; the meaning of acts of the latter kind, that something *is the case.*

The class of 'acts whose meaning is a norm' is not restricted to the issuance of obligations and prohibitions. It also encompasses, Kelsen says, the issuance of permissions and authorisations (ie attributions of power). Kelsen's 'ought', accordingly, is used in 'a broader than the usual sense': it 'includes "may" and

Perspectives on Kelsenian Themes (Oxford, Clarendon Press, 1998); and SL Paulson, 'Arriving at a Defensible Periodization of Hans Kelsen's Legal Theory' (1999) 19 *Oxford Journal of Legal Studies* 351. To some extent, such shifts justify my slightly eclectic approach to Kelsen's texts. Most of what I take up, however, pertains to the 'classical' (or 'Neo-Kantian') phase, which spans from the late 1930s until 1960, and encompasses the second edition of *The Pure Theory of Law.*

[2] H Kelsen, *The Pure Theory of Law*, 2nd edn, M Knight transl (Berkeley, University of California Press, 1967 [1960]) 4–5, 7.

[3] ibid 6–7.

[4] ibid.

[5] ibid 7.

"can"'.[6] Thus, when I speak of an 'order', I use the term (unless otherwise noted) as a paradigm for these other modalities. Note, moreover, that the point that this paradigm purports to convey is a conceptual point about the predicative structure of a norm. It is not a point specifically connected to what one currently calls 'speech act theory'. For speech acts (in particular 'directives') are only one way in which the 'ought-to-do' *qua* 'act of will' may be expressed. Gestures, signs or (today) mouse-clicking may also involve 'acts of will directed at the behavior of another'.[7]

Of course, to say that the 'meaning' of an order is, for example, that the addressee ought to be silent is not to say that the addressee *ought to be silent on all accounts*. It is to say only that *according to the individual giving the order* (ie 'from the point of view of the individual who has performed the act'[8]) the addressee ought to be silent. The correct way to describe the situation is by saying that 'The one individual wills that the other individual ought to behave in a certain way',[9] or that – as Kelsen also puts it – the 'subjective' meaning of the order (understood, to repeat, as an act of will directed toward the behaviour of another) is that the addressee *ought* to behave in a certain way. But, again, it is not necessarily the case that the order has the corresponding 'objective' meaning. It is not necessarily the case, in other words, that by issuing – or 'positing'

[6] ibid 5. *cf* ibid 77: '"Ought" usually expresses a command, not an authorization or permission. The legal "ought", however, the conjunction ['*die Kopula*', in the original German] which in the legal statement ['*Rechtssatz*'; I have altered the English translation] connects condition and consequence, embraces all three meanings: the command, the authorisation, and the positive permission of a consequence'. (See also Kelsen's 1962 essay 'Derogation', included in his *Essays in Legal and Moral Philosophy* (Dordrecht, Reidel, 1973), as well as his *General Theory of Norms*, M Hartney transl (Oxford, Clarendon Press, 1991 [1979]) 96ff, where 'derogation' is added to the spectre of 'normative functions'.) Here Kelsen is wrong, I think, on quite a number of points, though this is not the place to expand on the matter. 'Ought' is not an operator linking antecedent and consequent, but the copula in the consequent of a conditional norm. Authorisation is not a genuine deontic modality, but the precondition of institutional actions which themselves are the object proper of deontic qualification. A generic 'ought' is by no means characteristic of law; it comes with a certain level of abstraction at which any normative language may be discussed. But there is indeed a level of abstraction at which 'ought' can be taken as a placeholder for deontic modalities like 'obligatory' and 'permitted': see HN Castañeda, *Thinking and Doing. The Philosophical Foundations of Institutions* (Dordrecht-Boston, Reidel, 1975) 45ff.

[7] Kelsen, *The Pure Theory of Law* (n 2) 4f; and see also his reference to such acts' 'meaning as commands, as imperatives', at ibid 103. Kelsen's formulation is too simple on at least two counts. First, prescriptions can well be addressed to oneself (and in a democracy statutory laws are to be understood as commitments formulated in the first person plural). Second, he unhelpfully uses terms like 'command', 'permission', 'authorisation' etc, to refer both to kinds of (speech) acts, and to kinds of deontic modalities.

[8] ibid 7. This is contrasted with the 'objective' viewpoint of '*eines unbeteiligten Dritten*', ie of an impartial third person. (Again I have some issues with the English translation, which reads: 'a third individual not involved in the relation between the two [ie between the person who issues the prescription, and the person to whom the prescription is addressed]'.)

[9] ibid 5.

– the order the speaker or agent is 'objectively' creating a norm, ie that the content of the order has the 'meaning of a *valid* norm':[10]

> By the word 'validity' we designate the specific existence of a norm. . . . [W]e express by this the special manner in which the norm – in contradistinction to a natural fact – is existent. The 'existence' of a positive norm – that is to say, its 'validity' – is not the same as the existence of the act of will, whose objective meaning the norm is.[11]

To show that such an act has the objective meaning of a norm is, according to Kelsen, to show that the act is performed in compliance with a higher-order norm. In mature legal orders this is a power-conferring norm. Briefly to rehearse the paradigm:[12] a gangster who threatens me by demanding that I 'pay €18,000 before 1 May, or else' is not issuing or creating a norm. It is only 'subjectively', and not also 'objectively', that his command has the 'meaning' of a norm. It is only according to *him* that I ought to pay him that sum. If the next day he is killed in a fight, or if I successfully reciprocate by issuing a more frightening threat, I will rightfully get away without paying. Matters are different, however, if a similar demand is made in a letter from my tax inspector. If she is suddenly killed, of if I effectively threaten her into resigning, I am still under a duty to pay. For the tax inspector's demand amounts to the creation of a norm. Her requirement is premised, not merely on her subjective will, but on the exercise of a legal power – a power conferred by some other, higher-order norm. The 'subjective' meaning of her requirement – that I ought to pay €18,000 before 1 May – thus 'coincides', as Kelsen has it, with its 'objective' meaning, ie with 'the meaning the act has according to the law'.[13] Her requirement, then, does give rise to a norm; 'only the command of the official, not that of the gangster, has the meaning of a valid norm':[14]

> The mere fact that somebody commands something is no reason to regard the command as a 'valid' norm . . . Only a competent authority can create valid norms; and such competence can only be based on a norm that authorizes the issuing of norms.[15]

The creation of valid norms in law, then, according to Kelsen, is not (or not essentially) a content-related matter, as may be the case in underdeveloped legal orders or in most moral orders. It is a matter of whether the putative norm-issuer was indeed *authorised* to create norms, of whether the issuer stayed within the limits of the relevant competence, and whether the specific procedure deter-

[10] ibid 8.
[11] ibid 10.
[12] ibid 8ff.
[13] ibid 3.
[14] ibid 8.
[15] ibid 194.

mined by the relevant higher-order norms was followed. The creation of valid norms, Kelsen says, is a matter of a norm having been created 'in a certain way', rather than a matter of a norm having 'a certain content'.[16] In mature legal orders, it is essentially a 'dynamic' matter, rather than a 'static' one.[17]

Now, this process of law-creation is itself regulated by law; it forms therefore part of the object of what Kelsen calls the 'science of law'.[18] The science of law, he says, is 'cognition of the law',[19] and its object proper is legal *norms*. It concerns itself with human behaviour only indirectly:

> [T]he acts of law creation and law application that constitute the legal process are considered by legal cognition only to the extent that they form the content of norms – that they are determined by legal norms.[20]

The science of law, then, is not concerned with – and does not describe – such acts *qua* mere acts. It describes them as acts of norm-creation: it normatively *interprets* such acts as acts that produce valid norms and thus conform to – and apply – some higher-order authorising norm. It interprets them, in other words, as having 'objectively', and not merely subjectively, a normative 'meaning'. This *normative* interpretation is not, Kelsen stresses, the only possible interpretation of such acts. They can also be non-normatively interpreted; they can, for example, be interpreted as '[de facto] power relations', ie 'sociologically'.[21] But the *specifically legal* interpretation is the normative one: it is only under the normative interpretation that such acts can be understood as – *known* as – acts of law-creation.[22] The science of law, Kelsen writes, 'endeavours to comprehend its object "legally"', ie 'from the viewpoint of the law', and therefore 'represents a normative interpretation of its object'.[23]

This is a very important point. Kelsen stresses it in a lengthy and important footnote (unfortunately not reproduced in the English translation of *The Pure Theory of Law*):

[16] ibid 198.

[17] 'Essentially' is Kelsen's adverb. Kelsen allows for modes of norm-validation other than empowerment. A norm's validity can be simply a matter of its content being subsumable, 'as the particular under the general', under the content of another, higher-level norm (ibid 195). This is what he refers to as the 'static' principle of norm-validation (ibid 196). It is not Kelsen's point, of course, that the 'static' principle plays no role in actual legal systems; as he expressly notes, 'the static and dynamic principles may be combined in the same system', and this is often the case. But unless one accepts that there are 'directly evident' norms 'immanent in, or emanate[ing] from, reason', the 'dynamic' principle is more fundamental, Kelsen thinks, than the 'static' one (ibid 196); and in any event in a legal system norm-validation is ultimately a 'dynamic' matter.

[18] The science of law concerns itself *both* with norms *created, applied, or obeyed*; and with the normatively regulated process of law-*creation* and law-*application*; *cf* Kelsen's distinction between a 'static' and a 'dynamic' theory of law (ibid 70–71).

[19] ibid 72.

[20] ibid 71.

[21] ibid 218.

[22] See also ibid 4–5.

[23] ibid 70–71.

> To hold that *objective*, ought-validity is an essential element of the concept of law does not mean . . . that validity is something given in reality and thus something which can be verified in the same way as those properties of objects which can be apprehended by the senses. . . . Validity is not 'something *objectively given*'. . . . [What the Pure Theory of Law] emphatically holds [is] that the assertion that law is objectively valid, ie that the subjective meaning of a law-making act is also its objective meaning, is only a *possible* interpretation . . . of such acts, not a necessary one; it is entirely possible *not* to give those acts that [objective] meaning. . . . Belief in the authority of law-making organs – belief, that is, in the objective, 'ought' validity of law – is not belief in the existence of some non-existent reality. It is a certain interpretation of the meaning of real acts.[24]

Legal validity, for Kelsen, is solely a function of the normative, 'authorising' interpretation of certain facts – viz. actions, whether individual or collective – as norm-creating. Regarding norms *qua* norms as an object of knowledge is taking a viewpoint; and one can take it only together with its implications.

How, then, one is now led to ask, is such an interpretation *possible*? This is the question – the epistemological question – at the core of the Pure Theory of Law:

> [T]he Pure Theory of Law asks: 'How is it possible to interpret without recourse to meta-legal authorities, like God or nature, the subjective meaning of certain facts as a system of objectively valid legal norms ?

To see just where the problem lies, note that the chain of validity must come to an end: it is conceptually impossible that there is a 'highest' norm which is itself valid by virtue of having been enacted by an authorised agent or organ. No 'posited' norm, in other words, can be the highest – the ultimate – norm of a legal system. Why not? Consider the example of a judicial decision sentencing someone to death. This decision, says Kelsen, creates an 'individual' legal norm; more precisely, it is – or can be – interpreted as creating an individual legal norm. But:

> [t]his raises the questions: Under what conditions is such an interpretation possible, why is a judicial decision present in this case, why is the individual norm created thereby a legal norm? . . . The answer is: Because this individual norm was created in applying a criminal law that contains a general norm according to which (under conditions present in the case concerned) the death penalty ought to be inflicted.[25]

But we can now 'ask for the reason for the validity of this criminal law'; and

> the answer is: the criminal law is valid because it was created by the legislature, and the legislature, in turn, is authorized by the constitution to create general norms. If

[24] See H Kelsen, *Reine Rechtslehre*, 2nd edn (Vienna, Franz Deuticke, 1960) 218 fn (my translation; emphasis added). The footnote criticises Alf Ross's 'realist' account of validity in terms of (social) facts.

[25] *The Pure Theory of Law* (n 2) 199–200.

> we ask for the reason of the validity of the constitution . . . we may, perhaps, discover an older constitution; that means the validity of the existing constitution is justified by the fact that it was created according to the rules of an earlier constitution by way of a constitutional amendment.[26]

Eventually 'we arrive at a historically first constitution that cannot have been created in this way and whose validity, therefore, cannot be traced back to a positive norm created by a legal authority'. Constituent power – power to *make* constitutional norms – is irreducible to constitutional power – power *according to* constitutional norms. And yet we *do* interpret this first constitution as objectively valid. It follows, then, that

> if we ask for the reason of the validity of the historically first constitution, then the answer can only be (if we leave aside God or 'nature'[27]) that the validity of this constitution must be *presupposed*.[28]

The content of this presupposition is a norm. Kelsen famously calls it '*Grundnorm*' – 'basic norm'. It is the norm that authorises the act (or set of acts) by which the system's historically first constitution was laid down.[29] 'Historically' here refers to the normative pedigree of the constitution, not to the historical facts that brought it about from any non-normative point of view. It concerns the *genealogy* of a constitution, in the sense of a line of lawful heirs. So the validity of a system's highest positive norm is not something that epistemic enquiries into law are capable of tracking.[30] On the contrary: it is only *under* that constitutive presupposition or assumption – under that fiction – that one's engagement with law as a specific object of knowledge is possible:

> Only if this basic norm, referring to a specific constitution, is presupposed, that is, only if it is presupposed that one ought to behave according to this specific constitution – only then can the subjective meaning of a constitution-creating act and of the acts created according to this constitution be interpreted as their objective meaning, that is, as objectively valid legal norms, and the relationships established by these legal norms as legal relations.[31]

[26] ibid 200.

[27] This proviso is an expression of Kelsen's positivism; *cf* ibid 204: 'a positivistic science of law . . . cannot maintain that the norm to obey the commands of the creator of the constitution is the subjective meaning of the act of will of an authority *higher* than the creator of the constitution – such as God's or nature's'.

[28] ibid 200.

[29] The basic norm, Kelsen also writes, may 'be described as the *constitution in a logical-juridical sense* [*Verfassung im rechtslogischen Sinne*], in contradistinction to the *constitution in the positive legal sense* [*Verfassung im positive-rechtlichen Sinne*]' (translation altered, and emphasis added); indeed, the basic norm, Kelsen continues, is 'not a *positive* but a *presupposed* (*voraus-gesetzte*) norm': see ibid 199.

[30] ibid 204.

[31] ibid 201. This formulation of the basic norm – 'One ought to behave according to this specific constitution' – is but one of Kelsen's various paraphrases of the *Grundnorm*.

So the Pure Theory of Law offers an answer to that core question regarding the conditions under which the interpretation of 'the subjective meaning of certain facts as a system of objectively valid legal norms' is possible:

> The epistemological answer of the Pure Theory of Law is: 'By presupposing the basic norm that one ought to behave as the constitution prescribes . . .' The function of the basic norm is to found the objective validity of a positive legal order, that is, to interpret the *subjective* meaning of the acts of human beings by which the norms of an effective coercive order are created, as their *objective* meaning.[32]

It should be noted, however, that although this presupposition that the positive constitution *is* objectively valid – this presupposition that 'one ought to behave as that constitution prescribes' – is a necessary precondition of legal cognition, it is also at odds with Kelsen's own definition of a norm as the objective meaning of an *act of will*. The basic norm is not the product of any act of will: it is not a positive norm. Nor does the fact that it is necessarily presupposed by legal science – indeed by 'whoever interprets the subjective meaning of the constitution-creating act, and of the acts created according to the constitution, as the objective meaning of these acts'[33] – mean that the science of law posits, wills or prescribes the basic norm. For 'this interpretation', Kelsen insists, 'is a cognitive function, not a function of the will'.[34] The basic norm 'cannot be the meaning of an act of will'; 'it can only be the meaning of an act of thinking'.[35]

B. Advantages of Kelsen's Model

Good theoretical models of empowerment relations are not easy to devise (much as the slogan 'it's the competence, stupid!'[36] may appear neatly to summarise what is at stake). Legal practice is significantly varied and complex. For the sake of illustration, consider one of the key terms of empowerment relations: discretion.[37] Elsewhere I have commented on Somsen's analysis of 'discretion' with regard to decision-making in EU environmental law.[38] The

[32] ibid 202.

[33] ibid 204 fn 72.

[34] ibid

[35] ibid 204.

[36] Which I owe to Carole Lyons.

[37] From the vast literature, I would point to DJ Galligan, *Discretionary Powers. A Legal Study of Official Discretion*, 2nd edn (Oxford, Clarendon Press, 1990); T Spaak, *The Concept of Legal Competence* (Brookfield, Dartmouth, 1994); and T Spaak, 'Norms That Confer Competence' (2003) 16 *Ratio Juris* 89.

[38] *cf* H Somsen, 'Discretion in European Community Environmental Law: an Analysis of ECJ Case Law' (2003) 40 *Common Market Law Review* 1413; and B Van Roermund, 'Law at Cross-Purposes: Conceptual Confusion and Political Divergence' in S Prechal and B Van Roermund (eds), *The Coherence of EU Law. The Search for Unity in Divergent Concepts* (Oxford, Oxford University Press, 2008).

European Union is a paradigmatic case, if there ever was one, of a 'dynamic' normative order in Kelsen's sense. From its early beginnings it has been governed by the principle of explicit conferral of powers, laid down in a succession of binding treaties (and currently in articles 4.1 and 5 of the Treaty on European Union). In spite of these provisions, however, it often remains unclear who is empowered to what, in what exact sense, and under which particular constraints. On the basis of case law and policy document analysis, no less than eight meanings of 'discretion' have been found by Somsen to be at play. By paraphrasing them in more general terms one brings out the conceptual divergence that lurks in the background of issues of competence. Somsen's list illustrates that notions such as 'discretion', 'competence' and 'empowerment' stand in need of sustained conceptual elucidation if one wants to come to grips with politico-legal strategies on the fine line between challenging and violating European law (by private parties as well as Member States). Very practical matters – such as the immense problems of translation between the official languages of the European Union (in which, to begin with, there is typically no 'original' or 'authentic' language![39]) – make it necessary to draw distinctions such as that between an authorisation, a permission and a liberty to φ. And without a theoretical model one will not get very far on this road.

But though the risk that a theoretical model oversimplifies its object is high, the converse defect is also to be avoided. Indeed, as Richard Posner has pointed out, most jurisprudential models suffer from being too rich rather than too simple.[40] Just like a model which is too reductive, a model which is not reductive enough, allowing for too many variables (and, particularly, for too many *ceteris paribus* clauses), is a flawed one.

Kelsen's model of empowerment relationships – together with his definition of a norm – rises to this challenge. It is set at a fairly robust level of abstraction, which is a precondition for theory-construction and for the falsification of strong hypotheses. And it has the kindred virtues of explanatory parsimony and theoretical elegance.

Indeed, there is a noteworthy similarity between Kelsen's definition of a norm and Peter Strawson's equally parsimonious (and equally well-known) definition of facts. 'Facts', writes Strawson, 'are what statements, when true, state; they are not what statements are about'.[41] To see the parallel with

[39] *cf* L Mulders, 'Translation at the Court of Justice of the European Communities' in S Prechal and B Van Roermund (eds), *The Coherence of EU Law. The Search for Unity in Divergent Concepts* (Oxford, Oxford University Press, 2008).

[40] *cf* R Posner, *The Problems of Jurisprudence* (Cambridge, Mass., Harvard University Press, 1990) 362ff, 366 fn 12.

[41] PF Strawson, 'Truth' in G Pitcher (ed), *Truth* (Englewood Cliffs, Prentice Hall 1964 [1950]) 38. Or as Nelson Goodman would have it: 'facts are small theories, and true theories are big facts': *cf* N Goodman, *Ways of World-Making* (Indianapolis, Hackett Publishing Company, 1978) 96f.

Kelsen's account, keep in mind that for Kelsen the truth of statements and the validity of legal norms are *not* on a par:

> The statements formulated by the science of law that, according to a certain legal order, something ought to be done or not to be done . . . may be true or false. But the norms enacted by the legal authority, imposing obligations and conferring rights upon the legal subjects are neither true nor false, but only valid or invalid; just as facts are neither true nor false, but only existent or nonexistent, and only statements about facts can be true or false.[42]

It is with *facts*, then, not with statements, that legal norms are to be contrasted. Statements can be true or false – including the statements by which the science of law describes the law. But given Kelsen's view of legal norms as 'objectively valid' – which means, as we saw, that the subjective ought-meaning of a law-making act is also its objective meaning – there really can be no 'invalid' norms, any more than there can be 'non-existent' facts. By Kelsen's own definition, the idea of an 'invalid law' is just as oxymoronic as the idea of 'non-existent fact'. 'A valid norm', by the same token, is a pleonasm.[43] For validity is not a property or a value of norms. Validity is rather, Kelsen affirms, their specific mode of 'existence'[44] – and existence is not a predicate in (or a value of) judgements, be they practical or theoretical. Thus:

> The statement that a valid statute is 'unconstitutional' is a self-contradiction; for a statute can be valid only on the basis of the constitution. . . . Of an invalid statute one cannot say that it is unconstitutional, for an invalid statute is no statute at all; it is legally nonexistent.[45]

This result may seem counterintuitive. Do lawyers and legal authorities not constantly – and intelligibly – discuss whether some given norm is valid or invalid? Moreover, is Kelsen's own theory of legal validity not committed to the distinction between 'valid' norms (those which are authorised by a higher-order norm) and 'invalid' ones (those which are not)?

These doubts are misguided. The only implication is that for the sake of clarity we need to introduce and operate with the concept of a norm-*claim* – with the concept, if you will, of a *candidate* norm – ie the claim, made by any agent who performs an 'act of will directed at the behavior of another' (eg by commanding or requiring some action of someone), that the addressee *ought* to behave in a given manner. Kelsen himself appears to be aware of the need terminologically to distinguish 'norms' from what I have proposed to call

[42] *The Pure Theory of Law* (n 2) 73.

[43] *cf* Kelsen, *General Theory of Norms* (n 6) 171. That existence is not a predicate (or property) does not prevent Kelsen from submitting that 'a certain something . . . can have the quality [*Eigenschaft*] of is or of ought': see *The Pure Theory of Law* (n 2) 6. His philosophical idiolect is not always orthodox.

[44] ibid 10: 'By the word "validity" we designate the specific existence of a norm'.

[45] See *The Pure Theory of Law* (n 2) 271.

'norm-claims'. True, on the very first pages of *The Pure Theory of Law* he does use the term 'norm' to designate the practical thought-content – the 'subjective' meaning – of prescriptive acts, acts 'directed towards the behavior of others'.[46] Soon enough, however, the term 'norm' is largely reserved to refer to situations in which such acts can *also* be said 'objectively' to have the meaning that someone ought to behave in a given manner; and 'ought' is employed instead to refer to the 'subjective' meaning of prescriptive acts. We thus find passages like this:

> 'Ought' is the subjective meaning of every act of will directed at the behavior of another. But not every such act has also objectively this meaning; and only if the act of will has also the objective meaning of an 'ought,' is this 'ought' called a 'norm'.[47]

Let us then agree to use the term 'norm-claim' to refer to the characteristic prescriptive, practical thought-content – that someone *ought* to perform some given action – of such prescriptive 'acts of will directed at the behavior of others'.[48] This, to repeat, is the claim necessarily put forth by whoever performs any such act of will, whatever the guise under which it is performed (speech act, gesture, etc). Of course, that such a claim is made – that such a *candidate* norm is put forth – does not mean that it is warranted or in any way to be granted. Such a claim is to be granted only if the agent is empowered to perform the corresponding act – empowered, that is, to produce the corresponding 'objectively valid' norm. With this elementary distinction in hand, then, Kelsen's account may be simply recast as follows:

(1) A norm-claim N_c – as made by an agent *X* who performs an act of will φ directed at the behaviour of *Y* – is to be granted if, and only if, *X* is legally empowered to φ.
(2) In that case, by φ-ing, *X* creates – *X* 'posits' – the norm N_1 whose content is that *Y* ought to behave in accordance with φ.
(3) Empowerment is itself a normative status: to say that an agent *X* is empowered to φ is to say that there is a norm authorising *X* to φ; such a

[46] ibid 4–7.
[47] ibid 7.
[48] The difference between *prescriptive* and *descriptive* thought-contents is the difference between 'ought' and 'is' *qua* copulae: a difference at the level of (first-order predicate) logic. The copula indicates an act of thought; it can therefore be either theoretical (as in judging what the world is like) or practical (as in judging what is to be done). Both modes may be embedded (or embodied) in various actions (mental acts, speech acts and others). Thus the same practical thought-content ('John, turn the heating on if the temperature is $<15^{\circ}$ C'), though it is a prescription in the logical sense, is not necessarily, at the pragmatic level, a command (ie the content of a speech act of commanding): it may be a command, an advice, a suggestion etc. Kelsen acknowledged this distinction between 'is' and 'ought' as different logical 'modi', at least in his classical phase (*cf* ibid 7). Note, however, that in his philosophical idiolect 'copula' refers to the level of propositional operators rather than that of predication; see ibid 78.

norm – N_2 – can therefore figuratively be said to be 'higher' than the norm N_1 which *X* creates by φ-ing.

(4) N_2 will itself have been created by some agent's act of will; this agent must in turn be authorised by some higher norm N_3; and so on.

Such 'acts of will directed at the behavior of others', then, rather than norms, are on a par with statements. And the notion of a norm-claim helps bring out the parallel. Statements, of course, are not always true. By default, however, they raise truth-claims. To make a statement is to put forth its content as a *candidate* to the status of a fact; the statement stands to be tested in order to see if what is being asserted *as* true *is* true. If the statement passes the test, its content will be labelled a 'fact', and added to what we refer to as 'the world', added to 'reality'. If the statement fails the test, it will be relegated to the domains of fiction, error, perhaps even to the domain of lies. But even a lie is only successful if it raises a truth-claim. Similarly, acts of will directed at the behaviour of others by default raise norm-claims; and their content is called a 'norm' only if the norm-claim is warranted.

The similarity with Strawson's definition of a fact is even more clearly visible in another argument of Kelsen's against the idea that normative 'validity' parallels the 'truth' of statements:

> Since the validity of a norm is its specific existence, and existence occurs in time, the validity of a norm can be relative to time. Just as a norm *acquires* validity, it can also . . . *lose* its validity; it can begin to be valid at a certain point in time and then cease to be valid at a certain point in time. . . . But the truth of a statement is not relative to time. A statement does not begin to be true at some point or cease to be true at some point in time. *If* it is true, it is always true, has always been true, and will always be true.[49]

Validity, Kelsen says, is temporally determined – as everything else that exists. A norm exists *in time*, as it comes into existence, endures and disappears (ie as it gains, retains and loses its validity). The truth of a statement, on the other hand, is time-independent.[50]

[49] *General Theory of Norms* (n 6) 172–73.

[50] Of course, a statement may refer to states of affairs that exist in time. But its truth, as a value of its content, is timeless. 'That heat causes a metal to expand', Kelsen writes, '*if* true – is always true' (rather than something that *began* to be true when, say, *found* to be true). The same holds for 'statements about the existence of individual facts': 'That Kant was born in 1724 and died in 1804, and thus lived for eighty years, always remains true, and has always been true, even before Kant was born and before he died' (see *General Theory of Norms* (n 6) 173). This view can be accepted within the framework of a broader account of truth – of truth in the *modus essendi*. Systematic connections have to be drawn, however, with truth in the *modus cognoscendi*, ie with ways of *establishing* truth under certain presuppositions. (Strawson takes this crucial step. He linked the *truth* of a statement *S*, not (merely) to a way of finding out whether *S* is (or was, or will be) true, but (also) to the presuppositions which have to be in place if *S* is to have a truth-value at all. This was precisely the point that his famous rejoinder to Russell's theory of descriptions tried to hammer home: 'The present king of France is bald' – when France has no king. See PF Strawson, 'On Referring' (1950)

For Kelsen, then, the epistemic counterparts of norms existing in time are *facts* existing in time. And both norms and facts are understood as 'objective' thought-contents: practical, prescriptive thought-contents in the case of norms; theoretical, descriptive thought-contents in the case of facts. There is therefore no parallel between the 'validity' of norms and the 'truth' of statements. It is in the facticity of states of affairs, rather, that normative validity finds its correlate.

C. A Problem in Kelsen's Model – and How to Solve It

i. The Problem

Yet a difficulty has already begun to emerge. Suppose that Kelsen's account, the account that lies behind his model, is right. Suppose, that is, that norm-*claims* are to be granted – ie that the production of the corresponding valid norm is to be acknowledged – if and only if the agent or organ whose action raises the norm-claim enjoys (by virtue of some 'higher' norm) the competence to perform that action. Whose task, then, is it to decide on whether any given norm-claim is indeed to be interpreted as giving rise to a valid norm? Whose task is it to establish which norms are valid?

The only answer consistent with Kelsen's epistemological approach would seem to be: 'Legal scholarship (as well as anyone else pursuing knowledge of the law) – on the grounds of some theory of what would count as evidence for an agent's or organ's empowerment in a given legal system'. We entrust all those who epistemically concern themselves with law under its normative aspect, and professional legal scholars first of all, with the task of establishing whether or not some given norm-claim, as raised in some putative norm-creating act, is to be interpreted as an objectively valid norm in some legal system. They will often disagree, of course: but that is only to be expected in the context of epistemic endeavours, particularly if carried out in the realm of an academic discipline (as is the case with law). This disagreement should certainly not prevent legal scholars from developing theoretical models of authoritative decision-making, and from verifying whether individual decisions made by legal authorities – legislators, governments, judges, contracting parties, etc – can be described, explained and predicted in terms of

59 *Mind* 320.) Even if we accept that 'Kant was born in 1724' is true before 1724, we have no way of establishing, before 1724, whether Kant is born in 1724. One might say, though, that in 1723 it was a fact that he *would be* born in 1724, so that his being born in 1724 was the content of a predictive statement. To the extent that the truth of a predictive statement is something that can be established, eg by probability calculus, the thought-content of such a statement is a future 'fact'; but the thought-content itself is timeless.

such models.[51] And Kelsen's theory of the basic norm provides a sound basis for such an exercise. Its first tenet, as we saw, is that the possibility of legal scholarship rests on the presupposition – the fiction – that there is a highest norm, a norm the validity of which is not further scrutinised. But this is not the end of scholarly discussion – it is the beginning. For it is precisely against the backdrop of that presupposition that legal scholars formulate competing hypotheses about the normative hierarchy in any given legal system in response to the case (or case-type) at hand – hypotheses, that is, about how to recast the normative content of the system in such a way that it forms a coherent whole under the constitution, in view of any given case (or case-type). Legal scholars may also engage in developing proposals as to how this overall coherence may be improved (eg by enacting or repealing certain statutes, by articulating novel lines of interpretation which judges and other officials may wish to adopt, and so on). What they do, then, in essence, is to build theoretical models of legal competence for whatever legal system (or system-type) they may happen to be concerned with. And this is tantamount to establishing which legal consequences follow from which facts by virtues of the norms in that system – a perfectly Kelsenian stand.

However, scholarly disagreement will be less welcome if law is taken as a pragmatic enterprise, geared towards ending or precluding socio-political conflict by authoritative decision-making. From this viewpoint, scholarly disagreement about conclusions of law aggravates rather than mitigates the underlying dispute between the parties. And at any rate courts do certainly not wait for legal scholars to reach consensus before they decide *what the law is* in the case at hand. Binding and far-reaching decisions are very often taken by courts – in the full exercise of their competence – which are not only debatable, but indeed adopted with full conscience of their debatable character, and not infrequently even with *internal* disagreement. To *some* extent, of course, the court will remain engaged in an epistemic exercise in law; but it will undercut scholarly discussions by declaring how *it* sees things – by declaring what it takes to be law on the matter, and by deciding accordingly. A court thereby puts forth, *in the very process of exercising its characteristic decision-making competence*, a definite 'objective' interpretation – a definite interpretation as an

[51] Legal theory can here make use of contemporary methods and techniques in the social sciences; this would not amount to the kind of methodological syncretism that Kelsen rightly wanted to avoid, viz. the collapse of legal scholarship into social science: *cf* eg *The Pure Theory of Law* (n 2) 1. Even if methods and techniques of the social sciences are integrated, statements that some norm *N* is valid in some system *L* remain *Rechtssätze* – propositions *of* law – describing legal norms *qua* legal norms. (M Knight's translation of '*Rechtssatz*' by 'rule of law' – *cf* ibid 71ff – is dubious, to say the least. In their Appendix to H Kelsen, *Introduction to the Problems of Legal Theory*, BL Paulson and SL Paulson transl (Oxford, Clarendon Press, 1992 [1934]), Stanley and Bonnie Paulson explain why 'legal proposition', ie the propositional counterpart of a legal norm, is the correct translation of '*Rechtssatz*' in the second edition of the *Pure Theory* [though not in the first edition, where it's the equivalent of 'reconstructed legal norm'].)

'objectively valid norm' – of some norm-claim (as raised, for example, in some legislative provision), an interpretation which the norm validly produced by the court's decision embodies.

Kelsen is not unaware of this, of course. He very explicitly draws a contrast between, on the one hand, 'the interpretation of law by the science of law' – which he also calls 'jurisprudential interpretation' – which is 'purely cognitive ascertainment of the meaning of legal norms'; and 'the interpretation of law by legal organs', namely law-applying norms. The latter is 'authentic', says Kelsen; it 'creates law':

> In the application of law by a legal organ, the cognitive interpretation of the law to be applied is combined with an act of will by which the law-applying organ chooses between the possibilities [ie the different possible decisions within the 'frame' defined by the law which is to be applied[52]] . . . This act of will creates . . . a lower-level norm . . .. This act of will differentiates the legal interpretation by the law-applying organ from any other interpretation, especially from the interpretation of law by jurisprudence. . . . The interpretation by a law-applying organ is different from any other interpretation – all other interpretations are not authentic, that is, they do not create law.[53]

Furthermore:

> By way of authentic interpretation . . . not only one of the possibilities may be realized that [lie within the 'frame']. . . of the norm to be applied; but also a norm may be created which lies entirely outside the frame of the norm to be applied. By such authentic interpretation law can be created . . . as soon as the validity of [the individual norm created by the law-applying organ] cannot be rescinded, as soon as this norm has gained the force of a final judgment. It is well-known that much new law is created by way of such authentic interpretation, especially by courts of last resort.[54]

It seems to me, however, that Kelsen is trying to have it both ways. If, as he grants, a court can indeed produce a valid norm *N* even *outside* its sphere of empowerment as determined by some higher-order norm, then it must also be granted, it seems, that such a court is *making it the case* that it is empowered to create such a valid norm – indeed, that it is *creating* the corresponding power-conferring norm – simply *by claiming* that it is indeed empowered to produce N. But this seems to me to be at odds with Kelsen's equally explicit thesis, discussed in the previous sections, that 'if the question as to the reason for the validity of a certain legal norm is raised', then 'the answer can only consist . . . in the assertion that the norm was created according to the basic norm'. According to this test, as we saw, some given norm-claim (such as the

[52] *cf* ibid 351: 'the law to be applied constitutes only a frame within which several applications are possible, whereby every act is legal that stays within the frame'.

[53] ibid 354f.

[54] ibid.

norm-claim embodied in a court's decision) corresponds to an 'objectively valid norm' only if the norm-claim *is* made in accordance with some higher-norm (and, ultimately, with the *Grundnorm*). Yet Kelsen's remarks on 'authentic' interpretation amount to the recognition that a court's mere act of will – a court's mere norm-claim – may nonetheless bring about a valid norm. But if the test as to whether an act of will creates valid norms is itself decided, in the last resort, by an act of will – then why have a test in the first place?

There seems to be a fallacy in Kelsen's theory. How are we to deal with it?

ii. Solving the Problem

My suggestion is that one can only remain faithful to the fundamental tenets of the Pure Theory by introducing a distinction between (a) validity – to be understood as the ontological mode in which norms can be said to exist; and (b) bindingness – to be understood as the result of an authoritative pre-emption of validity. The latter is a status that authoritative decisions (with their corresponding norm-claims) may come to acquire pending the epistemological acknowledgment that they do amount to the production of valid norms. The former is a status assigned by those who – engaging epistemologically with the law with an eye to answer the question 'What should one do, as far as law is concerned, under the present conditions?' – interpret certain decisions (with their corresponding norm-claims) as producing valid norms. My argument runs as follows.

1. Let us grant Kelsen his theses (discussed above in subsection I.A) on the preconditions of legal cognition, ie the preconditions of one's knowledge that some norm *N* is valid in some legal system *L*. Let us also accept his view that validity is the specific ontological mode in which norms can be said to exist.
2. If legal cognition with regard to *L* is possible, then one should be able to make truth-apt statements with the form '*N* is valid in *L*' without authorised agents in *L* being able to disprove such statements at will. In other words, authorised and non-authorised agents must enjoy equal epistemic access to law.
3. The fulfillment of this epistemic requirement is supervenient on a sustained political programme of establishing and maintaining authority. The possibility of legal cognition with regard to *L* depends on political conditions and decisions. *L* has to be, by and large, efficacious and stable; indeed, *L* is the result of an interpretation of an efficacious order *as* a system of valid norms: efficacy, as Kelsen puts it, is a condition (though not a criterion) of validity.[55] But even though the possibility of legal cognition

[55] see ibid 211f.

thus depends on such conditions obtaining – and even though such conditions will typically include the making of decisions by political authorities – once such conditions are in place political authorities will be unable to interfere with legal cognition without losing authority both under and (eventually) over the law.[56]

4. Disputes may arise in any particular case about the correct outcome of epistemic engagements with law: the truth of any given statement with the form 'norm *N* is valid in some legal system *L*' may form the object of disagreement. Such disputes may fuel the very kind of socio-political conflicts that law is to resolve in the first place. There is therefore room in *L*, as well as need, for authoritative institutions capable of pre-emptively assigning truth-values to such statements while making decisions (and putting forth norm-claims) aimed at ending or precluding conflict. Such truth-value assignments, however, do not settle the validity issue; they do not *make* the corresponding statements true (or false), though they may contribute evidence either way.
5. Such decisions are binding in the double sense that (a) they are to be conformed to until modified by higher authoritative institutions of the same kind; and that (b) failure to conform is appropriately met with authoritatively determined sanctions.
6. Validity itself – that which is tracked by epistemic engagements with law – may well remain a moving horizon, ie provisionally established and essentially contested. While those epistemically engaged with *L* are interested in reconstructing the overall constitutional coherence of *L* (with regard to a specific case, type of case, etc) over and over again, those authoritatively involved in *L* seek to put an end to conflict (specific conflict, type of conflict, etc).

Though my proposal amounts to a deviation from the Pure Theory, it remains faithful to Kelsen's view that validity and bindingness are essentially connected or, indeed, conflate.[57] Bindingness is pre-empted validity; validity,

[56] It is beyond the limits of this chapter to argue for the view that the acquisition of legal authority is precluded if political agents never allow their norm-claims to count against themselves. As Kelsen remarks in the Preface to his *General Theory of Law and State*, 'the political authority creating the law and, therefore, wishing to conserve it, may doubt whether a purely scientific cognition of its products, free from any political ideology, is desirable. Similarly, the forces tending to destroy the present order and to replace it by another one believed to be better will not have much use for such a cognition of law, either': *cf* H Kelsen, *General Theory of Law and State*, A Wedberg transl (Cambridge, Mass., Harvard University Press, 1945) xvi. However, as soon as they intend to create a *legal* order, then by implication – or by Gricean implicature: *cf* section II – political authorities must intend to comply with a basic norm. For '(t)he basic norm of a positive legal order is nothing but the fundamental rule according to which the various norms of the order are to be created' (ibid 114).

[57] To say that 'a norm referring to the behavior of a human being is "valid"', according to Kelsen, is to say 'that it is binding – that an individual ought to behave in the manner determined by the norm': *cf The Pure Theory of Law* (n 2) 193.

reconfirmed bindingness. But each notion is associated to a different aspect of law. Bindingness relates to law *qua* authoritative practice geared towards ending or precluding social conflict. Validity relates to law *qua* object of cognition. The latter aspect I regard as the quintessential or primary one; in order authoritatively to make law, one must make it cognisable *qua* system of *norms* from which normative positions – rights, duties, powers, liabilities – can be gathered.

iii. Bindingness Without Validity and Vice Versa

There are further explanatory advantages to distinguishing legal validity from legal bindingness along the lines just sketched.[58] It makes room for the twin hypotheses (a) that we may be bound by invalid norms, and (b) that there may be valid norms by which we are not bound, at least not in the fullest sense. And both hypotheses can help us account for some familiar scenarios.

Consider, first, the possibility of bindingness without validity. There are indeed several familiar situations which can be plausibly described by saying that we *can* be bound – if only provisionally – in virtue of norm-claims which, though put forth by agents who are institutionally entrusted with legal authority to enact such claims, may turn out *not* to be valid under any plausible test that legal science may carry out. Our system of appeals provides one familiar set of examples. Take Mr and Mrs Van Aalen, who sought to obtain a formal judicial declaration that the defendant, a hospital, was liable in tort for the death of their three-year-old son Jeffrey.[59] They sought no remedies; they did not want to be awarded damages. They just felt that such a declaration would help them to cope with their loss. The county court granted the claim, but in appeal the district court reversed the decision: it saw no reason why law should deal with what it called 'purely emotional damage'. Both decisions were binding from the moment the respective judiciary authorities made them, and for as long as they stood. The Van Aalens then turned to the High Court, which upheld the district court's decision, thus confirming the denial of the Van Aalens' claim. This decision became final, and thus binding 'for good'. But was it justified under valid law? Legal scholars debated the case, and most agreed that the High Court had rendered a 'bad' decision. They offered reasons in support of the conclusion that the decision was at odds with

[58] Of course, nothing depends on the actual *terms* employed – we may reserve 'validity' for bindingness, and invent some alternative to refer to validity.

[59] I discussed the case in a different context in 'Seizing Sovereignty: The Law of Its Image' (2002) 11 *Social and Legal Studies* 395; and in 'No Harm Done. HR 9 oktober 1998, NJ 1998, 853 (Van Aalten / De Vereniging voor Christelijk Wetenschappelijk Onderwijs)' in R Janse, S Taekema and A Hol (eds), *Rechtsfilosofische Annotaties* (Nijmegen, Ars Aequi Libri, 2007).

valid law.[60] In this case, because consensus was notably strong, sustained and convincing, the High Court would come gradually to fine-tune, even abandon, its line of reasoning (though the decision in the Jeffrey case remained binding).[61] Another set of examples in which the distinction between legal bindingness and legal validity comes to the fore concerns legal decisions taken under political duress. Legal scholars in The Netherlands will usually not refer to decisions made by the High Court during the period of German occupation (1940–45), though they will not dispute the Court's jurisdiction at the time. They will regard such decisions, binding as they may have been, as invalid law – or at any rate as irrelevant for the reconstruction of valid law. (Note, in contrast, that legal scholars will be inclined to welcome judicial decisions that explicitly adopt the 'cognitive' approach, for example by discussing the relevant scholarly literature, or by engaging in comparative exercises with other jurisdictions. Note, also, that an important factor in getting appointed to the higher courts is one's cognitive performance with regard to the legal system under which one will be working.)

As for the possibility of valid norms that are not (fully) binding, think of situations in which authorities are unable, or feel reluctant, to impose sanctions for breach of valid norms (which norms are thus binding only in the sense that one undeniably ought to comply with them). This could come about if (a) there is (yet) no authority empowered to impose sanctions; (b) it is unclear what the empowered authorities actually are; or (c) if the authorities in place are relatively powerless in the situation at hand. The point could be illustrated by many a resolution of the UN Security Council (not to speak of decisions made by the International Court of Justice in The Hague). One could also say that in the development of EU law it has been precisely this cleft between validity and bindingness that has allowed the European Court of Justice to seize the initiative in a number of landmark cases, claiming to exercise its competence in the very process of overstepping it.[62] But ultimately these cases are more interesting for the direction they point to, than for the list of exceptions they may happen to suggest. Not only may supra-national polities have

[60] Vranken, for example, criticises the decision as follows: 'The Highest court decided coldly that civil law was not meant to protect such an emotional interest. One could call this a denial of the almost existential need in our culture to know who is responsible for something. But even if that were not the case, it can be said that there is something fundamentally wrong when the mother of Jeffrey is left empty-handed, but on the other hand a claim that crowing cocks cause psychological damage is allowed. The latter claim was even allowed to clog up the legal system on five different occasions'; *cf* JBM Vranken, *Exploring the Jurist's Frame of Mind. Constraints and Preconceptions in Civil Law Argumentation* (Deventer, Kluwer, 2006) 61.

[61] For a recent assessment *cf* E Van Maanen, 'Maakt Chipshol een einde aan Jeffrey?' (2010) 27 *Nederlands Tijdschrift voor Burgerlijk Recht* 189, after GE Van Maanen, 'Een arrest dat shockeert. HR 9 oktober 1998' (1999) 2 *Nederlands Tijdschrift voor Burgerlijk Recht* 47.

[62] *cf* H Lindahl, 'Dialectic and Revolution. Confronting Kelsen and Gadamer on Legal Interpretation' (2003) 24 *Cardozo Law Review* 769; L Corrias, *The Passivity of Law. Competence and Constitution in the European Court of Justice* (Dordrecht, Springer, 2011).

tighter or looser constitutional frameworks (the European Union being an instance of the former, the World Trade Organisation an instance of the latter),[63] the very parameters of constitutionalism are changing.[64]

A wider theory of law would be required to explain fully why these two aspects of law – law *qua* authoritative management of social conflict and law *qua* object of cognition – are complementary rather than antinomical. I would venture that it is precisely for the sake of *enhancing* authority that law-making authorities conduct themselves in such a way that the product of their actions and decisions constitutes a suitable object of cognition, ie that their actions and decisions can be interpreted as creating *norms*. There are at least two arguments here. First, an argument from effectiveness. It is much easier to remain in power if one's authoritative decisions can be known, interiorised and predicted, so that actual enforcement will be needed only in exceptional cases. Second, an argument from openness. Authority is not won by raising one's voice in an authoritarian manner; but it can be won and secured by allowing potential counter-voices to be heard, and by allowing other agents to prove one wrong. In mature legal systems, legal authorities can afford to entrust pursuers of legal cognition – scholars, experts, lawyers, laymen even – with such a task. As far as possible, authorities should await the results of such debates. On the other hand, legal scholars should acknowledge (as they usually do) that their epistemic exercise is premised on a political decision to expose legal validity to open dispute. But of course as disputes may continue, conflicts in society have to be settled, ended or precluded. Thus: if (1) law is geared to ending or precluding social conflict by having in place a sustainable system of norms; if (2) legal validity is not merely one of the guiding values, but indeed the *primary* guiding value of authoritative legal norm-claims; and if (3) legal validity may be permanently contested in epistemic debate; then it makes sense (a) to have institutions in place which are able provisionally to attribute that value – validity – in an authoritative way, and (b) to provide for a limited set of accountability and revision procedures. The decisions of such institutions do amount to a norm-setting interpretation of the law, in the sense that legal subjects will (within certain limits) be *bound* by them. But such decisions will bind neither higher authorities, nor the activities of legal scholars, who concern themselves with the study of norms *qua* norms, and thus with the *validity* of norm-claims (ie with the 'existence' of norms).

[63] G De Búrca and J Scott, 'The Impact of the WTO on EU Decision-making' in G De Búrca and J Scott (eds), *The EU and the WTO. Legal and Constitutional Issues* (Oxford, Hart Publishing, 2001) 2.

[64] As Neil Walker writes, 'constitutionalism in a plural order is *necessarily* conceived of not only as an internal property of polities but as a medium through which they interconnect – as a characteristic of the relationship between sites of authority as well as an internal characteristic of these authoritative sites'. *cf* N Walker, 'The EU and the WTO: Constitutionalism in a New Key' in De Búrca and Scott (eds), *The EU and the WTO* (n 63) 32f.

II. THE REFLEXIVE CHARACTER OF LEGAL VALIDITY

A. A Further Worry

In Kelsen's view, as we saw, political agents may bring about a system of legal norms. They can only do so (and intend to do so) by laying down rulings and prescriptions interpretable as creating norms whose validity can ultimately be traced to a basic norm. Note, however, that no political agent can lay down a basic norm: political agents can merely set forth a body of prescriptions which is open to being interpreted as a normative system under a basic norm. Indeed, as Kelsen writes,

> [t]o understand the nature of the basic norm it must be kept in mind that it refers directly *to a specific constitution, actually established by custom or statutory creation, by and large effective*, and indirectly to the coercive order created according to this constitution and by and large effective; the basic norm thereby furnishes the reason for the validity of this constitution and of the coercive order created in accordance with it. The basic norm, therefore . . . is not presupposed arbitrarily . . . Only if this basic norm, referring to *a specific constitution* is presupposed, that is, only if it is presupposed that one ought to behave according to *this specific constitution*, only then can the subjective meaning of a constitution-creating act and of the acts created according to this constitution be interpreted as their objective meaning, that is, as objectively valid legal norms.[65]

This means that political agents cannot possibly evade creating an epistemic stronghold for legal scholarship which may at times get in the way of political ambitions. On the other hand, it seems also to imply that the basic norm is the upshot of political rulings: that, in the last analysis, the only valid norms are those that political agents want to be valid.

But does this picture not lead us to the conclusion that the validity of legal norms is premised on the fact that legal subjects happen to *recognise* such norms as valid? Does it not lead us, in other words, to a 'recognition theory' – to an '*Anerkennungstheorie*' – of legal validity? And is such a conclusion not contrary to the basic tenets of the Pure Theory?

Since his earliest writings, Kelsen has indeed sought to reject recognition theories.[66] A weary footnote in the second edition of the *Pure Theory* summarises his views on the issue:

[65] *The Pure Theory of Law* (n 2) 201 (emphasis added).

[66] *cf* eg H Kelsen, *Hauptprobleme der Staatsrechtslehre, entwickelt aus der Lehre vom Rechtssatz*, 2nd edn (Aalen, Scientia Verlag, 1984 [1923]) 35f; or his *Allgemeine Staatslehre* (Vienna, Österreichische Staatsdrückerei, 1993 [1925]) 35f. In *General Theory of Law and State* (n 56), which seeks primarily to make a contribution to the Anglo-American discussion, one finds only weak echoes of this topic (ibid 376).

> [T]he doctrine of the basic norm is not a doctrine of recognition as is sometimes erroneously understood. According to the doctrine of recognition, positive law is valid only if it is recognized by the individuals subject to it, which means: if these individuals agree that one ought to behave according to the norms of the positive law. This recognition, it is said, actually takes place, and if this cannot be proved, it is assumed, fictitiously, as a tacit recognition. The theory of recognition, consciously or unconsciously, presupposes the ideal of individual liberty as self-determination, that is, the norm that the individual ought to do only what he wants to do. This is the basic norm of this theory. The difference between it and the theory of the basic norm of a positive legal order, as taught by the Pure Theory of Law, is evident.[67]

It does seem to go against the grain of law to argue that legal subjects are only under those obligations that they have imposed on themselves (or that can be reconstructed as being self-imposed). The same applies to legal officials, whose very status *as* legal officials is, in Kelsen's model, a product of higher-level norms. If Kelsen ever was a true Kantian – which I doubt – he was surely unimpressed by the typically Kantian views that inspired authors like Gustav Radbruch, for example, to hold that:

> a heteronomous obligation, an obligation by a foreign will, is a contradiction in itself. A Will may produce a Must if it is accompanied by the power to enforce; but neither a foreign Will nor even one's own Will may ever produce an Ought. We can understand the term "autonomy" only if by the obliging self of the self-obligation we understand not any Will, not even the desire of conscience, indeed, no empirical psychological reality whatever, but the moral personality, a purely normative, ideal, and unreal structure, in other words, the obligatory norm itself; what obliges us is not our conscience but the norm that speaks through it. So one arrives at the dilemma: either to regard the law as Will – which means to do without establishing its Ought, its obligatory force, its validity; or else to consider the law as an obligatory and valid Ought – which means to establish its validity as autonomous, as demanded by its subject's own moral personality.[68]

But while Radbruch thinks that a recognition theory keeps psychologism at bay, Kelsen thinks that a recognition theory *collapses into* psychologism.

I will argue that Kelsen expelled recognition theory from the Pure Theory of Law for the wrong reasons; and that he tacitly reintroduced it for the right reasons. In fact, as we will see, Kelsen had the wrong picture of what a recognition theory amounts to; he wouldn't therefore have noticed it reappearing at the back door.

[67] See *The Pure Theory of Law* (n 2) 218 fn 83.

[68] G Radbruch, *Legal Philosophy. The Legal Philosophies of Lask, Radbruch and Dabin* (Cambridge, Harvard University Press, 1932) 83f.

B. Norms and Indexical Reference

The '*self*-imposition' element which *Anerkennungstheorien* stress derives solely, I submit, from the intentional *structure* of one's engagement with law as a normative order. The project of recognition theories is not the oxymoronic one of suppressing the idea of authority from accounts of law and legal validity. Recognition theories do not hold that I am under a legal obligation only if what the legal authority wants me to do is *the same* as what I intend or prefer to do on the balance of reasons. What a recognition theory holds is, rather, that I am under a legal obligation only if what the legal authority wants me to do appeals to my being a *self*, ie appeals to my sense of identity in what one is to do. Tucked away in the simple question 'What should I do?' is – as Hector-Neri Castañeda, in particular, has argued – a self-referential structure that feeds on a first-person entity who takes *herself* as a subject in the practical sense, ie as an agent.[69] Perry has similarly pointed out that action depends on indexical beliefs (ie beliefs about what constitutes 'here', 'now', etc); for example, if *A* ought to go to a meeting at 5pm, she has to adopt the belief that it *now* is 5pm in order to comply with that norm. (*Quasi*-indexicals governed by the first-person are 'self' or (plural) 'together', 'one another', etc).[70]

To the extent that law is to be normatively regarded as imposing *duties* on the legal subject, then, law is dependent on the legal subject's free, intentional reconstruction of official utterances or actions as not only reasons for action in general, but as reasons for *her* action. The individual, in other words, reconstructs official behaviour as entailing a reason for *her* to act (indeed a potentially exclusionary reason: a reason that – depending on how the agent considers selfhood-preservation over time – may exclude, rather than simply contribute to the balance of reasons.)[71]

The agent's recognition of a duty as *hers* may well go together with individual disagreement, with disgust, even with fear. Antigone is the classical *topos*. She did fearfully what she believed she ought to do. Not only that; she also took liberty to *consider* the traditional laws of the polity as prima facie (valid) norms regarding how to dispose of her brother's remains, weighing such norms against the norm-claims set forth in Creon's commands. Both those traditional laws and Creon's commands were laws of *her* polis.[72] It is only the

[69] *cf* HN Castañeda, *Thinking, Language and Experience* (Minneapolis, University of Minnesota Press, 1989), which includes references to earlier work.

[70] *cf* J Perry, 'The Problem of the Essential Indexical' (1979) 13 *Noûs* 3. Indexicality, quasi-indexicality, reflexivity – all are ways of referring to the first-person perspective.

[71] The account of norms in terms of exclusionary reasons for action was famously put forth in J Raz, *Practical Reason and Norms* (London, Hutchinson, 1975). My 'potentially exclusionary' is simply meant as refinement.

[72] Antigone's agony is the choice between two forms of *positive* law, not – as some natural lawyers are inclined to think – between positive and supra-positive law.

first person, either individual or collective, that can reconstruct a threat – such as Creon's – as bringing about a prima facie norm, ie a prima facie, potentially exclusionary reason for action.[73]

To say this is not to say – contrary to Kelsen's opinion[74] – that legal obligation collapses into moral obligation. The reason is simple: though all norm-claims reflexively appeal to the self of the prospective agent, the parameters of validity are not set by the agent herself, and may well vary for legal and moral norms. But validity parameters are not the issue here; the very structure of normativity is. Indeed, the issue of legal validity presupposes that we have solved the issue of normativity – which concerns the structure of norms as authoritative elements of practical reasons. The force of recognition theories concerns the latter, not – as Kelsen mistakenly supposes – the former. Such theories stress that phenomena of all kinds, if they are to function as norms, depend on 'the eye of the beholder' recognising that 'this is about *me*' or that 'this is about *us*'. And *this* is something that Kelsen has no reason to reject. Note, in fact, that he employs similar wording in his early book on sovereignty (ie on supreme, 'highest' power):

> When do I, the beholder, presuppose an order to be sovereign? What are the grounds that cogently prompt me to the assumption in question, to the choice of the decisive presupposition?[75]

Indeed, when it comes to law, Kelsenian authority – and so normativity – is, like beauty, in the eye of the beholder. Its focal point is correlative with the viewpoint of what Raz called 'the legal man',[76] much as a vanishing point is correlative with a viewpoint in the theory of perspective.[77] For Kelsen, then,

[73] The first-person viewpoint already inherent to the position of the agent who asks herself 'What should I do' is in Antigone's case dramatically reinforced by the fact that she must ask this question with regard to her brother – a predicate which embeds a reflexive reference to a shared first-person position. One may recall the familiar example from introductory courses in predicate logic: 'John and Peter are sailors' means that John is a sailor and Peter is a sailor, whereas 'John and Peter are brothers' entails that they are each other's brothers, with 'each other' indicating self-reference.

[74] One he repeatedly pressed ever since *Hauptprobleme* (n 66) 346 ff.

[75] *cf* H Kelsen, *Das Problem der Souveränität und die Theorie des Völkerrechts. Beitrag zu einer Reinen Rechtlehre*, 2nd edn (Aalen, Scientia Verlag, 1981 [1928]) 14; authority, Kelsen says, is 'eine Voraussetzung im Denken des Staat und Recht erfassenden Betrachters' ('a presupposition in the thought of a spectator who is to understand state and law'). See also B Van Roermund, 'Authority and Authorisation' (2000) 19 *Law and Philosophy* 210, esp 218ff.

[76] J Raz, 'Kelsen's Theory of the Basic Norm' in Paulson and Paulson (eds), *Normativity and Norms* (n 1) 62ff.

[77] The vanishing point governs the position from where one *should* see a work of art in order to be 'captured' by it; but it is the viewer's viewpoint that will determine where the vanishing point *should* be construed. Seen from the viewer's viewpoint, the vanishing point may remain entirely virtual (it does not have to be a point *in* the painting); but the viewpoint *as seen from* the vanishing point may also remain virtual (for it does not have to coincide with the actual viewpoint of the spectator). Both viewpoint and vanishing point, then, may be given only obliquely, ie as a function of all sorts of depth clues.

the norm according to which murderers are to be sentenced with life imprisonment is ultimately not valid (in some legal system) simply because the King in Parliament (for example) says so. It is valid because it is 'assumed' by 'the beholder' that one ought to do what the King in Parliament says. And this 'beholder' is *not* an impartial spectator. She embodies the viewpoint of a first-person agent; she represents the capacity to exercise practical judgement in response to the question 'What should *I* do?', and it is this capacity that allows her to respond to certain facts as creating *norms*, ie reasons that potentially override the balance of reasons for action.

This responsiveness is just what is meant by 'recognition' in the sense of 'recognition theories'. It has nothing whatsoever to do with me *stipulating* what my duty is. Rather, it goes to acknowledging that a certain duty is mine. So the typical recognition that is involved in *responding* to some directive *as a norm* should be distinguished both from consent to what the norm requires, and from the judgement that it is (legally) valid. The latter, as discussed in section I, will be the result of the application of certain tests or criteria which vary from system to system, calibrated as they always are against some given body of (hierarchically structured) norms. The former is a *sequel* to the first-person 'What should I/we do?' question inherent to practical reasoning.

This first-person perspective, then, and to repeat, is inherent to our thinking *qua* agents. We do often discuss, of course, 'what I should do if I were you', or 'what one should do, whoever one is'; but this proves the very point I have been making: the viewpoint expressed by such questions is not a subjective viewpoint, but a strictly first-personal one. It is always as first-person agents that – seeking to filter out arbitrariness – we pursue objective answers to questions regarding how to act. Whether we adopt a utility-, a value- or a virtue-based view of what is required of us, such requirements become *norms* proper – they become *nomoi* – only to the extent that they become *auto*-nomoi. Therein – argues Kant in a crucial passage in *The Metaphysics of Morals* – lies the meaning of moral freedom:

> A *person* is a subject whose actions can be *imputed* to him. *Moral* personality is therefore nothing other than the freedom of a rational being under moral laws (whereas psychological personality is merely the ability to be conscious of one's identity in different conditions of one's existence). From this it follows that a person is subject to no other laws than those he gives to himself (either alone or at least along with others).[78]

Thus, this Kantian *giving oneself laws* has little to do with psychological attitudes of endorsement, agreement, or wholeheartedness that a person may adopt

[78] *The Metaphysics of Morals*, AK 6:223. I quote from I Kant, *Practical Philosophy*, MJ Gregor transl (Cambridge, Cambridge University Press, 1996) 378; *cf* also, in the same volume (at 269), *Critique of Practical Reason*, AK 5:162: '[The moral law] begins from my invisible self'.

with regard to (a) law.[79] That is not what makes a person a moral person. A moral person is one who acknowledges that what applies to all applies to her; that *she* is included in the set of those to whom a law applies.[80]

In precisely this respect, however, things are different with regard to ethical and legal norms. It is characteristic of ethics that some action φ constituting a duty is also a motive for φ-ing. It is characteristic of law, by contrast, that these two elements *may* but need not run together: it is one thing to regard φ as something that ought legally to be done, and another thing to have a motive to φ; I may recognise the legal duty to pay my taxes without that being my motive to pay them.[81] The motive may derive, surely, from φ being the content of a legal duty, but also from fear of sanctions, from a cost-benefit analyses, or from the reluctance to put in the amount of effort needed to evade φ-ing.[82] Moreover, one may have a motive to violate the norm, still acknowledging that it is a (valid) legal norm one is violating.

'Recognition', in sum, concerns the normativity of some given phenomenon – not the validity of what one considers to be a norm.

[79] Note that endorsement is distinct, again, from 'pleasure' in doing one's duty. Even in ethics one does not have to do one's duty with pleasure, but one is supposed to do it wholeheartedly. Both in ethics and in law we should acknowledge that human beings are not only 'rational' but also 'natural' beings: 'who are unholy enough that pleasure can induce them to break the moral law, even though they recognise its authority; and even when they do obey the law, they do it *reluctantly* (in the face of opposition from their inclinations)' (*The Metaphysics of Morals* AK 6:379): *cf* Kant, *Practical Philosophy* (n 78) 512.

[80] ibid 514: 'Another can indeed *coerce* me *to do* something that is not my end (but only as a means to another's end), but not to *make this my end*; and yet I can have no end without making it an end for myself. To have an end that I have not myself made an end is self-contradictory, and act of freedom which is yet not free. – But it is no contradiction to set an end for myself that is also a duty, since I constrain myself to it and this is altogether consistent with freedom' (*The Metaphysics of Morals* AK 6:381–82).

[81] ibid 383: 'In all lawgiving (whether it prescribes internal or external actions, and whether it prescribes a priori by reason alone or by the choice of another), there are two elements: first, a law, which represents an action that is to be done as *objectively* necessary, that is, which makes the action a duty; and second, an incentive, which connects a determining choice to this action *subjectively* with the representation of the law. Hence the second element is this: that the law makes duty the incentive. . . . The mere conformity or nonconformity of an action with law, irrespective of the incentive to it, is called its *legality* (lawfulness); but that conformity in which the idea of duty arising from the law is also the incentive of the action is called its morality' (*The Metaphysics of Morals* AK 6:218–19).

[82] Though one may argue that these all boil down to the same thing. With regard to the latter: increasingly, the reason to comply with copyright laws on computer software is that it is nearly impossible to copy it. *cf* EJ Koops, 'Criteria for Normative Technology: An Essay on the Acceptability of "Code as Law" in Light of Democratic and Constitutional Values' in R Brownsword and K Yeung (eds), *Regulating Technologies* (Oxford, Hart Publishing, 2008).

C. Reflexivity in the Basic Norm?[83]

That Kelsen misunderstood recognition theory and tacitly reintroduced its basic tenets in his own theory can best be shown by analysing one of the examples with which he seeks to illustrate the role of the basic norm. It is the homely story of a dialogue between father and son on going to school, parental authority and God's commands.

> A father addresses to his son the individual norm, 'Go to school.' The son asks his father, 'Why should I go to school?' That is, he asks why the subjective meaning of his father's act of will is its objective meaning, ie a norm binding for him – or, which means the same thing, what is the basis of the validity of this norm. The father responds: 'Because God has commanded that parents be obeyed – that is, He has authorized parents to issue commands to children.' The son replies: Why should one obey the commands of God? What all this amounts to is: why is the subjective meaning of this act of will of God also its objective meaning – that is a valid norm? or, which means the same thing, what is the basis of the validity of this general norm? The only possible answer to this is: because, as a believer, one presupposes that one ought to obey the commands of God.[84]

To bring out the very core of recognition theory, let us recast this story in the mould of real dialogue, suppressing all interjections of Kelsenian theoretical vocabulary:

(1) F: Go to school!
(2) S: Why should I go to school?
(3) F: Because I'm telling you to go to school.
(4) S: Why should I do as you say? Why should I obey you?
(5) F: Because God has commanded that parents be obeyed.
(6) S: Why should I obey God's commands?
(7) F: Because, as a believer, one presupposes that one ought to obey the commands of God.

The dialogue seems straightforward enough. But I submit that (7) *makes for a bad script*. It is not, in all likelihood, what the father would say. He would rather say something like (7′) or (7″):

[83] This subsection partially overlaps with B van Roermund, 'Kelsen Under the Low Skies. Recognition Theory Revisited and Revised' in R Walter, C Jabloner and K Zeleny (eds), *Hans Kelsen anderswo / Hans Kelsen Abroad. Der Einfluss der Reinen Rechtslehre auf die Rechtstheorie in verschiedenen Ländern, Teil III* (Vienna, Manz, 2010).

[84] I quote from Iain Stewart's translation: H Kelsen, 'The Function of a Constitution' in R Tur and W Twining (eds), *Essays on Kelsen* (Oxford, Clarendon Press, 1986 [1964]) 112; but variations of the example occur in several of Kelsen's writings: *cf* eg *The Pure Theory of Law* (n 2) 199; *General Theory of Norms* (n 6) 254. I am indebted to Iain Stewart for a discussion on this dialogue in the 2006 Kelsen seminar convened by Stanley L Paulson and John O'Haley at the Washington University in St Louis.

(7′) F: Because, as a believer, one ought to obey God's commands
(7″) F: Because, as believers, we ought to obey God's commands.

I actually ran a small test among 20 students in language and literature, and 98 per cent chose (7″) over (7) or (7′) as the best closing phrase to the dialogue. It is not difficult to see why. (7″) expresses three things in one fell swoop:

i. to obey God's commands is (part of) the definition of being a believer;
ii. this definition applies in the case at hand only from a first-person, plural perspective ('we'); and
iii. that perspective is shared between speaker and hearer, father and son: it is a common first-person, plural perspective.

Some of these features are suppressed in (7′), and (7) suppresses all of them. The first-person plural pronoun in (7″) takes up the third-person pronoun in (7) and (7′): here, indeed, the pronoun 'one' is a stand-in for 'we'. This 'we' does not come out of the blue; it has been governing the dialogue from the very first sentence. It is the pragmatic presupposition of a shared first-person plural perspective that accounts for the father's opening a dialogue with his son in the first place. Without such common perspective, the dialogue would have stopped at (3): 'Because I'm telling you to'. That is to say, the command in (1) would have been exclusively based on a subjective act of will. According to Kelsen's own definition of a norm, then, no norm would have emerged from the scene. What does the trick is not the detached view that, as a believer, 'one' should obey God's commands. What does the trick is the committed trust on the part of the speaker that he is sharing a viewpoint with the hearer, and the fact that the speaker expects the hearer to recognise this. Thus, it is the shared *recognition* – rather than the presupposition – that one has to obey God's commands, that defines religious belief in this story and lends objectivity to the father's reply in (5). To the extent that it is the *expectation* of shared recognition that feeds the dialogue as a joint action, one may even call it a Gricean 'implicature' rather than a presupposition.[85] As such, it may be cancelled or rejected, as the son might by saying something like (8):

(8) S: Your God or mine?

Such a reply would bring out the political backdrop against which the father's epistemic exercise is being carried out. As a 'joint' exercise,[86] it is premised on the expectation of joint recognition, and there is the risk that this expectation is frustrated. But no common epistemic exercise will ever take off the ground

[85] See P Grice, *Studies in the Way of Words* (Cambridge, Mass., Harvard University Press 1989) 24ff.

[86] See ME Bratman, *Faces of Intention. Selected Essays on Intention and Agency* (Cambridge, Cambridge University Press, 1999). According to Bratman, shared commitment does not necessarily amount to co-operative commitment; it may take the form of competition.

if such a risk is not taken. And this, it seems to me, is Kelsen's actual point with regard to law as an object of knowledge: that it rests on the political implicature of a shared recognition that some phenomenon is normative. This is the 'blind spot' in which justifications end; for that is where they emanate from.

That recognition theory was something that Kelsen actually accepted – in spite of his express claims to the contrary – is also apparent in another aspect of his doctrine of the *Grundnorm*. It is only by acknowledging the reflexive structure of norms that we can fully make sense of the claim that the basic norm directly points to the highest positive norm – ie to the constitution – and eventually to the *first* historical constitution. Kelsen's thought seems to be that by following the chain of history back to the system's 'first' constitution one will be able to answer the question of why the system's *present* constitution is valid. But this idea of 'following the chain of history' can be understood in two analytically different ways: one can *remember* the past, or one can *learn about* the past. While the latter is referential, the former is reflexive (as its translation into some languages indicates[87]). One may retrieve any 'past' that is properly documented; but one can only remember one's *own* past (which doesn't mean that one 'owns' one's past and is free to construe it according to one's likings.) And surely Kelsen *must* have meant to express the view that what counts as a system's 'historically first constitution' is something which is governed by (collective) memory, ie something *remembered from a first-person plural point of view*, rather than historiographically documented. Indeed, the fact that historians might offer a reconstruction of the Dutch 1813 Constitution as the effect of other constitutions would be completely irrelevant for whether or not the Dutch should call it *their* first constitution. What matters is whether some past constitution is recognised as *ours* – as *our* first constitution – now.[88] Here, again – at the heart of the Pure Theory – it is recognition theory that helps us make full sense of Kelsen's ideas.

III. CONCLUSION

I proposed in section I to distinguish between validity and bindingness as two modes of acknowledging the 'existence' of norms. A binding norm is one whose existence is authoritatively proclaimed; a valid norm, one whose existence is cognitively established. In mature legal systems, authorities impose norms (thereby proclaiming their bindingness) under the claim that their

[87] *cf* what ancient Greek calls the 'middle voice' between active and passive in μιμνήισκομαι; *se souvenir* (French); *sich erinnern* (German); *zich herinneren* (Dutch); *ricordarsi* (Italian); *recordar-se* or *lembrar-se* (Portuguese); etc.

[88] For a systematic account, see P Ricoeur, *La Mémoire, L'Histoire, l'Oubli* (Paris, Seuil, 2000) 388ff.

validity can be cognitively tracked; authorities thus expose themselves to a scholarly test which may well prove them wrong. But even if they are proven wrong, this self-exposure to such a test will generally enhance their authority; it undercuts the impression that officials behave arbitrarily, and correspondingly strengthens the belief that their decisions are predictable and reasonable. Thus, in the final analysis, the possibility that authoritative norm-claims are 'objectively' validated as a result of legal scholars' epistemic pursuits is contingent on a political decision to have such norm-claims submitted to a 'basic norm' validation test.

What, then, is the normative structure of such a test? Section II stressed the reflexivity of norms, which must be recognised from a first-person (plural) practical vantage point. In other words, the existence of norms – in both the validity and the bindingness modes – is ultimately correlated with, rather than dependent on, the viewpoint of a guidance-seeking plural subject. Such a subject – a society or a polity, say – cannot achieve this without mutual trust in a shared identity or selfhood. At bottom, without collective indexical self-reference, normative existence evaporates into thin air. Its format is not just based on the first-person pronoun 'we', but on its more elaborate reflexive form 'we, ourselves'.[89]

As we also saw, self-referential commitment does not amount to self-authorisation. Well on the contrary, it is typical of law that the joint commitment to a shared self takes the form of recognising *third*-person authority. Here first-person commitment and third-person authority are correlative, and describing this correlation is what legal cognition amounts to (particularly, though not exclusively, in its scholarly version). The legal scholar cannot cut loose from either of the two poles: from the vantage point of the legal community, and from the vanishing point of a highest norm attributing supreme authority. These two poles correlate in the strong sense of being mutually conditional or 'equi-primordial'; they correlate, as noted above, as both vanishing point and viewpoint in the theory of perspective. And things are similar in law. There can be no (virtually) supreme authority without a legal community appealing – with reference to the authority's very first decision – to what Kelsen calls an 'impartial third-person' viewpoint. But there can be no *legal* community prior to some political authority making binding decisions, decisions which effectively delineate the community into a bounded whole.

Living this correlation is what legal subjects and legal officials do. Their practice – one of 'doing things with rules', as Twining and Miers succinctly put it[90] – is not based on a 'presupposition'. It is based on commitment (and

[89] For the analysis of a reflexive 'we' in politico-legal context, see my essay 'First-Person Plural Legislature: Political Reflexivity and Representation' (2003) 6 *Philosophical Explorations* 235.

[90] W Twining and D Miers, *How To Do Things With Rules. A Primer of Interpretation*, 3rd edn (London, Weidenfeld and Nicholson, 1991).

detachment) and trust. Of course, if one wishes theoretically to *model* this practice of trust, one may operate, as Kelsen proposed, with this notion of a presupposition. It is, however, a theoretical or 'scientific' notion that does not resonate with legal agents concerned with the practical ramifications of law. And at the meta-theoretical level – which is the level at which the Pure Theory is placed – we may even come to the conclusion that this keystone of our model is a 'fiction' in the strong sense of the term, ie that it is, as Kelsen saw, self-contradictory.[91] This does not entail that the notion of a presupposition is self-contradictory *at the level at which the theoretical model is supposed to be of use* – any more than the fact that the notion of a presupposition features in our model entails that it is in virtue of the mere 'presupposition' that they are bound that legal agents *are* bound by the law. It is in virtue of self-commitment that they are bound.

[91] *cf General Theory of Norms* (n 6) 256.

3

The Great Puzzle: Kelsen's Basic Norm

STANLEY L PAULSON*

I. INTRODUCTION

THE BASIC NORM (*Grundnorm*) remains far and away the most notorious of the puzzles in Kelsen's legal philosophy. Many critics have found it simply baffling – to draw on Churchill, 'a riddle wrapped in a mystery inside an enigma'. The puzzle begins with the adjective 'basic'.[1] The connotations of 'basic' are close to those of 'fundamental' or 'foundational'. In the legal arena, basic norms, basic laws, basic principles and the like are understood not only as fundamental but as having substantive content. To take a single example, the opening articles of the post-War German Constitution or Basic Law (*Grundgesetz*) address the fundamental or basic rights (*Grundrechte*) of dignity, liberty and equality.[2] Kelsen's basic norm is different in having no substantive or material content.[3] Indeed, Kelsen's

* Special thanks to Bonnie Litschewski Paulson for wise counsel on every aspect of my work on Kelsen and to Robert Alexy for stimulating discussion and for his gracious hospitality in Kiel. I am indebted, too, to the editors' anonymous referees, who gave me helpful queries and suggestions.

[1] The expression 'basic' is the adjectival counterpart of Kelsen's substantive '*Grund*' (ground, basis, foundation) in the expression '*Grundnorm*'.

[2] German Basic Law, arts 1, 2 and 3 respectively. On post-War German constitutional law generally, see DP Currie, *The Constitution of the Federal Republic of Germany* (Chicago, University of Chicago Press, 1995); in an appendix to the treatise, Currie sets out the provisions of the Basic Law. See also R Alexy, *A Theory of Constitutional Rights*, J Rivers transl (Oxford, Oxford University Press, 2002 [1985]); Alexy, drawing on German law, develops a system of constitutional rights from the standpoint of 'principles theory'. Also in this genre: M Borowski, *Grundrechte als Prinzipien*, 2nd edn (Baden-Baden, Nomos, 2007); J Sieckmann, *Recht als normatives System. Die Prinzipientheorie des Rechts* (Baden-Baden, Nomos, 2009).

[3] The basic norm has no substantive or material content. Rather, it has structure, where 'structure' refers to elements that are common to every legal system, eg sanctions, empowering norms and the like. The distinction I have drawn between substantive or material content and structure reflects Kelsen's own distinction between, respectively, static and dynamic legal systems. See eg H Kelsen, *Introduction to the Problems of Legal Theory. A Translation of the First Edition* [1934] *of the* Reine Rechtslehre *or Pure Theory of Law*, BL Paulson and SL Paulson transl (Oxford, Clarendon Press, 1992) at §27 (55f), §31(a) (at 63f); H Kelsen, *General Theory of Law and State*, A Wedberg transl (Cambridge, Mass., Harvard University Press, 1945) at 110–13. Save for the temporal and

purity thesis[4] dictates that the basic norm cannot have substantive or material content.

Kelsen assigns to the basic norm the task of 'grounding' the law, of providing a foundation for the law, and the ensuing puzzle might be conceptualised in the form of a dilemma: Either the characterisation of the basic norm provides nothing remotely like a foundation for the law, generating instead a *petitio principii*, a begging of the question,[5] or – the other horn of the dilemma – despite this or that Kantian or Neo-Kantian[6] argument appearing to undergird the basic norm and to lend to it a grounding function, no such Kantian or Neo-Kantian argument proves to be sound.

An argument undergirding the basic norm has to be a Kantian or Neo-Kantian argument because Kelsen's self-imposed constraint, the purity thesis,[7] precludes every appeal to facts or values. That is to say, the purity thesis

territorial references of the basic norm, which identify it as the basic norm of this or that particular legal system, the structure of the basic norm – if only there were agreement on what that structure comes to – is the same in every legal system. In passing, it might be noted that this point is by itself enough to establish a distinction in kind between Kelsen's basic norm and Hart's rule of recognition, for Hart's rule of recognition is always a reflection of a particular legal system, see HLA Hart, *The Concept of Law*, 3rd edn (Oxford, Oxford University Press, 2012 [1961]) at 108f, 292f. The point is abundantly clear in recent work on the rule of recognition in American law, see MD Adler and KE Himma (eds), *The Rule of Recognition and the U.S. Constitution* (New York, Oxford University Press, 2009).

[4] See the text and note at n 7.

[5] This is the thrust of Robert Alexy's reply, as I read him, to Kelsen on the basic norm. See R Alexy, *The Argument from Injustice*, BL Paulson and SL Paulson transl (Oxford, Clarendon Press, 2002 [1991]) at 96–98.

[6] Of course there are significant – some would say enormous – differences between Kant's own philosophy and the philosophies developed by the Neo-Kantians, most prominently in the Marburg and Baden schools. Some of Kelsen's language on this front is sufficiently indeterminate to be understood as referring either to Kant's philosophy or to that of one or another of the Neo-Kantians. I attend, in section IV, to distinctions between Kant and the Neo-Kantians that raise questions about Kelsen's transcendental enterprise. For an uncommonly perceptive interpretation, see S Hammer, 'A Neo-Kantian Theory of Legal Knowledge in Kelsen's Pure Theory of Law?' in SL Paulson and BL Paulson (eds), *Normativity and Norms. Critical Perspectives on Kelsenian Themes* (Oxford, Oxford University Press, 1998) 177–94.

[7] Kelsen first introduces the language of a 'pure' theory of law in the subtitle of and foreword to his book, *Das Problem der Souveränität und die Theorie des Völkerrechts. Beitrag zu einer reinen Rechtslehre* (Tübingen, JCB Mohr, 1920), although the idea of purity is found in his work from the beginning. Kelsen's references to purity flag the so-called 'purity thesis', according to which the theory of the law is pure in so far as it is beholden neither to facts nor to values. In other words, no *arguments* reflecting either naturalism or morality can lend support to the Pure Theory of Law. This reflects something of Kant's view on purity, to which he gives effective expression in *Über den Gebrauch teleologischer Principien in der Philosophie* (first publ 1788), in Kant, *Gesammelte Schriften*, ed Royal Prussian Academy of Sciences and successor academies (29 volumes to date) (Berlin, Georg Reimer; later Berlin, Walter de Gruyter, 1902ff), commonly referred to as the *Akademie Ausgabe* [hereafter: *Ak* with volume number] vol 8, 157–84; Engl edn: 'On the Use of Teleological Principles in Philosophy', G Zöller transl, in Kant, *Anthropology, History, and Education*, G Zöller and RB Louden (eds) (Cambridge, Cambridge University Press, 2007) 192–218. As Kant writes, what is '*pure*' is 'not *dependent* on anything empirical', *Ak*8:184 (emphasis in original), Engl edn (above, this note) 218.

precludes any and every argument reflecting either a naturalistic standpoint or a moral point of view. What remains, Kelsen would have us believe, is a Kantian transcendental argument. But, as I argue in section III, no such argument undergirding the basic norm is sound.

The problems do not end here. Kelsen's appeal to the 'transcendental method' of Hermann Cohen and others in the Marburg School of Neo-Kantianism, ostensibly offering him the means to a sound argument, is not convincing either. This is my emphasis in section IV.

Is there an alternative? I turn, in section V, to an interpretation of Kelsen's Pure Theory of Law as a transcendental philosophy *without* transcendental argument.[8] My focus, with some textual support, is Arthur Schopenhauer. While the appeal to Schopenhauer may be of help in filling in a few of the blanks, it offers, *ex hypothesi*, no foundational argument.

My thesis, in a word, is that Kelsen fails to make a convincing case for his foundational claim. Part and parcel of my appeal to Schopenhauer is the possibility, as I note in section V, of understanding 'basic norm' simply as a shorthand reference to an explication of what, exactly, the jurist is doing in conceptualising 'the positive law as a valid system, as norm'.[9] The details of this interpretation must be left, however, to another paper.

Before turning to criticism, I examine, in section II, Kelsen's move to generate the foundational claim, which is found in the transition from his major treatise of 1911 to a paper of 1914.

II. GENERATING THE FOUNDATIONAL CLAIM

There is not a hint of a basic norm in Kelsen's first jurisprudential treatise, *Main Problems in the Theory of Public Law*, published in 1911,[10] and this, as we shall see, is no accident. The framework that Kelsen introduces here rules out the very possibility of a basic norm, however understood. Then, no later than 1914, Kelsen shifts ground, with an eye to introducing a basic norm.

The framework of *Main Problems*, for present purposes, consists of a distinction between 'how'-questions and 'why'-questions. Kelsen restricts the jurist to the former, the 'how'-questions.[11] The jurist addresses such questions as, for example, *how* legal norms are applied, *how* they are cognised or known,

[8] The phrase is Paul Guyer's. See P Guyer, 'Schopenhauer, Kant, and the Methods of Philosophy' in C Janaway (ed), *The Cambridge Companion to Schopenhauer* (Cambridge, Cambridge University Press, 1999) 93–137, at 93.

[9] Kelsen, *Introduction* (n 3) §29 (58).

[10] See H Kelsen, *Hauptprobleme der Staatsrechtslehre* (Tübingen, JCB Mohr, 1911) at 33–57, 142–88 and throughout, repr in M Jestaedt (ed), *Hans Kelsen Werke. Volume 2* (Tübingen, Mohr Siebeck, 2007).

[11] See Kelsen, *Hauptprobleme* (n 10) at 353.

how their logical form is to be understood[12] and so forth. In good Kelsenian parlance, these questions pose *formal* issues, and so they fall within the bailiwick of legal science. Indeed, elsewhere in *Main Problems*, Kelsen, with a nod to Hugo Preuß,[13] describes the concepts of legal science as '*formal* categories'.[14] These formal categories are what remain after Kelsen has eliminated the various material standpoints – teleological, psychological, sociological, political, moral and religious.[15] Their elimination is of course a central task of a pure theory of law, and Kelsen is busy at work on this front a decade before adopting, from Rudolf Stammler, the label 'pure theory of law'.[16]

In sharp contrast to these formal issues, posed as 'how'-questions, the overriding 'why'-question, Kelsen tells us, is addressed to the reason for compliance with the law and, likewise, to the reason for applying the law where compliance is not forthcoming.[17] 'Why'-questions pose *material* issues, that is, issues of explanation on the one hand and of justification on the other. Explanatory questions – say, the question of motives for compliance with the law – can be answered only by appeal to psychology or sociology, while justificatory questions can be dealt with, if at all, only by appeal to morality or religion.

> [T]he question of the basis of the validity of the law, on both of its possible [material] readings, turns out to be legally irrelevant. Either the question addresses the motive for lawful behaviour and is therefore a psychologico-sociological problem, or the question aims at moral justification and so finds itself in the realm of ethics.[18]

[12] See ibid at 237.

[13] Hugo Preuß is the draftsman of the *Weimar Verfassung*, and he is well known, too, for his work in legal theory, which reflected to a considerable extent the influence of Otto von Gierke. On ties between the theories of Kelsen and Preuß, despite the fact that their respective intellectual backgrounds are very different, see SL Paulson, 'Hugo Preuß und Hans Kelsen – überraschende Parallelen' in C Müller (ed), *Gemeinde, Stadt, Staat: Aspekte der Verfassungstheorie von Hugo Preuß* (Baden-Baden, Nomos, 2005) 65–83. On Preuß generally, see D Schefold, 'Hugo Preuß (1860–1925)' in H Heinrichs and others (eds), *Deutsche Juristen jüdischer Herkunft* (Munich, CH Beck, 1993) 429–53, and, with special attention to Preuß's legal theory, D Schefold, 'Einleitung' in H Preuß, *Gesammelte Schriften*, D Lehnert and C Müller (eds), vol 2: *Öffentliches Recht und Rechtsphilosophie im Kaiserreich*, Schefold (ed) (Tübingen, Mohr Siebeck, 2009) 1–76.

[14] Kelsen, *Hauptprobleme* (n 10) 92 (emphasis in original).

[15] See ibid at 92, 353 and throughout.

[16] Although the ultimate source of the notion of purity in Kelsen's purity thesis is Kant (see n 7), the immediate source of the 'purity' language is almost certainly Rudolf Stammler. Kelsen, in the foreword to *Das Problem der Souveränität* (n 7), refers to Stammler, and the work in question is Stammler's *Theorie der Rechtswissenschaft* (Halle, Waisenhaus, 1911). There Stammler speaks, inter alia, of 'the task' and 'the possibility' of constructing a 'pure theory of law', see ibid at 1–6, 10–23.

[17] This two-fold doctrine of the legal norm, speaking both to compliance and to the application of the norm (the imposition of a sanction should compliance not be forthcoming), counts as Kelsen's version of 'double institutionalisation', and it is already evident in *Hauptprobleme* (n 10) 49f and throughout. HLA Hart's talk of the intersection or 'union of primary rules of obligation with . . . secondary rules' as marking 'what is indisputably a legal system' is another reference to double institutionalisation; Hart, *The Concept of Law* (n 3) 94.

[18] Kelsen, *Hauptprobleme* (n 10) 353.

In short, these 'why'-questions are off limits for the jurist. And, by the same token, a basic norm is off limits, for it is directed to the overriding 'why'-question of the reason for compliance with the law or for applying the law where compliance is not forthcoming. The 'why'-questions pose material issues, and they are ruled out by a legal science that confines itself to questions posing formal issues, the 'how'-questions.

To trace these steps in *Main Problems*, I begin with the key passage on the overriding question of why the law ought to be complied with or why, should compliance not be forthcoming, the law ought to be applied. Kelsen argues that to pose this question from a legal standpoint is to engage in nonsense. 'Why', he asks, '*ought* the legal norm be complied with and applied?' Here is his answer:

> [T]he very posing of this question seems on first glance to be absurd. For it is intrinsic to the concept of the legal norm from the outset that the legal norm *ought* to be complied with and applied. The idea of the legal norm qua 'norm' already contains the qualification that the legal norm *ought* to be complied with and applied, so that this question would be tantamount to asking, say, why ought a norm that ought to be complied with be complied with?[19]

Kelsen's punchline is designed to show this line of enquiry to be patent nonsense, the result of proceeding as though legal science, with its distinctly formal stance, could sensibly pose and answer the overriding 'why'-question, which by its very nature is a material question. Or so Kelsen is arguing in 1911.

What happens, now, if everything is turned upside down? What happens if the formal stance of legal science is set aside and with it the idea of the legal norm as *sui generis*,[20] as a formal category? What then?

> If . . . one does not assume the normative character of the legal norm to be a self-sufficient, independent quality, not derivable from anything else, then the question of why a legal norm ought to be complied with can be understood as a question about the more general, higher norm that is superior to the legal norm at issue. For it is according to this higher norm that behaviour complying with the legal norm appears to be commanded, to be obligatory.[21]

This 'more general, higher norm' is a norm of morality or religion. From the standpoint of either morality or religion, one is free to pose the question of obligation as a material issue, as a genuine 'why'-question.

[19] ibid 352 (emphasis and quotation marks in original).

[20] This terminology stems from Alf Ross. See A Ross, *Theorie der Rechtsquellen* (Leipzig and Vienna, Deuticke, 1929) at 229, and A Ross, *Towards a Realistic Jurisprudence*, AI Fausbøll transl (Copenhagen, Einar Munksgaard, 1946) at 40f.

[21] Kelsen, *Hauptprobleme* (n 10) 352.

Unless everything is in fact turned upside down, however, the jurist will not have this freedom. It is for the moral philosopher to weigh critically an answer to the question of obligation, while for the jurist

> the normative character of the legal norm is an unshakeable presupposition, beyond all discussion. For the jurist, the knowledge that a legal norm conflicts with a moral norm cannot in any way change the fact that he recognizes even this legal norm as a norm, that is, he does not doubt that it ought to be complied with and applied. Any other stance on the part of the jurist would have him sawing off the very branch on which he sits. Resorting to a higher, moral order would mean the surrender of a self-sufficient legal system, the abandonment of an independent legal science and its disappearance without a trace into ethics. The jurist is not to question the *material* basis of the validity of the legal system. The only question the jurist is permitted to pose is a *formal* question. The jurist is to determine not the basis, not the 'why', but, rather, only the 'how'.[22]

The 'normative character of the legal norm' is presupposed, a point so obvious, Kelsen says, as to be 'beyond all discussion'.

So far, so good, from Kelsen's standpoint. The very possibility of addressing material questions, the genuine 'why'-questions, has been eliminated. This, after all, is what the formal stance of legal science requires.

Still, is Kelsen not left in a quandary? Simply to say that the 'normative character of the legal norm' is obvious and 'beyond all discussion' is a tad scanty. And Kelsen was too astute a thinker to leave it at that. So, as early as 1914, he shifts ground,[23] to wit: Alongside the possible material answers to the overriding 'why'-question, he now argues that there is also a formal answer that falls squarely within legal science. This formal answer to the overriding 'why'-question is the basic norm. The shift here is two-fold. First, Kelsen abandons the strict dichotomy between formal 'how'-questions and material 'why'-questions. The overriding 'why'-question, he is now saying, can lend itself to a formal answer. And, second, where the overriding 'why'-question is understood as lending itself to a formal answer, its character undergoes a profound change. It is no longer to be understood as a justificatory question, as the classical question of why the law ought to be obeyed. Instead, the 'why'-question emerges as Kelsen's foundational question, namely, the question of how the 'objective validity' of legal norms is to be grounded.

The result of Kelsen's shift, then, is to adhere to the formal stance but to open it up, now answering 'why'-questions in its name. To be sure, Kelsen's new 'why'-questions are most emphatically not justificatory questions. Rather, Kelsen's concern is with the nomological character of legal

[22] ibid 353 (emphasis and quotation marks in original).

[23] See H Kelsen, 'Reichsgesetz und Landesgesetz nach österreichischer Verfassung' (1914) 32 *Archiv des öffentlichen Rechts* 202–45, 390–438, at 215–20, repr in M Jestaedt (ed), *Hans Kelsen Werke. Volume 3* (Tübingen, Mohr Siebeck, 2010) 359–425, at 370–73.

science,[24] which, once established, assures that legal norms are 'objectively valid'. Kelsen now begins to explore in an altogether serious way the 'normative character' of the law, presupposed as obvious in 1911.

But how can Kelsen, having ruled out with the purity thesis every naturalistic argument and every moral argument, too, establish the nomological character of legal science or anything else? At various points in Kelsen's writings, his answer appears to take the form of a Kantian transcendental argument. Two questions arise here. First, why does Kelsen turn to a *transcendental* argument with its peculiarly 'transcendental' strategy rather than to something else? Second, why does Kelsen need any argument at all at this juncture? I have hinted at the answer to the first question. Since Kelsen's own constraint, the purity thesis, precludes both naturalistic and moral arguments, then, if there is to be an argument at all, it will have to be transcendental in character. Something of Kant's own quest, in the first *Critique*, for a form of argument that is altogether distinct from the rationalist and empiricist arguments of the tradition is present in Kelsen's reasoning, too. But, the second question, why does Kelsen need any argument here at all? Could he not simply set out the machinery of his Pure Theory of Law and invite the reader to compare his theory with other legal theories? Kelsen assumes, of course, that his theory has greater explanatory power than the competing theories, so why not rest the case with that? I believe he can,[25] but he wants to take the case further. Specifically, he wants to demonstrate that his legal theory is the only possible theory, the only possible means of establishing the objective validity of legal norms. And this leads him to take the steps that have him, in effect, adducing a transcendental argument.[26]

III. A KANTIAN TRANSCENDENTAL ARGUMENT IN LEGAL SCIENCE?

In *The Philosophical Foundations of Natural Law Theory and Legal Positivism* (1928) and in later writings, Kelsen poses his own transcendental question, identified by the characteristic Kantian language of 'possibility':

[24] See generally SL Paulson, 'A "Justified Normativity" Thesis in Hans Kelsen's Pure Theory of Law? Rejoinders to Robert Alexy and Joseph Raz' in M Klatt (ed), *Institutionalized Reason. The Jurisprudence of Robert Alexy* (Oxford, Oxford University Press, 2012) 61–111; H Dreier, 'Hans Kelsens Wissenschaftsprogramm' in H Schulze-Fielitz (ed), *Die Verwaltung, Beiheft 7: Staatsrechtslehre als Wissenschaft* (Berlin, Duncker & Humblot, 2007) 81–114.

[25] I return to this option in my brief concluding remark, suggesting that this is indeed Kelsen's alternative if, as I have argued, his transcendental argument is not workable.

[26] These are, to be sure, steps taken in a reconstruction. Kelsen does not at any point adduce a transcendental argument in a straightforward fashion, something he has in common with other philosophers and theorists of his day who drew on the work of the Marburg and Baden Neo-Kantians. In Kelsen's case, see the references to and quotations from his writings at nn 28, 31, 32 and 34. Here and elsewhere in his writings, one finds indications of his transcendental argument.

> How is positive law qua object of cognition, qua object of cognitive legal science, possible?[27]

Kelsen answers his transcendental question by appealing to the basic norm:

> Provided that only the presupposition of the basic norm makes possible the interpretation of the subjective sense of [certain material facts] as their objective sense, that is, as objectively valid legal norms, the basic norm can be described in its characterization by legal science as the logico-transcendental condition for this interpretation – if a concept of Kant's theory of knowledge may be applied by analogy.[28]

The language of 'possibility' is the key. The Kantian transcendental argument in its regressive form has the philosopher beginning with something that is given and then moving to the condition or conditions without which what is given would not be possible. Taking our cues from language such as this, what does Kelsen's transcendental argument look like? Here is a possible reconstruction:

(1) These legal norms, together representing a legal system, are objectively valid (*given*).
(2) The objective validity of these legal norms is possible only if the basic norm is presupposed (*transcendental premise*).
(3) Therefore, the basic norm is presupposed (*transcendental conclusion*).

The first premise – which, we may assume for the moment,[29] reflects the regressive form of Kant's own transcendental argument – introduces material that is given, whose existence is not in dispute. The characteristic Kantian language of possibility is found in the second premise, the transcendental premise. Then, by successive applications of *modus ponens*, the conclusion follows in a perfectly straightforward way.[30] This is to say that the problems with Kelsen's argument turn not on questions of logic, but on the question of the truth of the transcendental premise.

[27] H Kelsen, *Die philosophischen Grundlagen der Naturrechtslehre und des Rechtspositivismus* (in the series 'Philosophische Vorträge der Kant-Gesellschaft', no 31) (Charlottenburg, Pan-Verlag Rolf Heise, 1928) §36 (at 66).

[28] H Kelsen, *Reine Rechtslehre*, 2nd edn (Vienna, Deuticke, 1960) §34(d) (at 204f).

[29] I raise questions, in section IV, about the viability of this assumption.

[30] In schematic form, the transcendental argument in its regressive form looks like this:

(1) *P* (*given*).
(2) *P* is possible only if *Q* (*transcendental premise*).
(3) Therefore, *Q* (*transcendental conclusion*).

In the first premise, '*P*' stands for the material that is given, and, in the second premise and conclusion, '*Q*' stands for the presupposed basic norm. The argument is rendered formally valid by adding the trivial premise – call it premise 1a – to the effect that if *P* is given, as in premise 1, then *P* is possible. Then, from what is given, one regresses so to speak to the basic norm without which what is given would not be possible.

An evaluation of Kelsen's transcendental argument begins with a distinction between two perspectives. From a perspective *outside* the legal system, no transcendental argument addressed to the objective validity of legal norms is compelling. Kelsen himself points out that for, say, the anarchist, who stands outside the legal system and 'refuses to see anything but naked power where jurists speak of the law',[31] no transcendental argument can promise a demonstrative case on behalf of a position contrary to the anarchist's.[32]

While not arguing that a transcendental argument can make a difference from a perspective outside the legal system, Kelsen believes that from a perspective *inside* the legal system,[33] the transcendental argument is compelling. The familiar practice with the regressive form of the argument is to proceed from something given, and Kelsen begins with the fact of legal science.[34] All the steps taken by legal science in its restatement of the law are likewise given. Of course, it will be of interest that something is given only if there is a supporting argument, and this is precisely what the transcendental argument is supposed to provide.

By its nature, the transcendental argument will have force only if alternative approaches to the problem can be ruled out, that is to say, alternatives to Kelsen's Pure Theory of Law. This is the import of the transcendental premise in Kelsen's argument. The premise is true only if the peculiarly Kelsenian doctrine alone, the basic norm, can, indeed, do the work required. If alternatives – other doctrines from other legal theories – can do the same work, then Kelsen's transcendental premise is not true. Kelsen thinks he is on safe ground here. He draws on a tacit assumption of much work in the European tradition in legal philosophy and legal theory, namely, that the only approaches to the law are fact-based theories and natural law theory, that these two types of theory are not only mutually exclusive but jointly exhaustive of the possibilities.[35]

[31] Kelsen, *Introduction* (n 3) §16 (at 36).

[32] This point of Kelsen's simply underscores the limitations of the regressive version of the transcendental argument.

[33] See Alexy, *The Argument from Injustice* (n 5) at 109, where, in a characterisation of Kelsen's position, he writes: 'One can of course refuse . . . to participate in the (utterly real) game of the law. But if one gets into this game – and there are good reasons, at least in practice, to do so – then there is no alternative to the category of "ought" and thereby no alternative to the basic norm.'

[34] See quotation in the text at n 48.

[35] See eg H Kelsen, '"Foreword" to the Second Printing of *Main Problems in the Theory of Public Law*', BL Paulson and SL Paulson transl (from the *Vorrede* to Kelsen's *Hauptprobleme* (n 10)) in *Normativity and Norms* (n 6) 3–22, at 3f: 'The purity of the theory is to be secured against the claims of a so-called "*sociological*" point of view, which employs *causal*, scientific methods to appropriate the law as a part of natural reality. And it is to be secured against the *natural law theory*, which, by ignoring the fundamental referent found exclusively in the positive law, takes legal theory out of the realm of positive legal norms and into that of ethico-political postulates' (quotation marks and emphasis in the original). Horst Dreier neatly captures this aspect of the tradition, *tertium non datur*, with his talk of Kelsen's 'two-front strategy', see H Dreier, *Rechtslehre, Staatssoziologie und Demokratietheorie bei Hans Kelsen*, 2nd printing (Baden-Baden, Nomos, 1990) at 27–42. Kelsen's two-front strategy is also an overriding motif in Joseph Raz's work on Kelsen, see eg J Raz, 'The Purity

Kelsen proceeds with this assumption, *tertium non datur*,[36] as his point of departure. His stance on *tertium non datur* is, however, entirely a matter of strategy, for he believes the dictum to be mistaken. Neither of these two types of legal theory is defensible. By contrast, his own Pure Theory of Law – a third type of theory – is indeed defensible.

Kelsen does not, however, offer satisfactory arguments in support of his claim that natural law theory is indefensible, more often than not simply dismissing it out of hand. Natural law theory is left standing, then, as an alternative to Kelsen's own philosophy. What is more, even if Kelsen were able to offer sound arguments against the viability of both fact-based theories and natural law theory, he would not thereby settle the matter in his favour. For he undermines his first assumption, *tertium non datur*, by introducing his own philosophy, the Pure Theory of Law, as a distinct species of legal philosophy alongside and at the same level of abstraction as the two traditional approaches. Having opened up the field, he cannot now rule out the introduction of a fourth and even a fifth distinct species of legal philosophy.[37] Thus, even if Kelsen were to succeed in arguing against both fact-based legal positivism and natural law theory, he has no argument on behalf of *quartum non datur*. The presence of alternatives to Kelsen's philosophy means, in a word, that a transcendental argument, the only possible source of support for the Pure Theory of Law, is not sound, for its transcendental premise cannot be shown to be true.

The problems with attributing to Kelsen a Kantian or Neo-Kantian transcendental argument do not stop here. For it appears, in the end, that Kelsen is oscillating between Kant's transcendental argument and the argument developed in the name of a 'transcendental method' by the Marburg Neo-Kantians, most notably Hermann Cohen.

of the Pure Theory' (1981) 35 *Revue internationale de philosophie* 441–59, at 442, repr in *Normativity and Norms* (n 6) 237–52, at 238, and in J Raz, *The Authority of Law*, 2nd edn (Oxford, Clarendon Press, 2009) 293–312, at 294.

36 A distinguished historian of political and legal philosophy, Alexander P d'Entrèves, offers an illuminating statement on various legal theories divided according to the two rubrics in question, fact-based theories and natural law theory. See his paper 'Two Questions about Law' in T Würtenberger and others (eds), *Existenz und Ordnung. Festschrift für Erik Wolf zum 60. Geburtstag* (Frankfurt, Klostermann, 1962) 309–20, repr in AP d'Entrèves, *Natural Law*, 2nd edn (London, Hutchinson, 1970) 173–84.

37 Kelsen's introduction of a distinct species of legal philosophy alongside and at the same level of abstraction as the traditional approaches generates six possible species of legal philosophy. They stem from combinations of the *separation thesis* (complete separation of law and morality) with *juridico-fact thesis I* (no complete separation of law and fact), with *juridico-fact thesis II* (complete separation of law and fact), and with *juridico-fact thesis III* (reduction of law to fact), and, likewise, from combinations of the *morality thesis* (no complete separation of law and morality) with each of the three juridico-fact theses. Of course it does not follow that there are six prima facie defensible species. Some combinations of theses may well be nonsensical. The point lies elsewhere. Kelsen makes no effort to rule out these various species of legal philosophy, which is to say that there are possible alternatives to his own legal philosophy and this in turn undermines the transcendental argument.

IV. THE NEO-KANTIAN 'TRANSCENDENTAL METHOD' AND KELSEN'S OSCILLATION

In Kant's own philosophy, the so-called regressive form of the transcendental argument is to be understood in terms of its counterpart, the progressive form of the argument. The progressive form of the argument captures Kant's enterprise in the transcendental analytic of the first *Critique*, with the argument in regressive form serving as a shorthand version of the progressive form.[38] In particular, the progressive form of the argument takes as its point of departure a decidedly weak initial premise, a statement of the data of consciousness, and then, by way of an appeal to the necessary unity of consciousness, it proceeds, ultimately, to the objective experience of a phenomenal world. On one reading of the Kantian argument, the weak initial premise is designed to trap the sceptic, who calls into question the very idea of objective experience. The sceptic, however, cannot help but assent to Kant's initial premise, which simply records the data of consciousness. Having assented thereto, the sceptic is led inexorably to a position diametrically opposed to his own, namely, to the objective experience of the phenomenal world.

Whether the moves in the first *Critique*, understood as Kant's reply to the sceptic, are successful need not be pursued here. Kelsen, for his part, has no illusions about being able to answer the sceptic, and he says as much:

> [T]he Pure Theory of Law is well aware that one cannot prove the existence of the law as one proves the existence of natural material facts and the natural laws governing them, that one cannot adduce compelling arguments to refute a posture like theoretical anarchism.[39]

Kelsen refers here to what he understands as Kant's achievement, namely, Kant's transcendental demonstration of the objectivity of material facts and the laws of nature governing them. By contrast, no demonstration can 'prove the existence of the law'. Kelsen's sceptic, the anarchist, cannot be defeated by means of a transcendental argument. Recognising this, Kelsen turns to a perspective *inside* the legal system, where no issue of scepticism arises.[40]

Not simply owing to the absence of scepticism but for other reasons, too, Kelsen's transcendental argument appears to be far closer to Marburg Neo-Kantianism than to anything in Kant. The 'essential premise' of Kant's greater

[38] For a juxtaposition of the two arguments, regressive and progressive, with a comparison of their respective premises, see SL Paulson, 'The Neo-Kantian Dimension of Kelsen's Pure Theory of Law' (1992) 12 *Oxford Journal of Legal Studies* 311–32, at 328–30.

[39] Kelsen, *Introduction* (n 3) §16 (at 34).

[40] See also text and quotation at nn 31 to 33. One analogy to Kelsen's perspective *inside* the legal system is Hart's 'internal point of view', see Hart, *The Concept of Law* (n 3) at chs IV–VI.

argument, as Peter Strawson puts it,[41] is the necessary unity of consciousness or, in Kant's abstruse terminology, the transcendental unity of apperception.[42] In a notoriously difficult and prolix argument, Kant claims to show that the necessary unity of consciousness establishes objectivity, in Kantian parlance one's experience of objects. This means, inter alia, that the experiencing agent can distinguish these objects from particular experiences of them.[43] Here Kant spells out the argument by appealing to one's ability to ascribe to one's own consciousness conscious states that include the reidentification of numerically identical objects, thereby ruling out the 'reduction' of such objects to the conscious states themselves, as in empirical or dogmatic idealism.[44] Kant, in a word, makes a case in these terms for the existence of the phenomenal world.

Kelsen's interest, however, lies not in showing the existence of the phenomenal world, but in presupposing precisely this phenomenal world in the course of adducing his own transcendental argument addressed to legal science.[45] And, in the treatise of Kelsen's that comes closest to shedding light on how, exactly, his transcendental argument is to be understood,[46] his point of departure, the 'fact of legal science', appears to be the very point of departure found in the work of the Marburg Neo-Kantians, who speak *expressis verbis* of the 'fact of science'. As Hermann Cohen writes:

> If . . . I take cognition not as a form and manner of consciousness, but as a *Faktum* that has established itself in *science* and that continues to establish itself *on given foundations*, then the enquiry is no longer directed to a subjective fact; it is directed instead to a fact that *to whatever extent* self-propagating is *nevertheless* objectively given, a fact *grounded in principles*. In other words, the enquiry is directed not to the process and apparatus of cognition, but to its result, to science itself. Then the unequivocal question arises: From *which presuppositions* does this fact of science derive its certainty?[47]

[41] See PF Strawson, *The Bounds of Sense* (London, Methuen, 1966) at 24, 26.

[42] See I Kant, *Critique of Pure Reason* (first publ 1781/1787), NK Smith transl (London, Macmillan, 1929) at A107. Kant takes 'apperception' from Leibniz, who introduced the notion as a means of referring to self-consciousness. Apperception as conscious awareness is a step up, in Leibniz's philosophy, from 'unconscious perception'. See Leibniz, *Principles of Nature and of Grace, Founded on Reason* (first publ 1714), M Morris transl, in GW Leibniz, *Philosophical Writings*, GHR Parkinson (ed) (London, JM Dent, 1973) 195–205, at 197.

[43] For Peter Strawson's interpretation of Kant's objectivity thesis, on which I have drawn, see Strawson, *The Bounds of Sense* (n 41) at 89–112 and throughout.

[44] This, Kant argues, is Berkeley's position, see Kant, *Critique of Pure Reason* (n 42) at B71 and B274.

[45] On this point, see eg H Rickert, *Der Erkenntnis des Gegenstandes*, 6th edn (Tübingen, JCB Mohr, 1928) at 406f.

[46] I have in mind *Introduction* (n 3), where one finds a clear distinction between perspectives outside and inside the legal system, with Kelsen confining his transcendental argument to the latter (see text at nn 31 to 33), and also a clear statement on 'the fact of legal science', understood as Kelsen's point of departure in the argument (see text at n 48).

[47] H Cohen, *Das Princip der Infinitesimal-Methode und seine Geschichte* (Berlin, Ferd Dümmler, 1883) 5 (emphasis in original). See also H Cohen, *Begründung der Ethik*, 1st edn (Berlin, Ferd Dümmler, 1877) at 24f. The *locus classicus* on the transcendental method of the Marburg Neo-Kantians is P Natorp, 'Kant and the Marburger Schule' (1912) 17 *Kant-Studien* 193–221.

Kelsen's point of departure seems directly comparable:

> The possibility and the necessity of a normative theory of law is shown by the very fact of legal science (*das Faktum der Rechtswissenschaft*) over a millennium . . .[48]

It turns out, however, that the differences between Cohen's and Kelsen's respective points of departure are greater than their similarities. The key to these differences lies in Marburg Neo-Kantianism. I look in particular at the work of its leading figure, Hermann Cohen.[49] For it was Cohen who first introduced what he and others in the Marburg School called the 'transcendental method' with its point of departure in the fact of science.[50] Far from beginning with the data of consciousness, which would have him following Kant, Cohen takes his task to be determining the presuppositions from which 'this fact of science derive[s] its certainty'.

It is no accident that Cohen's understanding of the philosopher's task is different from Kant's. Philosophy in Germany was in a state of great flux at mid-century. The earlier Hegelian consensus had collapsed, and 'scientific positivism' took its place. So it was that psychologism, which in its early-nineteenth-century development had run counter to the prevailing post-Kantian idealism, gained enormously in prominence by mid-century. Psychologistic readings of Kant, familiar from Jakob Friedrich Fries and Friedrich Eduard Beneke in the early days of psychologism, were now being endorsed and, indeed, further developed by some of the leading theorists of the day, not least among them the physicist, physiologist and philosopher, Hermann von Helmholtz.

In his early work, in the 1860s, Cohen, too, proceeded from a psychological standpoint, having been influenced in his Berlin period by Heymann Steinthal and Moritz Lazarus, followers of Johann Friedrich Herbart. Cohen's early commitment to psychology is reflected in studies on Plato, for example his essay of 1866 entitled 'The Platonic Theory of Ideas Developed Psychologically'.[51] To be sure, in the first edition of his treatise on *Kant's Theory*

[48] Kelsen, *Introduction* (n 3) §16 (at 34) (translation amended).

[49] Hermann Cohen (1842–1918) was professor at the University of Marburg from 1876 to 1912, succeeding Friedrich Albert Lange, author of *The History of Materialism*, EC Thomas transl, 3 vols (London, Trubner, 1877–81 [1866]). Cohen published his first Kant treatise – *Kants Theorie der Erfahrung*, 1st edn (Berlin, Ferd Dümmler, 1871) – five years before his appointment as professor. Later he developed his own 'System of Philosophy'; his treatise *Logik der reinen Erkenntnis* (Berlin, Bruno Cassirer, 1902) is the central work here, though the 'System' reaches to ethics and aesthetics, with major treatises in these fields, too.

[50] For valuable discussion in the recent literature, see G Edel, *Von der Vernunftkritik zur Erkenntnislogik* (Freiburg and Munich, Karl Alber, 1988) at 100–62, 182–96 and throughout, 2nd edn (Waldkirch, Edition Gorz, 2010) at 81–129, 145–55 and throughout; J Stolzenberg, *Ursprung und System* (Göttingen, Vandenhoeck & Ruprecht, 1995) at 22–34; C Krijnen, *Nachmetaphysischer Sinn* (Würzburg, Königshausen & Neumann, 2001) at 55–57; G Kreis, *Cassirer und die Formen des Geistes* (Frankfurt, Suhrkamp, 2010) at 41–50.

[51] H Cohen, 'Die platonische Ideenlehre psychologisch entwickelt' (1866) 4 *Zeitschrift für Völkerpsychologie und Sprachwissenschaft* 403–64, repr in Cohen, *Schriften zur Philosophie und Zeitgeschichte*, A Görland and E Cassirer (eds), 2 vols (Berlin, Akademie-Verlag, 1928) vol 1, 30–87.

of Experience, published in 1871,[52] Cohen put considerable distance between his own programme and what he sees as psychological doctrines in Kant. In this early treatise, though, psychology continues to play a role, as shown, inter alia, by the lingering influence of Herbart's philosophy.[53] By 1883, however, with the publication of his monograph on the *Infinitesimal Method*,[54] the lengthy process of Cohen's emancipation from psychology was complete.[55]

Cohen's emancipation from psychology in his own philosophical research is not matched by any effort on his part to emancipate Kant from the nineteenth-century perception of Kant's philosophy as being fraught with psychological elements.[56] On the contrary. As Cohen puts it in the 1883 monograph, while Kant 'struggles with psychological ideas and demands', he, Cohen, seeks 'to render *objective*', in 'the letter and spirit of [Kant's] critical system, *reason in science*'.[57] In particular, Kant's transcendental aesthetic – his appeal to space and time as pure forms of sensibility or intuition – remains psychological through and through, according to Cohen, and is philosophically a 'triviality'.[58] For Cohen and others in the Marburg School, Kant's receptive faculty, standing between the categories of the understanding and the manifold of sensation, disappears. Moreover, Cohen's elimination of Kant's receptive faculty means that the 'constitutive' dimension of Kant's own philosophy is eliminated in Cohen's philosophy. Thus, if there is to be a constitutive dimension in Cohen's philosophy, it must be established independently of Kant's machinery in the transcendental analytic of the first *Critique*. That machinery is no more.

Similarly, mutatis mutandis, for Kelsen. He is outspoken on the constitutive dimension of legal science:

> It is also correct that, in terms of the Kantian theory of knowledge, legal science as cognition of the law, just as with all cognition, has a constitutive character and therefore 'creates' its object in so far as it conceives the object as a meaningful whole. Just as the chaos of sensory perceptions only becomes a cosmos through the ordering cognition of science, that is, becomes nature qua unified system, so likewise the collection of general and individual legal norms set down by legal officials

[52] See n 49.

[53] References to Herbart's philosophy in Cohen, *Kants Theorie der Erfahrung* (n 49), are found at 142–44, 152, 161–64.

[54] See n 47.

[55] See Edel, *Von der Vernunftkritik zur Erkenntnislogik* (n 50), for a lengthy and unusually rewarding examination of Cohen's philosophical development, on which I have drawn.

[56] As is well known, this is not only a 19th-century phenomenon. A part of Strawson's criticism of Kant in *The Bounds of Sense* (n 41) turns on what Strawson sees as an objectionable psychological dimension in Kant's philosophy. Wolfgang Carl responds to Strawson and earlier critics: see W Carl, *Die transzendentale Deduktion der Kategorien* (Frankfurt, Klostermann, 1992) at 79–94 and throughout

[57] Cohen, *Das Princip der Infinitesimal-Methode und seine Geschichte* (n 47) 6 (emphasis in original).

[58] ibid 23.

> – the material given to legal science – only becomes a unified, consistent system, a legal system, through the cognition of legal science.[59]

To say that legal science has a constitutive dimension is to say that a transcendental argument is at work, and, as we have seen, Kelsen would have his basic norm understood as a 'logico-transcendental condition', akin to a Kantian category. If, however, Kelsen is indeed following Cohen's Neo-Kantianism, he has no basis for appealing to a Kantian category, for conspicuous by its absence from Marburg Neo-Kantianism is the machinery present in Kant's philosophy that makes possible the constitutive dimension. Cohen's fundamental departure from Kant means that if Kelsen is still keen on pursuing what Cohen calls the transcendental method,[60] he must defend his work in that vein independently of Kant. But there is no textual evidence in Kelsen's *œuvre* that suggests he made such an effort.

This counts as yet another dead-end in searching Kelsen's philosophy for an undergirding for the objective validity of legal norms. Is the effort to work out the details of a transcendental argument simply mistaken? This was, in effect, Schopenhauer's position.

V. A TRANSCENDENTAL PHILOSOPHY WITHOUT TRANSCENDENTAL ARGUMENTS?

It is well known that Arthur Schopenhauer (1788–1860), after decades of neglect, caught on in the later-nineteenth century and was widely read, then and beyond. He was an unpopular outsider from the beginning, who, early in his ill-fated professional career, confidently insisted that his lectures in Berlin be scheduled at the same time as Hegel's, ending up, as it turned out, with virtually no students at all. He was initially so unpopular that some of the more prominent figures among his later readers discovered him, so to speak, by accident. For example, Nietzsche in the 1860s, then a soldier in the Prussian cavalry, had taken a fall and injured himself, and, while recuperating, he found Schopenhauer's *The World as Will and Representation* at a used-book stand. He began reading Schopenhauer casually, then avidly, growing ever more enamoured of this 'outsider'.[61]

[59] Kelsen, *Reine Rechtslehre* (n 28) §16 (74).

[60] For an interesting interpretation of the Kelsen-Cohen tie, markedly different from what I have written here, see G Edel, 'The *Hypothesis* of the Basic Norm: Hans Kelsen and Hermann Cohen' in *Normativity and Norms* (n 6) 195–219.

[61] See C Janaway, 'Schopenhauer as Nietzsche's Educator' in C Janaway (ed), *Willing and Nothingness. Schopenhauer as Nietzsche's Educator* (Oxford, Clarendon Press, 1998) 13–36, at 16–19, on which I have drawn here.

Schopenhauer's reception picked up, and in due course his works became standard fare. Wittgenstein is known to have read him,[62] as did Hans Vaihinger and many others, among them Hans Kelsen, as he reports in the longer of his autobiographies.[63] More significant than this testimonial is the fact that Kelsen draws on Schopenhauer chapter and verse in arguing, in *The Problem of Sovereignty*, that monism with the priority of state law leads in the end 'to a negation of the law and, therefore, to a negation of legal cognition and legal science'.[64] This juridico-theoretical contention of Kelsen's belies his own boilerplate on the matter, namely, that the choice between the two species of monism – the priority of state law versus the priority of international law – cannot be decided theoretically and is to be left to politics.

Schopenhauer's significance vis-à-vis Kelsen, however, lies elsewhere. In his doctoral dissertation, *The Four-Fold Root of the Principle of Sufficient Reason*, published in 1813,[65] Schopenhauer takes up the principle of sufficient reason. In its most general form, it says – here Schopenhauer quotes Christian Wolff – that 'nothing is without a ground or reason why it is rather than is not'.[66] Schopenhauer explicates the principle in four forms, in each case looking to the ground of the principle and then to the 'root' made possible by the ground, and, finally, linking the ground to possible objects of consciousness. The first ground of the principle of sufficient reason is causality, the root of 'becoming', and causality is linked to sensory representations (*Vorstellungen*). The second ground is reason, the root of 'knowing' (*Erkennen*), and reason is linked to concepts or abstract representations. The third ground is interdependence, the root of 'being', and interdependence is linked to the a priori forms of sensibility, space and time (Kant's pure forms of intuition). Finally, the fourth ground of the principle of sufficient reason is motive, the root of 'acting', and motive is linked to the will.

As one can imagine, the details of these grounds, their corresponding 'roots', and the link between ground and object of consciousness are philosophically difficult and complex. Schopenhauer built into his scheme an entire metaphysics with all that such a project portends. But here it is a single point that looms large, to wit: Schopenhauer was of the opinion that it is impossible to adduce an argument for the principle of sufficient reason. As he writes:

[62] See H-J Glock, 'Schopenhauer and Wittgenstein: Representation as Language and Will' in *The Cambridge Companion to Schopenhauer* (n 8) 442–58.

[63] See H Kelsen, 'Autobiographie 1947' in M Jestaedt (ed), *Hans Kelsen Werke. Volume 1* (Tübingen, Mohr Siebeck, 2007) 29–91, at 33.

[64] Kelsen, *Das Problem der Souveränität* (n 7), §63 (at 317) (emphasis in original).

[65] A Schopenhauer, *Ueber die vierfache Wurzel des Satzes vom zureichenden Grunde*, 1st edn (publ 1813) in: Schopenhauer, *Sämtliche Werke*, 4th printing, A Hübscher (ed) (Wiesbaden, FA Brockhaus, 1988) vol 7, 1–94, Engl edn: *Schopenhauer's Early Fourfold Root*, FC White transl (Aldershot, Avebury, 1997).

[66] Schopenhauer, *Ueber die vierfache Wurzel* (n 65) §5 (7), Engl edn (n 65) §5 (4).

> [T]he principle [of sufficient reason] does not lend itself to proof at all. What Aristotle says holds for all the failed proofs above: 'They seek a reason where no reason can be given, for the starting point of demonstration is not itself a matter of demonstration.' Every proof consists in tracing something questionable back to something recognized as true, and if we demand a proof of the latter again and again, whatever it may be, we will arrive in the end at certain principles that are the conditions for all thought and knowledge. Indeed, since all thought and knowledge consist in the application of these principles, and certainty, then, is nothing but concurrence with them, it follows that their own certainty cannot be demonstrated by appeal to still other principles.[67]

The principle of sufficient reason cannot, in any of its four forms, be demonstrated, for it stands behind and makes possible every demonstration.

I set aside here the question of whether Schopenhauer is correct in attributing to Aristotle the very view that he, Schopenhauer, defends, namely, that the principle of sufficient reason does not lend itself to any sort of demonstration, being presupposed in every demonstration. By contrast, Kant argues in an early work that the principle of non-contradiction is demonstrable,[68] and some have claimed that Aristotle and Kant are alike in that both seek to demonstrate the necessity of the principle of non-contradiction.[69]

Beyond all of this, the question is: Can one make sense of Kelsen's basic norm by arguing, by analogy, from Schopenhauer's stance on the principle of sufficient reason, namely, that the principle cannot be demonstrated? A related question is this: If no argument for the basic norm, no demonstration of it, is forthcoming, what then is its role? I return to this question below. But first, I look at two texts of Kelsen's on the basic norm that appear to track the suggested 'indemonstrability analogy'.

In *The Philosophical Foundations of Natural Law Theory and Legal Positivism*, Kelsen's monograph of 1928, he writes:

[67] Schopenhauer, *Ueber die vierfache Wurzel* (n 65) §13 (14f), Engl edn (n 65) §13 (9–11, at 10) (the quotation above is translated from the original, German text). Much later, in 1847, Schopenhauer published a second edition of the dissertation, expanding the text considerably, see Schopenhauer, *Sämtliche Werke* (n 65) vol 1, iii–ix, 1–160. The passage I have quoted from §13 of the first edition is largely unchanged in the corresponding §14 of the second edition. The quotation from Aristotle in Schopenhauer's text stems from the *Metaphysics*, IV.6. at 11–13, and I have drawn here on the translation by WD Ross, in *The Complete Works of Aristotle. The Revised Oxford Translation*, J Barnes (ed), 2 vols (Princeton, Princeton University Press, 1984) vol 2, 1552–728, at 1596. (Schopenhauer cites *Metaphysics* III.6. as his source, but this is a slip.)

[68] See I Kant, *Beweisgrund zu einer Demonstration des Daseins Gottes* (first publ 1763) in *Ak2* (n 7) 70–163, at 82, Engl edn: *The Only Possible Argument in Support of a Demonstration of the Existence of God*, D Walford transl, in Kant, *Theoretical Philosophy, 1755–1770*, D Walford and R Meerbote (eds) (Cambridge, Cambridge University Press, 1992) 107–201, at 126f.

[69] See eg DW Hamlyn, *Schopenhauer* (London, Routledge & Kegan Paul, 1980) at 11f, and on Aristotle's view generally, see TH Irwin, *Aristotle's First Principles* (Oxford, Clarendon Press, 1988) §§97–101 (179–88).

> [The basic norm] is not, say, the hypothesis of a special legal theory. It is merely the formulation of the necessary presuppositions for any positivistic grasp of legal materials.[70]

Similarly, but at greater length, Kelsen writes in the first edition of the *Pure Theory of Law*:

> The Pure Theory aims simply to raise to the level of consciousness what all jurists are doing (for the most part unwittingly) when, in conceptualizing their object of enquiry, they reject natural law as the basis of the validity of positive law, but nevertheless understand the positive law as a valid system, that is, as norm, and not merely as factual contingencies of motivation. With the doctrine of the basic norm, the Pure Theory analyses the actual process of the long-standing method of cognizing positive law, in an attempt simply to reveal the transcendental logical conditions of that method.[71]

The interpretation of the basic norm as a means of explication is, I think, tolerably clear here. Specifically, the basic norm counts as a shorthand reference to the assumptions made by jurists in treating the law 'as a valid system, as norm', without thereby appealing to natural law or, in modern parlance, moral philosophy. The task is one of explication, not demonstration.

Remarkably enough, Kelsen's tack here has a counterpart in Hermann Cohen's philosophy – or, more precisely, in one interpretation of Cohen's philosophy. As Jürgen Stolzenberg has argued, Cohen, having precluded every trace of the constitutive dimension of Kant's philosophy, argues that his own 'transcendental method' serves as 'an explication of the *recognition of the factum* of mathematical natural science itself – that is, an explication of what one ultimately accepts when one's point of departure is taken from the factum of mathematical natural science'.[72] This parallel in Cohen's philosophy to Kelsen's tack on the basic norm in the first edition of the *Pure Theory of Law* is clear; both Cohen's transcendental method and Kelsen's basic norm are understood as means of explication.

Less clear is the question of how much would have to be changed in Kelsen's greater legal philosophy in order to accommodate this interpretation of the basic norm. Two changes come to mind. First, this interpretation of the basic norm would require that Kelsen abandon his claim, conspicuous in the second edition of the *Pure Theory of Law*, that legal science plays a constitutive

[70] Kelsen, *Die philosophischen Grundlagen* (n 27) §4 (12).

[71] Kelsen, *Introduction* (n 3) §29 (58); see also Kelsen, *Reine Rechtslehre* (n 28) §34(d) (at 209).

[72] See Stolzenberg, *Ursprung und System* (n 50) 21–58, at 40 (emphasis in original). This text is reproduced, in part, in J Stolzenberg, 'The Highest Principle and the Principle of Origin in Hermann Cohen's Theoretical Philosophy', CJ Hahn transl, in RA Makkreel and S Luft (eds), *Neo-Kantianism in Contemporary Philosophy* (Bloomington, Indiana University Press, 2010) 132–49, at 136. (The quotation above is translated from the original, German text.)

role vis-à-vis the law.[73] This change is not a great loss, for the constitutive role presupposes that a Kantian transcendental argument applied in Kelsen's legal philosophy is sound, and there is no prospect whatever of making good on that presupposition. A second change comes to mind. Kelsen would have to abandon his claim, to which he gives expression again and again, that the Pure Theory of Law offers the only possible account of the normativity of the law – the only possible account, that is, apart from natural law theory or moral philosophy. Here, too, the change does not represent a great loss, for, just as with the first change, this claim of Kelsen's presupposes a sound Kantian transcendental argument applied in Kelsen's legal philosophy, and no such presupposition passes muster.

VI. CONCLUDING REMARK

I return to my central claim, that the foundational dimension of Kelsen's legal philosophy, ostensibly made out by appeal to the basic norm, does not withstand close scrutiny. This is not to say that the colossus known as Kelsen's legal philosophy has no claim on our attention. It is, rather, to say that Kelsen's philosophy will have to take its place alongside other positivistic legal philosophies. Its interest and worth will be determined by its explanatory force.

[73] See the quotation at n 59.

4

The Basic Norm Revisited

RICCARDO GUASTINI

I. THE BASIC NORM *QUA* NORM

A. Kelsen's Views

In the first edition of the *Reine Rechtslehre* (1934), every legal norm is, roughly speaking, a command.[1] In the second *Reine Rechtslehre* (1960), Kelsen distinguishes between commands, permissions and empowerments.[2] Finally, in the posthumous *Allgemeine Theorie der Normen* (1979), Kelsen further distinguishes four kinds of norms – commands, permissions, power-conferring (or 'empowering') norms and derogatory norms.[3]

I assume that this distinction of kinds of norms tracks differences in content and/or logical status. Thus commands and permissions both bear upon actions (or states of affairs brought about by actions), but ascribe different deontic statuses; derogatory norms bear, not upon actions, but upon (other) norms; commands and power-conferring norms can be mapped onto Hohfeldian modalities of a different sort (duty and power, respectively);[4] and so on.

Now, in the light of Kelsen's typology, what kind of norm is the basic norm of a positive legal system? In particular: is it a command (ie a deontic norm of conduct) or a power-conferring norm (a 'norm of competence', as it is also

[1] *cf* H Kelsen, *Introduction to the Problems of Legal Theory. A Translation of the First Edition of the* Reine Rechtslehre *or Pure Theory of Law*, BL Paulson and SL Paulson transl (Oxford, Clarendon Press, 1992 [1934]) 22ff, 43ff.

[2] *cf* H Kelsen, *The Pure Theory of Law*, 2nd edn, M Knight transl (Berkeley, University of California Press, 1967 [1960]) 4–5, 15ff.

[3] *cf* General *Theory of Norms*, M Hartney transl (Oxford, Clarendon Press 1991 [1979]) 96ff; and see also 'Derogation' in H Kelsen, *Essays in Legal and Moral Philosophy* (Dordrecht, Reidel, 1973). All such norms, however, are understood by Kelsen as expressions of what 'ought' (or 'ought not') to be the case – in a very wide sense of 'ought'. See also N Bobbio, '"Sein" and "Sollen" in Legal Science' (1970) 61 *Archiv für Rechts- und Sozialphilosophie* 7ff.

[4] *cf* WN Hohfeld, 'Some Fundamental Legal Conceptions as Applied in Judicial Reasoning' in WW Cook (ed), *Fundamental Legal Conceptions as Applied in Judicial Reasoning* (New Haven, Yale University Press, 1919) 23ff.

sometimes called[5])? There is in Kelsen's works, as far as I can see, no straightforward answer to this simple question.[6]

In the first *Reine Rechtslehre*, the basic norm is characterised as a norm 'delegating lawmaking authority',[7] the norm 'according to which the norms of the legal system are created'.[8] Nevertheless, Kelsen also provides a different – deontic – 'schematic formulation': 'Coercion is [ie ought] to be applied . . . as determined by the framers of the first constitution or by the authorities to whom they have delegated appropriate powers'.[9] Accordingly, he also states that 'the basic norm confers on the act of the first legislator . . . the sense of "ought"'.[10] The basic norm, hence, seems to have a mixed character – half conferring normative powers, half commanding (viz. commanding obedience to whatever further commands are issued by the organ to which the normative power is being conferred).

In the *General Theory of Law and State* (1945), Kelsen's mixed attitude is even clearer. On the one hand, Kelsen says that '[t]he basic norm merely establishes a certain authority, which may well in turn vest norm-creating power in some other authorities';[11] that the basic norm 'confers legal authority';[12] that its 'whole function' is 'to confer law-creating power on the act of the first legislator and on all the other acts based on the first act'.[13] On the other hand, however, when trying to articulate an explicit formulation of the norm at stake, Kelsen offers the following: 'One ought to behave as the individual, or the individuals, who laid down the first constitution have ordained'.[14] Once more, the basic norm appears to hang in the balance between an imperative or command and a power-conferring norm. It seems that, according to Kelsen, to attribute to some agent the power of issuing commands is tantamount to commanding (someone else) to obey or apply the commands issued by that agent.

[5] See GH von Wright, *Norm and Action. A Logical Enquiry* (London, Routledge & Kegan Paul, 1963) 192ff, or E Bulygin, 'On Norms of Competence' (1990) 11 *Law and Philosophy* 201–16.

[6] In 'Beyond the Basic Norm' in R Vázquez (ed), *Filosofía Jurídica. Ensayos en Homenaje a Ulises Schmill* (Mexico, Porrúa/UNAM, 2005), Stanley Paulson lists 10 Kelsenian 'formulations' of the basic norm. However, not all of them are, strictly speaking, 'formulations' *of* the basic norm; most are statements concerning its function and/or its status within the legal system. 'The basic norm *qua* ultimate basis of legal validity', for example, or 'the basic norm *qua* constitution in the juridical-logical sense', say nothing about the basic norm's 'formulation', strictly understood.

[7] Kelsen, *Introduction* (n 1) 59.

[8] ibid 56.

[9] ibid 57. Observe that, according to this formulation, the basic norm is addressed, not to legal subjects, but to legal officials (viz. those who 'apply' coercion).

[10] ibid 58.

[11] H Kelsen, *General Theory of Law and State*, A Wedberg transl (Cambridge, Mass., Harvard University Press, 1945) 113.

[12] ibid 120.

[13] ibid 116.

[14] ibid 115. Observe that, according to this new formulation, the basic norm is addressed, not to legal officials, but to legal subjects.

In the second *Reine Rechtslehre*, Kelsen repeats that 'the presupposed basic norm contains nothing but the determination of a norm-creating fact, the authorization of a norm-creating authority'.[15] As to its formulation, nonetheless, the basic norm looks definitely deontic: 'Coercive acts ought to be performed under the conditions and in the manner which the historically first constitution . . . prescribes. (In short: One ought to behave as the constitution prescribes.)'.[16]

In the *Allgemeine Theorie der Normen*, the basic norm once again exhibits its seemingly double nature. It 'empowers the individual or individuals who posited the historically first constitution to posit the norms which represent the historically first constitution;' as a consequence, 'one has [ie ought] to behave as the historically first constitution prescribes'.[17] In this late work, however, Kelsen does not suggest, as he (implicitly) had in previous works, that empowering is somehow identical or equivalent to (indirectly) commanding. Referring to empowering and commanding as two different normative 'functions',[18] he adds that when the power at stake is 'that of *positing norms*' (and thus, in the last analysis, the power of issuing commands), then 'empowering can *imply* a command'.[19] Thus 'by empowering the legislative organ to enact statutes *binding* on those subject to the law, the constitution . . . thereby makes the statutes he [the legislator] enacts *binding* on the subjects of the law'; such subjects are therefore 'commanded by the constitution to comply with the statutes'.[20] Nonetheless, Kelsen stresses that in these cases we have one and the same norm performing 'two different functions concerning two different subjects': it 'decrees (1) that the legislative organ can posit norms, and (2) that people whose behaviour is regulated by these norms are to comply with them'.[21]

In summary, Kelsen's basic norm appears to have a puzzling mixed nature. It both confers constituent power to the framers of the historically first constitution, and commands people to comply with the commands issued by such framers.[22]

[15] Kelsen, *The Pure Theory of Law* (n 2) 196.

[16] ibid 201. Observe that, according to this last formulation, the basic norm is addressed – once more – not to legal subjects, but to legal officials.

[17] Kelsen, *General Theory of Norms* (n 3) 255.

[18] ibid 96ff, and 103.

[19] ibid 103.

[20] ibid 104.

[21] ibid.

[22] *cf* J Raz, 'Kelsen's Theory of the Basic Norm' in *The Authority of Law. Essays on Law and Morality* (Oxford, Clarendon Press, 1979 [1974]) 126: 'The basic norm is power-conferring law. Kelsen, however, formulates it as duty-imposing'.

B. Discussion

Let us isolate for discussion three slightly different tenets which on the basis of the previous survey we can now ascribe to Kelsen:

1. To attribute to some agent the power of issuing commands, and to command that the (further) commands issued by that agent be obeyed or applied, *amount to the same*: these are just two different ways in which the same (basic) norm can be formulated.
2. The attribution to some agent of the power of issuing commands *implies* the command that the (further) commands issued by that agent be obeyed or applied (and perhaps vice versa).
3. The basic norm simultaneously decrees *both* that the framers of the historically first constitution are authorised to posit norms *and* that legal subjects ought to comply with such norms.

i. The First Tenet

The first tenet is implausible. It seems evident that an authorisation and a command – although somehow connected – amount to two different norms. They have different contents, different objects, different addressees, and map onto different Hohfeldian modalities:

1. Different contents (different 'phrastics', in Hare's terms[23]): the *issuance* of (further) norms, in the case of authorisation; *compliance* with (future) norms (to be enacted by the authorised agent), in the case of command.
2. Different objects: the authorisation bears upon (future) normative *acts*;[24] the command, in turn, is a blanket meta-norm bearing upon compliance with (future) *norms*.
3. Different addressees: the authorisation is addressed to the *framers* of the first constitution; the command, to legal *subjects* and/or *law-applying organs*.
4. Different Hohfeldian modalities: *power* and *duty*, respectively.[25]

ii. The Second Tenet

Can it nevertheless be maintained that the command, though not directly *expressed*, is *implied* in the authorisation, as Kelsen's second tenet suggests? The answer depends on the kind of implication one has in mind.

[23] RM Hare, *The Language of Morals* (Oxford, Oxford University Press, 1952) 17ff.
[24] By a 'normative act' I mean an act of issuing norms.
[25] Power-conferring norms, however, can also be understood as permissions: see von Wright, *Norm and Action* (n 5) 192. If one accepts this view, then one should say that authorisation and command map onto different *deontic* modalities.

a. Pragmatic Implication

If understood by reference to some sort of 'pragmatic implication' (a Gricean 'implicature',[26] perhaps), the thesis seems sound. It seems a matter of course that the point of authorising someone to issue commands is to make such future commands binding on their addressees.[27]

This is only true, however, under certain conditions concerning the actual formulation of the norms at stake. Take, for example, articles 54 and 70 of the Italian constitution. Article 54 provides that 'All citizens have the duty to . . . comply with the constitution and the statutes'. Article 70, in turn, stipulates that 'Legislative [ie statute-making] power is exercised jointly by the Chambers'. It is not fully clear that one could plausibly maintain that article 70 'implies' – in some unspecified 'pragmatic' way – article 54, ie that this particular authorisation implies this particular command. At any rate, the opposite is certainly not true. The command to comply with statutes does not by itself imply any particular authorisation; and indeed amounts to nothing unless statute-making power is conferred to some definite state organ by a further norm. Article 54, arguably superfluous in view of article 70, would be empty and pointless if left unaccompanied.

b. Logical Entailment

If, on the contrary, the 'implication' in Kelsen's second tenet is understood in terms of logical entailment, the underlying argument would run, it seems, along the following lines:

1. The framers of the first historical constitution are authorised to issue commands (or norms).
2. Validity is the characteristic property (the 'specific existence') of authorised commands (or norms).[28]
3. The commands (norms) issued by the framers of the first historical constitution are valid.
4. Validity is (or entails) binding force.[29]
5. The commands (norms) of the framers of the first historical constitution are binding.
6. 'Binding' means 'obligatory'.[30]
7. The commands (norms) of the framers of the first historical constitution are obligatory, ie they ought to be obeyed.

[26] See P Grice, 'Logic and Conversation' in his *Studies in the Way of Words* (Cambridge, Mass., Harvard University Press, 1989).

[27] This seems to be Alf Ross's suggestion in *On Law and Justice* (London, Stevens & Sons, 1958) 32.

[28] *The Pure Theory of Law* (2) 10.

[29] ibid 193.

[30] ibid.

The conclusion actually follows from the premises. The key premise of this argument, however, is premise 4: the highly disputable statement of equivalence (or entailment) between validity and binding force. This is in fact one of the central theses of the Pure Theory of Law.[31] And without it, the conclusion no longer follows. We can agree that authorisation is a necessary and perhaps even a sufficient condition of validity (whatever 'validity' may exactly mean); but if 'valid' does not entail 'obligatory', the fact that a command is authorised, and thus valid, does not entail it is obligatory to obey it.

There are good and well-known reasons to reject premise 4. The equation of validity and binding force amounts to the statement that there is a general obligation to obey the law. But, first, such an obligation cannot be a *legal* one. This is so for plain logical reasons. The sentence 'The law ought to be obeyed' takes as its object *the law as a whole.* So that sentence does not belong to the language of law itself; it belongs to a second-order language *about* the law. It follows that the putative obligation to obey the law cannot be a *legal* obligation; it can only be a meta-legal, and thus non-legal, obligation: viz. a moral or political obligation.

Second, the statement that there is a moral or political obligation to obey the law is incompatible with the purely cognitive enterprise of methodological positivism, which Kelsen himself espoused. Legal cognition can certainly not command obedience to positive law;[32] that much is a plain consequence of Hume's law. The statement that there is a moral or political obligation to obey the law is to be understood as a piece of 'ideological positivism' instead.[33]

[31] For discussion, see B Celano, 'Validity as Disquotation' in P Comanducci and R Guastini (eds), *Analisi e Diritto* 1999. Ricerche di Giurisprudenza Analitica (Turin, Giappichelli, 2000) 35–77; B Celano, *La Teoria del Diritto di Hans Kelsen. Una Introduzione Critica* (Bologna, Il Mulino, 1999) 291ff; and B Celano, 'Cuatro Temas Kelsenianos' in PE Navarro and MC Redondo (eds), *La Relevancia del Derecho. Ensayos de Filosofía Jurídica, Moral, y Política* (Barcelona, Gedisa, 2002) 153–84.

[32] Even though this seems to be precisely what the conceptual framework of the Pure Theory seems (inconsistently) to require: see B Celano, 'Kelsen's Concept of the Authority of Law' (2000) 19 *Law and Philosophy* 173–99, esp 188.

[33] I use Norberto Bobbio's familiar distinction between (a) methodological positivism, understood as the neutral description of the law in force; (b) theoretical positivism, understood as a set of substantive theses about the law (such as the thesis that law is imperative, coercive, etc); and (c) ideological positivism, understood as the thesis that there is a general obligation to obey the law. See N Bobbio, 'Sur le Positivisme Juridique' in *Mélanges en l'Honneur de Paul Roubier*, vol 1 (Paris, Dalloz-Sirey, 1961) 53ff; as well as his *Il Positivismo Giuridico* (Turin, Giappichelli, 1996 [1961]). On ideological positivism (which he calls 'quasi-positivism'), see A Ross, 'Validity and the Conflict between Legal Positivism and Natural Law' in SL Paulson and BL Paulson (eds), *Normativity and Norms. Critical Perspectives on Kelsenian Themes* (Oxford, Clarendon Press, 1998 [1961]) 147–63, esp §VI; and *cf* also Raz, 'Kelsen's Theory of the Basic Norm' (n 22) 144: Kelsen 'uses the natural law concept of normativity, ie the concept of justified normativity'.

iii. The Third Tenet

Kelsen's third tenet, taken literally, cannot be accepted; it is hard to see how one and the same norm could both authorise someone and command someone else.

Can this tenet be non-literally construed instead as the claim that one and the same normative *sentence* – the so-called basic 'norm' – simultaneously expresses *two* different norms: (1) an authorisation and (2) a command? Well, there is certainly nothing peculiar about the idea that one single sentence can express a plurality of norms. Think, for example, of a constitutional provision stipulating that 'All citizens are equal before the law, without regard to their sex, race, language, religion, and political opinions'. Under what seems to be the natural way of interpreting such a provision, it expresses not one, but five norms: 'Discrimination on the grounds of sex is prohibited'; 'Discrimination on the grounds of race is prohibited'; 'Discrimination on the grounds of language is prohibited'; and so on.

Kelsen, however, would not accept this non-literal construction of his tenet. He clearly thinks of his basic 'norm' as a *norm* – and indeed as *one* norm – rather than as a *sentence* expressing a plurality of norms.

My unsurprising conclusion: Kelsen had no definite, coherent view about the nature – the content and logical status – of the basic norm.

II. THE BASIC NORM *QUA* BASIC

Within the Pure Theory of Law, and because of Kelsen's well-known conflation of a norm's (a) existence, (b) binding force and (c) validity, the basic norm is a conceptual necessity.

'By the word "validity"' – says Kelsen – 'we designate the specific existence of a norm';[34] and to say 'a norm is "valid"' means 'that it is binding',[35] ie 'that it *ought* to be obeyed and applied'.[36] Existence being no predicate, Kelsen's equivalence entails that he takes validity and binding force to be definitional features of 'norm'. A non-existent norm is not a norm at all. Hence, according to Kelsen, since existence is the same as validity, an invalid norm is not a norm; and since validity is the same as binding force, a non-binding norm is not a norm.[37] By the same token, his doctrine that validity depends on authorisation

[34] Kelsen, *The Pure Theory of Law* (n 2) 10.

[35] ibid 193.

[36] ibid 10f.

[37] Kelsen's stipulations, of course, are seriously at odds with ordinary legal discourse. In ordinary discourse we do not take the phrases 'valid norm' or 'binding norm' to be redundant, nor do we take 'invalid norm' or 'non-binding norm' to be self-contradictory. In other words, we treat validity and binding force as contingent properties – rather than definitional features – of norms.

by a higher norm is equivalent to the doctrine that existence, and thus also binding force, depends on authorisation by a higher norm.[38]

Because he cannot accommodate the idea of an invalid norm – which is for him a contradiction in terms – Kelsen is forced to search for a reason for the validity (and thus for a higher, authorising norm) of any existent norm. When faced with the historically first constitution, therefore, he has but two possibilities. He must either (a) deny its validity, binding force and existence – which would be a rather odd move, given that, from the standpoint of the Pure Theory, the entire legal system would lose its validity, binding force and existence; or (b) postulate a meta-constitutional (and thus non-positive) norm which confers validity, binding force and existence to the constitution and to the entire legal system.

The postulation of this 'basic' meta-constitutional, non-positive norm is nevertheless subject to two main criticisms.

A. Needless Reduplication

As Hart pointed out, the basic norm is a 'needless reduplication' of the (first) constitution:

> If a constitution specifying the various sources of law is a living reality . . . then the constitution is accepted and actually exists. It seems a needless reduplication to suggest that there is a further rule to the effect that the constitution (or those who 'laid it down') are to be obeyed.[39]

The charge of reduplication is grounded on the fact the basic norm and the (first) constitution share two distinctive features: both are effective; and both are non-valid,[40] their validity being merely presupposed. It is true that unless the basic norm is presupposed, the constitution cannot be *said* to be 'valid', given that validity admittedly depends on authorisation by a higher norm, and that there simply is no higher positive norm authorising the issuance of the constitution. As a matter of course, however, the basic norm itself is also non-valid: were it valid, there would be no need of presupposing its validity.

There is nothing surprising in the non-validity of the constitution. It is logically impossible for all the norms of a legal system to be valid. The ultimate,

[38] cp Raz, 'Kelsen's Theory of the Basic Norm' (22) 132: 'The basic norm is necessarily presupposed when people regard the law as normative'.

[39] HLA Hart, *The Concept of Law*, 3rd edn (Oxford, Oxford University Press, 2012 [1961]) 293.

[40] I use 'non-valid' (instead of 'invalid') because it can be argued that both validity and invalidity are norm-relative concepts, ie that a norm is valid or invalid 'relative to another norm permitting its issuing'; as a consequence, strictly speaking, the supreme (or 'sovereign') norm of a normative system is *neither* valid *nor* invalid: *cf* von Wright, *Norm and Action* (n 5) 196, 199. See also R Caracciolo, *El Sistema Jurídico. Problemas Actuales* (Madrid, Centro de Estudios Constitucionales, 1988) 31ff.

supreme norm of the system cannot itself be valid; indeed it makes no sense to ask about its validity (or invalidity) at all.[41] The entire system, in other words, must necessarily rest upon a non-valid norm.

But then, if the very basis of the legal system cannot but be an effective, non-valid norm, why should one need this idea of a presupposition of a non-positive norm beyond the constitution – instead of just admitting that the positive constitution itself is non-valid? Why not plainly acknowledge that the constitution – a positive norm (or set of norms) whose binding force[42] is simply assumed in virtue of its effectiveness – is *the* basic, supreme norm of the system? It is 'basic', to echo Kelsen himself, 'because nothing further can be asked about the reason for its validity'.[43]

B. Paradoxical Consequence

The historically first constitution is the product of the so-called 'constituent power' (Sieyès's '*pouvoir constituant*'). By definition, constituent power – in opposition to 'constituted powers' such as the legislative power – is neither conferred nor regulated by any previous (or 'higher') norm. It is *extra ordinem* power: it is, in other words, de facto, non-legal, power. This is why the (first) constitution is necessarily non-valid. It does not rest on any previous ('higher') authorisation.

Now, the presupposition of the basic norm – understood as a norm which empowers the framers of the historically first constitution[44] – has the paradoxical result of turning the constituent power into a constituted one. Given that, under the basic norm, the framers of the historically first constitution enjoy a *legal* (legally 'constituted') power – the norm-creating power conferred by the basic norm – constituent power is converted into a legally conferred, de jure power.

In the posthumous *Allgemeine Theorie der Normen*, Kelsen seems eventually to be aware of this paradox. He states – indeed he 'confesses'[45] – that the basic

[41] *cf* Hart, *The Concept of Law* (n 39) 108ff, though Hart is discussing the 'rule of recognition' rather than the constitution.

[42] *Pace* Kelsen, binding force is not to be conflated with validity; authorisation by a higher norm entails no obligation to obey.

[43] *General Theory of Norms* (n 3) 255.

[44] *cf* H Kelsen, 'The Function of a Constitution' in R Tur and W Twining (eds), *Essays on Kelsen*, I Stewart transl (Oxford, Clarendon Press, 1986 [1964]) 112ff, esp 114f: 'If the historically first constitution was laid down by a resolution of an assembly, the basic norm authorizes the individuals forming that assembly; if the historically first constitution arose by way of custom, the basic norm authorizes this custom – or, more correctly, authorizes the individuals whose conduct forms the custom giving rise to the historically first constitution'.

[45] The verb is used by Kelsen in the following passage: 'In my earlier writings . . . I represented my entire doctrine of the basic norm as a norm that is not the meaning of an act of will but, rather, that is presupposed in thought. Now I must unfortunately confess to you, gentlemen, that I can no longer

norm, a 'merely thought norm', is a 'fictitious' norm (ie one 'contrary to reality'), and that it is 'self-contradictory, since it represents the empowering of an ultimate . . . legal authority and so emanates from an authority – admittedly, a fictitious authority – even higher than this one'.[46]

III. FROM FOUNDATION TO RECOGNITION

The basic norm is meant to provide the normative foundation of the legal system; it is supposed to be its ultimate, supreme norm. Our discussion of the 'needless reduplication' and the 'paradoxical consequence' worries, however, suggests that the problem of the ultimate *normative* foundation of a legal system is simply a false problem. The basis of a legal system is simply its (historically first) constitution. No further 'foundation' is required.

But in giving up the basic norm a different problem is now left open: the problem of the identification of each legal system as such. This is not the same as the foundational problem which we have just discussed. The latter is the problem of determining the ultimate norm of a system; the former is the problem of determining the *identity* of each system: the problem, in other words, of identifying which norms belong to it.

This is the problem that Hart seeks to address in *The Concept of Law* by means of his doctrine of the 'rule of recognition': a rule which, 'providing criteria for the *identification* of other rules of the system',[47] is seemingly meant to differentiate any one system from another. Unfortunately, Hart's solution is unpersuasive. Here is why.

That Kelsen's basic norm amounts to a 'needless reduplication' is 'particularly clear', Hart writes,

> where, as in the United Kingdom, there is no written constitution: here there seems to be no place for the rule 'that the constitution is to be obeyed' in addition to the rule that certain criteria of validity (e.g. enactment by the Queen in Parliament) are to be used in identifying the law. This is the accepted rule and it is mystifying to speak of a rule that this rule be obeyed.[48]

maintain this doctrine. I have to give it up' (H Kelsen, 'Diskussionsbeitrag' (1963) 13 *Österreichische Zeitschrift für öffentliches Recht* 119; as quoted by R Alexy, *The Argument from Injustice. A Reply to Legal Positivism*, BL Paulson and SL Paulson transl (Oxford, Clarendon Press, 2002 [1994]) 110 fn 189).

[46] *General Theory of Norms* (n 3) 256. See also Kelsen, 'The Function of a Constitution' (n 44) 116f. A further problematic consequence of Kelsen's late views is pointed out by Alexy, *The Argument from Injustice* (n 45) 111: '[A] further basic norm would have to be invented to empower the fictitious authority to issue the basic norm, which would amount to not only denying the original basic norm its character as a basic norm, but also – since the further basic norm, too, could only be the content of an act of will – presupposing *ad infinitum* further fictitious authorities and the fictitious basic norms empowering them'.

[47] *cf The Concept of Law* (n 39) 111 (emphasis added).

[48] ibid 293.

This passage seems to imply that – at least when an unwritten, customary constitution is in force – the rule of recognition (the set of 'criteria of validity . . . to be used in identifying the law') and the fundamental rules *of* rule-production (by setting criteria of validity such as 'enactment by the Queen in Parliament'), which Hart calls 'rules of change', are, after all, one and the same thing.[49] And such fundamental rules of change – a set of power-conferring rules – are but *the constitution itself*, which provides the criteria of validity of legislation and any further 'lower' rules. But then, as Bobbio has argued, Hart's rule of recognition seems *itself* to be but a 'needless reduplication' of his own fundamental 'rules of change'.[50] From this standpoint, moreover, it appears that the constitution, understood as a set of criteria of recognition of the law, is in a sense not itself (part of the) law.[51] The law is thereby reduced to ordinary, infra-constitutional norms only.

This is a rather implausible stance. From a juristic point of view, it seems a matter of course that the constitution is not an extra-legal criterion of recognition, but part of the law itself. Moreover, the constitution, written or unwritten, *is* – or includes, at any rate[52] – a set of power-conferring rules of change: and power-conferring rules are not, as such, *criteria* of recognition (though of course they may be connected to criteria of recognition[53]); they are, rather, genuine (albeit non-deontic) norms. Finally, the constitution, too, needs to be 'recognised', which means that the rule of recognition, properly understood

[49] Note that this reading suggests that the rule of recognition is to be read as a power-conferring rather than a duty-imposing rule.

[50] *cf* N Bobbio, 'Per un Lessico di Teoria Generale del Diritto' in *Studi in Memoria di Enrico Guicciardi* (Padua, Cedam, 1975) 47–55, at 52: 'the norms regulating the production of norms ['rules of change', in Hartian parlance] provide the necessary and sufficient criteria to "recognise" the valid norms of the system'; such norms and the rule of recognition are 'one and the same thing' (my translation). In light of this identification of constitution and rule of recognition, Hart's remark about Kelsen's 'needless reduplication' can be given a slightly different reading. Prima facie Hart's suggestion is that Kelsen's basic norm is a needless reduplication of the constitution; but he can now be seen as holding that the basic norm is a needless reduplication of the rule of recognition, too. (It is unclear whether the same implication would hold for systems with written constitutions, ie whether where a written constitution does exist, the rule of recognition is also precisely the set of empowering norms provided by the constitution. Hart seems not to have held consistent views on these matters.)

[51] I am taking for granted that any criterion of recognition *of the law* is necessarily *meta-legal*, for plain logical reasons; *cf The Concept of Law* (n 39) 111: the rule of recognition 'is not a rule on the same level as the "laws strictly so called" which it is used to identify'. Hart adds that 'the case for calling the rule of recognition "law" is that the rule providing criteria for the identification of further rules of the system may well be thought a defining feature of a legal system, and so itself worth calling "law"'.

[52] Some authors (including Kelsen) view the constitution (in the 'material' sense) as amounting to just a set of power-conferring norms. See eg *General Theory of Law and State* (n 11) 124: 'The constitution in the material sense consists of those rules which regulate the creation of the general legal norms, in particular the creation of statutes'.

[53] Namely, a criterion of recognition can *refer to* a power-conferring norm; this is the sort of connection I have in mind.

– and in spite of what Hart seems at least sometimes to suggest – (a) cannot be the constitution itself, and (b) must provide a criterion for the identification of the constitution, too.

Hart is right to think that the rule of recognition is logically a necessary condition of our knowledge of the law. (The same is not true of Kelsen's basic norm, as I tried to argue.) The description of (the normative contents of) a legal system presupposes the identification of the system itself.[54] Hart's own picture of the rule of recognition, however, is unsatisfactory.

The rule of recognition, as I understand it, is *no legal norm*. It is no *norm*; it neither prescribes nor authorises. It is not *the* constitution itself, though it refers to the constitution. It is instead a conceptual tool for the identification (the 'recognition') of each particular legal system (its constitution included). Each rule of recognition, to put it differently, is a *definition* of the legal system to which it refers.[55] It is also not *legal*, because it is not a member of the system to which it refers; it is an extra-systematic criterion for identifying the system itself.

For any given legal system, its rule of recognition would run more or less along the following lines:

The legal system includes:

1. the norms expressed by its (historically first) constitution (which is supposed to be by and large effective), whether written or customary; and
2. the norms issued (and not derogated) by any organ authorised to do so by the constitution.[56]

There is no need to insist, I think, that such a rule – differently from Kelsen's basic norm – neither authorises nor commands anyone to do anything.[57]

[54] See *The Concept of Law* (n 39) 104, 108.

[55] See E Bulygin, 'Sobre la Regla de Reconocimiento' in CE Alchourrón and E Bulygin, *Análisis Lógico y Derecho* (Madrid, Centro de Estudios Constitucionales, 1991 [1976]) 383–91.

[56] See E Bulygin, 'Sobre la Regla de Reconocimiento' in CE Alchourrón and E Bulygin, *Análisis Lógico y Derecho* (Madrid, Centro de Estudios Constitucionales, 1991 [1976]) 383–91.

[57] For a different view, however, see J Ruiz Manero, *Jurisdicción y Normas. Dos Estudios Sobre Función Jurisdiccional y Teoría del Derecho* (Madrid, Centro de Estudios Constitucionales, 1990) 99ff.

Part II

Law's Empirical Existence

5

The Efficacy of Constitutional Norms

PABLO E NAVARRO*

I. INTRODUCTION

EFFICACY IS A neglected topic in contemporary legal philosophy.[1] Although it is often said that an understanding of efficacy forms a necessary part of a complete account of the existence of legal systems, one would be hard-pressed to find in the literature a thorough analysis of this feature of positive law. The following remark, made more than 30 years ago by Joseph Raz, remains true today:

> The tests for identity and existence of a legal system contain three basic elements: efficacy, institutional character, and sources. Efficacy is the least controversial of these conditions. Oddly enough it is also the least studied and least understood.[2]

Hans Kelsen is among those who emphasise the crucial role played by efficacy in an explanation of the nature of law. He views the relationship between 'the validity and the efficacy of law' as 'a special case of the relationship between the "ought" of the legal norm and the "is" of natural reality':[3] for the validity

* I am grateful to two anonymous reviewers for very helpful comments on an earlier version.

[1] It would seem, generally speaking, that legal philosophers tend to regard efficacy as a sociological, empirical problem, rather than as a conceptual one. But see E Bulygin, 'Der Begriff der Wirksamkeit' (1965) 41 *Archiv für Rechts- und Sozialphilosophie* 39ff; J Raz, *The Concept of a Legal System*, 2nd edn (Oxford, Clarendon Press, 1980) 203ff; P Ingram, 'Effectiveness' (1984) 69 *Archiv für Rechts- und Sozialphilosophie* 484–503; PE Navarro, *La Eficacia del Derecho* (Madrid, Centro de Estudios Constitucionales, 1990); PE Navarro and JJ Moreso, 'Applicability and Effectiveness of Legal Norms' (1997) 16 *Law and Philosophy* 201–19; or L Hierro, *La Eficacia de las Normas Jurídicas* (Barcelona, Ariel, 2004).

[2] *cf* J Raz, 'Legal Positivism and the Sources of Law' in *The Authority of Law*, 2nd edn (Oxford, Oxford University Press 2009 [1979]) 42.

[3] H Kelsen, *The Pure Theory of Law*, 2nd edn, M Knight transl (Berkeley, University of California Press, 1967 [1960]) 211. Here and in the following quotations I modify the English-language translation, which indistinctly renders as 'effectiveness' both Kelsen's '*Wirksamkeit*' (which I shall translate as 'efficacy') and Kelsen's '*Effektivität*' ('effectiveness'). (The latter is used eg to draw the contrast between 'legitimacy and effectiveness' at ibid 208, or in Kelsen's discussion of the 'principle of effectiveness' in international law at ibid 336f.) In translating '*Wirksamkeit*' as 'efficacy' I follow Bonnie and Stanley Paulson in their translation of the first edition of Kelsen's *Reine Rechstlehre*: *cf* H Kelsen, *Introduction to the Problems of Legal Theory*, BL Paulson and SL Paulson transl (Oxford, Clarendon Press, 1992 [1934]) eg 28f, 60f.

of a norm 'is an *ought* and not an *is*', whereas its efficacy 'is an "is-fact"'[4] – and the Pure Theory strives to view law as both a normative order and a complex social fact.

In this essay I will be concerned with some issues surrounding the efficacy of constitutional norms in the context of the Pure Theory of Law. Kelsen characterises a legal system's constitution as the 'highest level of positive law',[5] and constitutional norms as the ultimate positive ground of legal validity.[6] The efficacy of constitutional norms thus emerges as a particularly challenging subject – given Kelsen's view that the relationship between validity and efficacy is 'one of the most important and at the same time most difficult problems of a positivistic legal theory'.[7]

The scope of my inquiry will be restricted in two ways. The first restriction concerns the sense in which I will be using 'constitution' and its cognates. By 'constitution' Kelsen almost always means 'the norm or norms that determine how (that is, by what organs and by what procedure – through legislation or custom) the general norms of the legal order that constitute the community are to be created'.[8] Sometimes in his later work, however, he also uses the term in a broader, 'relativised' sense, to refer to *any* given norm which can be said to regulate the creation of any other ('lower') norm. Thus in the *General Theory of Norms*, for example, he says that

> [a] norm stands to another norm as higher to lower, if the validity of the latter is founded on the validity of the former. If the validity of the lower norm is founded on the validity of the higher norm in that the lower norm is *created* in the way prescribed in the higher norm, then the higher norm has the character of a constitution with respect to the lower norm, since the essence of a constitution is that it regulates the creation of norms. Thus a statute regulating the procedure by which law-applying organs, courts in particular, create individual norms is a 'constitution' with respect to the procedure of these organs, just like the 'constitution' in the narrower specific sense of the word with respect to legislative procedure . . . The concept of a constitution is thus relativized.[9]

In this chapter I will not refer to this new, 'relativised' concept; I use 'constitution' instead (as does Kelsen throughout most of his writings) in the 'narrower specific sense of the word'.

The second restriction is that, for the most part, I will not be concerned with the various subtle changes (very often made *sub silentio*) in Kelsen's views

[4] Kelsen, *The Pure Theory of Law* (n 3) 10.
[5] ibid 222.
[6] ibid 200.
[7] ibid 211.
[8] ibid 198f.
[9] H Kelsen, *General Theory of Norms*, M Hartney transl (Oxford: Clarendon Press, 1991 [1979]) 257. There is a similar passage in H Kelsen, 'The Function of a Constitution' in R Tur and W Twining (eds), *Essays on Kelsen* (Oxford, Clarendon Press, 1986 [1964]) 118.

on efficacy – as on several other issues – as his impressive body of work progressed.[10] Thus while in the 1945 *General Theory of Law and State*, for example, the efficacy of single norms (as opposed to the efficacy of the legal system 'on the whole') is not (not explicitly, at least) a condition of their validity,[11] in the second edition (1960) of *The Pure Theory of Law* Kelsen expressly maintains that

> the efficacy of a legal order as a whole and the efficacy of a single legal norm are . . . the condition for the validity; efficacy is the condition in the sense that a legal order as a whole, and a single legal norm, can no longer be regarded as valid when they cease to be efficacious.[12]

It can be argued, however, that this had always been Kelsen's view; for he had acknowledged since his earliest works that single norms might cease to be legally valid because of *desuetudo*.[13] So for the sake of simplicity I shall mainly refer to the second edition of the *Pure Theory*, and gloss over some minor variations (as well as some perplexing details) of Kelsen's evolving views on the topic.[14]

My strategy in this chapter will be to consider and discuss two candidate reconstructions of Kelsen's account of the efficacy of constitutional norms. I begin, in section II, with what might at first sight appear to be Kelsen's adopted view, and which I dub the 'internal account', viz. that constitutional norms are efficacious only to the extent that they are followed by their addressees. I will argue that Kelsen's strong theses about the structure and function of legal norms – both of legal norms in general, and of constitutional norms in

[10] Many legal philosophers have drawn attention to several important changes undergone by the Pure Theory along the decades. For one example, see E Bulygin, 'An Antinomy in Kelsen's Pure Theory of Law' in SL Paulson and BL Paulson (eds), *Normativity and Norms. Critical Perspectives on Kelsenian Themes* (Oxford, Clarendon Press, 1998).

[11] H Kelsen, *General Theory of Law and State*, A Wedberg transl (Cambridge, Mass., Harvard University Press, 1945) 41f.

[12] *The Pure Theory of Law* (n 3) 211f. This point is sometimes overlooked by commentators. Andrei Marmor, eg, asserts that in the Pure Theory '[e]fficacy is not a condition of legal validity of individual norms. Any given norm can be legally valid even if nobody follows it', a statement which the second edition of the *Pure Theory* does certainly not support; *cf* A Marmor, *Philosophy of Law* (Princeton, Princeton University Press, 2011) 19; or his entry 'The Pure Theory of Law' in *The Stanford Encyclopaedia of Philosophy* (Fall 2010 edn), EN Zalta (ed), URL = http://plato.stanford.edu/archives/fall2010/entries/lawphil-theory/. Marmor moreover mentions that according to Kelsen 'a norm is *efficacious* if it is actually (generally) followed by the relevant population'. This is also wrong: Kelsen repeatedly stresses – including in the *General Theory of Law and State* (n 11) eg at 62 – that the fact that a norm is *applied* by the competent legal organs is just as relevant in this regard as the fact that a norm is followed or obeyed by the population at large; *cf Pure Theory of Law* (n 3) 11f, 212. This latter dimension cannot be ignored, as we shall see, in a discussion of the efficacy of constitutional norms.

[13] See eg Kelsen, *Introduction to the Problems of Legal Theory* (n 3) 63; *General Theory of Law and State* (n 11) 119f; and *The Pure Theory of Law* (n 3) 212f.

[14] An example of what I consider a perplexing detail is Kelsen's claim, in *General Theory of Law and State* (n 11) 40, that while validity is 'a quality of law', efficacy 'is a quality of the actual behaviour of men and not, as linguistic usage seems to suggest, of law itself'.

particular – are incompatible with the adoption of the internal account. I then turn, in section III, to what I call an 'external' account of efficacy. It comes in two varieties. One is the view that the efficacy of constitutional norms turns on the efficacy of other, 'lower' (ie infra-constitutional) norms. The other is the view that the efficacy of constitutional norms turns on whether the lower norms of the system have been created in the way the constitution prescribes. There is evidence in Kelsen's writings supporting the attribution to him of either one of these views. But both views, as we shall see, are at odds with Kelsen's explanation of the systematic nature of law. In section IV, finally, I discuss the implications, for his treatment of efficacy, of Kelsen's doctrine of the constitutive character of judicial decisions. My conclusion will be that the Pure Theory offers no satisfactory account of the efficacy of constitutional norms.

II. THE INTERNAL ACCOUNT

It is often suggested that a legal norm is efficacious if and only if it is more often than not complied with by its addressees.[15] I will refer to this view as the 'internal' account of efficacy. The account is 'internal' in the sense that it looks only into the content of the norm in order to establish its efficacy: it makes the efficacy of a norm turn solely on some measure of coincidence between the factual circumstances which the norm regulates and the behaviour of the individuals to whom the norm applies; no other facts are necessary. According to this view, for example, many of the norms in the Argentinian Constitution (the 'historically first' version of which dates from 1853), such as those which establish the end of slavery or the abolishment of noble titles, can be said to have been efficacious; for they clearly have been complied with.

At first glance at least, this does seem to be a reasonable view. A constitution, of course, is a *set* of norms rather than a single norm. But the internal account can also be used to characterise the notion of a constitution that is *as a whole* efficacious; for it seems just as reasonable to claim that to say that a constitution is efficacious is to say that most of its norms are efficacious.[16] Provided that one accepts the equally common view that there is 'no neces-

[15] See eg HLA Hart, *The Concept of Law*, 3rd edn (Oxford, Oxford University Press, 2012 [1961]) 103; E Bodenheimer, *Jurisprudence. The Philosophy and Method of the Law*, revised edn (Cambridge, Mass., Harvard University Press, 1974) 260; LW Sumner, *The Moral Foundations of Rights* (Oxford, Clarendon Press, 1987) 29 fn 58; R Shiner, *Norm and Nature* (Oxford, Clarendon Press, 1992) 163.

[16] Some legal norms can be more important or relevant (in some respect) than others; a complete theory of the efficacy of constitutional norms would have to take into account the connections between the efficacy of a constitution and the continuity of a political system. See J Raz, 'The Identity of Legal Systems' in *The Authority of Law*, 2nd edn (Oxford, Oxford University Press 2009 [1971]) 100.

sary connection between the validity of any particular rule and *its* efficacy',[17] an inefficacious constitutional norm could still validly belong to an efficacious constitution. Thus section 24 of the Argentinean Constitution, for example, which prescribes that trial by jury be implemented, but which (apart from a few attempts) has largely been ignored by Congress, can be said to remain by and large inefficacious even though the Argentinean Constitution is efficacious as a whole.

Plausible as this account of efficacy may seem, it is not one that Kelsen could be said to have adopted as an account of the efficacy of constitutional norms.[18] Indeed, as we will see, the internal account of the efficacy of constitutional norms is incompatible with Kelsen's views on both the structure and the reconstruction (by legal science) of legal norms.

To be sure, Kelsen does hold a general view on the efficacy of legal norms which is in line with the internal account. He often speaks of a norm's efficacy as 'the fact that the norm is actually applied and obeyed, the fact that people actually behave according to the norm':[19]

> By efficacy of a legal norm, which attaches a sanction to a certain behaviour and thus qualifies the behaviour conditioning the sanction as illegal, that is, as 'delict', two facts may be understood: (1) that this norm is *applied* by the legal organs (particularly the law courts), which means that the sanction in a concrete case is ordered and executed; and (2) that the norm is *obeyed* by the individuals subjected to the legal order.[20]

Now this characterisation does qualify as 'internal' in the sense in which I have introduced the term. Yet this can't be Kelsen's characterisation of the efficacy of constitutional norms. For this internal notion of efficacy is inextricably associated with Kelsen's peculiar account of the structure of legal norms: and under that account constitutional norms do not qualify as legal norms – as 'complete' legal norms – in the relevant sense. Let me elaborate.

As I mentioned in the Introduction, Kelsen views the relation between validity and efficacy as one aspect of the relation between the *normative* and the *factual* dimensions of law:

> A positivistic legal theory is faced by the task to find the correct middle road between two extremes which both are untenable. The one extreme is the thesis that there is no connection between validity as something that ought to be and

[17] *cf* Hart, *The Concept of Law* (n 15) 103 (emphasis in original).

[18] By saying that the internal account seems plausible I don't mean to suggest that it is a satisfactory account of the efficacy of constitutional norms (whether or not it was Kelsen's own). One worry would be that many (if not most) constitutional norms are power-conferring rather than duty-imposing; but power-conferring norms cannot strictly be 'complied' with, cannot be obeyed or disobeyed.

[19] *The Pure Theory of Law* (n 3) 10.

[20] ibid 11.

> efficacy as something that is; that the validity of the law is entirely independent of its efficacy. The other extreme is the thesis that validity and efficacy are identical.[21]

Efficacy, he holds, 'is a condition for validity – but it is not validity':

> If the validity, that is, the specific existence of the law, is considered to be part of natural reality [and thus identified with efficacy], one is unable to grasp the specific meaning in which the law addresses itself to reality and thereby juxtaposes itself to reality, which can be in conformity or conflict with the law only if reality is not identical with the validity of the law.[22]

Kelsen's resistance to identifying (normative) validity and (factual) efficacy is reflected in his main claims about the relation between the two notions. Even though 'a minimum of efficacy is a condition of validity',[23] and even though a general norm 'is regarded as valid only if the human behaviour that is regulated by it actually conforms with it, at least to some degree',[24] efficacy is certainly not, Kelsen maintains, the 'reason' for validity ('that is, the answer to the question why the norms of this legal order ought to be obeyed and applied').[25] Validity and efficacy, he points out, do not 'coincide in time' – 'a norm becomes valid before it becomes efficacious, that is, before it is applied and obeyed'[26] – and 'a legal order does not lose its validity when a single legal norm loses its efficacy':

> A legal order is regarded as valid, if its norms are *by and large* efficacious (that is, actually applied and obeyed). Nor does a single legal norm lose its validity if it is only exceptionally efficacious in single cases . . . [T]he possibility of an antagonism between that which is prescribed by a norm as something that ought to be and that which actually happens must exist.[27]

In opposing the reduction of law to empirical facts – the collapse of validity into efficacy – and by insisting that the specific existence of law lies in its *normativity*, and not merely on its empirical facticity, Kelsen sets forth a positivist theory which differs significantly from the sort of positivism that had been prominent in the philosophy of science for the past century. This latter strand was characterised as follows by GH von Wright:

> One of the tenets of positivism is *methodological monism*, or the idea of the unity of scientific method amidst the diversity of subject matter of scientific investigation. A second tenet is the view that the exact natural sciences, in particular mathematical physics, set a methodological ideal or standard which measures the degree of

[21] ibid 211.
[22] ibid 213.
[23] ibid 11.
[24] ibid.
[25] ibid 213.
[26] ibid 11.
[27] ibid 212f.

> development and perfection of all the other sciences, including the humanities. A third tenet, finally, is a characteristic view of scientific explanation. Such explanation is, in a broad sense, 'causal'. It consists, more specifically, in the subsumption of individual cases under hypothetically assumed general laws of nature.[28]

Kelsen rejects these three tenets. His is a positivist theory in the sense that it is 'a theory of positive law': a theory that 'attempts to answer the question what and how the law *is*, not how it ought to be'.[29] But he characterises legal science as an autonomous *normative* science – a science of *positive* legal systems qua *normative* systems:

> By defining law as norm (or, to be precise, as a system of norms or as a normative order) and by limiting the science of law to the cognition and description of legal norms and to the norm-constituted relations between the norm-determined facts . . . the science of law as a science of norms is delimited against all other sciences that are directed toward causal cognition of actual happenings.[30]

But if such a science, methodologically 'different from natural science', exists, then, says Kelsen, 'it must describe its object according to a principle different from causality'.[31] This principle – which Kelsen calls 'imputation' – is the principle 'applied' in legal propositions ('*Rechtssätzen*'), ie in 'the sentences by which the science of law describes its object'.[32] 'Although analogous to causality', imputation is 'characteristically different from it':[33]

> Precisely like a law of nature, the legal proposition connects two elements. But the connection expressed in the legal proposition has a meaning entirely different from causality, the connection expressed in a law of nature. . . . The legal proposition does not say, as the law of nature does: when *A* is, 'is' *B*; but when *A* is, *B* 'ought' to be.[34]

Specifically, the science of law represents 'the specific meaning with which the legal order addresses itself to the individuals subject to it' by describing the law in propositions stating that 'according to a certain legal order under the condition that a certain delict determined by that legal order has been committed, a certain sanction determined by that legal order ought to take place'.[35] In other words:

> The law-describing legal proposition appears as the statement that under certain conditions, determined by the legal order, a certain coercive act, likewise determined by the legal order, ought to be performed.[36]

[28] GH von Wright, *Explanation and Understanding* (Ithaca, Cornell University Press, 1971) 4.
[29] *The Pure Theory of Law* (n 3) 1.
[30] ibid 75.
[31] ibid.
[32] ibid 76; again I modify the English-language translation, which equivocally renders '*Rechtsätze*' as 'rules of law'.
[33] ibid.
[34] ibid 77.
[35] ibid 78.
[36] ibid 108.

This, according to Kelsen, is the 'scheme of the legal proposition formulated by legal science'[37]: the unitary scheme according to which legal science reconstructs and describes the norms of any given legal system, the single pattern to which all 'legally relevant material' can be reduced.[38]

Thus it is Kelsen's anti-reductionist stance on normativity – his rejection of any attempt to conflate 'is' and 'ought', empirical facticity and normativity, efficacy and validity – that underlies his account of the basic structure of legal norms.[39] This account is itself reductionist, of course, though in a very different sense of the adjective. For in jurisprudence, as Brian Bix remarks, the term 'reductionism' can be used to refer to at least two kinds of theoretical projects. One is the project of reducing 'law or legal rules to essentially one type of norm'; this is the sense in which Kelsen can be said to have been a reductionist. The other is the project of 'trying to restate normative phenomena in purely empirical terms'; and in this sense Kelsen was not a reductionist (and was indeed an anti-reductionist).[40]

It is in this light that one should read such initially puzzling claims of Kelsen's as his well-known assertion that 'law is the primary norm, that stipulates the sanction'.[41] Kelsen is referring here to what he regards as the basic type of legal norm: addressed at legal officials, and stipulating that a coercive act be ordered if certain conditions obtain.

As Michael Hartney notes, this view that 'all legal norms (when reconstructed) have the same canonical structure: "If A does B, the official C is to (*soll*) order that sanction D be imposed on A" ' – the view, in other words, that 'the central kind of legal norm is addressed to an official and "directs" him to order a coercive act' – is a longstanding one; it remains unchanged at least since the first edition (1934) of the *Pure Theory of Law*.[42]

Equally well-known is Kelsen's claim that the notion of a duty-imposing legal norm addressed at *citizens* is, 'so to speak', says Kelsen, an 'epiphenomenon' of the sanction norm. He grants that 'the representation of law is greatly facilitated if we allow ourselves to assume also the existence of the first norm [ie the norm 'which demands the omission of the delict']' – and 'it is only if

[37] ibid 58.

[38] See also *General Theory of Law and State* (n 11) 45.

[39] As Bobbio puts it: 'Kelsen's theory of law as a coercive order is grounded mainly on the notion that law is made of norms, and that the characteristic trait of such norms is not that they prescribe (and even less that they authorise) certain courses of conduct, but that they establish a nexus of imputation between the delict ['*l'illecito*'] and the sanction': *cf* N Bobbio, 'Verso una Teoria Funzionalistica del Diritto' in *Dalla Struttura alla Funzione. Nuovi Studi di Teoria del Diritto* (Milan, Edizione di Comunità, 1970) 70 (my translation).

[40] *cf* B Bix, 'Reductionism and Explanation in Legal Theory' in T Endicott, J Getzler, and E Peel (eds), *Properties of Law. Essays in Honour of Jim Harris* (Oxford, Oxford University Press, 2006) 44 and fn 10.

[41] *General Theory of Law and State* (n 11) 61.

[42] *cf* M Hartney, 'Introduction: The Final Form of the Pure Theory of Law' in H Kelsen, *General Theory of Norms*, M Hartney transl (Oxford, Clarendon Press, 1991) xxii, xxxv.

one makes use of the concept of secondary norms in the presentation of law that the subject "ought" to avoid the delict and perform the legal duty' – but this 'secondary' norm is, he says, 'certainly superfluous in an exact exposition of law'[43]:

> Only the organ [to which the sanction norm is addressed] can, strictly speaking, 'obey' or 'disobey' the legal norm, by executing or not executing the stipulated sanction. As ordinarily used, however, the expressions 'obeying the norm' and 'disobeying the norm' refer to the behaviour of the subject. The subject can 'obey' or 'disobey' only the secondary norm. If we countenance this common mode of expression according to which the subject obeys or disobeys law, it commends itself to say that the organ 'applies' or does not 'apply' law. Only by adopting some such terminological distinction shall we be able to see clearly the difference between law's relation to the subject, the potential delinquent, and its relation to the organ.[44]

We are now in a position to see how the internal criterion of efficacy – according to which, as was said, a norm is efficacious when it is either applied by the legal courts, or obeyed by legal subjects[45] – fits with Kelsen's general account of legal norms, both 'primary' and 'secondary':

> As far as by law we understand the genuine, primary legal norm, law is efficacious if it is applied by the organ – if the organ executes the sanction. And the organ has to apply law precisely in the case where the subject 'disobeys' law: this is the case for which the sanction is stipulated. There is, however, a certain connection between factual obedience and the factual application of law. If a legal norm is permanently disobeyed by the subjects, it is probably no longer applied by the organs either. Therefore, though the efficacy of law is primarily its being applied by the proper organ, secondarily its efficacy means its being obeyed by the subjects.[46]

But remember that our topic in the present chapter is the efficacy of *constitutional* norms. And constitutional norms – which organise the process of law-creation and law-application in a legal system – are neither typically, nor usually, Kelsenian 'primary', sanction-imposing norms; nor are they Kelsenian 'secondary', duty-imposing norms, 'superfluous in an exact exposition of the law'. Kelsen acknowledges this explicitly. 'Constitutional norms', he grants, 'do not stipulate coercive acts'. They do, however, determine 'one of the conditions of the coercive act stipulated by other norms':

> The court that has to apply the general valid norms of a legal order to a concrete case, must decide the question whether the norm to be applied is constitutional, that is, created in a legislative procedure determined by the constitution or by

[43] *General Theory of Law and State* (n 11) 60f.
[44] ibid.
[45] See text to n 20.
[46] *General Theory of Law and State* (n 11) 62.

> custom delegated by the constitution. This fact . . . is as much a condition for the sanction stipulated by the court in a concrete case as the fact . . . that a delict had been committed.[47]

Indeed, he says, the 'complete' formulation of the sanction norm will make explicit the various different elements – apart, that is, from the commission of the delict – the joint ascertainment of which is the condition of the sanction. Thus:

> The [complete] proposition of law describing this situation – for example when a criminal law of a democratic legal order is applied – is this: if the constitutionally elected parliament, by way of a procedure prescribed by the constitution, has passed a statute, according to which a certain behaviour ought to be punished, as a crime, in a certain way; and if the court has ascertained the fact that a certain individual has behaved in that way; then the court ought to impose the punishment prescribed by the statute.[48]

'This formulation of the legal proposition', Kelsen continues, 'reveals the position of the so-called constitutional law (that is, the norms regulating the creation of general legal norms) within the framework of a legal order'.[49] Such norms are not 'independent, complete norms'.[50] Rather, they are 'intrinsic parts of all the legal norms which the courts and other organs have to apply'[51]; they determine but one of the several conditions to which – in 'complete' legal norms – the sanction is attached as a consequence.[52]

Make of this doctrine what you will.[53] For my present purposes it is sufficient to remark that such 'incomplete', 'dependent' norms are not the sort of thing that can (in Kelsenian terms) be either obeyed or applied. For, as we have seen, these two notions are defined by Kelsen by reference to the 'complete', sanction-stipulating legal norm.[54] What follows, of course, is not that constitutional norms cannot be efficacious. What follows is rather that Kelsen's internal account of efficacy is inadequate as an account of the efficacy of constitutional norms. He needs a different sort of account; he needs an external account of the efficacy of constitutional norms: an account, that is, which appeals to something other than the contents of such norms. As we will

[47] *The Pure Theory of Law* (n 3) 238; and cp *General Theory of Law and State* (n 11) 143f.

[48] *The Pure Theory of Law* (n 3) 238.

[49] ibid.

[50] ibid.

[51] *General Theory of Law and State* (n 11) 144.

[52] On Kelsen's 'complete' norms see also ibid 53, 129. In *The Pure Theory of Law* (n 3) Kelsen favours a different terminology, preferring almost always to speak instead of 'autonomous' norms ('*selbständige Normen*', in the original text) – *cf* ibid 55ff – but 'complete norms' ('*vollständige Normen*') occurs as well, and he seems to use the terms pretty much synonymously, as suggested by the phrase just quoted to n 50 (or indeed by the identical passage in *General Theory of Law and State*, at 143).

[53] A very well-known discussion is of course HLA Hart's, in *The Concept of Law* (n 15) 35ff.

[54] Recall the passage quoted to n 44.

now see, there are two different external accounts which can be attributed to Kelsen. But neither is devoid of problems.

III. EXTERNAL ACCOUNTS

A. The Efficacy of Lower-Level Norms

Kelsen's doctrine of the 'complete' sanction-norm is part of his discussion of the 'static' aspect of law.[55] But it seems that his views on legal 'dynamics' – and particularly his doctrine of the basic norm – allow us to isolate, and attribute to him, a different account of the efficacy of constitutional norms.

Indeed, the notion of an efficacious constitution plays a central role in Kelsen's doctrine of the basic norm. 'To understand the nature of the basic norm', he writes,

> it must be kept in mind that it *refers directly to a specific constitution, by and large efficacious*, and indirectly to the coercive order created according to this constitution and by and large efficacious; the basic norm thereby furnishes the reason for the validity of this constitution and of the coercive order created in accordance with it. The basic norm, therefore, is not the product of free invention.[56]

More clearly even:

> [T]he basic norm prescribes: 'Force ought to be exerted under the conditions and in the manner prescribed by the *by and large efficacious constitution* and by the by efficacious general and efficacious individual norms created according to the constitution'. Efficacy is stipulated as a condition for the validity by the basic norm.[57]

And 'a constitution is efficacious,' he tells us in passing, 'if the norms created in conformity with it are by and large applied and obeyed'.[58] This contention allows us to isolate the following *external* account of the efficacy of a constitution:

> (E1) A constitution *C* is efficacious if and only if the lower-level norms created in conformity with *C* are efficacious (ie by and large applied and obeyed).

This account is 'external' in the sense that it refers to facts *other* than the facts that feature in the content of the norms – the constitutional norms – the efficacy of which (E1) purports to define. (E1) accounts for the efficacy of some given constitutional norm N1 in terms of the efficacy of *another*, lower-level norm N2 that has been created in accordance with N1.

[55] On the distinction between 'static' and 'dynamic' legal theory, see *Pure Theory of Law* (n 3) 70f.

[56] ibid 211 (my emphasis); again I substitute 'efficacious' for 'effective' in the English translation (the original German is '*wirksam*'): see n 3.

[57] ibid 208 (my emphasis).

[58] ibid 210.

Now (E1) accommodates the fact that constitutional norms are not 'complete' norms in the sense explained in the previous section; as we saw, it is precisely because constitutional norms do not qualify as 'complete' norms that an external account of their efficacy is required within the frame of the Pure Theory. (E1) is also compatible with the fact that, as was also noted,[59] constitutional norms are (typically, at least) power-conferring norms, not duty-imposing ones.

But (E1) is also not a satisfactory account of the efficacy of constitutional norms. It is incompatible with the role assigned by the Pure Theory of Law to the constitution of a legal system. Here is why. 'The function of a constitution', according to Kelsen, is 'the grounding of validity';[60] and, as is well-known, Kelsen maintains that

> the validity of [a system's historically first] constitution – the assumption that it is a binding norm – must be *presupposed* if we want to interpret (1) the acts performed according to it as the creation or application of valid general legal norms; and (2) the acts performed in application of these general norms as the creation or application of valid individual norms.[61]

This presupposition 'must be a norm'[62] – it is Kelsen's basic norm:

> [A] positive legal order represents a system not of co-ordinate but of superordinate and subordinate norms – that is, a hierarchy of norms, whose highest tier is the constitution, which is grounded as valid by the presupposed basic norm, and whose lowest tier is the individual norms positing a particular concrete mode of conduct as obligatory. In this way the validity of the higher norm regulating the creation of the lower norm always grounds the validity of that lower norm.[63]

Consequently, lower-level legal norms are valid only if the constitution is valid. But, as we saw, Kelsen maintains that the basic norm 'is not the product of free invention', in that it refers 'directly' to some given 'constitution . . . by and large efficacious', and 'indirectly' to a 'coercive order created according to this constitution and by and large efficacious'.[64] This means that in order to assume (to 'presuppose') that some given constitution is valid we need to determine both that it is efficacious, and that the corresponding lower-level norms are efficacious. Now if (E1) were sound, then if such lower-level norms were inefficacious, the constitution would also be inefficacious; the basic norm would then not be presupposed; and such lower-level norms would therefore not be valid. This would carry two problematic consequences. First, if in order to determine whether the infra-constitutional norms enacted by legal authori-

[59] *cf* n 18.
[60] Kelsen, 'The Function of a Constitution' (n 9) 119.
[61] *The Pure Theory of Law* (n 3) 200.
[62] ibid.
[63] 'The Function of a Constitution' (n 9) 119.
[64] See the passage quoted to n 56.

ties are valid we had first to determine whether such norms are efficacious, then it couldn't be the case that such legal norms could be valid *before* they were efficacious – which is a conclusion which not only seems wrong, but which, as we have already noted,[65] Kelsen actually rejects. Second, and more dramatically, if the efficacy of a constitution is reduced – as proposed in (E1) – to the efficacy of lower-level norms, then there would no longer be any point to Kelsen's claim that the basic norm is presupposed if and only if a specific *constitution* is efficacious: for this would be just another way of saying that the basic norm is presupposed if and only if the lower-level norms are efficacious, which in turn would entail that the actual efficacy of the constitution would in fact be irrelevant. Therefore Kelsen cannot adopt (E1) as his account of the efficacy of constitutional norms.

We can unfold this argument in a different and perhaps clearer way. Here are four propositions, subscription of which can be attributed to Kelsen, concerning validity and its relation to efficacy:

A. If a legal norm N is efficacious, then N is valid.[66]
B. If a legal norm N is valid, then its constitutional ground – that is, a certain constitutional norm CN – is also valid.[67]
C. If a constitutional norm CN is valid, then a basic norm is presupposed.[68]
D. The basic norm is presupposed only if the constitution is efficacious.[69]

Assume, for the sake of simplicity, that a constitution contains one single norm CN. We have, then, that, according to Kelsen, and for some infra-constitutional norm N,

(1)	If N is efficacious, then N is valid.	(From (A))
(2)	If N is valid, then CN is valid.	(From (B))

It follows by transitivity that

(3)	If N is efficacious, then CN is valid.	(From (1) and (2))

[65] See the passage quoted to n 26.

[66] The justification for attributing (A) to Kelsen is that, given that Kelsen treats efficacy a predicate of norms, the statement that some norm N is efficacious presupposes that N exists, which – since for Kelsen 'the existence of a legal norm is its validity': *cf* eg *General Theory of Law and State* (n 11) 48, or *The Pure Theory of Law* (n 3) 10 – is to say that N is valid. See also R Caracciolo, 'Interpretación de Sentido y Conocimiento Jurídico' in *El Derecho Desde la Filosofía. Ensayos* (Madrid, Centro de Estudios Políticos y Constitucionales 2009 [1977]) 18. Note, too, that in 'Geltung und Wirksamkeit des Rechts' in R Walter, C Jabloner and K Zeleny (eds), *Hans Kelsens stete Aktualität* (Vienna, Manz, 2003 [about 1965]) 21, Kelsen explicitly states that efficacy is, in the Pure Theory, a 'sufficient' condition of validity ('*Wirksamkeit ist – der Reinen Rechtslehre nach – zwar die hinreichende . . . Bedingung der Geltung einer Rechtsnorm*'); and at 12, fn 10, moreover, he registers his agreement with Larenz's claim that 'in social life' efficacy already 'presupposes' validity.

[67] See the passage quoted to n 61, and *cf* generally *The Pure Theory of Law* (n 3) 193ff, 198ff.

[68] See eg *The Pure Theory of Law* (n 3) 201ff.

[69] See ibid, and recall the passage quoted to n 56.

Now given that

(4) If CN is valid, a basic norm is presupposed, (From (C))

the conclusion follows that

(5) If N is efficacious, then a basic norm is presupposed. (From (3) and (4))

We know, however, that Kelsen also holds that

(6) If a basic norm is presupposed, then CN is efficacious. (From (D))

Now according to (E1) – the external criterion we are discussing in this subsection – a constitution is efficacious if and only if the lower-level norms created in conformity with it are efficacious. Consequently

(7) If CN is efficacious, then N is efficacious. (From (E1))

It follows, then, that

(8) If a basic norm is presupposed, then N is efficacious. (From (6) and (7))

From (5) and (8), nevertheless, we obtain

(9) A basic norm is presupposed if and only if N is efficacious.

But this means that we cannot determine the validity of a legal system's lower-level norms without establishing that they are efficacious, and thus that only efficacious norms are valid, and indeed that they are valid only to the extent that they are efficacious. And this is tantamount to saying that the efficacy of a constitution plays no independent role in the presupposition of a basic norm – a conclusion that Kelsen would evidently have to reject.[70]

So (E1), too, must be rejected. What we need – what Kelsen needs – is an external account of the efficacy of constitutional norms which does not refer to the efficacy of the lower-level norms in the system.

B. The Creation of 'Lower-Level' Norms

In his discussion of scenarios in which a revolution brings about a change in constitution (and therefore a change in the basic norm) Kelsen seems to suggest that a constitution is efficacious when the lower-level norms of a system are created in accordance with it – or, more precisely, when the acts of will by which certain agents purport to bring about such norms are indeed 'objec-

[70] The fact that the efficacy of the constitution requires only the efficacy the *majority* of its norms – ie, as Kelsen puts it, that the constitution is 'by and large' efficacious: see passage quoted to n 56 – does not affect this conclusion. According to (E1), the efficacy of the majority of constitutional norms CN1, CN2, . . . CNn is still nothing else but the efficacy of other, lower-level norms N1, N2, . . . Nn. See Caracciolo, 'Interpretación de Sentido y Conocimiento Jurídico' (n 66) 18f.

tively' interpreted as norm-creating according to that constitution.[71] In his 1965 essay 'The Function of a Constitution', moreover, Kelsen remarks that the basic norm refers directly

> to a particular constitution that has in fact been laid down, whether created by custom or by formal statement. That is to say, it refers to the facts in which the norms of the constitution are posited, which norms are the subjective meaning of these facts – yet indirectly refers to the general and individual norms of the legal order which are in fact posited in conformity with the constitution, i.e. the basic norm refers indirectly to the facts whose subjective meaning these norms are.

So far this seems to parallel the similar passage from the second edition of the *Pure Theory of Law* which we quoted and discussed in the previous subsection.[72] But now Kelsen adds:

> That means that the basic norm refers only to an efficacious constitution – *that is, to a constitution in conformity with which statutes, and judicial and administrative decisions in conformity with statute, are in fact made.*[73]

On the grounds of these passages it is possible to formulate, and again ascribe to Kelsen, another account of the efficacy of a constitution:

> (E2) A constitution *C* is efficacious if lower-level norms are created in conformity with it (ie by the organs and according to the procedures that *C* prescribes for norm-creation).

This criterion retains the advantages while avoiding the specific shortcomings of (E1), the external account discussed in the previous subsection. Like (E1), (E2) is an external account that is perfectly compatible with the fact that, from a 'static' perspective, constitutional norms would not qualify, according to Kelsen, as 'complete' norms. Like (E1), moreover, (E2) is consistent with the typical power-conferring character of constitutional norms. But, differently from (E1), (E2) does not require that a system's infra-constitutional norms are themselves efficacious – complied with – in order for a constitution to be efficacious. What (E2) requires instead is solely that the constitution is actually used – 'applied', as Kelsen would put it[74] – in the *creation* of lower-level norms.

Note, also, that this external account is logically weaker than (E1): (E1) entails (E2), but (E2) does not entail (E1). This means that although the rejection of (E1) does not commit us to rejecting (E2), if there are independent grounds to reject (E2), then those grounds will also constitute additional arguments for rejecting (E1). So now the question before us is: is (E2) satisfactory?

[71] *The Pure Theory of Law* (n 3) 210.

[72] See the passage quoted to n 56.

[73] Kelsen, 'The Function of a Constitution' (n 9) 115.

[74] cf *The Pure Theory of Law* (n 3) 234: 'A norm that determines the creation of another norm is applied by the creation of that other norm. Application of law is at the same time creation of law . . . In application of the constitution the general norms are created by legislation or custom'.

One problem with (E2) is that it is rendered useless by Kelsen's own explanation of the phenomenon of irregular norms such as 'unconstitutional' legislative norms, or 'illegal' individual norms posited by judicial decisions. In modern legal systems there are institutions – like the Supreme Court of the United States, or the Constitutional Courts of several European countries – empowered to solve conflicts between norms of different hierarchical 'levels'. Think, for example, of a conflict between a norm enacted by a legislative body, such as a Parliament, and a constitutional norm. Now the legislative norm may come to be declared unconstitutional by a system's Constitutional Court; in that case, the norm will (normally) be eliminated from the system, and other specific consequences may follow. But even before any such decision – and indeed irrespective of whether any such decision actually comes to be made – lawyers and jurists might naturally refer to the legislative norm as 'unconstitutional', and hence as 'invalid'. One could non-problematically accept, that is, as Stephen Munzer, for example, puts it, that there *exist* 'invalid' norms:

> [C]onsider the case where a State law of long-standing is declared invalid or unconstitutional by the Supreme Court of the United States. The existence of this law would not be in dispute: if 'offenders' have been tried and convicted under its provisions for many years, it would be impossible to deny its existence. Yet this law is held to be invalid, i.e. not to conform to the Constitution. Hence, at some point the law both exists and is invalid. Therefore validity and existence are not identical.[75]

But this is a conclusion that Kelsen – because, as noted above,[76] he views a norm's 'validity' as its 'specific existence' – cannot draw. He maintains that such 'traditional' expressions as 'illegal judicial decision' or 'unconstitutional statute', which 'give the impression that such a thing as a "norm contrary to a norm" in general and a "legal norm contrary to a legal norm" were possible', cannot in fact be taken literally; for according to Kelsen there can *be* no invalid norms:

> A 'norm contrary to a norm' . . . is a self-contradiction; a legal norm which might be said to be in conflict with the norm that determines its creation could not be regarded as a valid legal norm – it would be null, which means that it would not be a legal norm at all. That which is null cannot be annulled.[77]
>
> The statement that a valid statute is 'unconstitutional' is a self-contradiction; for a statute can be valid only on the basis of the constitution. If one has reason to assume that a statute is valid, the reason for its validity must be the constitution. Of an invalid statute one cannot say that it is unconstitutional, for an invalid statute is no statute at all; it is legally non-existent, and no legal statement can therefore be

[75] S Munzer, *Legal Validity* (The Hague, Martinus Nijhoff, 1972) 13f.
[76] *cf* n 66.
[77] *The Pure Theory of Law* (n 3) 267.

> made about it. If the assertion, usually made by traditional theory, that a statute is unconstitutional, were to have a possible juristic meaning, it cannot be taken literally.[78]

These claims of Kelsen's are motivated by his account of the systematic existence of legal norms. He holds that the validity of any given legal norm N1 is a matter of N1 having been created in in accordance with some 'higher' norm N2, which is the 'reason for the validity' of N1.[79] Consequently, N1 cannot possibly 'conflict' with N2; for a conflict would mean that N1 was not valid, and thus that it would not exist *qua* norm of the system:

> No conflict is possible between a higher norm and a lower norm, that is, between one norm which determines the creation of another norm and this other norm, because the lower norm has the reason for its validity in the higher norm. If a lower norm is regarded as valid, it must be regarded as being valid according to a higher norm.[80]

How, then, does Kelsen account for what jurists – and many legal theorists as well – normally refer to as 'invalid' legal norms? Famously, his contention is that every power-conferring norm is to be read as *alternatively*, if tacitly, authorising the lower-level organs to create norms that either conform or do not conform to the specified requirements of content or procedure:

> The provisions of the constitution which regulate legislation have an alternative character. The constitution includes a direct and an indirect regulation of legislation; and the legislative organ has to choose between them.[81]

The fact that 'the constitution confers upon an organ different from the legislative organ the power to examine the constitutionality of statutes and authorizes this organ to repeal a statute considered as "unconstitutional" '[82] shows merely, according to Kelsen, 'that the constitution, while being unable to exclude the second path, prefers the first';[83] but unless and until the statute is rescinded

> the statute is valid and has to be applied by all law-applying organs. . . . The so-called unconstitutional statutes are constitutional statutes which, however, may be rescinded in a special procedure . . . [P]rovisions of the constitution regulating legislation have the mentioned alternative character. The legislative organ has the choice between two paths: the one prescribed explicitly by the constitution and the one to be decided by the legislative organ itself.[84]

78 ibid 271.
79 *cf* ibid 193ff.
80 ibid 208.
81 ibid 273.
82 ibid.
83 ibid 274.
84 ibid.

The same solution is offered for the hypothesis of 'the "unlawful" judicial decision'.[85] According to this doctrine, then, legislators can *validly* enact laws *whether or not* they conform to the actual (explicit) content of the relevant power-conferring norms; and judges can *validly* issue decisions (and thus individual legal norms) *whether or not* they conform to the actual (explicit) content of the general norms which they apply. In short, the legislator's norms are *always* valid, irrespective of their content; as are the judge's decisions. Hence there can be no invalid norms; and law is properly speaking a normative *system*, since 'no conflict is possible between a higher and a lower norm'.[86]

I am not concerned in this chapter with the critical assessment of this strategy of Kelsen's.[87] What I wish to emphasise is its profound impact on the issue of the efficacy of constitutional norms, and particularly for (E2), the external account presently under consideration. If one accepts that lower-level norms are always validly created, (E2) leads to the conclusion that the constitutional norms that regulate the creation of lower-level norms are *always* efficacious. More precisely, if one agrees with the doctrine that those constitutional norms which regulate the law-making process always tacitly authorise the creation of norms by means of irregular procedures or with explicitly proscribed contents, then if one adopts (E2) as an account of the efficacy of constitutional norms – if, that is, one takes the valid creation of lower-level norms as the criterion for deciding whether a constitution is efficacious – then one cannot but reach the conclusion that constitutions are always efficacious. The problem, of course, is that it (E2) is thereby rendered useless; it becomes pointless to insist that the efficacy of a constitution turns on the 'valid' creation of lower-level norms.

There is a second problem with an account like (E2), and it is a problem which also directly affects (E1). In Kelsen's reconstruction of legal 'dynamics', as we saw, the reason for the validity of any given legal norm is always another, 'higher' norm.[88] Accordingly – the constitution being the 'highest' positive norm grounding the validity of all the other norms in a legal system – we need to establish the validity of the constitution (again by reference to a 'higher' norm, which is the basic norm) in order to determine the validity of any 'lower' norm. Now according to either (E2) or (E1), the efficacy of a constitution turns on other, 'lower'-level norms. Therefore the efficacy of a constitution can be established only if such lower-level valid norms exist. But given

[85] ibid 267ff.

[86] ibid 276.

[87] For discussion, see eg R Vernengo, 'La Función Sistemática de la Norma Fundamental' (1960) 1–2 *Revista Jurídica de Buenos Aires* 207ff; CS Nino, *La Validez del Derecho* (Buenos Aires, Astrea, 1985) 32ff; J Ruiz Manero, *Jurisdicción y Normas* (Madrid, Centro de Estudios Constitucionales, 1990) 51ff; or E Bulygin, 'Cognition and Interpretation of Law' in SL Paulson and L Gianformaggio (eds), *Cognition and Interpretation of Law* (Turin, Giappichelli, 1995) 16ff.

[88] See text to n 79.

that the efficacy of a constitution is in turn a condition of *its* validity – for it is only if the constitution is efficacious that it makes sense to presuppose a basic norm, and thus to presuppose that certain acts of will (eg commands) by certain agents amount 'objectively' to the creation of valid norms – then it is impossible, without vicious circularity, for the constitution to ground the validity of the lower-level norms.[89] One would be simultaneously determining the validity of lower norms by reference to the efficacy of the constitution, and determining the efficacy of the constitution by reference to the validity of lower norms.

IV. EFFICACY, VALIDITY AND LEGAL DYNAMICS

I should now like to return to the matter – discussed in section II – of the efficacy of general legal norms in the context of the Pure Theory, in order to note and discuss an intriguing remark of Kelsen's in the posthumously published *General Theory of Norms* (1979).

We already know that in Kelsen's theory of law, efficacy and legal dynamics are intrinsically connected, and that this connection plays a crucial role in Kelsen's understanding of the relations between efficacy and validity. As Kelsen remarks in the *General Theory of Law and State* (1945):

> [T]he relationship between validity and efficacy is cognizable . . . only from the point of view of a dynamic theory of law dealing with the problem of the reason of validity and the concept of the legal order. From the point of view of a static theory, only the validity of law is in question.[90]

The idea seems clear. Legal dynamics concerns the creation and application of positive law – legal dynamics answers the question 'whether or not and why a certain norm belongs to a system of valid legal norms'[91] – and the facts of efficacy (as well as, of course, the facts of inefficacy) condition the creation (and the elimination) of legal norms just as much as the facts of norm-*positing*, whether intentional or custom-based, do. In contrast, when we are interested in the 'static' aspect of law our concern, according to Kelsen, is with the 'essence of law', and thus with the 'role of coercion in defining the concept of law':[92]

> What, from a dynamic point of view, is the creation of a general norm determined by a higher norm, the constitution, becomes in a static presentation of law one of the conditions to which the sanction is attached as a consequence in the general

[89] See also PE Navarro and JJ Moreso, 'Eficacia y Constitución' (1992) 10 *Revista del Centro de Estudios Constitucionales* 55ff, esp 58; and L Hierro, *La Eficacia de las Normas Jurídicas* (n 1) 186.

[90] *General Theory of Law and State* (n 11) 42.

[91] ibid 122.

[92] ibid.

> norm (which, from the dynamic point of view, is the lower norm in relation to the constitution). In a static presentation of law, the higher norms of the constitution are, as it were, projected as parts into the lower norms.[93]

We are already familiarised with this notion – the notion of the 'complete' general, sanction-stipulating norm.[94] We also know that according to Kelsen the efficacy of a general sanction norm lies 'primarily' in 'its being applied by the proper organ'[95]: we saw in section II how an *internal* account of efficacy – although inadequate as an account of the efficacy of constitutional norms – appears to be suited to Kelsen's general sanction-stipulating norms.

In the *General Theory of Norms* Kelsen seems, generally speaking, to continue to endorse similar views. But after presenting them, in chapter 34, Kelsen remarks that

> The preceding explanations – inasmuch as they concern general legal norms – are based on the usual formulation of a general norm: 'If an illegal situation (delict) occurs, then a legal consequence (sanction) is to occur'. But they require an important correction if the general norm is given its correct formulation: 'If a competent law-applying organ (especially a court) ascertains that a state of affairs specified abstractly in a general legal norm has occurred concretely, the competent court is to posit an individual norm which decrees to be obligatory a concrete coercive act which agrees with the coercive act specified abstractly in the general norm'.[96]

This is a puzzling passage. On the one hand Kelsen offers this 'correct formulation' as a revised formulation – as a restatement, as it were – of '*the*' general norm. On the other hand, the revised formulation itself *refers to* 'the general norm', and to circumstances and consequences 'specified abstractly' in 'the general norm'. Is Kelsen now referring to a norm which – *parallel* to the 'abstract', sanction-stipulating general norm – stipulates that the competent court, when it has ascertained that some concrete state of affairs is an instance of the state of affairs generically described in the general norm, is to issue an individual decision ordering a coercive act that specifies the consequence also generically described in the general norm?

In any case Kelsen seems clear that when it comes to the characterisation of the role of legal officials, and particularly of courts, this revised formulation is to be preferred – after all it is the 'correct formulation' – to the 'usual formulation' of the relevant general norm. And indeed he had already maintained in the second edition of the *Pure Theory of Law* that

> the legal proposition does not say: 'If a certain individual has committed murder, then a punishment ought to be imposed upon him.' The legal proposition says: 'If

[93] ibid 144.
[94] See text to n 48.
[95] See passage quoted to n 46.
[96] *General Theory of Norms* (n 9) 140.

> the authorized court in a procedure determined by the legal order has ascertained, with the force of law, that a certain individual has committed a murder, then the court ought to impose a punishment upon that individual'.[97]

Likewise in the *General Theory of Law and State*:

> [T]he correct formulation of the legal proposition is not 'If a subject has committed a delict, an organ shall direct a sanction against the delinquent', but 'If the competent organ has established in due order that a subject has committed a delict, then an organ shall direct a sanction against this subject.[98]

But this shift brings with it some important consequences with regard to efficacy. If indeed this is the 'correct formulation' of general norms, then Kelsen's original internal account of efficacy seems no longer to be satisfactory. For one, observance by legal subjects can no longer be a ground of efficacy: under this revised formulation, the general norm is efficacious only when it *is* applied, ie when the competent courts do 'posit an individual norm which decrees to be obligatory a concrete coercive act', and when the sanction is executed. As Kelsen now puts it:

> Whether a general norm [in its 'correct formulation'] is efficacious . . . does not depend on the actual observance of the norm we have called the 'secondary' norm (i.e. on behaviour which avoids the sanction) but on the judicial finding that there obtains a concrete state of affairs which is the condition for a sanction.[99]

It would seem, then, that the efficacy of the correctly formulated general norms would turn only on whether legal officials happen to apply them to the cases that such norms do *actually* regulate. But this can also not be Kelsen's conclusion. For Kelsen holds throughout his works that judicial decisions are 'constitutive' in character, both with regard to the so-called 'finding' of the applicable law, *and* with regard to the so-called 'finding' of the relevant facts of the case:

> [E]ven the ascertainment of the fact that a delict had been committed represents an entirely constitutive function of the court . . . Not the fact in itself that an individual has committed a murder is the condition stipulated by the legal order, but the fact that an organ, authorized by the legal order, in a procedure prescribed by the legal order, has ascertained that an individual has committed murder.[100]

Again, this is not the place to discuss this rather dubious doctrine,[101] which seems to go hand-in-hand with Kelsen's views on the 'correct formulation' of general legal norms. I mean only to draw attention to the radical consequences

[97] *The Pure Theory of Law* (n 3) 240.
[98] *General Theory of Law and State* (n 11) 136.
[99] *General Theory of Norms* (n 9) 141.
[100] *The Pure Theory of Law* (n 3) 239; see also *General Theory of Law and State* (n 11) 135f.
[101] For discussion, see eg Bulygin, 'Cognition and Interpretation of Law' (n 87) 18ff.

that follow on the matter of efficacy. Kelsen comes to acknowledge in the *General Theory of Norms*, such views lead to the conclusion that the revised general norm is efficacious *not only* when

> the competent courts, once they have found a concrete state of affairs *subsumable under the state of affairs specified abstractly in the general norm*, posit an individual norm which decrees to be obligatory a concrete coercive act subsumable under the coercive act specified abstractly in the general norm,[102]

but *also* when

> the court finds that the concrete state of affairs which is the condition for the sanction . . . *does not* exist, and so dismisses the plaintiff's case or acquits the defendant, that is, posits an individual norm which specifies that *no* coercive act is to be performed.[103]

Moreover, Kelsen adds that the general norm can even be considered to be efficacious even if it is '*never* applied' (provided 'the courts are never in a situation to find a concrete state of affairs which is the condition for sanctions').[104] And to this list of consequences one would have to add that the general norm is also efficacious (and 'applied'), even when judges happen to convict a person who happens in fact to be *innocent* – a conclusion that follows from Kelsen's doctrine of the constitutive character of judicial decisions.

But then, given that in order to count as efficacious, the (correctly formulated) general norm no longer has to be observed; given that it also does not have to 'applied' at all; and given, moreover, that it counts as having been 'applied' (and thus efficacious) even when innocents are found guilty and convicted; it would be exceedingly difficult to find *any* inefficacious general norm at all.

V. CONCLUDING REMARKS

The result of our inquiries is that the Pure Theory of Law fails to offer a satisfactory account of the relations between validity, efficacy and legal dynamics. To conclude, I wish briefly to note that Kelsen's difficulties in this regard are only exacerbated by his late distinction – set forth in the *General Theory of Norms* – between 'conditional validity' and 'full validity'. 'A general legal hypothetical norm is valid as soon as it is posited', he says in chapter 13; 'but it is valid only conditionally, and . . . cannot be immediately observed (or violated) and applied':

[102] *General Theory of Norms* (n 9) 141 (my emphasis).
[103] ibid (emphasis in the original).
[104] ibid (my emphasis).

> If the validity of a norm means that it *ought* to be observed and applied . . . then a general hypothetical norm can be valid only mediately, that is, through the *intermediary* of the validity of the corresponding individual categorical norm in which the behaviour abstractly decreed to be obligatory in the general hypothetical norm is concretely decreed to be obligatory. . . . The validity of a general hypothetical norm begins when it is posited. But this conditional validity is not full validity. The process by which a general hypothetical norm becomes valid does not end with the positing of the norm. It must be continued, once the condition abstractly specified in this general hypothetical norm is concretely satisfied, by the positing of an individual categorical norm which corresponds to the general norm.[105]

But this means that a general norm is valid – 'fully' valid – only in so far as it *is* applied – which is tantamount to saying that the norm is fully valid only if it is efficacious. In order to determine a norm's 'full' validity, in other words, we must look at its application:

> [T]he judge's positing of the individual norm corresponding to the general norm must supervene in order for it to be possible to speak of the full validity of the law, of law being valid in the full sense of the word.[106]

Given that in the *General Theory of Norms* the fact that a norm is 'applied' still features as a sufficient condition of its efficacy,[107] it follows that only efficacious norms can be fully valid in a legal system.

This late view is difficult to square with other Kelsenian theses. Given that both legal systems (as a whole), and not only single norms, can be said to be valid, does the distinction between 'full' and 'conditional' validity apply to legal systems as well – and, if so, what conclusions should we draw on the subject of a the relation between a system's validity and efficacy? What about the basic norm of a legal system? Is it *fully* valid, or only conditionally so? These and other questions that could be raised in connection with Kelsen's final work – questions which I cannot address here – are pointers to further difficulties brought into what was already a highly problematic account of the relations between the validity and the efficacy of norms and normative systems.

[105] ibid 50.
[106] ibid 300.
[107] ibid 139.

6

The Realist Hans Kelsen

UTA BINDREITER*

I. INTRODUCTION

WE ARE ACCUSTOMED to thinking of Kelsen as *the* legal positivist: less often he is spoken of as Kelsen the realist. And yet, nothing, as he sees it, would be more natural. The Pure Theory is a positivistic theory of law, he says, and this is to say that it is a realistic theory of law.[1] And what is more (as he declares in another passage): The Pure Theory is, in a certain sense, a 'radically realistic' theory.[2] Radically realistic – how?

While the *Reine Rechtslehre* was being prepared for a second edition, Kelsen read *On Law and Justice*, a work written by his erstwhile student Alf Ross and published, in an English translation, in 1958.[3] Evidently, the perusal of this work did not add to Kelsen's cheer: greatly provoked by the charges, both outspoken and implied, which Ross once again[4] had levelled against the Pure Theory, Kelsen decided then and there to launch a counter-attack by way of a review article with the title 'A "Realistic" Theory of Law and the Pure Theory of Law: Remarks on Alf Ross's *On Law and Justice*'.[5]

* Many warm thanks to Professor Stanley L Paulson, who read the first version of the chapter, for his comments and valuable advice.

[1] H Kelsen, *Reine Rechtslehre*, 2nd edn (Vienna, Franz Deuticke, 1960) 403.

[2] H Kelsen, *The Pure Theory of Law*, 2nd edn, M Knight transl (Berkeley, University of California Press, 1967 [1960]) 106; *Reine Rechtslehre* (n 1) 112.

[3] A Ross, *On Law and Justice*, M Dutton transl (London, Stevens & Sons, 1958). This work was first published in Danish in 1953; the second edition – which, apart from correcting some misprints, retains unchanged everything that appeared in the 1953 edition – appeared in 1966: *cf Om Ret og Retfærdighed. En Indførelse i den analytiske Retsfilosofi* [On Law and Justice. An Introduction to Analytic Philosophy of Law] (Copenhagen, Nyt Nordisk Forlag Arnold Busck, 1966). In the present chapter, I have used both the original Danish text from this second, 1966 edition, and the 1958 English translation. Longer English quotations from the Danish edition are my own translations.

[4] *cf* n 6.

[5] H Kelsen, 'A "Realistic" Theory of Law and the Pure Theory of Law. Remarks on Alf Ross's *On Law and Justice*' (1959), transl L Duarte d'Almeida, in this volume. My quotations follow this English-language translation, but my page references will be to the original, H Kelsen, 'Eine "Realistische" und die Reine Rechtslehre. Bemerkungen zu Alf Ross: On Law and Justice' (1959/60) 10 *Österreichische Zeitschrift für öffentliches Recht* 1–25: because the English version helpfully

It was the title of this article that first attracted my attention: I was intrigued, I confess, by the quotation marks encircling the word 'realistic'. What function might they have?

1. Are they indicating that Ross's professedly realistic theory was not realistic at all? And if so, what was Kelsen's understanding of the word 'realistic'?
2. Are they indicating that Ross's theory was not realistic according to his own definition of that word?
3. Or was Kelsen, perhaps, 'hitting back', that is to say, using quotation marks in order to set Ross straight on a vital point, namely, that it was an extraordinary presumption, not to say impertinence, on his part to launch his theory as the first genuinely realistic theory, thereby neatly implying that all other legal theories, both traditional and current, were *not* realistic?[6]
4. And did Kelsen take his cues from Ross himself who, in *On Law and Justice*, frequently had encircled the word 'validity' in quotation marks, thereby intimating his awareness that the term, as such, was meaningless, but that he was nevertheless forced to use it for lack of anything better?[7]

Any or, indeed, all of these reasons may have contributed to Kelsen's decision to employ quotation marks when referring to Ross's 'realistic' theory.[8] It was a means of expressing sarcasm, no doubt – but the tantalising question remains: what exactly was Kelsen alluding to? To arrive at a plausible answer to this question is the purpose of the present chapter.

In his article, Kelsen restricted himself to a discussion of those views of Ross's that were in direct opposition to his own. The five views discussed are: I. The term 'empirical science'; II. Legal cognition; III. The dualism of *Sein* ('is') and *Sollen* ('ought') and Ross's attempt to dissolve it; IV. Ross's reinterpretation of validity and his so-called 'predictive' theory of valid law; and V. The reproach of metaphysical speculation with reference to Kelsen's concept of objective *ought*-validity and the role of the basic norm.

These five sections represent the structure of Kelsen's article. Each provides an exhaustive treatment of the issue in question,[9] elucidating the views of the

displays the original page numbers, my references can be easily followed. This piece indicates Kelsen's first preoccupation with the Scandinavian variant of legal realism. He reviews both *On Law and Justice* and Ross's earlier work, *Towards a Realistic Jurisprudence. A Criticism of the Dualism in Law*, AI Fausbøll transl (Copenhagen, Einar Munksgaard, 1946 [1934]).

[6] Kelsen may have had another grudge against Ross, namely the latter's scathing 'Book Review: Kelsen, *What is Justice?*' (1957) 45 *California Law Review* 564–70. See also n 180.

[7] In this, Ross may have been imitating his Swedish colleague AV Lundstedt (1882–1955), who had initiated the device (and indeed was famous for it) of encircling 'metaphysically'-coloured words with quotation marks.

[8] This applies not only to the title of the article but also to running text.

[9] The article is not easy to read, owing inter alia to its 'compact' form. This may explain why the article has been leading a rather discreet and little-noticed existence. Laudable exceptions are

parties and eventually leaving Kelsen as, so to speak, the undisputed conqueror on the field of battle.[10] His article is not merely a thoroughly convincing defence of the Pure Theory: with ruthless logic and exemplary *akribeia*, Kelsen pins down the flaws in Ross's theory and exploits them mercilessly.[11]

In light of the purpose of my chapter, I decided on the following delimitations. Firstly, I shall concentrate on those sections of Kelsen's article – its sections I and IV – in which he most poignantly comments on the 'realism' of Ross's theory.[12] Secondly, I shall leave aside the complex issue of the relationship between legal positivism and legal realism generally. Thirdly and lastly, I shall not undertake a detailed study of the precise sense in which Kelsen uses the term 'realistic' in jurisprudential contexts, an issue involving both philosophical and linguistic problems, which fall outside the scope of my chapter. Instead, I shall submit my personal and merely preliminary views on that issue when trying to answer the question set out above, viz. what Kelsen might have been alluding to by employing quotation marks.

My chapter is structured as follows. Section II is given over to *On Law and Justice* and Ross's endeavour, prompted by logical positivism, to render scientific (in a specific sense, as we will see) traditional, normative jurisprudence. Taking as my point of departure his programmatic statements in the 'Preface' to his work, I shall first set out what he requires from a science of law if it is to count as a 'genuine' science, and then describe his effort to eliminate the dualism of *Sein* and *Sollen*. I deal in section III with Kelsen's critique of Ross's theory: first, I shall render Kelsen's views on the term 'empirical science' and the object of a science of law; and, second, I take up in some detail his reasoning with respect to Ross's (reinterpreted) concept of validity and the implications of this concept. Finally, in section IV, I take stock and suggest inter alia that Kelsen had at least one good reason for using quotation marks when alluding to Ross's theory, namely the fact that Ross, in his juridico-scientific work, failed to pay attention to an essential prerequisite for any science: logical consistency.[13]

M Schmidt's essays 'Reine Rechtslehre und Skandinavischer Rechtsrealismus' in R Walter (ed), *Untersuchungen zur Reinen Rechtslehre II* (Vienna, Manz, 1988); and 'Reine Rechtslehre versus Rechtsrealismus' in R Walter (ed), *Schwerpunkte der Reinen Rechtslehre* (Vienna, Manz, 1992).

[10] Indeed, the article seems to have been written in a militant spirit.

[11] It is not an exaggeration to say that this article represents the climax of Kelsen's preoccupation with what are commonly called 'realistic' theories.

[12] Thus, I shall not enlarge on Ross's reproach of 'metaphysical speculation' and Kelsen's defence of his position.

[13] On the issue of inconsistencies in Ross's theory, see subsection III.C, as well as section IV, text to n 173 and n 174; and *cf* Schmidt, 'Reine Rechtslehre und Skandinavischer Rechtsrealismus' (n 9) 105.

II. ALF ROSS: JURISPRUDENTIAL REALISM

A. Introduction

Alf Ross's main interests are directed towards providing jurisprudence with a methodological foundation. Taking as his point of departure a strictly empirical, anti-metaphysical stance, his objective is the description of the law in purely factual terms, with reference to psychological processes. His object of investigation – *the law* – is actual human behaviour, with special attention to psychological influences.

In the 'Preface' to *On Law and Justice*, Ross carefully outlines his jurisprudential approach by issuing a series of programmatic statements. The first of these statements concerns his overall objective: to arrive at a realistic interpretation of law. By 'realistic interpretation' he means an interpretation 'in accordance with the principles of an empirical philosophy',[14] the leading idea of his work being 'to carry, in the field of law, the empirical principles to their ultimate conclusions'.[15]

This 'leading idea', in turn, prompts two demands: first, the *methodological* demand that the study of law must follow the patterns of observation and verification, that is, the patterns employed by modern empirical science; and, second, the *analytical* demand that the fundamental legal concepts must be interpreted 'as conceptions of social reality, the behaviour of man in society, and as nothing else'.[16] Hence – Ross goes on to say in the 'Preface' – he is bound to reject the following three ideas:

1. The idea that there is a specific a priori 'validity', raising the law above the world of facts; instead, Ross reinterprets validity in terms of social facts.
2. The idea of an a priori principle of justice *qua* guide to legislation; instead, Ross would have the problems of legal politics discussed in a relativistic spirit.
3. The idea that legal cognition is a specific normative cognition, expressed in *ought*-propositions; instead, Ross means to interpret legal thinking formally, 'in terms of the same logic as that on which other empirical sciences are based (*is*-propositions)'.[17]

[14] Ross, *On Law and Justice* (n 3) ix.

[15] ibid. The text in Ross's English 'Preface' to the 1958 edition diverges from that in his Danish 'Forord' to the 1953 (and 1966) editions. In the latter, Ross stresses that his basic outlook on legal science is anti-metaphysical, and announces his 'programmatic demand that legal science must be based upon, and built up, as an empirical science, in a relativist spirit and following the methodological patterns employed by all modern science that is not of a purely formal logical nature': *cf* Ross, *Om Ret og Retfærdighed* (n 3) 3 (my translation).

[16] *On Law and Justice* (n 3) ix.

[17] ibid x.

According to Ross, there have been in the recent past two main tendencies in jurisprudence – metaphysical idealism and scientific realism.[18] With an eye to characterising his own approach, he advances the umbrella-term 'jurisprudential realism'[19] – a term obviously coined to mark the difference between his own approach and that of so-called 'idealistic' theories.[20] What characterises 'jurisprudential realism', Ross explains, is the desire

> to understand the science of law in conformity with the conceptions concerning the nature, task and method of science as worked out by modern, empiricist philosophy . . . There is only one world and one species of cognition. All science is ultimately concerned with the same body of facts.[21]

Given these premises, the study of law turns out to be a study of social phenomena: in Ross's words, the task for jurisprudence has to be

> the interpretation of the 'validity' of the law[22] in terms of social efficacy, that is, a certain correspondence between a normative idea-content and social phenomena.[23]

The 'real' law, then, is the effective law, and the effective law is the law applied by the courts:

> It is here [ie in the application of the law by the courts] that we must seek for the efficacy that defines the validity of the law.[24]

As announced in the 'Preface', Ross's scientific program marks a new phase in his philosophical development. Before entering this phase, however, he deemed it as no more than proper to bid farewell, as it were, to his earlier stages, and to mention two persons to whom he was particularly indebted for

[18] ibid 68; *Om Ret og Retfærdighed* (n 3) 83.

[19] In Danish: '*retsfilosofisk realisme*'; *cf Om Ret og Retfærdighed* (n 3) 79; *On Law and Justice* (n 3) 64. On 'jurisprudential realism', see also section IV, text to n 177.

[20] On 'jurisprudential idealism', see Ross, *Om Ret og Retfærdighed* (n 3) 79ff; *On Law and Justice* (n 3) 64ff; and *cf* S Wedar, *Realism and Validity. Studies in the Legal Theory of Alf Ross* (Höganäs, Tryckeri AB Höganäs, 1985) 3.

[21] *Om Ret og Retfærdighed* (n 3) 82 (my translation); *cf On Law and Justice* (n 3) 67.

[22] In Danish: '*rettens gælden*'; *cf Om Ret og Retfærdighed* (n 3) 82; the quotation marks are Ross's. Svein Eng recently explained that the Danish noun form '*gælden*' is not a living option, neither in everyday language nor in professional contexts. The form may, nevertheless, be used as a technical term. This is what Ross does when speaking of '*retssystemets gælden*' (usually translated as 'the validity of the legal system'). As Eng points out, Ross's '*gælden*' can only be understood within the context of Ross's theory – it corresponds neither to '*Geltung*' in ordinary German nor to '*Geltung*' in Kelsen's work; see S Eng, 'Lost in the System or Lost in Translation? The Exchanges between Hart and Ross' (2011) 4 *Ratio Juris* 199f. As used in Ross's theory, the noun '*gælden*' is related to '*Wirksamkeit*' in Kelsen's work; it is different from both '*Sollgeltung*' and '*Gültigkeit*' in Kelsen, as emphasised by the latter in 'A "Realistic" Theory of Law and the Pure Theory of Law' (n 5) 9–11; see Eng, ibid 217 fn 39.

[23] *Om Ret og Retfærdighed* (n 3) 82 (my translation); *cf On Law and Justice* (n 3) 68. On the issue of correspondence, see subsection III.C, text to n 143.

[24] In Danish: '*rettens gælden*': *cf Om Ret og Retfærdighed* (n 3) 47; *On Law and Justice* (n 3) 34f; and see n 22.

guidance and inspiration: Hans Kelsen and Axel Hägerström.[25] To Kelsen, Ross expresses his indebtedness for having introduced him to jurisprudence, and to Hägerström, for having opened his eyes 'to the emptiness of metaphysical speculations in law and morality'.[26] What is more, Ross extends thanks to Kelsen for something special as well, namely, for having taught him 'the importance of consistency'.[27]

Retrospectively, one might say that mentioning consistency was, perhaps, a somewhat hasty thing to do.[28]

B. 'Empirico-Realistic' Legal Science

Let us return to Ross's 'Preface', in which he firmly rejects the idea that legal cognition might count as a specific normative cognition.[29] For Ross, there is only empirical cognition, for, in his view, it is impossible to have cognition of a supernatural object that cannot be perceived through the senses. There are two facets to the empirical character of cognition; I will label them 'Criterion 1' and 'Criterion 2'.

i. Criterion 1: Focus on Empirical Facts

The empirical character of cognition manifests itself in its exclusive focus on empirical facts. If there is to be a genuine 'science' of law, Ross claims, then law must be conceived as fact:

> All science is ultimately concerned with the same body of facts, and all scientific statements about reality . . . are subject to empirical test.[30]

Consequently, basic legal concepts – such as, for example, valid law – must be interpreted 'as conceptions of social reality, the behaviour of man in society,

[25] I am referring to the 'Preface' to *On Law and Justice* (n 3). In the 'Preface' to *Om Ret og Retfærdighed* (n 3) 5, Ross had – apart from Kelsen and Hägerström – also mentioned the Danish civil law professor Viggo Bentzon.

[26] *On Law and Justice* (n 3) x.

[27] ibid.

[28] In his review of *On Law and Justice*, Kelsen frequently draws attention to the inconsistencies ('*Widersprüche*') in Ross's theory; *cf* n 13, and n 149.

[29] *Om Ret og Retfærdighed* (n 3) 3; *cf On Law and Justice* (n 3) x.

[30] *Om Ret og Retfærdighed* (n 3) 82 (my translation); *cf On Law and Justice* (n 3) 67. And also: '[The verification procedure], then, is about testing the truth of the statement; at the same time, it defines the meaning content of the statement. If it is not possible to proceed in this way (for instance, with respect to the assertion that the world is governed by an invisible demon), then we find ourselves completely at a loss for an answer to the question, whether or not the assertion is true. Assertions of this type are said to lack (logical) meaning and are called metaphysical': *Om Ret og Retfærdighed* (n 3) 52 (my translation); and *cf On Law and Justice* (n 3) 39f. According to Ross, it is more accurate to speak of 'testing' than of 'verifying', since 'a definite confirmation of the truth of a scientific proposition is not possible': *On Law and Justice* (n 3) 40 fn 1; *Om Ret og Retfærdighed* (n 3) 53 fn 1.

and as nothing else'.[31] In Ross's view, it goes without saying that the propositions of an empirical legal science must be *is*-propositions; only *is*-propositions can have cognitive meaning.

In his classification of linguistic utterances, Ross distinguishes between:

1. utterances of *assertion* (in Danish: '*påstande*'), that is, utterances with representative meaning;
2. *exclamations* (in Danish: '*udbrud*'), that is, utterances without any representative meaning, and without any intent to exert influence; and
3. *directives*, that is, utterances without any representative meaning but with the intent to exert influence.[32] Ross employs the word *directive* by way of general term, denoting intention-borne, emotive-volitional expressions. To this group belong inter alia commanding, suggesting, wishing, admonishing, requesting and the like.[33]

To the three categories of utterances named above there correspond – to a certain extent – the grammatical concepts 'indicative sentence', 'interjection' and 'imperative sentence': only to a certain extent, however, for a linguistic utterance in the grammatical form of an assertion in the indicative mood can very well be a directive (an order, a command) and not an assertion. Thus, for example, the sentence: 'Now you close the door' may – depending on circumstances – be an assertion (informing about what is happening), but it may also be a directive (to be followed, in writing, by an exclamation mark).[34]

Marking the language of positive law, directives can be found in statute books. According to Ross, directives are 'emotional expressions that can be used as a means to direct people'.[35] What is decisive is that the law works in the same way as directives emanating from an individual, and that legislation is grounded in 'social intent' analogous to individual intent.[36] The law – Ross insists in a famous quote – is not written in order to impart theoretical truths:

[31] *On Law and Justice* (n 3) ix.

[32] Svein Eng points out that Ross's characterisation of directives as utterances without any representative meaning but with intent to exert influence – *cf Om Ret og Retfærdighed* (n 3) 18; *On Law and Justice* (n 3) 8 – may give rise to perplexities. On the one hand, it is tempting, linguistically, to read 'representative meaning' as synonymous with 'cognitive patterns of action'; on the other hand, norms, in order to influence action, must represent cognitive patterns of action comprehensible to the addressee (something which Ross seems to deny in the first part of his definition of 'directive'). Things become clearer, however, if we consider that 'representative meaning', in Ross, not only refers to cognitive patterns of action but also to the modality of description and the properties of truth and falsehood: *cf Om Ret og Retfærdighed* (n 3) 17; *On Law and Justice* (n 3) 7. Thus, Ross does not deny that directives are action-guiding; what he denies, is that directives can be said to be true or false. See Eng 'Lost in the System or Lost in Translation? The Exchanges between Hart and Ross' (n 22) 227 fn 57.

[33] *Om Ret og Retfærdighed* (n 3) 18; *On Law and Justice* (n 3) 7.

[34] *Om Ret og Retfærdighed* (n 3) 18; *On Law and Justice* (n 3) 8.

[35] *Om Ret og Retfærdighed* (n 3) 19; *On Law and Justice* (n 3) 8.

[36] *Om Ret og Retfærdighed* (n 3) 18 fn 3; *On Law and Justice* (n 3) 8 fn 2, with reference to Karl Olivecrona's term 'independent imperative'.

rather, is it written in order to direct people, judges and citizens alike, to act in a certain way: 'The *Riksdag* [ie the Parliament] is not an information bureau but, rather, a central organ for social direction'.[37]

Directives, then, are *pre*-scribing a certain course of conduct. *Doctrinal propositions*, on the other hand – that is, the sentences formulated by legal science – are propositions *about* the law, *de*-scribing legal norms. Since directives and doctrinal propositions may have exactly the same grammatical form, there must be a difference in their *logical* meaning. Or so Ross claims.[38]

Legal writing purports 'to be cognition of what is actually the law in force',[39] that is, what is commonly called 'valid law' within a certain legal system. And it is precisely for this reason, Ross insists, that legal writing must consist of assertions, not directives. Since, however – as mentioned above – assertions may have the same grammatical form as directives, it is necessary to 'rewrite' the former in a specific way, such as for example: 'D is valid (Illinois, California, common, etc) law'. This assertion (or doctrinal proposition) is an *is*-proposition, and it is a proposition *about* the law. It is a logical assertion, Ross maintains, 'to the effect that certain directives are valid law'.[40]

ii. Criterion 2: Absence of Metaphysical Speculation

Ross believes his case on behalf of the empirical character of cognition is strengthened by the absence of metaphysical speculation (as he calls it). As I said in the Introduction to this chapter, I shall not take up this issue in greater detail. Suffice it to say that Ross rejects all ideas of validity in the sense of *ought*-validity, be it in terms of an a priori idea of justice or as a formal category, as understood in Kelsen's theory.[41] In Ross's view, ideas of *ought*-validity are merely 'metaphysical constructions, grounded in our moral consciousness, which experiences suggestive notions and their – curiously automatic – motivating force'.[42]

In light of Ross's requirements for a genuine – an empirical – legal science, and also in light of his characterisation of 'jurisprudential realism', one can state the following with respect to Kelsen's theory.

[37] *Om Ret og Retfærdighed* (n 3) 19 (my translation); *cf On Law and Justice* (n 3) 8.

[38] Ross speaks of a 'radical diversity' between the sentences formulated by 'the law' and the sentences formulated by legal science (that is, the doctrinal propositions in textbooks): while the former are (alogical) directives, the latter are (logical) assertions, stating that certain directives are valid law; *cf Om Ret og Retfærdighed* (n 3) 20 fn 6; *On Law and Justice* (n 3) 9 fn 4. On Ross's and Kelsen's classifications of legal utterances, see J Bjarup, 'Alf Ross' in R Walter, C Jabloner, K Zeleny (eds), *Der Kreis um Hans Kelsen. Die Anfangsjahre der Reinen Rechtslehre* (Vienna, Manz, 2008) 434ff. On Kelsen's *Sollsätze*, see U Bindreiter, 'The Modality of Kelsen's *Sollsatz*' (2005) 21 *Rechtstheorie* 167–78.

[39] *On Law and Justice* (n 3) 9.

[40] ibid fn 4.

[41] On 'formal idealism' in Kelsen, see *Om Ret og Retfærdighed* (n 3) 80ff; *On Law and Justice* (n 3) 66ff.

[42] In Danish: '*motiverende kraft*': *cf Om Ret og Retfærdighed* (n 3) 82 (my translation). *cf On Law and Justice* (n 3) 68: 'Ideas of validity are metaphysical constructions built on a false interpretation of the "binding force" experienced in the moral consciousness'.

The Pure Theory of Law does not focus on facts but on norms. Grounded in the (metaphysical) idea of *ought*-validity,[43] the Pure Theory upholds the (idealistic) dualism of *Sein* and *Sollen*, thereby giving rise to *ought*-sentences (which Ross would regard as unscientific).[44] What is more, there is, underlying this construction, the initial hypothesis of a harmless[45] but nevertheless metaphysical basic norm, whose sole function, Ross believes, consists in investing the positive constitution with (*ought*-)validity.[46] Hence, from Ross's perspective, the Pure Theory of Law can hardly be said to meet the requirements of an empirical science.

Ross omits to mention, however, that there is no standard definition of what an 'empirical science' amounts to.[47]

C. 'Reinterpreting' Validity

It was the view that the dualism of validity and reality is 'a fundamental source of error'[48] that initially triggered Ross's approach towards a realistic jurisprudence: validity, he says, is nothing but 'subjective experiences of impulse'[49] towards certain behaviour. In the concept of an objective *ought*-validity (as in Kelsen's theory), these impulses are unwarrantedly 'rationalised' – or so Ross maintains[50] – for such rationalisation is an epistemological impossibility,[51] and consequently meaningless,[52] or 'nonsense'.[53]

The dualism Ross is fighting – the dualism between reality and validity – maps onto the contrast between empirical cognition of reality and a priori

[43] According to Kelsen, the belief in the objective *ought*-validity of the law is not a belief in the existence of a reality that does not exist; rather, it is a certain interpretation of the *meaning* appertaining to real acts. The interpretation is justified if one presupposes a basic norm which legitimises the subjective meaning of the law-positing acts as their objective meaning: see 'A "Realistic" Theory of Law and the Pure Theory of Law' (n 5) 23; and *cf Reine Rechtslehre* (n 1) 218 fn, as well as n 115.

[44] One of the standard objections to the Pure Theory of Law, on the part of realistic legal scholars, is that Kelsen's theory is metaphysical owing to its being concerned with (supra-empirical) *ought*-prescriptions. On this issue, see Schmidt, 'Reine Rechtslehre und Skandinavischer Rechtsrealismus' (n 9) 107, and 'Reine Rechtslehre versus Rechtsrealismus' (n 9) 149–52.

[45] *Om Ret og Retfærdighed* (n 3) 85; *On Law and Justice* (n 3) 70; and *cf* 'A "Realistic" Theory of Law and the Pure Theory of Law' (n 5) 25.

[46] *Om Ret og Retfærdighed* (n 3) 81; *On Law and Justice* (n 3) 66.

[47] On Kelsen's conception of 'empirical science', see subsection III.B.

[48] Ross, *Towards a Realistic Jurisprudence* (n 5) 11.

[49] ibid 12.

[50] ibid 80.

[51] ibid 91.

[52] ibid 95.

[53] 'Validity in the sense of a category or sphere of existence co-ordinated with reality is nonsense in the literal meaning of the word: validity (value or duty) is nothing objective or conceivable whatsoever, it has no meaning, is a mere word': *cf* ibid 77.

cognition of a specific validity beyond all reality.[54] Ross proposes to do away with it. In his view, the way to 'dissolve' this dualism is not to deny the individual experiences of validity (as did the American realists), but to reinterpret them as rationalisations of certain emotional experiences and 'thus [to] include them in the world of fact'.[55] After all, for Ross, 'validity' is nothing objective or conceivable, but only a word, a common term for expressions 'by which certain subjective experiences of impulse are rationalised'.[56]

There is, however, a dilemma here. On the one hand, Ross characterises objective *ought*-validity as an erroneous and meaningless rationalisation of a psychological fact; but on the other, he is perfectly aware that 'normative ideas' are essential to the concept of law. As his earlier work *Towards a Realistic Jurisprudence* also makes clear, he has no real wish to eliminate – or as he put it: to 'spirit away'[57] – all normative points of view and thereby to end up with a purely behaviouristic theory.[58] What, then, is he to do?

Over the course of seven years – between 1946 and 1953 – Ross's views on validity and valid law, and how to interpret these notions, underwent modifications. The problem underlying these modifications was, of course, how the term 'validity', deprived of its '*ought*-ness', can possibly be conceived as standing for an element of empirical reality.[59] Pondering this problem, Ross was influenced by certain aspects of American Legal Realism (particularly by its focus on courts, and by the element of prediction), as well as by logical positivism. And at the end of the day, the term 'valid law' – deprived of any trace of 'ought' – would stand for 'the law that is being applied by the courts' (that is, the law that is effective).

Several steps were implied in the process of 'reinterpreting' validity. In *Towards a Realistic Jurisprudence*, Ross had distinguished between a 'disinterested behaviour attitude having the stamp of validity' and an 'interested behaviour attitude'.[60] The former means that the rule-positing and rule-applying organs are considered, by the legal subjects, as competent to issue and apply legal rules. The subjects believe in the legal competence of the

[54] *Om Ret og Retfærdighed* (n 3) 41 fn 1; this note is omitted in the English translation. In Ross's view, a typical dualism is the law belonging 'at the same time to the world of empirical facts and the supersensual world of the eternal ideas, the realm of validity': *cf Towards a Realistic Jurisprudence* (n 5) 9 f. This typical dualism stems – or so Ross claims – from the opposition between a realistic conception of the legal phenomena (that is, a conception which considers the law as a set of social facts) and the traditional continental view 'which, since the days of Natural Law and Kant's idealistic philosophy, has tried to interpret the law in principle as a system of binding norms deriving their validity from certain *a priori* principles of justice'; *cf* ibid 9.

[55] *Towards a Realistic Jurisprudence* (n 5) 10.

[56] ibid 12.

[57] ibid 49.

[58] Other so-called realistic theories have done precisely that, and have been criticised by Ross for doing so: *cf* ibid 49, 145.

[59] *cf* Wedar, *Realism and Validity* (n 20) 8.

[60] *Towards a Realistic Jurisprudence* (n 5) 78.

authorities, and this 'belief' constitutes their respect vis-à-vis legal organs *qua* authorities.[61] According to the earlier Ross, then, 'belief in validity' is an essential element of the phenomenon of law,[62] an element that enables rule-issuing individuals to induce legal subjects to behave according to the legal norms.[63] An 'interested behaviour attitude', on the other hand, is the 'impulse of fear of compulsion':[64] it is in the subjects' interest that they obey the legal norms, and thus evade sanctions.

These two psychological attitudes – the 'disinterested' and the 'interested' behaviour-attitudes – are facts; and such facts, Ross maintained, constitute the *motive* for rule-corresponding behaviour, the motive underlying the efficacy of the law:

> In reality . . . there is an intimate fusion and real inductive interaction between the two factors, compulsion and authority, interest and disinterested compliance.[65]

'Validity' is precisely this psychological fact; it is the impulse towards a certain course of conduct. Thus validity itself 'becomes a phenomenon of reality',[66] and all aspects of the putative dualism found in legal phenomena seem thereby to have vanished into thin air. One problem remains, however: if validity is a (psychological) fact in reality, then validity has obviously disappeared *qua* normative idea. But did not Ross declare that nothing was to be gained by 'spiriting away' normative ideas?[67]

How, then, does one arrive at a defensible interpretation of legal validity?[68] According to the 'middle-period'[69] Ross – that is, the Ross of *On Law and Justice* – this can only be achieved by means of a synthesis. At this point,

[61] ibid 80.
[62] ibid 147.
[63] ibid 80.
[64] ibid 78.
[65] ibid 82.
[66] ibid 90.
[67] 'If the law is defined as a certain actual behaviour, dualism is, indeed, avoided . . . Statements about the law will be purely theoretical statements about what happens or what will happen. But this results in a complete disruption of the concept of law': ibid 49.
[68] Ross's 'working hypothesis' was that the concept 'valid (Danish) law' could, in principle, be defined and explained in the same way as the concept 'valid norm of chess': '[the] norms of chess are the abstract idea-content (of a directive nature) which make it possible, as a scheme of interpretation, to understand the phenomena of chess (the actions of the moves and the experienced patterns of action) as a coherent whole of meaning and motivation – as a game of chess; and, along with other factors, within certain limits to predict the course of the game. It should be observed that the phenomena of chess and the norms of chess are not distinct phenomena existing independently [in Danish: 'med selvstændig real eksistens']; they are merely abstract sides of the same thing . . . The law, too, can be conceived as partly legal phenomena, partly legal norms in mutual correlation': *cf Om Ret og Retfærdighed* (n 3) 26 (my translation); *On Law and Justice* (n 3) 17. The quality of '*at gælde*' (that is, to be valid) is ascribed to the norms, not to the phenomena: *Om Ret og Retfærdighed* (n 3) 41f.
[69] The late period in Ross's work starts with *Directives and Norms* (London, Routledge and Kegan Paul, 1968).

another 'nuance' in Ross's understanding of the word 'realism' comes into the picture. For even if Ross did not ascribe great informative import to the term 'jurisprudential realism',[70] he took pains, in *On Law and Justice*, to be clear that by 'realistic' he meant an understanding of law 'as a social phenomenon determined by the application of the law by the courts'.[71] And his own realistic standpoint, as he declares in 1953,[72] is neither purely behaviouristic nor purely ideological. It is *behaviouristic* in so far as it is directed towards finding consistency and predictability in the externally observed verbal behaviour of the judge;[73] and it is *ideological*[74] in so far as the consistency referred to is

> a coherent whole of meaning and motivation, only possible on the hypothesis that in his spiritual life, the judge is governed and motivated by a normative ideology of a certain content.[75]

In Ross's synthesis, courts are accorded a central position, and judges are assumed to be motivated by a common 'normative ideology'. In each case, the judge has to discover the norm of conduct on which his decision will be based. If prediction is at all possible, it must be because the mental process by which the judge decides to base his decision on one rule rather than another, is not an arbitrary matter,

> but a process determined by attitudes and conceptions,[76] a normative ideology, present and active in the Danish judges' minds when acting in their capacity as judges. To be sure, we cannot observe directly what is going on in the mind of the judge, but we can set up hypotheses thereon, and their value can be tested exactly because they lend themselves to predictions. This ideology is the subject of the doctrine of the sources of law. The ideology is a constituent part of valid Danish law and consists of directives.[77]

Ross's concept of validity involves two aspects: one external, the other internal. On the one hand, the observable and regular compliance with a pattern of action (on the part of judges); on the other, the experience of this pattern as a socially binding norm.[78] In Ross's view, the definition of 'valid law' must necessarily comprise both objective determinants and a subjective (psychological) factor. 'Valid (Danish) law' means

[70] See section IV, text to n 177.

[71] *On Law and Justice* (n 3) 68; *Om Ret og Retfærdighed* (n 3) 83.

[72] That is, in the first edition of *Om Ret og Retfærdighed*: see n 3.

[73] *Om Ret og Retfærdighed* (n 3) 89; *On Law and Justice* (n 3) 73f.

[74] In *Om Ret og Retfærdighed* (n 3) §14, Ross speaks about 'behaviouristic' and 'ideological' realism; in the English-language translation this was changed to 'behaviouristic' and 'psychological' realism: *cf On Law and Justice* (n 3) §14.

[75] *Om Ret og Retfærdighed* (n 3) 89 (my translation); *cf On Law and Justice* (n 3) 74.

[76] In Danish: '*indstillinger og forestillinger*'.

[77] *Om Ret og Retfærdighed* (n 3) 90–91 (my translation); *On Law and Justice* (n 3) 75f.

[78] *Om Ret og Retfærdighed* (n 3) 50; *On Law and Justice* (n 3) 37.

> the abstract set of normative ideas which serve as a scheme of interpretation for the phenomena of Danish law in action, which, in turn, means that these norms are followed efficaciously, and followed because they are felt to be socially binding.[79]

As reinterpreted by Ross, then, the concept 'valid law' is a purely factual concept, comprising both a behaviouristic element (the behaviour of the judges: efficacy) and a psychological element (the motive underlying efficacy: a feeling). Since Ross identifies validity and efficacy, the statement that a certain norm is valid means solely that the norm is being applied, and applied *because* it is conceived, by the judge, as socially binding.

So it is that Ross thinks he has proved that the concept of law does not require metaphysical explanations.[80] A system of norms is 'valid' if it can serve as a scheme of interpretation for a corresponding[81] set of social actions, and in such a way that we can comprehend this set of actions 'as a coherent whole of meaning and motivation, and within certain limits to predict them'.[82] And this ability – to serve as a scheme of interpretation – is based on *fact*, namely, the fact that the norms are complied with efficaciously, because they are felt to be (socially) binding.

Felt to be binding – by whom? By the judge and other law-applying authorities.[83] And what precisely are these social facts which, as legal phenomena, constitute the counterpart of the legal norms? These social facts are the human actions regulated by rules which, directly or indirectly, concern

> the exercise of *physical force against a person through specially appointed public authorities* . . . [T]he law consists of directives concerning an *order, to the courts, to exercise physical force.*[84]

A typically Kelsenian definition, one might think. It is, however, Ross's. And Ross arrives at the conclusion that the 'real' counterpart of legal norms[85] – that is, the relevant 'social facts' – must be the application of the law by the courts; in short, the decisions of the courts.[86] This conclusion, in turn, implies that scientific propositions *about* the law – such as, for instance, '§28 is valid Danish law' – have cognitive meaning: they can be verified, or tested, by reference to the (future) decisions of the courts.

[79] *Om Ret og Retfærdighed* (n 3) 27 (my translation); *On Law and Justice* (n 3) 18. In a note, Ross adds: 'By the judge and other legal authorities applying the law'; *cf On Law and Justice* (n 3) 18 fn 2 (and see also 34–35); *Om Ret og Retfærdighed* (n 3) 27 fn 2 (and see also 47ff).

[80] *Om Ret og Retfærdighed* (n 3) 27–28; *On Law and Justice* (n 3) 18.

[81] See subsection III.C, text to n 143.

[82] *Om Ret og Retfærdighed* (n 3) 47; *On Law and Justice* (n 3) 34.

[83] *Om Ret og Retfærdighed* (n 3) 27 fn 2; *On Law and Justice* (n 3) 18 fn 2; *cf* n 79.

[84] *Om Ret og Retfærdighed* (n 3) 46 (my translation; Ross's italics). cp the same passage (with my italics) in *On Law and Justice* (n 3) 34: 'determining the conditions under which physical force *shall be* exercised against a person . . . A national law system is the rules for the establishment and functioning of the State machinery of force'.

[85] In Danish: '*normernes reale modstykke*'; *cf Om Ret og Retfærdighed* (n 3) 47.

[86] ibid 47; *On Law and Justice* (n 3) 34.

To have included a predictive element in his theory of legal validity seems to have been a necessary measure for Ross, for (as he himself would grant) there are obvious problems with his reinterpretation of validity. Consider the following situation. A judge faces a so-called 'hard case'; as a judge, he has a duty to apply what is termed 'valid law'. There exists a certain statute, recently promulgated, which seems to be applicable in this case. The problem, however, is that the statute has not yet been applied: according to Ross's reinterpreted concept of validity ('valid' meaning 'being applied', 'being efficacious') the statute is not yet valid.[87] According to most people, on the other hand – and also according to Kelsen – the statute, being part of a system of norms, and having been issued and promulgated correctly, is already valid.

Realising that something was amiss, Ross ventured to modify his theory. Contrary to what he had said in *Towards a Realistic Jurisprudence*,[88] he declared in *On Law and Justice* that statements about valid law at the present time must be understood 'as referring to hypothetical future decisions under certain conditions'.[89] In a nutshell, then, this is Ross's so-called predictive theory (or prognosis theory) of legal validity: a validity statement – ie a statement that some rule or law is legally valid – can be understood as a scientific and true empirical statement *if* one can predict that it will make part of the motivation of a future judicial decision; or, in Ross's words, *if*

> on some basis other than previous practice of the courts there is reason to assume that the rule will be applied in any future legal decision.[90]

Thus a doctrinal proposition to the effect that a certain rule is valid is a prophecy or a prediction that the rule will play an essential part in the motivation of future judicial decisions and of decisions by other legal organs.[91]

Such a prediction, however, will always be uncertain. Ross grants this point: a validity statement, he says, 'continues to be in principle an uncertain prediction regarding legal decisions in the future'.[92] We can never predict the court's decision with absolute certainty, for the rule in question may possibly not be applied at all, or only in a few individual cases.

Ross's 'predictive' theory has met with a great deal of criticism.[93] An issue that has attracted particular attention is Ross's claim that a legal norm can be

[87] What is more: in principle, the judge may apply any rule he likes (eg a purely moral rule) since, according to Ross's theory, this rule would be considered valid as soon as it has been applied.

[88] *Towards a Realistic Jurisprudence* (n 5) 106; *cf* 'A "Realistic" Theory of Law and the Pure Theory of Law' (n 5) 15.

[89] *Om Ret og Retfærdighed* (n 3) 54; *On Law and Justice* (n 3) 41.

[90] *On Law and Justice* (n 3) 41; *Om Ret og Retfærdighed* (n 3) 54.

[91] On this issue, Ross deviates from his mentor Axel Hägerström (1868–1939), who had dismissed the idea that is was possible to make scientific statements about valid law.

[92] *Om Ret og Retfærdighed* (n 3) 56; *On Law and Justice* (n 3) 42.

[93] The Danish scholar Preben Stuer Lauridsen first pointed out that Ross's version of predictivism suffered from circularity: *cf* P Stuer Lauridsen 'On a Fundamental Problem in the Legal Theory of Prediction' (1976) 20 *Scandinavian Studies in Law* 194 ff.

valid to a greater or lesser degree, depending on the degree of probability with which it can be predicted that the rule will be applied.[94] To Kelsen, as we will see in subsection III.C, the idea that validity is a matter of degree is not only erroneous but preposterous, its single merit lying in the fact that the necessity of upholding the dualism of validity and efficacy is thereby emphasised further.

In summary, Ross's legal theory relies on two basic assumptions. First, the juridico-philosophical assumption that 'real' law is efficacious law, ie the law that is being applied by the courts; second, the meta-scientific assumption (which Ross gleans from logical positivism) that every statement of fact claiming to be scientific presupposes verification by means of observation data.

It emerged from subsection II.B that Ross takes 'empirical' to be synonymous with 'realistic', and that both these terms stand for 'scientific'.[95] Whether (and, if so, to what extent) Ross is justified in employing these synonyms in his theory, is the issue at the core of Kelsen's critique. From subsection II.C, on the other hand, it emerged that Ross, by 'reinterpreting' validity (and thereby equating it with efficacy), seems to conceive of the 'realism' of his theory in a special sense (not easily defined) directly connected to his behaviouristic-psychological outlook. Although he had tried in 1946 to unveil the concept of *ought*-validity as primarily a psychological fact (albeit erroneously rationalised), he decided in 1953 to switch the focus to the external aspect, that is, to the behaviour of the courts. By restricting the concept of efficacy to the behaviour of legal officials, however, Ross jeopardised – at least in Kelsen's view – the 'sociologico-realistic' outlook of his theory. Focusing on 'social facts' in the form of judicial decisions, Ross would come to ignore what Kelsen calls 'social reality' ('*soziale Realität*'), as distinct from 'natural reality' ('*natürliche Realität*').[96]

III. HANS KELSEN: A POSITIVISTIC-REALISTIC THEORY OF LAW

A. Introduction

When *On Law and Justice* was published, Kelsen was already acquainted not only with his Danish colleague's leanings towards a realistic jurisprudence[97]

[94] *Om Ret og Retfærdighed* (n 3) 58f; *On Law and Justice* (n 3) 45.

[95] That far, the Uppsala school of philosophy and logical positivism are in agreement. Interestingly, Ross's erstwhile mentor Hägerström had rejected logical positivism as constituting a version of metaphysics. In this view, Hägerström was followed by both Vilhelm Lundstedt and Karl Olivecrona, thus leading to a division between the Scandinavian Realists. For a discussion of Hägerström's 'legacy', see J Bjarup, 'The Philosophy of Scandinavian Legal Realism' (2005) 18 *Ratio Juris* 10 ff.

[96] Kelsen, *Reine Rechtslehre* (n 1) 90; see subsection III.A and section IV, particularly 181.

[97] From around 1930 onwards, Ross seems to have given up the idea of building upon Kelsen's work.

but also with American Legal Realism. Referring to the latter, Kelsen had formerly used the term 'sociological or realistic jurisprudence'.[98] In the second edition of the *Pure Theory of Law*, by contrast, he mentions the representatives of 'the American so-called "realistic" jurisprudence'[99] – *with* quotation marks, which suggests that the term 'realistic' might be inadequate, in his view, for denoting purely behaviouristic theories.

Ross's theory was not purely behaviouristic. As we saw in subsection II.C, it was meant to represent a synthesis of psychological and behaviouristic realism. Nevertheless, Kelsen used quotation marks in the title of his review essay on *On Law and Justice*. Why?

As I indicated in the Introduction, I cannot, within the framework of the present essay, engage in a thorough investigation of Kelsen's understanding of the term 'realistic'. In light of my overall purpose, however, it may be useful to mention the following. (Because important nuances are easily lost in translation, I shall in this part of the text make frequent use of Kelsen's own German-language expressions). Kelsen draws a contrast between, on the one hand, '*Naturwirklichkeit*', ie natural reality, and, on the other hand, '*Rechtswirklichkeit*', juristic reality (or reality in the realm of the law).[100] The Pure Theory of Law is not a theory about what happens in natural reality;[101] it is a theory about what 'ought to' happen according to positive law.[102] In brief, the object of the Pure Theory of Law is not nature or natural reality – an 'is' – but norms – an 'ought'. In spite of this, however, the Pure Theory does not aim at cognition of what the law *ought* to be. It aims instead at cognition of what the law *is*. As Kelsen puts it, the Pure Theory of Law is

> [a] theory of positive law, and this is to say: a theory of the 'real' existing law, not of an ideal law; a theory of a juristic reality.[103]

In contradistinction to an 'ideal' law, then, positive law is the 'real' existing law ('*das wirkliche Recht*').[104] The object of the Pure Theory is such positive, real law: [t]he law as it is: a juristic reality.[105] When the Pure Theory of Law maintains that its object is positive law, then, it conceives of positive law as an 'is' ('*als Sein*') in relation to justice (which grounds demands about how law *ought to*

[98] *cf* eg Kelsen, *General Theory of Law and State*, A Wedberg transl (Cambridge, Mass., Harvard University Press, 1945) 162f.

[99] '*Vertreter der amerikanischen sogenannten "realistischen" Jurisprudenz*': *Reine Rechtslehre* (n 1) 91.

[100] ibid 111.

[101] '[*v*]*on dem, was natürlich ist*': H Kelsen, 'Was ist die Reine Rechtslehre?' in H Klecatsky, R Marcic and H Schambeck (eds), *Die Wiener Rechtstheoretische Schule* (Vienna, Europa Verlag, 1968 [1953]) 614.

[102] '[*v*]*on dem, was positiv-rechtlich sein soll*': ibid.

[103] ibid (my translation); in German: '*eine Lehre vom positiven, und das heißt, vom wirklichen, nicht von einem idealen Recht, eine Lehre von der Rechtswirklichkeit*'.

[104] ibid.

[105] ibid (my translation); in German: '*das Recht so wie es ist, also eine Rechtswirklichkeit*'.

be). The distinction between *Sein* and *Sollen* – between that which is real ('*wirklich*') and that which 'ought to' be – is merely relative: from a scientific point of view, there is no reality in the sense of 'absolute reality'.[106]

B. Legal Cognition and the Object of Legal Science

As he announces in the 'Preface' to his book *On Law and Justice*,[107] Ross rejects the idea that legal cognition constitutes a specific normative cognition, expressible in *ought*-sentences. Instead, he interprets legal thinking formally 'in terms of the same logic as that on which other empirical sciences are based'.[108]

We have seen that for Ross there is only one world and one species of cognition – empirical cognition – and that the empirical character of cognition resides both on its focus on facts and on the total absence of what Ross calls 'metaphysical speculation'. These were the two criteria mentioned above in subsection II.B. If jurisprudence aspires to the level of a genuine science, it must, thinks Ross, meet these two criteria. And Kelsen's Pure Theory, in Ross's view, does not.

Now, for Kelsen, too, there is only one world – the natural world that we inhabit. In contrast to Ross, however, he holds that there are different species of cognition, and that we can look upon this world of ours from different perspectives and explain its phenomena according to different methods. Depending on our object of investigation, there is not only empirical cognition, but normative cognition as well. Cognition can refer to facts (to '*eine Seinstatsache, einen Seinsakt*') but it can also refer to norms (to a '*Soll-Sinn*'). Cognition can therefore concern itself with different objects – with a 'real' (in German: '*real*') object, or with an 'ideal' ('*ideell*') object.[109] The important thing, however, is that science, by focusing on an ideal object – as does legal science – does not sacrifice its 'scientific character'.

Legal (normative) science[110] focuses, *not* on describing human relations according to the principle of causality, but on interpreting these relations

[106] ibid.

[107] *cf* subsection II.A.

[108] *On Law and Justice* (n 3) x.

[109] 'A "Realistic" Theory of Law and the Pure Theory of Law' (n 5) 2.

[110] The Pure Theory of Law provides the methodological foundation for legal science '*als einer normativen Gesellschaftswissenschaft*', that is, for legal science *qua* normative social science: see Kelsen, 'Was ist die Reine Rechtslehre?' (n 101) 615. On jurisprudence *qua Gesellschaftswissenschaft*, see Kelsen, *Reine Rechtslehre* (n 1) 1, 78ff, 89ff. On Kelsen's characterisation of jurisprudence qua '*normative Gesellschaftswissenschaft*', see *Reine Rechtslehre* (n 1) 90, or *The Pure Theory of Law* (n 2) 85f. On jurisprudence *qua Geisteswissenschaft*, that is, *qua* human science, see the editors' supplementary note 3 in the 'Appendix I' to H Kelsen, *Introduction to the Problems of Legal Theory*, BL Paulson and SL Paulson transl (Oxford, Clarendon Press, 1992 [1934]) 130f.

according to the principle of imputation.[111] Legal science does not describe how human relations actually take place 'within the realm of natural reality';[112] it describes how human relations, determined by positive norms, 'ought to' take place.

Obviously, the object of a science of law must be the law. But what *is* the law? According to the Pure Theory of Law – and actually also according to Ross in *On Law and Justice*, as Kelsen was quick to point out[113] – the law is a system of *norms*. The object of legal science must therefore be these norms (that is, an *ought*), and the sentences of legal science, which describes such norms, must be *ought*-sentences. The '*ought*' of these sentences is, however, an '*ought*' in the descriptive sense,[114] and for precisely this reason the propositions of legal science are genuinely scientific, theoretical propositions. It is totally out of the question, says Kelsen, that there should be anything 'at all "metaphysical" in the assertion that the meaning of a certain norm-creating human act is that people ought to behave in a certain way'.[115]

In Kelsen's view, it cannot be the task of legal science that it describe – or predict, for that matter – the behaviour of the legal officials. Rather, the task of legal science is to give expression to the *specific sense* in which the law addresses those human beings whose behaviour it regulates: the specific sense which 'is' the legal norm.[116] In Kelsen's words:

> [T]he statements of legal science are not statements about how people actually behave. They are statements about how people *ought to* behave according to a certain national or international legal system.[117]

Kelsen's interpretation of the term 'empirical science' is considerably wider than Ross's. A science is *empirical* (in contradistinction to *metaphysical*), not only when it describes objective facts and natural processes in the reality of

[111] On Kelsen's conception of science, see A Carrino, 'Reflections on Legal Science, Law, and Power' in SL Paulson and BL Paulson (eds), *Normativity and Norms. Critical Perspectives on Kelsenian Themes* (Oxford, Clarendon Press, 1998) 514 ff.

[112] '[*i*]*m Bereich natürlicher Realität*': *Reine Rechtslehre* (n 1) 90.

[113] 'A "Realistic" Theory of Law and the Pure Theory of Law' (n 5) 3.

[114] ibid 8.

[115] Here is Kelsen's German-language original: 'Es ist völlig unerfindlich, was "Metaphysisches" in der Behauptung liegt, daß der Sinn eines durch Menschen gesetzten, Norm erzeugenden Aktes ist: daß sich Menschen in bestimmter Weise verhalten sollen': *cf* ibid 22. Here it may be worth comparing HLA Hart's mode of expression in his review of Ross's *On Law and Justice* (emphasising the necessity of Kelsenian 'ought-propositions' in the analysis of legal thinking): 'In fact the elucidation of the internal aspect of any normative discourse requires such propositions, and if we carefully study them we shall see that there is nothing "metaphysical" about them, though their "logic" or structure is different from statements of fact or expressions of feeling'; *cf* HLA Hart, 'Scandinavian Realism' in *Essays in Jurisprudence and Philosophy* (Oxford, Clarendon Press, 1983 [1959]) 166.

[116] 'A "Realistic" Theory of Law and the Pure Theory of Law' (n 5) 5.

[117] ibid (my italics).

time and space;[118] a science is just as empirical[119] when it describes the *meaning* that is tied to certain human acts; that is, when it describes norms (an *ought*).[120]

And what is more: in Kelsen's view, a theory of law – and here he clearly has his own theory in mind – remains 'empirical' as long as it restricts itself to describing those norms that constitute the meaning of empirical acts (the meaning, that is, of acts posited *by humans* within the spatio-temporal reality), as opposed to norms originating with non-*human* authorities (ie by super-human authorities like God or Nature).[121] For if a theory of law goes beyond positive law 'and makes statements about some presumed natural law',[122] it will lose its empirical character and turn 'metaphysical'.[123]

Hence Kelsen submits an interpretation of the term 'empirical science' that includes norms *qua* object of cognition. In light of this interpretation, the Pure Theory can be said to be just as *empirico-scientific-realistic* as the theory proposed by Ross.

On the other hand: given Ross's narrower interpretation of the term 'empirical science' – that is, conceiving of 'science' as exclusively focusing on empirical facts – then the object of legal science ('the law') must be seen as pure fact, and what are commonly called legal norms must be conceived as '*Seinsregeln*': as 'rules' describing actual human behaviour.

Kelsen frankly grants that it is possible (and perhaps even useful) to look at law in this way. He doubts, however – and he expresses himself very carefully[124] – that any such theory would be able to grasp the *specific sense* in which the law addresses human beings. Kelsen's point here is that Ross, insisting on his extremely narrow interpretation of 'empirical science', is bound to end up with a sociological and purely descriptive theory that is doomed to fail to grasp this specific sense. In *On Law and Justice*, however, Ross does not hold on

[118] As Kelsen frequently puts it: '*im Bereich der natürlichen Wirklichkeit*', that is, in the realm of natural reality; *cf Reine Rechtslehre* (n 1) 90.

[119] Already in 1945 Kelsen had pointed out that it was wrong to characterise sociological jurisprudence 'as an "empirical" or "descriptive" discipline in contradistinction to normative jurisprudence as a "non-empirical" or "prescriptive" discipline. The connotation of the term "empirical" is tied up with the opposition between experience and metaphysics. An analytical description of positive law as a system of valid norms is, however, *no less empirical* than natural science restricted to a material given by experience . . . *Like any . . . other empirical science*, normative jurisprudence describes its particular object. But its object is norms and not patterns of actual behavior. The statements by means of which it describes the norms in their specific connection with a legal order are not themselves norms. Only the law-creating authorities can issue norms. The ought-statements in which the theorist of law represents the norms have a merely descriptive import; they, as it were, descriptively reproduce the "ought" of the norms': *cf* Kelsen, *General Theory of Law and State* (n 98) 163 (my italics).

[120] 'A "Realistic" Theory of Law and the Pure Theory of Law' (n 5) 5.

[121] ibid.

[122] *General Theory of Law and State* (n 98) 163.

[123] ibid.

[124] 'A "Realistic" Theory of Law and the Pure Theory of Law' (n 5) 2.

to his narrow interpretation; and, as emerges from his earlier work, he never meant to do so, either.

In *On Law and* Justice, his programmatic statements in the 'Preface' notwithstanding, Ross speaks of 'legal norms';[125] he characterises the national legal system as an integrated body of 'rules';[126] and, more tellingly even, he employs *ought*-formulations in speaking *about* the law.[127] With this glaring aspect of *On Law and Justice* before him, Kelsen is able to show that Ross's theory, too, is concerned with *ought*-validity (in the form of 'normative idea content', 'normative ideology', etc) and that Ross, too, uses the language of normative jurisprudence. For what is this 'normative idea content', Kelsen asks rhetorically, if not the idea of the *ought*?[128]

Therefore, Kelsen is correct to point out that the object of Ross's ostensibly empirical, legal science is actually an *ought*, not an *is*.[129] In Kelsen's opinion, Ross fails to realise this owing to his determination (bordering on obsession) to establish legal science as an empirical science: Ross desperately clings to an interpretation of 'empirical science' that is too narrow by far.[130] In order to count as an empirical science, legal science should not strive to attain the unattainable goal of describing norms (an *ought*) by means of *is*-propositions. Ross's essential mistake, Kelsen believes, is to hold that it is possible to conceive of the law

> as a norm (in the sense of an *ought*-prescription) and simultaneously to characterise legal science as a science descriptive of *is*-facts (and in *this* sense as an 'empirico-realistic' science).[131]

From the perspective of the Pure Theory of Law, then, the domain of empirical science is more extensive than that of causal-explanatory science. Therefore, Kelsen's theory claims to be an 'empirico-realistic' theory, too: but, in contradistinction to Ross's theory, 'empirico-realistic' in *another*, more comprehensive sense.

[125] *Om Ret og Retfærdighed* (n 3) 10; *On Law and Justice* (n 3) 1.

[126] *Om Ret og Retfærdighed* (n 3) 46; *On Law and Justice* (n 3) 34.

[127] That is to say, *On Law and Justice* (n 3): here, the word 'shall' appears, for eg, on pp 34 and 35 – which was noticed by Kelsen in 'A "Realistic" Theory of Law and the Pure Theory of Law' (n 5) 3, 20. In *Om Ret og Retfærdighed* (n 3) 46, 47, however, Ross does not use the Danish words for 'must', 'shall' or 'ought to'.

[128] 'A "Realistic" Theory of Law and the Pure Theory of Law' (n 5) 23.

[129] ibid 3.

[130] ibid 5.

[131] ibid 4 (emphasis added); *cf* J Bjarup, *Skandinavischer Realismus. Hägerström – Lundstedt – Olivecrona – Ross* (Freiburg/Munich, Alber, 1978) 88f.

C. Validity: Prophecy and Matter of Degree?

In 1946, Ross had claimed,[132] as we saw, that validity was nothing but the subjective experiences of impulse towards certain courses of conduct, and that such experiences are 'rationalised' in the concept of an objective *ought*-validity (as it figures in Kelsen's theory). But this rationalisation, Ross maintained, is an epistemological impossibility,[133] and therefore 'nonsense in the literal meaning of the word'.[134] From this, Kelsen naturally assumed that Ross was bent on eliminating the concept of normative validity altogether, as the concept of something that was alien to reality, to '*Seins-Wirklichkeit*'. He moreover remarked, rightly, that if 'validity' is a meaningless term, then it ought not to be used at all in a theory claiming to be 'realistic'.[135]

Ross, however, continued to speak of 'validity', albeit in another sense. In reinterpreting validity he had endowed the term with a wholly different meaning: 'valid' now means, simply, 'being applied'; to say that a norm is valid is the same as saying that it is being applied by the courts (and thus that it is efficacious). Naturally, Kelsen reacted strongly to this identification of validity and efficacy – an identification that challenges the dualism of *Sein* and *Sollen* (or, as an aspect of it, the dualism between the validity of the law and its efficacy)[136] which forms the very heart of the Pure Theory of Law.

Let us return to our example of a judge who, facing a 'hard case', is called to apply 'valid law'.[137] A certain statute has been promulgated, say, on 31 December. According to Kelsen, all one can say about this statute on 1 January is that the statute is valid at that date, and that it may become efficacious at some future time. Should it happen that the statute is not applied at all during a considerable period of time, then it may become obsolete and lose its property of being valid. On 1 January, however, the statute is considered valid, and the distinction must be drawn between this actual property and its possible future efficacy.

According to Kelsen, moreover, a legal norm can be efficacious in either of two senses. A norm is efficacious, first, if it is obeyed, ie if legal subjects behave in such a way as to evade the sanction that is tied to the norm; second, a norm is efficacious when it is applied, *qua* sanction, by the legal organs. What is important, however, is that a norm is valid even when it is *not* obeyed by the

[132] *Towards a Realistic Jurisprudence* (n 5) 12, 81.

[133] ibid 91.

[134] '[v]alidity in the sense of a category or sphere of existence co-ordinated with reality is nonsense in the literal meaning of the word: validity (value or duty) is nothing objective or conceivable whatsoever, it has no meaning, is a mere word': ibid 77.

[135] 'A "Realistic" Theory of Law and the Pure Theory of Law' (n 5) 11.

[136] *cf The Pure Theory of Law* (n 2) 10ff; *Reine Rechtslehre* (n 1) 10f.

[137] See subsection II.C, text to n 87.

subjects, and that the norm is valid even when it is *not* applied by the legal organs (for instance when it cannot be applied because the offender cannot be arrested).[138]

The fact that Ross's concept of efficacy narrowly refers to legal officials only,[139] and not also to individual citizens, is incomprehensible to Kelsen. After all, Ross agrees with Kelsen in conceiving of legal norms as sanction-stipulating norms – a conception that enables one clearly to discern the difference between the application of the law (on the part of legal officials) and compliance with the law (on the part of subjects, who thereby evade sanctions). 'Efficacy', then, comprises two factual elements – judicial application *and* compliance with the law. So to reject, as Ross does, a concept of efficacy that encompasses compliance with the law by legal subjects is, in Kelsen's view, simply indefensible (all the more so from the standpoint of a psycho-sociological theory of law, which Ross's 'realistic' theory claims to be). After all, sanction-stipulating legal norms purport to *prevent* the offences (the occurrence of which is a condition of the stipulated sanction).[140]

And there is more. As we have seen, Ross's concept of efficacy comprises two factors – an external, physical factor (the externally observable regularity in the judge's behaviour when applying the law), and an internal, psychological factor (the experience, on the part of the judge, of this pattern of behaviour as being a socially binding norm).[141] In contrast to his former work *Towards a Realistic Jurisprudence*, in which Ross's focus was on the internal, psychological factor (validity *qua* disinterested behaviour attitude), his focus in *On Law and Justice* is on the physical factor, ie on the efficacy of the law:

> the task for jurisprudence must be the interpretation of the validity of the law ['*rettens gaelden*'] as social effectiveness, that is, a certain correspondence between a normative idea content and social phenomena.[142]

In Kelsen's view, these words are in two respects decisive. First, Ross seems to be unaware of the import of the word 'correspondence' in his definition of 'validity'. Correspondence between two items presupposes the existence of a certain relationship between them, and exactly because of this relationship,

[138] 'A "Realistic" Theory of Law and the Pure Theory of Law' (n 5) 17–21; *The Pure Theory of Law* (n 2) 11f; *Reine Rechtslehre* (n 1) 10f.

[139] 'The efficacy that conditions the validity of the norm ['*normens gælden*'] can . . . solely be sought in the application of the law, not in the law in action among the citizens': *Om Ret og Retfærdighed* (n 3) 48 (my translation); *cf On Law and Justice* (n 3) 35. In this respect there is a difference between *On Law and Justice* and *Towards a Realistic Jurisprudence* (n 5). In the latter, Ross's concept of efficacy was more comprehensive in so far as it referred to the behaviour of the legal community in its entirety, that is, to both legal officials and individual citizens; the efficacious law is the law that is obeyed and applied.

[140] 'A "Realistic" Theory of Law and the Pure Theory of Law' (n 5) 17.

[141] *Om Ret og Retfærdighed* (n 3) 50; *On Law and Justice* (n 3) 37; *cf* subsection II.C, text to n 78.

[142] *Om Ret og Retfærdighed* (n 3) 82 (my translation); *cf On Law and Justice* (n 3) 68.

the items in question cannot be identical: 'The law is a different thing from the behaviour that either corresponds or fails to correspond to it'.[143]

And second, if validity is defined as efficacy, then, Kelsen contends, it is simply 'a mistake'[144] to tie the behaviour representing efficacy (that is, the sanction-imposing behaviour of legal officials) to a certain motive or motivation, or to the 'feeling' of being bound by the legal norms. This is incorrect, Kelsen insists, because not only legal subjects, but also legal officials frequently obey the law from motives other than a 'feeling' of being bound. In many instances, the courts certainly do apply the norms they *ought to* apply, but not necessarily out of a feeling of being bound: instead, judges may think that applying the legal norms strictly will lead to a politically desirable judicial decision.[145]

In Kelsen's view, it is simply wrong to combine (as Ross does) a perspective directed at the 'social reality of the facts of human behaviour'[146] with motives or 'feelings'. A theory of law claiming to focus on social fact but nevertheless including feelings has forfeited – or so Kelsen seems to think; and in this he is not alone[147] – any claim to be called 'realistic'.[148]

Taking his critique one step further, Kelsen looks more closely at Ross's claim that validity, 'reinterpreted' as efficacy, actually is a matter of degree. Here Kelsen detects, not a genuine inconsistency,[149] but a glaring instance of illogical thinking.

Ross had been driven to concede that a rule can be understood as valid even *before* it has had the chance of being efficacious (that is, before it has been applied) – *if* one can predict that it *will be* efficacious.[150] In Ross's view, there is a relationship of correspondence between the degree of validity and the degree of probability with which the efficacy of the rule is predicted. In other words, according to Ross's predictive theory, a rule can be said to be valid law to a greater or lesser degree, depending on the prediction regarding the likelihood that the rule will be applied.[151]

This likelihood, in turn, depends on the empirical material the prediction is based on, ie on the sources of law. The likelihood is high, Ross maintains, and

[143] 'A "Realistic" Theory of Law and the Pure Theory of Law' (n 5) 7.

[144] In German: '*unzutreffend*': ibid 18.

[145] ibid.

[146] '*die soziale Wirklichkeit des tatsächlichen menschlichen Verhaltens*': ibid.

[147] Feelings 'have no place in the world of fact': *cf* G MacCormack, 'Scandinavian Realism' (1970) 11 *The Juridical Review* 48.

[148] 'A "Realistic" Theory of Law and the Pure Theory of Law' (n 5) 18.

[149] There is seemingly no end to what Kelsen calls Ross's '*Widersprüche*', that is, contradictions: see eg ibid 5, 12, 15, 20.

[150] 'It is often said that a rule is valid law when it is *applied in the practice of the courts*. However, this is a very clumsy formulation that requires greater precision in several respects': *Om Ret og Retfærdighed* (n 3) 53 (my translation; Ross's italics); *cf On Law and Justice* (n 3) 40.

[151] *Om Ret og Retfærdighed* (n 3) 58; *On Law and Justice* (n 3) 45.

the rule possesses a correspondingly high degree of validity, if the prediction is based on a statutory provision, the interpretation of which has been established in long and consistent practice. On the other hand, the likelihood of application is low, and the rule has a correspondingly low degree of validity – it is only 'slightly valid', one might say – if the prediction is based on neither legislation nor practice, but only on so-called theories, that is, on such principles and evaluations that are assumed to have decisive weight with the courts.[152]

Kelsen agrees with Ross that efficacy – that is, efficacy in the sense of judicial application – is a matter of degree.[153] However, he completely rejects the rest of Ross's argument. Yes, efficacy as such is indeed a matter of degree, but the degree of probability with which one can predict, at a certain stage, that a legal norm *will be* efficacious, may be very low, whereas the actual efficacy of the norm can, at a later stage, prove to be very high, and vice versa. Hence, it is *not* the case that the degree of probability with which one can predict the efficacy of a legal norm corresponds to a certain degree of validity. Kelsen's point here is that the norm is considered valid even in those cases in which it is *not* applied, although it *ought to* be applied; that is to say, the norm is valid even in those cases in which it is *not efficacious*. For even in those cases, the norm must be conceived of as 'existing', and this existence cannot, consequently, be the fact of the norm's being applied. This 'existence' can only be the *ought*-validity of the norm.[154]

With the upshot of Ross's so-called 'predictive' theory of valid law in mind,[155] Kelsen points out, and in no uncertain terms, that this theory actually proves that it is imperative to distinguish between validity qua *ought*-validity ('*Sollgeltung*') and efficacy *qua is*-fact ('*Seinsfaktum*').[156] For if validity really were identical with efficacy, then, Kelsen insists, one could only say about a law promulgated but not yet applied that this law probably will be valid, but not that it is already valid.[157] Still, Ross himself grants that such a law, under certain conditions, can be understood as 'valid'; however unconsciously, he subscribes to Kelsen's thesis of the relation between validity and efficacy when he says that

[152] *Om Ret og Retfærdighed* (n 3) 58f (my translation). The English text in *On Law and Justice* (n 3) 45 deviates slightly from the Danish.

[153] 'A "Realistic" Theory of Law and the Pure Theory of Law' (n 5) 21.

[154] ibid.

[155] According to Kelsen – who was acquainted with the predictive theory of the American realists: see *General Theory of Law and State* (n 98) 165ff – to predict decisions of the courts is not a task for legal science: 'The prediction of a future court decision might be considered part of the business of a practical lawyer counselling his client. But cognition of the law must not be confounded with legal advice'; *cf The Pure Theory of Law* (n 2) 89; *Reine Rechtslehre* (n 1) 93.

[156] 'A "Realistic" Theory of Law and the Pure Theory of Law' (n 5) 19.

[157] ibid 20.

> the efficacy which conditions the validity of the norm can . . . solely be sought in the application of the law by the courts.[158]

Kelsen says exactly the same: efficacy is a *condition* of validity, but it is not identical with it.[159]

In summary: it emerged from subsection III.B that Kelsen and Ross have different views about the kind of information imparted by legal science – while Ross's legal science offers empirical information about the future behaviour of the courts, Kelsen's legal science offers normative information about how the courts *ought to* behave.[160]

Kelsen does not (at least not in principle) object to Ross's equating of 'realistic' and 'empirical' with respect to the science of law – *provided*, that is, that the term 'empirical science' is extended to norms *qua* object of cognition. In this case, the Pure Theory of Law fulfils what in subsection II.B above we identified as Ross's Criterion 1.[161] With respect to Criterion 2 (absence of metaphysical speculation), Kelsen feels compelled to point out to Ross that it is a *distinctive* trait of the Pure Theory that it expressly rejects any metaphysical element.[162]

On the other hand, subsection III.C has brought out Kelsen's strong reaction to the alleged 'realism' of Ross's theory with respect to what Ross calls 'social facts'. According to Kelsen, legal science is concerned with the validity of norms, as opposed to their efficacy – a distinction he arrived at *via* an analysis of legal thought. Ross, by contrast, maintains that the essential factor as concerns the 'validity' of a legal norm is 'solely the fact that it is efficaciously upheld by the courts'.[163] In Kelsen's view, it is not justifiable for a professedly

[158] *Om Ret og Retfærdighed* (n 3) 48 (my translation); *On Law and Justice* (n 3) 35.

[159] 'A "Realistic" Theory of Law and the Pure Theory of Law' (n 5) 20. Efficacy is a condition of validity 'in the sense that a legal order as a whole, and a single legal norm, can no longer be regarded as valid when they cease to be efficacious': *cf The Pure Theory of Law* (n 2) 212; and *Reine Rechtslehre* (n 1) 218f, and also 92 and 215ff (including the long footnote on Ross's *Towards a Realistic Jurisprudence*; this note is not included in the English-language translation).

[160] On this issue, see Bjarup, 'Alf Ross' (n 38) 438.

[161] In 'Validity and the Conflict between Legal Positivism and Natural Law' in SL Paulson and BL Paulson (eds), *Normativity and Norms. Critical Perspectives on Kelsenian Themes* (Oxford, Clarendon Press, 1998 [1961]) 160, Ross would speak of the 'admittedly empiricist programme of the Pure Theory of Law'.

[162] 'A "Realistic" Theory of Law and the Pure Theory of Law' (n 5) 5. Ross claims, albeit indirectly, that Kelsen's dualism is of a metaphysical nature since it 'leads consistently to a metaphysical assertion that existence itself in its innermost being is valid'. And within brackets, he refers to Hegel: *cf Om Ret og Retfærdighed* (n 3) 51; *On Law and Justice* (n 3) 38. This was a splendid opportunity for Kelsen to set Ross right about Hegel, and that it was, there, actually a question of monism and not dualism. Ross had failed to see that Kelsen's distinguishing between efficacy and validity had precisely to do with his objective to evade metaphysical monism. The 'ought' is not immanent in the 'is' but is something different – just as the validity of a norm is different from the norm's efficacy; see Kelsen ibid 21f.

[163] *Om Ret og Retfærdighed* (n 3) 48; *On Law and Justice* (n 3) 35.

socio-psychological theory to employ a concept of efficacy that has been narrowed to comprise only the actions of officials.[164]

IV. CONCLUSION

Let us return to the question raised in the Introduction to this chapter: what, exactly, did Kelsen mean to convey by the quotation marks with which he refers to Ross's 'realistic' theory of law?

As far as I can see (and without putting too fine a point on it), Kelsen wished to make Ross understand that there was no reason for him, Ross, to launch his theory of valid law as particularly 'realistic': Ross's reinterpreted concept of validity (*qua* efficacy) was not realistic enough *if* 'realistic' is understood in the sense of 'sociological'; and Ross's equation of 'realistic' and 'scientific' appeared negligible in view of the fact that he failed to observe an essential prerequisite of all science – logical consistency.

It seems to be universally acknowledged in our day that no legal philosopher would feel inclined to characterise his or her theory as being anything other than 'realistic'. Unfortunately, this does not assist us in establishing what it actually means for a legal theory to be 'realistic'. The fact that this term is used in so many different ways seems to turn every attempt of this kind into a hopeless undertaking.[165]

However, it has been pointed out[166] that the use of the word 'realistic' in literary or artistic contexts often intimates that certain movements are to be seen as a reaction to other schools – schools that had been dominant previously and, in contrast to the present approach, had described life in an idolising or romanticising manner; and that the adjective has also been used in this sense in jurisprudence.[167] Under this hypothesis, which does not seem implausible, what is commonly called 'Scandinavian Legal Realism' can be said to be 'realistic' in the sense of representing a reaction against the influ-

[164] Ross did not respond to Kelsen's review article. In 'Validity and the Conflict between Legal Positivism and Natural Law' (n 161) 161 fn 31, however, he mentioned it, in seemingly guarded terms, as a 'penetrating analysis and critique of my views'. Kelsen, on the other hand, continued his critique of Ross in *Reine Rechtslehre* (n 1) 19, 124 and 215ff. This critique, however, referred to Ross 1946 only.

[165] On the various uses of the term 'realism' (in epistemology, ontology and the philosophy of science), see M Martin, *Legal Realism: American and Scandinavian* (New York/Washington, Peter Lang, 1997) 2.

[166] ibid. The similarity of the meaning of 'realism' in 'legal realism' and its meaning in literary contexts was first observed by RS Summers, 'On Identifying and Reconstructing a General Legal Theory – Some Thoughts Prompted by Professor Moore's Critique' (1984) 69 *Cornell Law Review* 1021 fn 27.

[167] In literature, realism refers to an approach that purports to describe life as it *really* is – as it is *in reality* – and *not* from an idealising perspective; *cf* Martin, *Legal Realism* (n 165) 2.

ence, hitherto dominant, of idealistic metaphysics on legal thinking.[168] Scandinavian Legal Realism is in principle grounded in the teachings of the so-called 'Uppsala school' of philosophy and the founder of this school, philosopher Axel Hägerström.[169] This school's 'realism' manifests itself in its views about what legal phenomena and legal rules *are*, namely in the idea that they are part of the only reality there is – the reality of time and space, accessible to knowledge through observation and experience. When Hägerström employed the word 'realistic' he used it as a synonym for 'scientific' (in the specific sense in which he used this latter adjective).[170] So did Alf Ross.

Section II has shown that Ross aimed at a theory that, being 'realistic' in the sense of being based on empirical facts, sought nonetheless to account for the notion of legal validity, the essential element of law. This aim created a dilemma. Ross's predicament was already discernible in 1946: in *Towards a Realistic Jurisprudence*, while rejecting as untenable the view that law consists of norms, or rules, *qua* meanings of law-creating acts,[171] he nevertheless maintained that a workable theory of law should not seek to 'spirit away entirely all normative points of view, all notions of validity'.[172] He was well aware that such 'spiriting away' would amount to eliminating the specifically *legal* element from one's theory of law; and he had no wish of doing that.

But in that case – or so Kelsen asked rhetorically[173] – how is it possible for legal science, understood as an 'empirical' science (in the sense in which Ross used the term), to be exclusively concerned with facts? How can Ross demand, in the name of a 'realistic jurisprudence' (as he does in his 'Preface'), 'that the fundamental legal notions must be interpreted as conceptions of social reality, the behaviour of man in society, and as nothing else'?[174] These two desiderata – the wish to retain normative points of view, but also, nonetheless, to arrive at a legal science exclusively concerned with facts – simply do not go together.

[168] With respect to Sweden, the term as such signals the opposition to a school of thought that was dominant during the greater part of the 19th century, namely, the idealism of Christopher Jacob Boström (1797–1866), who called his idealistic approach 'rational idealism'; Axel Hägerström, in turn – purporting to do away with Boströmianism – called his own philosophy (anchored in the law of contradiction) 'rational naturalism'. On Hägerström's 'recipe' for realism, see J Bjarup, 'Reason and Passion. A Basic Theme in Hägerström's Legal Philosophy' (1980) 11 *Rechtstheorie* 152ff.

[169] For an overview of Scandinavian Legal Realism, see L Björne, *Realism och skandinavisk realism. Den nordiska rättsvetenskapens historia, Del IV. 1911–1950* (Stockholm, Institutet för rättshistorisk forskning, 2007) ch III.

[170] On Hägerström's philosophy of reality and knowledge, see Bjarup, 'Reason and Passion' (n 168) 2ff.

[171] *Towards a Realistic Jurisprudence* (n 5) 78, 93.

[172] ibid 49.

[173] 'A "Realistic" Theory of Law and the Pure Theory of Law' (n 5) 4.

[174] *On Law and Justice* (n 3) ix. The 'Preface' to *Om Ret og Retfærdighed* (n 3) does not contain this phrase.

In this, however, Ross's theory does not deviate from other realistic theories. It has been pointed out more than once that what is problematic with all so-called 'realistic' theories is that they wish on the one hand to distance themselves from the idea of legal norms *qua* 'ought'-prescriptions, but on the other hand are dependent on that very idea – since they want to describe, or predict, human behaviour under the impact of such norms.[175] Indeed, one might say that Ross's dilemma actually proves the soundness of Kelsen's view that sociological jurisprudence *presupposes* the concept of law as defined by normative jurisprudence.[176]

It can be inferred from the overall tenor of Kelsen's review that what hurt him most in *On Law and Justice* was Ross's exclusion of the Pure Theory of Law from the realm of what he calls 'jurisprudential realism'[177] (thereby dismissing it automatically as a case of 'jurisprudential idealism').[178] Actually, Kelsen needed not to have grieved all that much about this relegation. For as regards the expression 'jurisprudential realism', Ross did not ascribe any particular weight to it; he appears to have considered it to have little, if any, explanatory significance, and simply to have seen it as a 'battle-cry' of sorts – as a slogan[179] – in the fight against idealistic approaches in general (and not specifically against the Pure Theory).[180]

To Kelsen, in contrast, the meaning of the term 'realistic' seems to have been crystal clear, indeed self-evident, so as to require no further explanation. As I have intimated previously, an investigation into Kelsen's understanding of 'realistic' would call for a comprehensive linguistic-philosophical inquiry which I am unable to pursue within the scope of this chapter.[181] Nonetheless,

[175] Schmidt, 'Reine Rechtslehre versus Rechtsrealismus' (n 9) 142f; Bjarup, 'Alf Ross' (n 38) 436.

[176] In Kelsen's view, normative jurisprudence is a precondition for purely sociological theories: 'sociology can define the phenomenon of law . . . only by having recourse to the concept of law as defined by normative jurisprudence. Sociological jurisprudence presupposes this concept. The object of sociological jurisprudence is not valid norms – which form the object of normative jurisprudence – but human behavior. What human behavior? Only such human behavior as is, somehow or other, related to "law"'; *cf General Theory of Law and State* (n 98) 175.

[177] See subsection II.A.

[178] Ross distinguishes between *material* and *formal* jurisprudential idealism: *cf Om Ret og Retfærdighed* (n 3) 79f; *On Law and Justice* (n 3) 65f. According to the *material* variant, nothing is 'law' unless the idea of justice is part of the content of the law, as the 'validity-making' property; this view has dominated natural law at all times. *Formal* idealism, on the other hand, holds that the validity of positive law can be identified without any recourse to moral values. In Ross's view, formal jurisprudential idealism has found its most striking expression in Kelsen; see *Om Ret og Retfærdighed* (n 3) 80; *On Law and Justice* (n 3) 66.

[179] '[m]ore by way of a slogan than because the term is informative': *Om Ret og Retfærdighed* (n 3) 79 (my translation); this phrase is omitted in the English-language translation.

[180] Over the years, Ross had been influenced by various schools of philosophy, and he did not hesitate to incorporate some of these influences into his own theory. This success may have prompted him to look upon himself as the founding father of a completely new approach to the law and legal science.

[181] The adjective 'realistic' derives from the adjective 'real' (in German: '*real*', '*reell*' and '*wirklich*'). That which is 'real', exists in empirical nature – 'in reality'. In the English language,

I venture to suggest[182] that the word 'realistic', in Kelsen's works, ought to be understood in terms of the human act of 'positing' norms. Kelsen used the terms 'positivistic' and 'realistic' in the same breath.[183] He defines the 'real', existing law ('*das reale Recht*') as 'the positive law, posited by human beings and hence changeable'.[184] To Kelsen, the quality of being 'real' law seems to be tied to its having been 'posited' by humans and not by superhuman authorities. In his own words:

> A realistic theory of law . . . is not concerned with an ideal law . . . and, alongside, with a 'real' existing law, posited by humans; it is concerned with *one* kind of law only: with positive law, posited by human beings.[185]

Therefore, I believe that we ought to pay attention to Kelsen's words when he points out to us that it was the Pure Theory of Law that first had discerned, and tried to solve, what he calls 'the problem surrounding the specifically juristic reality understood as the problem of the positivity of the law'.[186] From the point of view of the Pure Theory, the issue of a specifically *juristic* reality and the issue of the *positivity* of the law seem to be one and the same.[187]

there is, by way of noun, only the word 'reality'; in the German language, on the other hand, there are two nouns for 'reality', namely '*Wirklichkeit*' and '*Realität*'. In everyday language, '*Wirklichkeit*' and '*Realität*' are frequently used interchangeably, meaning one and the same thing (namely, physical reality). In juridico-philosophical language, however – specifically, in the language used by legal scholars well-grounded in Kantian philosophy – '*Wirklichkeit*' and '*Realität*' refer to different things. Both Kelsen and Ross were well-grounded in Kantian philosophy. Within the compass of this chapter, it is not possible to pursue the complex issue of how Kelsen and Ross differentiated between the use of '*Realität*' and '*Wirklichkeit*' and how this differentiation informed their understanding of the term 'realistic'. I consider this issue to be deserving of a special study, however. Within this context, Enrico Pattaro's impressive investigation into the three (non-synonymous) Swedish adjectives '*real*', '*verklig*' and '*existerande*' (that is, 'real', 'real' and 'existing') in Hägerström's ontology must be mentioned: E Pattaro, 'I Will Tell You about Axel Hägerström: His Ontology and Theory of Judgment' (2010) 23 *Ratio Juris* 135 ff.

[182] My views are derived in part from what Kelsen says about the term 'realistic' in the second edition of the *Pure Theory of Law*, in part from scattered evidence in some of Kelsen's articles published around 1960.

[183] See eg H Kelsen, 'Vom Geltungsgrund des Rechts' in H Klecatsky, R Marcic and H Schambeck (eds), *Die Wiener Rechtstheoretische Schule* (Vienna, Europa Verlag, 1968 [1960]) 1423–24; 'On the Basis of Legal Validity', SL Paulson transl (1981 [1960]) 26 *The American Journal of Jurisprudence* 185–86; *Reine Rechtslehre* (n 1) 112, 402, 403.

[184] Kelsen, *Reine Rechtslehre* (n 1) 404.

[185] ibid 403.

[186] In German: The Pure Theory had discerned, and tried to solve, '*das Problem der spezifischen Rechtswirklichkeit als Problem der Positivität des Rechts*': *cf* 'Was ist die Reine Rechtslehre?' (n 101) 614 (my translation).

[187] According to Kelsen, 'The Pure Theory of Law discerns the positivity of the law in the fact that the legal norms are posited through human acts, performed within natural reality but regulated by higher norms . . . The peculiar relationship between, on the one hand, the "Is" of the norm-positing and norm-corresponding acts (in the realm of nature) and, on the other hand, the "Ought" of the legal norms, posited and obeyed – this relationship constitutes *a specific juristic reality or, which is the same thing, the positivity of the law*': *cf* ibid 614f (my translation and italics).

7

Wiener *Realism*

PIERLUIGI CHIASSONI*

I. THE SPELL OF PERIODISATION

MANY DIFFERENT ATTEMPTS have been made over the past three decades to discern the philosophical 'periods' undergone by the Pure Theory of Law, from its beginnings around 1910 up to the posthumously published *General Theory of Norms* (1979).[1] Such exercises in periodisation are certainly worthwhile; in the long run, there were indeed noteworthy changes in Kelsen's thought. But there is a risk that the Pure Theory is thereby depicted as rife with instability and internally afflicted by conflicting pulls[2] – an impression which is, I think, ultimately untrue, and which it is important to counterbalance. For there is, it seems to me, one deep, enduring

* I am grateful to audiences in Oxford and Barcelona, to an anonymous reviewer, and to the editors of the present volume, for very helpful comments and suggestions.

[1] *cf* O Weinberger, *Normentheorie als Grundlage der Jurisprudenz und Ethik. Eine Auseinandersetzung mit Hans Kelsens Theorie der Normen* (Berlin, Duncker & Humblot, 1981) 160ff; MG Losano, 'La dottrina pura del diritto dal logicismo all'irrazionalismo' in H Kelsen, *Teoria generale delle norme* (Turin, Einaudi, 1985) xvii–lxi [Losano is to be credited with an earlier attempt at periodisation: *cf* his 'Saggio Introduttivo' in H Kelsen, *La dottrina pura del diritto* (Turin, Einaudi, 1966) xiiiff]; D Beyleveld and R Brownsword, 'Normative Positivism: The Mirage of the Middle-Way' (1989) 9 *Oxford Journal of Legal Studies* 463ff; E Bulygin, 'An Antinomy in Kelsen's Pure Theory of Law' in SL Paulson and BL Paulson (eds), *Normativity and Norms. Critical Perspectives on Kelsenian Themes* (Oxford, Clarendon Press, 1998 [1990]) 297ff; D Beyleveld, 'From the "Middle-Way" to Normative Irrationalism: Hans Kelsen's *General Theory of Norms*' (1992) 56 *Modern Law Review* 104ff; C Heidemann, *Die Norm als Tatsache, Zur Normentheorie Hans Kelsens* (Baden-Baden, Nomos, 1997) – on which *cf* SL Paulson, 'Four Phases in Hans Kelsen's Legal Theory? Reflections on a Periodization' (1998) 18 *Oxford Journal of Legal Studies* 153ff; SL Paulson, 'Introduction' in SL Paulson and BL Paulson (eds), *Normativity and Norms. Critical Perspectives on Kelsenian Themes* (Oxford, Clarendon Press, 1998) xxiiiff; and my own periodisation of Kelsen's epistemology in P Chiassoni, *L'indirizzo analitico nella filosofia del diritto. I. Da Bentham a Kelsen* (Turin, Giappichelli, 2009) 303ff.

[2] In 'Four Phases in Hans Kelsen's Legal Theory?' (n 1), for example, Stanley Paulson explains what he calls Kelsen's 'Hybrid' period – a sub-stage of the 'classical' phase (1921–60) – as a product of a 'schism' between two conflicting theoretical directions: one represented by the import of Adolf Merkl's ingenious *Stufenbau* doctrine, the other by the 'normativity problem'. A comparable picture is proposed in 'An Antinomy in Kelsen's Pure Theory of Law' (n 1) by Eugenio Bulygin.

idea, present in Kelsen's works for more than six decades, which can be said to lie at the very core of the Pure Theory of Law. To put it as plainly as possible, Kelsen always strove to develop and promote a realistic jurisprudence. Underlying the Pure Theory as a whole, in other words, there is a stable epistemological preference for legal realism. Or so I mean to argue in the present essay.

Evidence for the persistent realistic orientation of Kelsen's jurisprudence can be found, as we will see, since the earliest stages of its development, and particularly since his 'strong' Neo-Kantian constructivist stage (which started in the 1910s and culminated with the first edition, in 1934, of *The Pure Theory of Law*).[3] In fact, Kelsen himself often described the Pure Theory as a 'radically realistic' theory of law – a characterisation that can be found in texts ranging from as early as 1933 to as late as 1960.[4] The evidence has often been overlooked by Kelsen scholars, who, preferring to concentrate almost exclusively on specific single components of the Pure Theory of Law, have lost sight of Kelsen's overall and lifelong goal – viz. to account for *real* law, for law as it really is.[5] From this overarching perspective, however, it is quite possible to give a *unified* account of the different 'periods' of Kelsen's work. Indeed, the Pure Theory's many twists and turns – including some momentous swerves, like the final demise of its Neo-Kantian ingredient – can all be seen as having been dictated by the constant need to refine or replace whatever claims and methodological tools prove on each renewed inspection to be less than adequate.

In attempting to vindicate the deep realistic orientation of the Pure Theory, I shall thus also try to rescue its jurisprudential integrity. My argument will proceed in three steps. I begin, in section II, by emphasising the realistic orientation of the Pure Theory from the standpoint of an abstract characterisation of legal realism. I then suggest, in section III, that some features commonly identified by Kelsen scholars as characteristic of Kelsen's final period – the so-called 'sceptical' period – are by no means so dramatically at odds with his

[3] See my *L'indirizzo analitico nella filosofia del diritto* (n 1) 315ff.

[4] See eg H Kelsen, 'Methode und Grundbegriff der Reinen Rechtslehre' (1933) 3 *Annalen der critische Philosophie* 78; *Introduction to the Problems of Legal Theory*, BL Paulson and SL Paulson transl (Oxford, Clarendon Press, 1992 [1934]) 18; 'The Pure Theory of Law and Analytical Jurisprudence' (1941) 55 *Harvard Law Review* 49; *General Theory of Law and State*, A Wedberg transl (Cambridge, Mass., Harvard University Press, 1945) 13; H Kelsen, *The Pure Theory of Law*, 2nd edn, M Knight transl (Berkeley, University of California Press, 1967 [1960]) 106.

[5] Such excessive focus on details has also led to some uncharitable criticisms of the Pure Theory. For one example, Alf Ross famously claimed that the Pure Theory is paradoxically committed, at its core, to a 'quasi-positivist', ideologically compromised view of law and legal science: *cf* A Ross, 'Validity and the Conflict Between Legal Positivism and Natural Law' in SL Paulson and BL Paulson (eds), *Normativity and Norms. Critical Perspectives on Kelsenian Themes* (Oxford, Clarendon Press, 1998). For discussion, see CS Nino, 'Some Confusions Surrounding Kelsen's Concept of Validity' in the same volume; and B Celano, *La teoria del diritto di Hans Kelsen. Una introduzione critica* (Bologna, Il Mulino, 1999) 369ff.

previous periods as is often claimed: his earlier periods, as we will see, are similarly infused by 'scepticism'. In section IV, finally, I turn my attention to Kelsen's theory of legal science – one of the most controversial aspects of the Pure Theory – and argue, on the basis of a fresh account, that it, too, is realistic in essence.

I am aware that many Kelsen scholars will regard my proposed reading of the Pure Theory's overall orientation as utterly misguided. This is not surprising. Kelsen's realism has endured a fate similar to that of Poe's 'Purloined Letter'; so blatantly evident, so plain, that it is overlooked by those bewitched by the intricacies of its surroundings: as if hidden in plain sight.

II. THE PURE THEORY AS A REALISTIC THEORY OF LAW: THE WHOLESALE ARGUMENT

The characteristic traits of legal realism – and by 'legal realism' I have in mind a meta-theoretical abstraction building on those otherwise diverse theoretical strands known as 'American Legal Realism', 'Scandinavian Legal Realism', 'Italian Legal Realism' and so on – can be brought out from at least three perspectives: (1) from the perspective of the history of Western legal culture, legal realism represents a critical reaction against nineteenth-century legal positivism, particularly against its formalism and conceptualism, as well as against its grip upon twentieth-century legal thinking; (2) if one thinks instead in terms of jurisprudential pigeonholes, then legal realism can be said to represent the 'law as fact' variety of legal positivism; realism is therefore to be contrasted with the 'law as norm' variety of legal positivism (ie with 'normative positivism', or 'normativism', as it is also sometimes called); and (3) with regard to its background philosophy, lastly, realism accords with empiricism, and opposes idealism and metaphysics.

My claim will be that the Pure Theory of Law can be regarded as an instance of a peculiar form of realism – I propose to label it '*Wiener* realism' – which had both Kelsen and Adolf Julius Merkl as its foremost representatives. The distinctiveness of *Wiener* realism can be seen, I will argue, from each of those three perspectives: not merely from the perspective of the history of Western culture, which should be less controversial, but from the standpoints of empiricism and of the normativism/realism debate as well.

To support this claim at a wholesale level – my goal in this section – I will first offer an inventory of realist claims, which I hope won't sound too self-serving. I shall then turn to those aspects of the Pure Theory of Law that constitute evidence that it embodies a realistic outlook.

A. Realistic Jurisprudence in a Nutshell

I shall take the following as the eight characteristic tenets of a realistic jurisprudence:

1. *Positive law as institutionalised ideology*. Positive law – the man-made regulation of human relations through the social organisation of coercion – is inevitably driven by material and spiritual interests; it always embodies *some* set of values, which it imposes on legal subjects.
2. *Natural law as ideology in search of institutionalisation*. Natural law – one of the most powerful philosophical ideas in Western culture – is an intellectual, ideological artefact; it can be put to the normative use of justifying either the existence or the change of positive legal orders.
3. *Law's changeability*. Positive legal orders, far from being static sets of norms, can and do continuously change in order to meet the current needs and interests of societies.
4. *Law's instrumentality*. Positive legal orders are not ends in themselves; nor are they ultimate values; they are *means* of promoting whatever goals any given society may happen to consider worth pursuing at any given moment.
5. *Rule-scepticism, judicial discretion, interpretative non-cognitivism, fact-scepticism*. General legal norms (ie legal rules), as brought about by means of legislation and precedent, do not fully determine the solutions of individual cases; general legal norms do not operate automatically as standards of individual human behaviour; indeed, the application of law is not a pure matter of logic and cognition: rather, it necessarily involves acts of will and acts of law-making. Legal interpretation is also not a pure matter of cognition: it always involves decisions about the correct meaning to be ascribed to legal source-materials. As for argumentation concerning matters of law (*quaestiones juris*), it is usually but a rhetorical device for the ex post facto justification of decisions – decisions that are independently arrived at because of their substantive value; and argumentation concerning matters of fact (*quaestiones facti*), though it may resort to scientific theories and standards, is nonetheless always ridden with discretionary choices that make the very idea of judicial fact-*finding* a misleading fiction.
6. *Law's lack of intrinsic systematicity*. Positive legal orders are not, in and of themselves, ordered, consistent, coherent or complete: in and of themselves, they do not amount to normative *systems*; it is jurists – within the boundaries of so-called legal 'science' – that set forth systematisations of previously unordered bodies of legal source-materials.
7. *Empiricism and meta-ethical non-cognitivism*. Legal realism is empiricism applied to the study of law. A realistic theory of law is committed to an

empiricist ontology and epistemology; it holds that there is no reality beyond empirical reality, and no knowledge apart from empirical and formal knowledge. Suggested by this empiricist stance, moreover, is a commitment to meta-ethical non-cognitivism – the view that there are no objective, absolute moral values; that all values and ideals in the domain of normative ethics and justice are ultimately subjective, relative and thus contingent. Men do not 'discover' moral values, which are not 'out there' in some metaphysical dimension of 'reality'; men rather *create* and ultimately *choose* such values by acts of will (whether or not they happen to be aware of this crucial feature of their practical lives).

8. *Realistic epistemology*. Owing to its empiricist allegiances, legal realism approaches law as a social and cultural phenomenon; it seeks to articulate an epistemologically sound theory of law along the following lines: (1) While dealing with positive legal orders, realistic inquiries do not dwell at the superficial level of what legal norms and officials 'say'; rather, realist inquiries pay attention to, and purport to account for, both (a) the way legal orders actually *are* and *work*, and what their officials actually *do*, and (b) the (likely) practical consequences of such officials' decisions. Legal realism, in other words, does not concern itself with the *validity* of legal norms only; rather, it concerns itself with their *efficacy*. (2) While dealing with positive legal orders, realistic inquiries seek (a) to bring to the fore the ideologies that are afoot in legal discourse – from comprehensive normative outlooks to interest-driven representations of the legal and the social world – and (b) to analyse such ideologies in their semantic, logical and pragmatic dimensions. By the same token, realistic analyses of general legal concepts ('state', 'legal source', 'legal norm', 'legal right', 'legal duty', 'validity', 'binding force', 'responsibility', 'legal person' and so on) seek to depurate them from metaphysical, fictional or even 'magical' elements, and to replace them, if that is the case, by clearer and empirically sounder concepts. (3) While dealing with the idea of natural law, realism strives to make manifest its value-laden and ideologically committed character, and to expose what it perceives as the basic shortcomings of natural law theory – so that this influential intellectual widget, stripped of any tinge of self-delusion, can be appreciated for what it really is. (4) In pursuit of its lines of enquiry, a realist theory of law strictly sticks to epistemic values (truth, logical consistency, explanatory power, advancing knowledge, clarity, simplicity, elegance); subscribing to what we may call the 'candour postulate', it professes to make explicit its own epistemological principles and options; and it strives to keep moral and political values at bay, relegating them to the domain of legal politics (a domain in which each jurist must make her own choices, take her sides – and accept the moral responsibility associated to her institutional role).

B. The Pure Theory's Realism

Given this characterisation of legal realism, the realistic orientation of the Pure Theory of Law should seem a matter of course. At both the epistemological and the theoretical levels, Kelsen's views on positive law and natural law are, we may say, decidedly realistic.

i. A Realistic Epistemology

At the epistemological level, the Pure Theory's realism manifests itself in three respects: (1) It views law as a social phenomenon belonging to the realm of empirical reality. It rejects any idea of a metaphysical, transcendental legal reality, and opposes 'natural law' theories of all sorts.[6] (2) The Pure Theory maintains that genuinely scientific knowledge of the law is possible, and takes a firm stand against methodological syncretism, fictions, metaphysics and against hidden ideological choices and political allegiances. The fact that Kelsen sought explicitly to defuse many of the unwarranted dualisms that pervaded legal thought at the turn of the century – such as the notorious dualism of state and law – is strong evidence of a programme painstakingly carried out (rather than merely announced). (3) The Pure Theory is committed to the distinction between *Sein* (is) and *Sollen* (ought); its immanentist, rationalist and empiricist philosophical outlook combines Kantian epistemology with the empiricist methodology of twentieth-century social sciences, and opposes any return to 'pre-Kantian metaphysics' ('*vorkantische Metaphysik*').[7]

Now, it is true the *Sein/Sollen* distinction is commonly regarded among Kelsen scholars as providing conclusive evidence in favour of an 'idealistic' reading of the Pure Theory. They quote several passages in which Kelsen maintains that norms are not facts in the world of *Sein*, but rather ideal entities in the world of *Sollen*. And from such passages they conclude that Kelsen's idea of a normative jurisprudence – of legal science as a science of *norms* – is the idea of a science, not about reality, but about some mythical *Sollen*; they conclude, in other words, that legal cognition is for Kelsen not a form of empirical knowledge but rather something like the a priori knowledge of idealistic philosophy: something dependent on 'a priori reasoning'.[8]

[6] See Kelsen, 'Methode und Grundbegriff der Reinen Rechtslehre' (n 4) 86ff; *Introduction to the Problems of Legal Theory* (n 4) 28ff; the 'Preface' to *General Theory of Law and State* (n 4); *Reine Rechtslehre*, 2nd edn (Vienna, Franz Deuticke, 1960) 218 fn; 'A "Realistic" Theory of Law and the Pure Theory of Law. Remarks on Alf Ross's *On Law and Justice*' (1959), transl L Duarte d'Almeida, in this volume; and 'Naturrechtslehre und Rechtspositivismus' (1961) 4 *Revista Jurídica de Buenos Aires* 8ff.

[7] 'Methode und Grundbegriff der Reinen Rechtslehre' (n 4) 83.

[8] *cf* A Ross, *On Law and Justice* (London, Stevens, 1958) 64ff.

Unfortunately, those who argue along these lines are wrong. First, Kelsen makes it abundantly clear on many occasions that legal norms, in his view, even though they are ideal entities, are nonetheless the 'meanings' of acts of will performed by legal authorities in determinate spatio-temporal contexts. From this standpoint, legal norms are indeed *empirical* entities, in the sense of being endowed with an existence in time and space. Indeed, for a legal norm to exist, it is necessary, according to Kelsen, that there be either a *custom* – ie a 'generally observed course of action' combined with a general normative *opinio iuris sive necessitatis* on the part of some social group – or some discreet expression of the will of some legal authority (by means of observable bodily gestures, non-verbal symbols or spoken or written sentences).[9]

Second, proponents of an idealistic reading of the Pure Theory appear mistakenly to assume that empirical knowledge is the same as *causal* knowledge. But Kelsen, in the course of presenting his views on (normative) legal science, makes it clear that there are two kinds of empirical knowledge about the law: causal knowledge and normative knowledge. The former is the business of sociological jurisprudence, ie of the sociology of law. An example of this sort of inquiry would be an investigation into the motives ('reasons') that explain why judges in some given legal order have decided cases of some sort in such-and-such way, or why legislatures have enacted such-and-such statutes. The latter kind of knowledge about the law, however – normative knowledge – is the business of legal science, whose task is to provide descriptions of the valid norms of some given legal order. We shall come back to Kelsen's theory of legal science in section IV. For now let me just emphasise that these norms that form the object of legal science are not mere 'paper rules'; they are 'real' rules, rules – norms – belonging to a legal order which is by and large effective.[10]

Third, it is on the basis of the 'hypothesis' (or the 'fiction') of a basic norm (a '*Grundnorm*') that legal science describes the valid norms of any given legal order. Here, again, three related points are clearly and constantly pressed by Kelsen from the first edition (1934) of the *Reine Rechtslehre* on. One is that presupposing the basic norm is an *option*; the presupposition is a condition on which the very possibility of understanding law as a system of valid *norms* depends: but law can also be looked at solely in terms of acts of will and (de

[9] See eg *General Theory of Law and State* (n 4) 114–15; Kelsen's letter to Ulrich Klug dated 4 July 1960 in H Kelsen and U Klug, *Rechtsnormen und Logische Analyse. Ein Briefwechsel 1959 bis 1965* (Vienna, Franz Deuticke 1981) 42ff; *The Pure Theory of Law* (n 4) 4ff, 71ff; 'Naturrechtslehre und Rechtspositivismus' (n 6) 8, 18, 26ff, 40; *General Theory of Norms*, M Hartney transl (Oxford, Clarendon Press, 1991 [1979]) 163ff. Furthermore, 'a legal norm may lose its validity by never being applied or obeyed – by so-called *desuetudo*': *cf The Pure Theory of Law* (n 4) 213; norm-existence is, for Kelsen, entirely a fact-dependent matter.

[10] 'Methode und Grundbegriff der Reinen Rechtslehre' (n 4) 75, 88f; *Introduction to the Problems of Legal Theory* (n 4) 13–14; *General Theory of Law and State* (n 4) 162ff; *The Pure Theory of Law* (n 4) 59ff, 70ff, 71ff, 85ff.

facto) power relationships. A second point is that the presupposition of the basic norm is an *epistemological* option, rather than an ideological one; the doctrine of the basic norm is meant to depurate the notion of validity of any idea of an absolute, intrinsic, metaphysical binding force. Lastly, this epistemological option establishes the autonomy of normative legal science *qua* genuinely scientific enterprise: a science distinct from legal sociology, and capable of dealing with the issue of legal validity (or, as we would say nowadays, the problem of legal 'normativity') without violating science's methodological postulate of value-neutrality ('*Wertfreiheit*').[11]

At the end of subsection II.A I mentioned the 'candour postulate' – the methodical disposition always to identify and make explicit one's (ethical, political, epistemological) options – as one of the basic aspects of jurisprudential realism. Now is the moment to note that Pure Theory displays an unswerving commitment to this postulate. It makes explicit both its own and other theories' meta-theoretical premises and assumptions: and indeed Kelsen's doctrine of basic norm consists precisely in an attempt to render explicit the presupposition on which knowledge of the law *qua* normative order ultimately depends.[12]

ii. A Realistic Theory of Law

The Pure Theory *qua* (general) theory of law may also be regarded as realistic. Here two ingredients come to the forefront: the ('*Stufenbau*') theory of the hierarchical structure of legal systems, and Kelsen's theory of legal interpretation. Both theories represented, in their day, a veritable revolution in legal thought, and their importance has not since diminished. They are the pillars of Kelsen's 'radically realistic' theory of law, which moreover embraces a moderate form of norm-scepticism. General legal norms, Kelsen thinks, are always *in*determinate standards; they are 'semi-manufactured' products, as he puts it, 'which are finished only through the judicial decision and its execution'.[13] Legal interpretation is always the outcome of an act of will, an act by which interpreters *decide* on the 'proper' or 'correct' meaning of a norm (usually some general norm which is to be 'applied' to some individual case).[14] Accordingly, jurisdictional activity is never declarative in character; it is never an exclusive matter of cognition and logical inference. Rather, jurisdictional activity is fully *constitutive* in character; 'the function of adjudication', as he puts it for example

[11] 'Methode und Grundbegriff der Reinen Rechtslehre' (n 4) 75ff; *Introduction to the Problems of Legal Theory* (n 4) 73ff; *The Pure Theory of Law* (n 4) 101ff; 'Naturrechtslehre und Rechtspositivismus' (n 6) 32f; *General Theory of Norms* (n 9) 252ff.

[12] See eg *Introduction to the Problems of Legal Theory* (n 4) 58; *The Pure Theory of Law* (n 4) 204f.

[13] *General Theory of Law and State* (n 4) 135.

[14] I leave aside, for the moment, Kelsen's views on *scientific* interpretation, which will be considered in section IV.

in 1934, 'is constitutive through and through; it is law creation in the literal sense of the word'.[15] By acts of will, judges *constitute* the general norm(s) to be 'applied',[16] the facts of the case to which such norms are to be applied and, of course, the individual norm by which the case is decided. Indeed, the Pure Theory has consistently subscribed to the idea that there is '*kein Imperativ ohne Imperator*' ('no imperative without an imperator'): the idea, that is, that no legal norm exists which has not been produced by a legal authority; an idea, it is worth stressing, which – far from being a distinctive feature of Kelsen's final period (the so-called 'irrationalist' period)[17] – is well and clearly present since the 1934 edition of the *Reine Rechtslehre*.[18]

Other characteristic claims and focal points of the Pure Theory which reflect its ingrained realistic orientation towards the knowledge of legal norms *in action*, as it were – knowledge of how legal systems *in fact* operate, of what sorts of relations obtain between legal organs (and legal norms) placed at different 'levels' in the *Stufenbau*, and so on – include the following: (1) positive law is an ideology-ridden and an interest-ridden social phenomenon: law itself, so to speak, is necessarily 'impure';[19] (2) legal systems are *dynamic* orders: changeable, and indeed constantly changing;[20] (3) positive law is a specific 'social technique' which can be put to use as a means to whatever goals or interests legal authorities may choose to pursue;[21] (4) legal validity is conditioned by efficacy (and thus also by *desuetudo*);[22] (5) general legal norms are to be understood as embedding a tacit 'alternative clause': for 'illegal' lower-level norms (viz. individual norms created by judicial decisions) are nonetheless to be recognised as valid (albeit only 'restrictedly' so – 'so to speak' – if subject to

[15] *Introduction to the Problems of Legal Theory* (n 4) 68; see also *General Theory of Law and State* (n 4) 135; *The Pure Theory of Law* (n 4) 237–38.

[16] 'A judicial decision does not have merely declaratory character as is sometimes assumed. The court does not merely "find" . . . the law whose creation had been previously entirely completed . . . The finding of law is present only when the general norm to be applied in the concrete case is to be ascertained; and *even this ascertainment has a constitutive, not merely a declaratory, character*': *cf The Pure Theory of Law* (n 4) 237–38 (my italics).

[17] *cf* H Kelsen, 'Law and Logic' in *Essays in Legal and Moral Philosophy* (Dordrecht, Reidel, 1973 [1965]) 237f; *General Theory of Norms* (n 9) 3.

[18] *cf* Kelsen, *Introduction to the Problems of Legal Theory* (n 4) 63ff; *General Theory of Law and State* (n 4) 132ff; *The Pure Theory of Law* (n 4) 236ff.

[19] *Introduction to the Problems of Legal Theory* (n 4) 18–19, 33f, 117; *General Theory of Law and State* (n 4) 5ff; *The Pure Theory of Law* (n 4) 33, 101.

[20] *Introduction to the Problems of Legal Theory* (n 4) 63ff; *General Theory of Law and State* (n 4) 110ff; *The Pure Theory of Law* (n 4) 193ff.

[21] 'Methode und Grundbegriff der Reinen Rechtslehre' (n 4) 86; *Introduction to the Problems of Legal Theory* (n 4) 28ff, esp 31; 'The Law as a Specific Social Technique' in *What is Justice? Justice, Law, and Politics in the Mirror of Science* (Berkeley, University of California Press, 1957 [1941]) 231ff; *General Theory of Law and State* (n 4) 15ff.

[22] *Introduction to the Problems of Legal Theory* (n 4) 60ff; *General Theory of Law and State* (n 4) 29ff, 41ff, 119f; 156; *The Pure Theory of Law* (n 4) 211ff.

further annulment);[23] and accordingly (6) the common jurist's notions of an act's 'nullity', a statute's 'unconstitutionality', a judicial decision's 'illegality' and so on, must be redefined if they are to correspond to the actual workings of the law.[24]

One may disagree with any or all of these ideas. But one cannot plausibly deny, I think, that they represent the elements of an empirical, anti-ideological, anti-metaphysical, realistic general theory of law.

III. THE PURE THEORY AS A REALISTIC THEORY OF LAW: THE ARGUMENT FROM SCEPTICAL FEEDBACK

The argument from sceptical feedback runs as follows. Kelsen scholars by and large agree that the Pure Theory's last 'period' is a 'sceptical' one, and that it bears the marks of a 'crude legal realism'.[25] But the ideas commonly singled out as evidence of this putative 'sceptical' turn were already present (if inchoately articulated, or infelicitously phrased) at earlier stages of the Pure Theory. Hence, scepticism is no novelty of the 'late' Kelsen – though of course it may be argued that it was at this final stage that it reached its summit.

I will illustrate this argument by turning to some representative claims made by Stanley Paulson and Derick Beyleveld.

A. A Continuous Vein of Scepticism

Stanley Paulson identifies three 'dramatic' changes in the Pure Theory of Law, as it moved from a 'classical phase' (circa 1921–60) to a 'sceptical phase' (after 1960):

> First, Kelsen abandons his earlier view to the effect that legal norms are subject to constraints imposed by logic. Second, he gives up the idea that legal science has a 'normative' dimension. Third, he defends an utterly emaciated version of the basic norm thesis, namely, the basic norm qua fiction.[26]

Should we agree with this assessment? Let us separately consider each one of these supposed 'changes'.

[23] *Introduction to the Problems of Legal Theory* (n 4) 71ff; *General Theory of Law and State* (n 4) 159; *The Pure Theory of Law* (n 4) 267. On this point *cf* also text to n 33.

[24] 'In this respect the law is like King Midas: just as everything he touched turned to gold, so everything to which the law refers assumes legal character. Within the legal order, nullity is only the highest degree of annulability': *cf The Pure Theory of Law* (n 4) 278.

[25] *cf* Beyleveld, 'From the "Middle-Way" to Normative Irrationalism' (n 1) 119.

[26] Paulson, 'Introduction' (n 1) xliii.

i. Abandonment of the Claim that Legal Norms are Subject to Logical Constraints?

As for the first of Kelsen's alleged changes singled out by Paulson, I would counter that even in the second edition of the *Reine Rechtslehre* – a work where logicism is seemingly at its peak – it is not quite true that legal norms are characterised as being 'subject to constraints imposed by logic'. Though he acknowledges that legal norms may (and do often) conflict, he makes clear that such conflicts are not tantamount to *logical* contradictions:

> To be sure, it is undeniable that legal organs may create conflicting norms – that they perform acts whose subjective meaning is an 'ought' and which may be in conflict with each other if their subjective meaning is interpreted as their objective meaning . . . This conflict, however, . . . is not a logical contradiction in the strict sense of the word, even though it is usually said that the two norms 'contradict' each other. For logical principles, especially the principle of the exclusion of contradictions, are applicable to assertions that can be true or false . . . But a norm is neither true nor false, but either valid or invalid.[27]

Only legal propositions – the statements by which legal science describes the content of the law – can be true or false; logical principles are accordingly applicable *only*, says Kelsen, to such propositions, and not to legal norms.[28] Now, it is true that he comes – or rather jumps – to the notorious conclusion that

> [l]ogical principles are applicable, *indirectly*, to legal norms to the extent that they are applicable to the legal propositions which describe the legal norms and which can be true or false. Two legal norms are contradictory and can therefore not both be valid at the same time, if the two legal propositions that describe them are contradictory.[29]

Yet if we go on to ask what such an 'indirect' applicability of logical principles to legal norms consists in, we will find that what causes normative conflicts to disappear at the level of legal science's admittedly *descriptive* discourse is actually not logic, but *interpretation* – informed, to be sure, by the epistemological principle of consistency; for

> [t]he cognition of law, like any cognition, seeks to understand its subject as a meaningful whole and to describe it in noncontradictory statements [and thus] starts from the assumption that conflicts of norms within the normative order which is the object of this cognition can and must be solved by interpretation.[30]

[27] *Pure Theory of Law* (n 4) 205.
[28] ibid 74.
[29] ibid; I modified the English translation, which misleadingly translates as 'rules of law' Kelsen's '*Rechtssätze*' – which I render as 'legal propositions': see *Reine Rechtslehre* (n 6) 77.
[30] *Pure Theory of Law* (n 4) 206.

Given a conflict between any two norms belonging to the same hierarchical 'level' and enacted at different times, legal science 'presumes' that – in a legal order in which there is an organ 'normally authorized to prescribe changeable and therefore abolishable norms' – the principle *lex posterior derogat prior* is, if not expressly stated, then implicitly 'included in the authorization'.[31] Legal science may then proceed to the conclusion that those two norms can 'not both be valid at the same time' – for the latter has derogated the former. Likewise, given conflicting norms that have been 'prescribed simultaneously, by the same act and by the same organ', legal science will face

> the following possibilities for the solution of the conflict . . . : Either the two norms can be understood [viz. by *interpretation*] to be subject to a choice by the law-applying organ, e.g., the judge; or if . . . the two norms are only partly contradictory, then the one norm can be understood to be limiting the validity of the other. The law-describing proposition does not say: 'Adultery ought to be punished *and* ought not to be punished'; it says: 'He who commits adultery ought to be punished *or* ought not to be punished'.[32]

And if a conflict occurs between two norms belonging to different hierarchical 'levels' – one 'higher' relative to the other – then again legal science will, again by interpretation, read *in* the 'higher' norm a tacit alternative clause authorising the production of 'lower' norms which do *not* correspond in content to the explicit part of that 'higher' norm; which is why 'between a higher norm and a lower norm' it is also the case, for Kelsen, that 'no conflict is possible'.[33] (In fact, both Kelsen's doctrine of the 'tacit alternative clause' and his theory of the constitutive character of adjudication[34] ought to be kept in mind by anyone who considers his remarks on the 'indirect' applicability of logical principles to legal norms. For example, his claim that 'one legal norm may be deduced from another if the rules of law that describe them can form a logical syllogism'[35] should be read in conjunction with his contention that 'the individual norm stipulating that a certain sanction ought to be directed against a certain individual has been *brought into existence* by the judicial decision; it *did not exist before*'.[36] Kelsen scholars who think that Kelsen's late period was calamitous have perhaps underestimated the relevance of both his doctrine of the *Stufenbau* and of the associated account of the law-making process.)

The conclusion suggested by the foregoing remarks is that the change from the 'classical' to the 'sceptical' phase, which Paulson detects, did not concern Kelsen's view of *the law*. It concerned instead his view about the proper task of

[31] ibid.
[32] ibid 206f.
[33] ibid 208, 267ff; *cf* also text to n 23.
[34] *cf* text to n 15.
[35] *Pure Theory of Law* (n 4) 74.
[36] ibid 238; *cf* also the passage quoted in n 16.

legal science. It was legal science – not the law, not legal *norms* – that was, in Kelsen's 'classical' phase, subject to the constraints of logic. Legal science's task, Kelsen then thought, was to 'understand' the law 'as a meaningful whole and to describe it in noncontradictory statements'.[37] And it is *this* constraint that is abandoned in Kelsen's late, 'sceptical' period, partly because he came to acknowledge a blunder.[38] For if legal science, *qua* science, is to present the law *as it is* – then it cannot really assume or presuppose (differently from what Kelsen said in the second edition of *The Pure Theory*, as we have just seen) that no two conflicting norms can be simultaneously valid. Rather than seeking to dispel any conflicts by means of interpretation, legal science is to see whether *or not* the relevant conflict-solving (meta-)norms happen to be in place; *lex posterior derogat priori* is 'a principle of positive law and not a logical principle'.[39] Note, moreover, that this correction does by no means amount to a fundamental change in Kelsen's understanding of legal science; and also that Kelsen's former views about conflicts between norms of different levels, and about 'unconstitutional laws', are likewise preserved in this last phase.[40]

In short, then: Kelsen was *always* aware that positive law, being a human artefact, can be rife with conflicting norms; it can at points be meaningless, even absurd. His 'change' boils down to merely this: during his 'classical' phase he thought that legal science should, *qua* science, remedy, as far as possible, the positive law's possible meaninglessness; in the 'sceptical phase, the law's possible meaninglessness becomes, for legal science, a fact simply to be identified and exposed.

ii. Giving Up the 'Normative' Dimension of Legal Science?

As for the second of Kelsen's supposedly 'dramatic' changes as he entered his 'sceptical' phase – that 'he gives up the idea that legal science has a "normative" dimension', as Paulson puts it – I am not sure that I understand what such a 'normative dimension' amounts to. But let me try and proceed by guess-work.

Since the earlier stages of Kelsen's 'classical' period, namely since what Paulson calls the 'Neo-Kantian period' (circa 1921–35) of the 'classical' phase, Kelsen holds that legal science can be a genuine science, maintaining that the 'cognition of norms' is 'a function different from both making and applying the law'.[41] Legal science is 'normative' in that it *deals with* norms – it is 'a

[37] *Pure Theory of Law* (n 4) 206.

[38] See Kelsen and Klug, *Rechtsnormen und Logische Analyse* (n 9) 49f; and *cf* also H Kelsen, 'Derogation' in *Essays in Legal and Moral Philosophy* (Dordrecht, Reidel, 1973 [1962]) 261ff; and 'Law and Logic' (n 17) 228ff.

[39] *General Theory of Norms* (n 9) 126; and see generally ibid 123ff, 57ff.

[40] *cf* ibid 125.

[41] *Introduction to the Problems of Legal Theory* (n 4) 13.

cognitive science of norms'[42]) – and not in the sense that it *creates* norms. From the early 1940s on, moreover, Kelsen explicitly introduces in his work a distinction between legal norms ('*Rechtsnormen*') and legal propositions ('*Rechtssätze*') – the latter being truth-apt statements *about* (ie, *purporting to describe*) valid legal norms, and characteristically expressed in sentences in which deontic terminology is used descriptively[43] (he speaks in this regard of an 'ought' with a 'descriptive' meaning[44]) – and he comes to make the ex post facto claim that this distinction had always been, if only implicitly, at the heart of the Pure Theory since his 1911 *Hauptprobleme*.[45]

Now, if this is how the 'normative' dimension of legal science is to be understood, then it seems to me that Kelsen 'gives up' no aspect thereof whatsoever in his final, 'sceptical' phase. He maintains, as before, that legal science is 'normative' in the sense that it *deals with* (and not in the sense that it creates) norms; he maintains, as before, that the function of legal science and the function of legal authority are quite distinct; he maintains, as before, that the discourse of legal science is made of legal propositions, which describe (rather than prescribe) legal norms.[46] If there is novelty, it is a purely *notational* one: Kelsen demystifies the awkward notion of a *de*scriptive 'ought' by more clearly stressing both that (a) deontic sentences are semantically ambiguous, and may in fact be used, according to context, either prescriptively, to express norms, or descriptively, to express legal propositions;[47] and that (b) legal propositions may well be expressed by plainly descriptive (ie grammatically indicative) sentences.[48]

But perhaps Paulson has something else in mind when he refers to the 'normative' dimension of legal science: something having to do instead with the role of the basic norm as the ultimate basis of the objective validity of the legal norms of a positive legal order – and so something specifically connected with legal science's ability to cope with the so-called issue of the 'normativity' of law. If this conjecture is right, then Paulson's second charge collapses into his third – to which I now turn.

[42] ibid.

[43] *Hauptprobleme der Staatsrechtslehre* (Tübingen, JCB Mohr, 1911). See eg Kelsen, 'The Pure Theory of Law and Analytical Jurisprudence' (n 4) 51; *General Theory of Law and State* (n 4) 45ff; *Pure Theory of Law* (n 4) 71ff).

[44] *General Theory of Law and State* (n 4) 163; *Pure Theory of Law* (n 4) 75.

[45] See *Reine Rechtslehre* (n 6) 83 fn; this is one of the several lengthy and important footnotes included in the original, German-language edition which were not included in the English translation.

[46] *General Theory of Norms* (n 9) 2, 23, 152ff.

[47] ibid 163f.

[48] 'A textbook on Austrian criminal law can contain the sentence: "According to Austrian law the norm 'A thief is to be punished with imprisonment' is valid." That is an is-sentence. But the same thought can also be expressed in a *sollen*-sentence: "According to Austrian law, a thief is to be punished with imprisonment"': *cf* ibid 164.

iii. An 'Utterly Emaciated Version of the Basic Norm Thesis'?

Paulson seems to view Kelsen's late characterisation of 'the basic norm qua fiction' as a particularly 'dramatic' change; for Kelsen employs 'fiction' in the specific sense in which Hans Vaihinger had used the term, and in such a sense fictions are admittedly 'self-contradictory':

> Kelsen's talk of the 'self-contradictory' character of the basic norm may be a contrivance . . ., but the general significance of his use of Vaihinger is unmistakable. By means of the basic norm, now a fictitious construct, one proceeds *as though* the material of the law were irreducibly normative. And this, it scarcely need to be added, amounts to a fundamental concession on Kelsen's part: The normativity thesis, claiming the irreducibly normative character of the law, is not defensible.[49]

Here we face, I think, the following alternative: either Kelsen has now really abandoned his 'normativity thesis' as Paulson conceives it; or his explicit characterisation of the basic norm as a Vaihingerian 'fiction' amounts to nothing more than an attempt simply to provide a clearer account of a doctrine which in fact he continued to endorse rather than retract – in which case the 'normativity thesis', as Paulson conceives it, is really not a proper part of the Pure Theory. This latter hypothesis – which is at any rate very much worth exploring, if only for the sake of argument – is, I think, the correct one. What reasons are there for defending it?

For one, what Kelsen seems to mean to emphasise in the *General Theory of Norms* is that though he had previously referred to the basic norm as a 'hypothesis', strictly speaking 'the Basic Norm is not a hypothesis *in the sense of Vaihinger's philosophy of As-If* . . . but a fiction'.[50] It is, more precisely, a 'cognitive' fiction, ie a fiction consciously adopted for theoretical reasons:

> According to Vaihinger, a fiction is a cognitive device used when one is unable to attain one's cognitive goal with the material at hand . . . The cognitive goal of the Basic Norm is to ground the validity of the norms forming a positive moral or legal order, that is, to interpret the subjective meaning of the norm-positiving acts as their objective meaning (i.e. as valid norms) and to interpret the relevant acts as norm-positing acts.[51]

There seems to me to be no substantial change from what Kelsen had maintained, for example, in the second edition of the *Pure Theory*, where one finds the following, nearly identical, description of the 'function of the basic norm', namely to render epistemically possible a normative interpretation of the social phenomenon of law:

[49] Paulson, 'Introduction' (n 1) xlv.
[50] *General Theory of Norms* (n 9) 256, my emphasis.
[51] ibid.

> [O]nly the presupposition of the basic norm makes it possible to interpret the subjective meaning of the constitution-creating act (and of the acts established according to the constitution) as their objective meaning, that is as objectively valid legal norms . . . The function of the basic norm is to found the objective validity of a positive legal order, that is, to interpret the *subjective* meaning of the acts of human beings by which the norms of an effective coercive order are created, as their *objective* meaning.[52]

And likewise in the *General Theory of Law and State* Kelsen had maintained that

> [t]he whole function of the basic norm is to confer law-creating power on the act of the first legislator and on all the other acts based on the first act. To interpret these acts of human beings as legal acts and their products as binding norms, and that means to interpret the empirical material which presents itself as law as such, is possible only on the condition that the basic norm is presupposed as a valid norm. The basic norm is only the necessary presupposition of any positivistic interpretation of the legal material.

There seems therefore to be no momentous change of mind about the basic norm in Kelsen's 'late' period. The conclusion to draw must then be that Paulson's 'normativity thesis', which he believes Kelsen *abandoned* in his 'late' period, is a thesis that perhaps Kelsen never really endorsed after all. The 'normativity thesis', as Paulson formulates it, is the thesis of the 'irreducibly normative character of the law':[53] the thesis, that is to say, that law is irreducibly made of norms, that it cannot be reduced to (social or natural) facts. But recall, in this regard, the following passage from the second edition of the *Pure Theory*:

> The Pure Theory describes the positive law as an objectively valid normative order and states that this interpretation is possible only under the condition that a basic norm is presupposed according to which the subjective meaning of the law-creating acts is also their objective meaning. The Pure Theory thereby characterizes this interpretation as possible, not necessary, and presents the objective validity of positive law only as conditional – namely conditioned by the presupposed basic norm. The fact that the basic norm of a positive legal order *may* but *need not* be presupposed means: the relevant interhuman relationships may be, but need not be, interpreted as 'normative', that is, as obligations, authorizations, rights, etc. constituted by objectively valid norms. It means further: they can be interpreted without such presupposition (i.e., without the basic norm) as power relations (i.e., relations between commanding and obeying or disobeying human beings) – in other words, they can be interpreted sociologically, not juristically.[54]

Nor is this a late addition to Kelsen's understanding of the basic norm. Here is a passage from 1934:

[52] *Pure Theory of Law* (n 4) 202
[53] Paulson, 'Introduction' (n 1) xlv.
[54] *Pure Theory of Law* (n 4) 217f.

> The Pure Theory of Law is well aware that the specifically normative meaning of certain material facts, the meaning characterized as 'law', is the result not of a necessary interpretation but of a possible interpretation, possible only given a certain basic interpretation [ie the basic norm].[55]

These passages suggest that Paulson's attribution of the thesis of the 'irreducibly normative character of the law' to Kelsen must be either qualified (ie reinterpreted) or else rejected. Perhaps it could be qualified as the claim that Kelsen believed that there is something both distinctive and worthwhile – from the standpoint of our knowledge of the law, and in view of how legal experience actually is (we think and speak of ourselves as having legal rights, duties, powers, etc) – about a normative interpretation of the social phenomenon of law: an interpretation according to which such a phenomenon is (also, and meaningfully) seen as a *normative* order, that is, as a social phenomenon made of norms and not merely of human acts (of commanding, obedience and disobedience). This reading would be in tune with what I referred to above (at the end of subsection II.B.i) as the Pure Theory's epistemological 'candour'. Read along such lines, however, the 'normativity thesis' was by no means abandoned, *pace* Paulson, by Kelsen's late-period characterisation of the basic norm as a 'fiction'. On the contrary, the underlying idea was in fact a cardinal feature of the Pure Theory since earlier times.

B. The Backlash of Normative Irrationalism

Derick Beyleveld, too, in a review of Kelsen's posthumously published *General Theory of Norms*, lists a number of supposedly 'radical' consequences brought into Kelsen's general jurisprudence by his late 'normative irrationalism'. 'Most significantly', Beyleveld writes, Kelsen's final views require him to abandon his earlier attempt – which, according to Beyleveld, the second *Pure Theory* embodied – 'to forge a "middle-way" between legal idealism and legal realism'[56] – leaving him with 'a rather crude legal realism'.[57] Is this assessment warranted? Let us consider these allegedly 'disastrous'[58] features of Kelsen's final work.

(A) According to Beyleveld, Kelsen's late claim that conflicting norms *can* be simultaneously valid[59] entails that 'municipal and international law can be considered as independent of each other' – which is, Beyleveld says, 'an

[55] *Introduction to the Problems of Legal Theory* (n 4) 34.
[56] 'From the "Middle-Way" to Normative Irrationalism' (n 1) 104.
[57] ibid 119.
[58] ibid.
[59] See text to n 40.

unrecognised change of position' from his previous views.[60] In fact, however, Kelsen had already advanced such a view in the second edition of *The Pure Theory*, maintaining – on the grounds of a telling analogy – that 'what is regarded as a conflict between the norms of international law and the norms of national law is not a conflict of norms at all':

> For example: A state can be obligated by treaty to grant the members of a minority the same political rights as the members of the majority, but a national statute deprives the members of the minority of political rights – this contrast, however, *does not affect the validity of either the treaty or the statute.* The situation is exactly analogous to a situation within the state's legal order, without, on that account, causing any doubt as to its unity. The so-called unconstitutional statute, too, is a valid norm and stays valid until its validity is abolished by another decision.[61]

We have seen that this view on the 'unconstitutional statute' is one which Kelsen holds also during his final 'period'.[62] He holds on such grounds that two conflicting norms – eg a norm of conventional international law, and a conflicting national norm – are *both* valid, even though the enactment of the conflicting national norm may be a condition for the application of an international law sanction, or even though the national norm may be liable to being declared null and void by a competent international court. Therefore Kelsen's late adoption of the view that a normative conflict *presupposes* that conflicting norms are *both valid* at the same time – itself a consequent 'realistic' development of his theory of law (as I suggested at the end of subsection II.B.ii above), in so far as it more closely reflects the way in which legal systems actually operate – has no effect on his theory of the unity of national and international law.

(B) Another supposedly 'dramatic' consequence, according to Beyleveld, follows from Kelsen's insistence that 'an individual norm cannot follow logically from a general one because it is possible for a judge to recognise the validity of the general norm, but fail to posit the individual one';[63] and the worry here is that

> [i]f there is no logical derivation of an individual norm from a general one, then it seems that general norms can never guide action. Kelsen attempts to solve this problem by treating the relation between a general norm and an individual one as a function of an act of will. . . . [L]egal duties are not constituted by general rules, but only by a corresponding act of the individual judge. This is very radical, for it follows logically that there can be no binding precedents and that is impossible for any legally empowered official to act *ultra vires*. The doctrine of acceptance also

[60] 'From the "Middle-Way" to Normative Irrationalism' (n 1) 118.
[61] *Pure Theory of Law* (n 4) 330.
[62] Again, see text to n 40.
[63] 'From the "Middle-Way" to Normative Irrationalism' (n 1) 109.

> entails that it is not possible to know what individual norm 'corresponds' to what general one prior to acceptance.[64]

These may indeed be shocking consequences. But they do not constitute that much of a novelty in the Pure Theory: for, again, they were already held by Kelsen in works pertaining to his 'classical' period. At most, this late phase amounts to a refinement and perhaps a radicalisation – not to any sort of U-turn. (Let me be clear, once again, that in saying this I am by no means committing myself to an endorsement of Kelsen's claims as theoretically sound; I am presently concerned with mistakes in existing critiques of the Pure Theory of Law, rather than with critiques of the Pure Theory's existing mistakes.[65]) The questions, then, are, first, whether Kelsen *ever* maintained that general norms can *always* 'guide action', and second, whether his final view was that general norms can *never* 'guide action'.

To begin with, Kelsen would certainly have treated the issue of action-guidance by norms as a psychological and sociological one having to do with the *motives* by which people obey, disobey, apply or fail to apply, a norm. If judges do usually apply certain general norms in certain ways to certain individual cases, thereby issuing certain individual norms, so that the general norms can be said to be to some degree efficacious, then legal subjects at large may be induced, by knowledge of these facts, to be 'guided' by such general norms (understood in the terms in which they have actually been applied by courts). But this picture – which is the standard Kelsenian picture[66] – has nothing whatsoever to do with the possibility of logically deriving individual norms from general ones.

Second, it was never Kelsen's view that general norms are 'automatically' or 'logically' applicable by themselves, as it were, to people's conducts. On the contrary, his longstanding view was that general norms are but an intermediate stage in the process of law-creation and law-application, from the initial establishment of the historically first constitution to the individual acts by which judicial decisions and administrative orders are eventually executed.[67] General norms are 'semi-manufactured' products;[68] and they are 'frames' within which several different routes of 'application' to individual cases are possible.[69] Moreover, whenever the doctrine of *res judicata* holds, general norms, according to Kelsen (as we have already seen) are to be understood as

[64] ibid 118.

[65] In this I follow the exact same approach adopted almost 60 years ago by N Bobbio, 'La teoria pura del diritto ed i suoi critici' in *Studi Sulla Teoria Generale del Diritto* (Turin, Giapicchelli, 1995) 75ff.

[66] *cf* eg *Introduction to the Problems of Legal Theory* (n 4) 31; *General Theory of Law and State* (n 4) 24; *Pure Theory of Law* (n 4) 26f; *Reine Rechtslehre* (n 6) 217f n.

[67] *Introduction to the Problems of Legal Theory* (n 4) 67ff; *General Theory of Law and State* (n 4) 132ff; *Pure Theory of Law* (n 4) 233ff.

[68] See text to n 13.

[69] *Introduction to the Problems of Legal Theory* (n 4) 80f; *Pure Theory of Law* (n 4) 350ff.

including a tacit 'alternative' clause authorising even the performance of the so-called 'illegal' lower-level act.[70] And the same account extends, of course, to judicial decisions which fail to follow 'binding' precedents: for binding precedents are but general norms, though originating in individual judicial decisions rather than in legislative acts proper.[71] So while it is true, yes, that according to Kelsen, as Beyleveld puts it, 'it is impossible for any legally empowered official to act *ultra vires*' – assuming that we are dealing with officials acting at the final stage of the legal process – this is clearly a constant feature of the Pure Theory, rather than a late twist.

(C) Another worry stemming from Kelsen's late 'denial of a logic of norms' is, according to Beyleveld, this:

> The denial of a logic of norms entails that all authorisation . . . must be dynamic. Alongside this we get the theory that derogation is not a logical function but requires a derogating norm to be posited. However . . . although Kelsen holds that a derogating norm does not conflict with the norm it derogates, the notion of derogation rests on the idea that there is a logical incompatibility between norms. Without this derogation is impossible; and, if it is impossible, then a dynamic theory of law is incoherent.[72]

Although there is much that could be said about this passage, a few remarks will suffice to dispose of Beyleveld's unwarranted concerns. The key claim here is that 'the notion of derogation rests on the idea that there is a logical incompatibility between norms'. This claim is wrong. Derogation does not necessarily (ie conceptually) presuppose the existence of either a conflict or a logical incompatibility between norms. Derogation may, for example, target an entire code – a Civil Code, say – replacing it with an entirely new one which may not conflict with the former. Or derogation may simply be a means of getting rid of some norm which the present law-maker deems pointless or obnoxious, even if it does not conflict or in any sense contradict any other norm (old or new) of the legal system.

Note, moreover, that Kelsen had always maintained – prior to his late period – that the *resolution* of any given normative conflict is something that necessarily turns on the existence of some meta-norm.[73] Semantics – 'logic' – can tell us only whether any two given norms conflict; it cannot tell us *which* of the conflicting norms is to be given preference, which is something that will depend on conflict-resolution criteria (to be identified by legal science by means of interpretation). So Kelsen never maintained (and rightly so, it may be said in passing) that derogation is a 'logical function'.

[70] See text to n 23 and to n 33.
[71] *General Theory of Law and State* (n 4) 149f; *Pure Theory of Law* (n 4) 250f.
[72] 'From the "Middle-Way" to Normative Irrationalism' (n 1) 118.
[73] See *General Theory of Law and State* (n 4) 155–56, 263; *Pure Theory of Law* (n 4) 205ff, and recall the discussion in section III.A.i.

Given that derogation does not rest on an assumption of logical incompatibility, derogation remains perfectly *possible* even if we think, with Kelsen, that normative conflicts are an altogether different matter from logical contradictions. Hence, *pace* Beyleveld, there is nothing 'incoherent' in Kelsen's dynamic theory of law.

(D) Lastly, according to Beyleveld, even though in *General Theory of Norms* the role of the basic norm is, 'as before', to be 'the reason for the validity of [the] norms of an order, by validating the authority of the norm-creators of the order', Kelsen faces the following concern:

> [F]or one norm to validate another requires a practical syllogism (which implies the intelligibility of the notion of practical reason). Kelsen's normative irrationalism precludes this (and Kelsen is adamant that the concept of practical reason is a contradiction in terms). In line with this, Kelsen portrays the validation effected by the basic norm in a *theoretical* syllogism (involving statements of legal science, not norms themselves). He also claims that the basic norm is a fictitious norm, not a positive one. But all of this is thoroughly inconsistent. According to Kelsen, a fictitious norm cannot validate a positive one and statements of legal science cannot validate or create norms. If Kelsen wants a middle way [between legal idealism and legal realism], he must abandon normative irrationalism. Without a logic of norms and practical reason, he is left with a rather crude legal realism.[74]

But this charge does not stand – and again some brief remarks are enough to dismiss it. First, we have already seen that the idea that the basic norm is a 'fictitious' norm amounts to no revolutionary change within the Pure Theory.[75] It is but a clarification destined to present the basic norm, in line with Vaihinger's epistemology, in its proper light, viz. as an epistemological device for interpreting as objectively valid the norms of positive legal orders. That being the case, Kelsen's jurisprudence may indeed be regarded as a *realistic* variety of legal positivism – but one consistently endorsed since his 'classical' period.

Second, the idea of the 'theoretical syllogism' as a 'validating' device is by no means inconsistent with Kelsen's rejection of a logic of norms. To deny that there is a logic of norms is to deny that in order for any given norm N_1 to be legally valid it is either necessary or sufficient that the content of N_1 is logically derived from the content of some other norm N_2. (That there is '*kein Imperativ ohne Imperator*'[76] was already Kelsen's view, as we saw, in the 'classical' period: it goes hand-in-hand with his theory of the constitutive character of adjudication.[77]) But to show that the *content* of some individual norm N_1 does derive from the *content* of some previously identified valid general norm N_2

[74] 'From the "Middle-Way" to Normative Irrationalism' (n 1) 118f.
[75] See subsection III.A.iii.
[76] See text to n 17.
[77] See subsection II.B.ii.

cannot *but* have justificatory force: for it will justify (and so in a sense 'validate') the individual norm as derivable, content-wise, from the general norm, and thus provide an argument against its reversal on appeal (if the possibility of appeal exists). Kelsen's main point, however, is that an individual norm N_1 *would still be legally valid* (until repealed by some further authoritative 'act of will') even if it could not be shown to derive, *content*-wise, from any higher-level general norm N_2.

IV. THE PURE THEORY AS A REALISTIC THEORY OF LAW: THE RETAIL ARGUMENT

A. 'Legal Science' and 'Theory of Legal Science'

'Legal science' is an ambiguous expression, as are its counterparts in other languages,[78] and this ambiguity has often been the cause of some misunderstandings.

The phrase is sometimes meant as a straightforward translation from the Latin expression '*scientia iuris*',[79] which comes to us through Roman culture, and which came to be used to refer to the doctrinal study of law (or 'legal dogmatics', from the nineteenth-century German term '*Rechtsdogmatik*', which seems to have been coined by Rudolph von Jhering[80]). The doctrinal study of law, however, does not necessarily amount to a 'scientific' investigation about the law. It concerns itself with the *content* of particular positive legal orders, aiming at providing definite answers to '*Quid juris*?' ('What is the law [on the matter]?') questions; and in doing so, what it usually sets forth is proposals *de iure condito*, eg proposals regarding the correct way to interpret some given statutory clause or as to the correct way to solve, under existing law, a normative conflict. Such proposals, although concerned with the content of existing law (rather than with how the law *should* be), belong nonetheless to the domain of practical reason and legal politics.

Sometimes, though, if less often, 'legal science' is used to refer to any inquiry into law which *can* be described as 'scientific' (in some sense of the adjective), whether it concerns itself with the law in general or with the content of some particular positive legal order. In this case 'legal science' is not the same as the doctrinal study of law as conceived and undertaken in Western cultures.

[78] eg '*scienza del diritto*' or '*scienza giuridica*' in Italian, '*ciencia del derecho*' or '*ciencia jurídica*' in Spanish, '*Rechtswissenschaft*' in German, '*science du droit*' or '*science juridique*' in French.

[79] See A Peczenick, *Scientia Juris. Legal Doctrine as Knowledge of Law and as a Source of Law*, vol 4 of E Pattaro (ed), *A Treatise of Legal Philosophy and General Jurisprudence* (Dordrecht, Springer, 2005) 1–2.

[80] *cf* W Fikentscher, *Methoden des Rechts in vergleichender Darstellung. Band III: Mitteleuropäischer Rechtskreis* (Tübingen, Mohr Siebeck, 1976) 228.

Of course one does encounter in the literature occurrences of 'legal science' which, though meant to *refer* to the doctrinal study of law as traditionally undertaken by jurists, simultaneously purport to convey that such doctrinal inquiries *do* have the property of being genuinely 'scientific'. But precisely because the claim that such a link can be established between the two senses of 'legal science' is very much open to discussion – and indeed such a claim has offended the epistemological sensibilities of many a theorist from the mid-nineteenth century onwards – one ought to keep the disambiguation in mind.

The phrase 'theory of legal science' suffers from a related ambiguity; it can be used to refer to three kinds of theoretical inquiries. First, it can be understood as referring to *descriptive methodological inquiries* into the different kinds of operations actually involved in the *doctrinal* study of law (encompassing analyses of the techniques and methods which jurists do employ or may – given their actual institutional and cultural context – employ). Second, it can be used to refer to *prescriptive methodological inquiries* into the different kinds of operations that *ought* to be involved in the *doctrinal* study of law (encompassing analyses of the techniques and methods which jurists *ought* to employ). Third, it can be used to refer to *epistemological inquiries* into the conditions and the ideal model (put forth on the grounds of some presupposed general theory of scientific knowledge) of a genuinely *scientific* knowledge of positive law.

In this section I should like to suggest that the latter is the sense in which the Pure Theory of Law can be said to be (or to include) a theory of legal science. Kelsen opens the second edition of the *Reine Rechtslehre* by stating that

> [t]he Pure Theory of Law is a theory of positive law. It is a theory of positive law in general, not of a specific legal order. It is a general theory of law, not an interpretation of specific national or international legal norms; but it offers a theory of interpretation.[81]

But this is too modest a description of the scope and multi-layered content of Kelsen's jurisprudential project. The Pure Theory of Law is more than a general theory of law. It also offers a theory – strictly, a meta-theory – of the conditions under which both general legal theory *and* the doctrinal study of law may be regarded as genuinely scientific inquiries into positive law. It offers, in other words, an *epistemology* of law.

I have already made a few comments, in subsection II.B.ii, on the realistic orientation of Kelsen's epistemology. Now is the moment to strengthen this aspect of my argument, by considering the details of Kelsen's theory of the scientific knowledge of law.

[81] *The Pure Theory of Law* (n 4) 1.

B. The Pure Theory of Legal Science as a Realistic Theory

Thorough scientific knowledge of the law is, for Kelsen, something that depends on the collaborative pursuit of several different lines of inquiry. Three disciplines feature as the basic components of his map of legal learning: the analytical philosophy of justice;[82] sociological jurisprudence (ie sociology of law); and normative jurisprudence.[83]

Now, in a review essay on Alf Ross's *On Law and Justice*, Kelsen explicitly refers to his own conception of normative jurisprudence – which encompasses both the general theory of law, and the doctrinal study of law (ie, in Austinian terms, both 'general' and 'particular' jurisprudence[84]) – as a *realistic* conception:

> [A] science is 'empirical' – as opposed to 'metaphysical' – not only when it describes facts occurring in time and space, but also when it describes the *meaning* of certain human acts. A theory of law remains empirical if it confines itself to the description of norms that are the meaning of empirical human acts occurring in space and time, and if it does not concern itself with norms arising from supra-human instances such as God or a god-created Nature. Provided that the 'ought' of the norms it describes is not the 'ought' of some sort of metaphysical justice, a theory of law remains empirical. The Pure Theory of Law meets these conditions. With the utmost emphasis – and like hardly any other theory of law – the Pure Theory discards from its scope all metaphysical elements. It can therefore claim to be regarded as no less empirical, and in this sense as no less 'realistic', than Ross's 'realistic' theory.[85]

But what, precisely, does such an empirical 'description of norms' amount to?

[82] With which Kelsen himself engages in the many essays collected in his 1957 volume *What is Justice? Justice, Law and Politics in the Mirror of Science* (Berkeley, University of California Press, 1957), and also in the long essay 'Das Problem der Gerechtichkeit', published as an Appendix (not included in the English translation) to the second edition of the *Reine Rechtslehre*. (He states in the Preface – also omitted from the English-language edition – that though the 'problem of justice, as a value-problem' does not belong to the 'analysis of positive law qua legal reality', it needs to be discussed nonetheless, because of its utmost importance for 'legal politics': *cf Reine Rechtslehre* (n 6) viii.)

[83] *cf* 'The Pure Theory of Law and Analytical Jurisprudence' (n 4) 44ff; and see *Pure Theory of Law* (n 4) 101ff.

[84] *cf* J Austin, 'Outline of the Course of Lectures' in *Lectures on Jurisprudence or The Philosophy of Positive Law*, vol 1, 5th edn, R Campbell (ed) (London, Murray, 1885) 31f.

[85] Kelsen, 'A "Realistic" Theory of Law and the Pure Theory of Law' (n 6) 5 (my page reference is to the original 'Eine "Realistische" und die Reine Rechtslehre. Bemerkungen zu Alf Ross: On Law and Justice' (1959/60) 10 *Österreichische Zeitschrift für öffentliches Recht* 1–25: the English version, in this volume, includes references to the page numbers of the original text); *cf* also 'Law and Morality' in *Essays in Legal and Moral Philosophy* (Dordrecht, Reidel, 1973 [1960]) 93 fn 1; and, for earlier statements of the Pure Theory's 'realism', 'Methode und Grundbegriff der Reinen Rechtslehre' (n 4) 78f; *Introduction to the Problems of Legal Theory* (n 4) 18; *Reine Rechtslehre* (n 6) 60 n; and *Pure Theory of Law* (n 4) 106.

This is one of the most elusive claims of the Pure Theory of Law, and many different interpretations have been proposed by Kelsen scholars.[86] In what follows I will offer my own fresh reconstruction – guided both by the principle of charitable interpretation, and by the hermeneutic canon of totality – of Kelsen's theory of legal science, as laid down from his *General Theory of Law and State* up to the posthumous *General Theory of Norms*.

Let me begin by observing that 'description of norms' ('*Beschreibung von Normen*') is a term of art within the Pure Theory: indeed, one would do better simply to ignore the ordinary meaning of the verb 'description', and to concentrate instead on the peculiar set of activities that Kelsen has in mind. (Kelsen's use of 'description' can be simply explained by the need to signpost the contrast with norm-*creation*). And here there is an immediate general distinction to be drawn, a distinction which in turn will enable us to differentiate between two *kinds* of activity which can be characterised as activities of norm-'description'. A couple of paragraphs ago I mentioned a division of labour *within* normative jurisprudence, between the general theory of law and the doctrinal study of law. The former is concerned with the actual formal or structural features of legal norms and legal systems, whatever their particular content may be. The latter is concerned with the identification of the valid laws of some particular legal system, and with stating what it is that such laws in fact prescribe or stipulate.

We can accordingly distinguish, fully in line with the Pure Theory of Law, between two *kinds* of endeavours which can be referred to as in some sense 'descriptive' of legal norms: on the one hand, the *theoretical description* of structural and formal features of legal norms and legal systems; and, on the other hand, the *doctrinal description* of the contents of the norms of actual given legal systems. Let us separately consider and flesh out each one of these kinds of endeavour.

i. *Theoretical Description*

Theoretical description – the task of *general* legal theory – can be said to encompass three closely related subtasks: conceptual analysis; the static theory of legal norms; and the dynamic theory of legal norms.

1. *Conceptual analysis* occupies itself with general legal concepts: 'law', 'state', 'legal norm', 'validity', 'efficacy', 'source of law', 'legal duty', 'legal right', 'legal sanction', 'legal responsibility' and so on.[87]

[86] Some even think that Kelsen's own characterisation of the Pure Theory as 'empirical' is misleading, not to say abusive, on the grounds that the features of any *truly* empirical legal science would surely differ significantly from the model of legal science associated with the Pure Theory; see M Troper, 'Ross, Kelsen et la validité' (2002) 50 *Droit et Societé* 43ff, with persuasive rejoinders to Ross's charge – in the already referenced 'Validity and the Conflict Between Legal Positivism and Natural Law' (n 5) – that the Pure Theory is only 'quasi-positivist'.

[87] See eg *General Theory of Law and State* (n 4) 3ff; *Pure Theory of Law* (n 4) 108ff; and also 'Professor

2. The *static theory of legal norms* occupies itself with the logical form of norms (as opposed to their superficial grammatical form);[88] with the functional variety of legal norms;[89] and with relations between norms from the point of view of their *content*.[90]
3. The *dynamic theory of legal norms* occupies itself with the structure of legal orders; with relations between norms from the point of view of their production or creation;[91] with the issue of the 'unity' of legal systems;[92] with the difference and relations between validity and efficacy (both of legal systems as a whole, and of legal norms individually considered);[93] with the problem of so-called legal 'gaps';[94] with the possibility of conflicts between norms belonging to different hierarchical levels of a legal system;[95] and with the possibility of conflicts between norms of the same level, and the criteria which positive legal orders may adopt for their resolution.

Theoretical description, then, amounts to much more than mere 'description'. It also necessarily involves comparative empirical investigations of different actual and historical legal orders, the analysis of positive 'legal conscience', and theory-construction. Conceptual analysis, in particular, far from being purely 'descriptive', is a critical exercise in rational reconstruction: for (in Kelsen's view) it should provide *re*-definitions of jurists' common sense notions (of jurists' 'intuitions', as we would put it nowadays) in such a way that is compatible with the epistemological postulate of purity. Conceptual analysis, according to this view, performs a *therapeutic* function, as it were: it

Stone and the Pure Theory of Law' (1965) 17 *Stanford Law Review* 1130ff.

[88] Kelsen holds here that the form of general legal norms is the hypothetical (ie conditional) 'If A is, then B *ought* to be'; individual norms, in turn, can be either hypothetical or categorical; see *Introduction to the Problems of Legal Theory* (n 4) 24f; *General Theory of Law and State* (n 4) 45ff; *Pure Theory of Law* (n 4) 76ff.

[89] Kelsen differentiates between commands, permissions and authorisations, and comes eventually to add 'derogation' to his taxonomy: see eg *Pure Theory of Law* (n 4) 15ff; 'Derogation' (n 38) 261; *General Theory of Norms* (n 9) 96ff.

[90] In this regard, Kelsen differentiates between 'dependent' and 'independent' norms: *cf* eg *Pure Theory of Law* (n 4) 54ff.

[91] The Pure Theory of Law endorses the *Stufenbau doctrine*: *cf* eg *Introduction to the Problems of Legal Theory* (n 4) 55ff, 63ff; *General Theory of Law and State* (n 4) 123ff; *Pure Theory of Law* (n 4) 221ff; *General Theory of Norms* (n 9) 258.

[92] *Introduction to the Problems of Legal Theory* (n 4) 54ff, *General Theory of Law and State* (n 4) 110ff; *Pure Theory of Law* (n 4) 193ff.

[93] *Introduction to the Problems of Legal Theory* (n 4) 62-3; *General Theory of Law and State* (n 4) 115ff, 122; *Pure Theory of Law* (n 4) 211ff.

[94] The Pure Theory endorses the claim that legal system are structurally complete: *cf* Kelsen, *Introduction to the Problems of Legal Theory* (n 4) 84ff; *General Theory of Law and State* (n 4) 146ff; 'Science and Politics' in *What is Justice? Justice, Law, and Politics in the Mirror of Science* (Berkeley, University of California Press, 1957 [1951]) 374f; *Pure Theory of Law* (n 4) 15ff, 245ff; *General Theory of Norms* (n 9) 131f, 227ff. For criticism, see E Bulygin, 'Kelsen on the Consistency and Completeness of Law', in this volume.

[95] The Pure Theory endorses the notorious doctrine of the 'tacit alternative clause': see text to n 33.

purports, as already mentioned,[96] to cure legal thought from its traditional ideological biases. That this is Kelsen's view is made clear, for example, in his unrelenting undoing of value-laden dualisms – false antinomies, he claimed – embodied in traditional jurisprudence. These include the dualism of law and state; the dualism of law ('*Recht*') in an objective and a subjective sense; the dualism of public and private law; the dualism of physical and legal person; the dualism of law-creation and law-application; and so on.[97] And just how longstanding project this project was is something that can be gathered from a 1922 essay in which Kelsen vindicates 'epistemic anarchism' as the way to establish a '*purely legal theory* of the state', ie a '*stateless theory of the state*', which 'gets rid of the idea of a state as distinct from law', and is thus the necessary step by which 'legal and political theory first push forward from the level of theology into the ranks of modern science':

> Since modern science seeks everywhere to dissolve substance into function, and has long since thrown the concept of soul overboard, along with that of force, modern psychology has become a soulless theory of the soul, and modern physics a forceless theory of force. . . . [S]o likewise is the reduction of the supralegal concept of the state to the concept of law the indispensable precondition for the development of a genuine science of law, as a *science of positive law* purified of all natural law. That is the aim of the pure theory of law, which is simultaneously the pure theory of the state, because a theory of the state is possible only as a theory of state-law, while all law is state-law, because every state is a legal state.[98]

ii. Doctrinal Description

Under this heading we can further distinguish between *static* and a *dynamic* doctrinal inquiries into law. Static description is backward-looking; it purports to account for the general and individual norms of some *given* legal order, as they have in fact been produced and applied at the moment at which the description takes place; it concerns, as we might put it, legal norms *in actu*. Dynamic description, in contrast, concerns legal norms *in potentia*: it is a forward-looking inquiry into the general norms of some given legal order *in view of their application*.

Together, these two forms of doctrinal description represent the Pure Theory's alternative to the traditional, unscientific 'legal science', which had had its origins with nineteenth-century theorists. In considering in further detail, as I now propose to do, what each of these two forms of inquiry involve, I will make use of some fresh terminology which was not Kelsen's own; but my goal, as I said, is that of presenting Kelsen's theory in its best light.

[96] *cf* point 8 in subsection II.A.

[97] See *Introduction to the Problems of Legal Theory* (n 4) 37ff, 92ff, 97ff; *General Theory of Law and State* (n 4) 78ff, 132ff, 181ff; *Pure Theory of Law* (n 4) 125ff, 191f, 233ff, 284ff, 318ff.

[98] See H Kelsen, 'God and the State' in *Essays in Legal and Moral Philosophy* (Dordrecht, Reidel, 1973 [1922]) 81–82.

1. *Static doctrinal description* of the valid norms of some given legal system at some given moment in time involves a complex series of operations which we may group into three stages.
   1.1 The first stage is the *identification of the prima facie valid legal materials* that make up a community's written and unwritten law: its written constitution, if any, its statutes, regulations, judicial decisions, customary practices and so on. This is a matter of empirical investigation, often carried out on the basis of the materials' 'self-interpretation'[99] (as 'constitution', 'law', 'regulation', 'executive order' and so on) and some legal education.
   1.2 The second stage is the *identification of all-things-considered valid norms*, understood as the 'meanings' of those authoritative acts of will which have brought about the community's valid legal materials (constitution, statutes, judicial decisions and so on). Kelsen very much leaves the point to his readers' discernment; this being the case, the following can be said about the kind of interpretative activity (*static interpretation*, as we might dub it) involved at this stage: it seems to consist in an isomorphic (or at any rate plainly iterative) interpretation of legal materials with the goals of (a) sorting out genuine materials from spurious materials, ie from those materials which, appearances notwithstanding, are unfit to express valid norms because of the absolute incompetence of the issuing agency;[100] (b) sorting out those genuine materials which are nevertheless for *semantic* reasons unfit to express valid norms;[101] (c) sorting out those genuine materials which are nevertheless *no longer* fit to express valid norms because of their persistent inefficacy (*desuetudo*);[102] (d) sorting out those genuine legal materials which are no longer fit to express valid norms because they have been repealed by valid derogatory norms; (e) sorting out conflicts between norms placed at the same hierarchical level, and the conflict-resolution criteria that officials 'ought' *according to positive law* to apply;[103] (f) sorting out conflicts between norms placed at different

[99] *cf Introduction to the Problems of Legal Theory* (n 4) 9; *Pure Theory of Law* (n 4) 3; the German term is '*Selbstdeutung*': see eg 'Methode und Grundbegriff der Reinen Rechtslehre' (n 4) 69; *Reine Rechtslehre* (n 6) 2.

[100] See the example of the 'orders' issued by the notorious 'captain' of Köpenick in 'Methode und Grundbegriff der Reinen Rechtslehre' (n 4) 78f; *Introduction to the Problems of Legal Theory* (n 4) 9.

[101] eg 'in the form of a constitutionally established statute the nation's congratulations may be conveyed to the head of the state on an anniversary of his accession to power': see *Pure Theory of Law* (n 4) 52, and *cf* also *General Theory of Law and State* (n 4) 123.

[102] *Introduction to the Problems of Legal Theory* (n 4) 63; *General Theory of Law and State* (n 4) 119ff; *Pure Theory of Law* (n 4) 211ff.

[103] We have already seen (*cf* subsection III.A.i) that Kelsen's views on the role of legal science in the *resolution* of these kinds of conflicts has evolved; thus while eg in 1960 Kelsen claims that legal science is capable of solving such conflicts 'by interpretation' (*Pure Theory of Law* (n 4) 206), in later texts he maintains instead that 'legal science is no more competent to resolve – e.g. by interpreta-

hierarchical levels, and the conflict-resolution criteria that officials 'ought' *according to positive law* to apply;[104] (g) identifying those putative legal 'gaps' which judges have claimed to be 'filling' by creating new legal norms;[105] and eventually (h) casting the all-things-considered valid norms resulting from these previous inquiries and selections in their proper logical form.

1.3 The third, and last, stage is the *description of valid legal norms*, ie the exposition of those previously identified all-things-considered valid norms (and meta-norms) in the form of *legal propositions* ('*Sollsätze*') stating what it is that one 'ought' to do according to the law.[106] It goes without saying that this description is time-dependent: it stands in need of constant readjustment in view of any new law-making, law-applying or law-repealing act (for law is a dynamic order).

2. *Dynamic doctrinal description*, in turn, and as I previously said, is forward-looking. It amounts to a 'scientific' interpretation of the general norms of some given legal system – an interpretation performed *as a service*, as it were, to judges and other officials, whose task it is to apply such general norms. It normally consists in the identification of the set of all the possible meanings of the wording of some given general norm (eg a constitutional norm, or a statutory norm) in view of its application, from the viewpoint of the community's interpretative methods, canons and criteria. Two points must be stressed. One is that scientific interpretation is not sociology of interpretation; it is, rather, the methodological unpacking of general norms in light of accepted interpretative methods: but of course this also makes it an activity bound by legal experience, presupposing empirical knowledge of a particular legal culture and of its

tion – existing conflicts of norms . . . than it is to posit them in the first place' (*General Theory of Norms* (n 9) 127). In both phases, however, Kelsen is clear that legal science *identifies* the applicable conflict-resolution criteria *according to positive law*.

[104] *General Theory of Law and State* (n 4) 153ff; *Pure Theory of Law* (n 4) 267ff; *General Theory of Norms* (n 9) 126ff.

[105] As mentioned above (see n 94), Kelsen holds, as a matter of *theoretical description*, that there are no real gaps in the law.

[106] See text to n 47 and to n 48. We could further differentiate, always in Kelsenian spirit, between (what we might call) *simple* legal propositions (which describe individual sanction-stipulating norms) and *complex* legal propositions (which describe clusters of one primary norm and its ancillary, 'dependent' laws (including power-conferring laws, legal definitions, laws providing for exceptions, procedural laws and so on: what Kelsen refers to as norm-'fragments'). *Simple* legal propositions, in turn, can be either elliptical ('If *A*, then it ought to be the case that *B*') or full-blown ('According to legal system *S*, if *A*, then it ought to be the case that *B*'). One may of course wonder whether such an exercise is really viable; the Kelsenian jurist would find herself, it seems, in the same predicament as Dworkin's Hercules: see R Dworkin, *Taking Rights Seriously* (Cambridge, Mass., Harvard University Press, 1977) 105ff. But for my present purposes it is not necessary to address the question whether Kelsen ought to be understood as setting forth an ideal, regulative standard (rather than an actually achievable goal).

methodological attitudes and commitments. A second point is that, from the standpoint of scientific interpretation, any general valid norm is really, not *a* norm, but a *set* – a 'frame'[107] – of alternative norms. This is why I characterised the dynamic description as being about valid norms *in potentia*. Here is an illustrative passage:

> [T]he task of a legal scientist interpreting a legal instrument is to show its possible meanings and to leave it to the competent legal authority to choose in accordance with political principles the one which this authority thinks the most appropriate. In showing the possibilities which the law to be applied opens to the legal authority, the legal scientist scientifically serves the law-applying function; and in revealing the ambiguity, and thus the necessity for improving the wording, he serves the law-creating function in a scientific way. If the legal scientist recommends to the legal authority one of different meanings of a legal norm, he tries to influence the law-making process and exercises a political, not a scientific, function; if he presents this interpretation as the only correct one, he is acting as a politician in the disguise of a scientist.[108]

iii. Conclusion

Let me again emphasise that I have not been concerned with the question of whether Kelsen's account of the doctrinal study of law is a satisfactory one. My concern was instead with establishing (as I believe I have done) whether Kelsen's views on the subject can be seen – or rationally reconstructed – as providing a model of a kind of *empirical* knowledge of positive law which is at once different from sociological knowledge (which is causal knowledge); from general legal theory (which is analytical-comparative study); and from legal politics *de iure condito* (which is not a form of knowledge at all).[109]

[107] *cf* text to n 69.

[108] 'Science and Politics' (n 94) 368; and see also 'Methode und Grundbegriff der Reinen Rechtslehre' (n 4) 78f; *Introduction to the Problems of Legal Theory* (n 4) 86ff; *Introduction to the Problems of Legal Theory* (n 4), 77ff; the opening note 'On Interpretation' in *The Law of the United Nations. A Critical Analysis of its Fundamental Problems* (New Yore, FA Praeger, 1950) xiii ff; and *Pure Theory of Law* (n 4) 348ff. Kelsen says nothing about the logical form of the sentences that express the propositions which are the outcomes of scientific interpretation. With some philosophical imagination, however, one might perhaps distinguish between (a) *conjectural interpretative statements* and (b) *interpretative legal propositions*. The logical form of the former would be something along the lines of 'In view of its application, valid legal norm N means: N_1 (according to interpretative method IM_1) *or* N_2 (according to interpretative method IM_2) *or*... N_n (according to interpretative method IM_n)'. The logical form of the interpretative legal propositions, in turn, would be 'According to valid legal norm N of legal system L, it is prescribed that if C_1, then it ought to be the case that S_1 (according to interpretative method IM_1) *or* that if C_2, then it ought to be the case that S_2 (according to interpretative method IM_2) *or*... that if C_n, then it ought to be the case that S_n (according to interpretative method IM_n)'.

[109] Some authors have maintained that Kelsen's theory of legal science is at odds with his theory of scientific interpretation: *cf* eg R Guastini, 'Kelsen on Legal Knowledge and Scientific Interpretation' in L Gianformaggio and SL Paulson (eds) *Cognition and Interpretation of Law* (Turin,

V. SUMMING UP

My claims in this chapter can be summarised as follows.

1. The three basic attitudes of a realistic theory of law are: anti-formalism, empiricism and anti-normativism.
2. The Pure Theory of Law offers a radically anti-formalistic and anti-conceptualist theory of law. It mounts a comprehensive critique of traditional methodological and theoretical claims characteristic of nineteenth-century Continental legal positivism.
3. The Pure Theory of Law also embodies a highly sophisticated attempt to apply an empiricist epistemology to the study of law. Kelsen strove to establish the autonomy of empirical doctrinal inquiries into law, as a different enterprise from, on the one hand, both legal sociology and general jurisprudence (which he regarded as worthwhile kinds of inquiry in their own right), and, on the other hand, traditional 'legal science' (which he viewed as not in the least scientific, but rather as legal politics in disguise).[110] In so doing, Kelsen opposed mainstream legal 'realists' who tended to reduce the scientific knowledge of law to legal sociology and thus to conceive the doctrinal study of law as irredeemably value-laden, practical and unscientific.
4. As for its anti-normativist attitude, the Pure Theory rejects the 'law as fact vs law as norm' shibboleth and suggests that we abandon both naïf realism and naïf normativism in favour of a sounder middle-way represented by (what we might call) *realistic normativism*. By 'naïf realism' I mean that sort of purely behaviourist jurisprudence which dismisses all norm-talk as pretence, and seeks to wipe off legal rights and legal duties on the back of purely 'predictivist' theories. By 'naïf normativism' I mean the notion that to know the law is to know its norms *in some objective sense*, ie the notion that norms are somehow objects 'out there' waiting to be discovered by jurists. Kelsen opposes both these routes, each of which unwarrantedly assumes that there is only one theoretically acceptable standpoint, and both of which fail to realise that the matter ultimately depends on an epistemological option. (Naïf normativism moreover espouses a view of norms which Kelsen deems false.)

Giappichelli, 1995) 107ff. On the contrary, the account I have just set forth allows us to understand both theories as perfectly compatible, and indeed as two facets of Kelsen's conception of the doctrinal study of law as a genuinely scientific enterprise.

[110] See the passage quoted to n 108 and, again, *Reine Rechtslehre* (n 6) 60 fn; 'Methode und Grundbegriff der Reinen Rechtslehre' (n 4) 78f; *Introduction to the Problems of Legal Theory* (n 4) 79ff, 90.

Kelsen's realistic normativism, by contrast, while it does assume that the law is made of norms, does so on the grounds of an explicitly acknowledged epistemological option; and it views legal norms simply as either norms *in actu* (ie as they have in fact been produced and applied at the moment at which the description takes place), which are the object of (what I proposed to call) 'static' description; or as norms *in potentia* (ie as 'frame'-norms), which are the object of (what I proposed to call) dynamic description.

8

Kelsen and Hägerström: Clearing Up Misunderstandings and Mapping Out the Common Ground

JES BJARUP*

I. INTRODUCTION

IN 1933, THE leading politics journal in Sweden featured a long essay by Hans Kelsen containing, in Swedish translation, most of his (soon to be published) *Reine Rechtslehre*.[1] At the end of March that year, Kelsen accepted an invitation to lecture in Lund, Stockholm and Uppsala.[2] In Uppsala he was introduced to Axel Hägerström (1868–1939), often considered the leading philosopher in Sweden. Hägerström, who held the Chair of practical philosophy at Uppsala University from 1911 until his retirement in 1935, was familiar both with Kelsen's *Hauptprobleme*[3] and with his *Allgemeine Staatslehre*,[4] which he thought

* I am grateful to the Edvard Cassel Stiftelse, Stockholm Universitet, for supporting my participation in the *Legal Science and Legal Theory* conference at the University of Oxford (September 2010). I am also very grateful to two anonymous reviewers, and to the editors, for comments and suggestions on an earlier version.

[1] *cf* H Kelsen, 'Den rena rättsläran. Dess Metod och Grundbegrepp' (1933) 36 *Statsvetenskaplig Tidskrift* 193–244. The text corresponds largely (though not exactly) to chs I to VIII in the *Reine Rechtslehre*; and the section on international law (ch IX in the book) is omitted. The first edition of the *Reine Rechtslehre* is available in English as *Introduction to the Problems of Legal Theory*, BL Paulson and SL Paulson transl (Oxford, Clarendon Press, 1992 [1934]). In turn, a Swedish translation of the second edition has recently been prepared by Uta Bindreiter: *cf* H Kelsen, *Den rena rättsläran* (Stockholm, Thales, 2008). This new translation will hopefully stimulate the discussion of Kelsen's doctrines in the Nordic countries.

[2] *cf* RA Métall, *Hans Kelsen. Leben und Werk* (Vienna, Franz Deuticke, 1969) 61.

[3] H Kelsen, *Hauptprobleme der Staatsrechtslehre entwickelt aus der Lehre vom Rechtssatze*, which I will quote (using original pagination) from the new edition in M Jestaedt (ed), *Hans Kelsen Werke. Volume 2* (Tübingen, Mohr Siebeck 2009 [1911]). Unless otherwise noted, translations – from this as well as other works quoted in the present chapter – are mine.

[4] H Kelsen, *Allgemeine Staatslehre* (Berlin, Julius Springer, 1925).

> well worthy of attention both for the philosopher of law and for the jurist. The prevailing theory is not just a harmless doctrine of principles with no practical importance; on the contrary, it plays an important part in the juridical interpretation of laws and other juridical decisions.[5]

Like Kelsen, Hägerström had criticised the 'will-theory' (or 'imperative-theory') of law, in a 1916 essay, in which he engaged critically with the former's 1911 *Hauptprobleme*.[6] The two philosophers share some philosophical terrain, as we shall see; but between them there is certainly room for discussion on some fundamental questions about law and legal science.

Kelsen would likely have preferred such a discussion to be dialogic. As he puts it in the *Hauptprobleme*:

> Dialogue, the most suitable form for expressing my understanding, may well have been acceptable in ancient philosophy, but is, regrettably, no longer countenanced in the modern philosophic-scientific literature.[7]

What Kelsen has here in mind is not so much, I surmise, the use of dialogue as a literary form, but the actual constructive exchange of views with his colleagues. In the 'Foreword' to the second printing of the *Hauptprobleme* he credits Alfred Verdross, Leonidas Pitamic and Adolf Merkl with theoretical developments and insights which he, Kelsen, adopted and incorporated into his own views.[8] By contrast, Hägerström does resort to the dialogical form – in his monograph *The Botanist and the Philosopher*, in which he presents a (popular) version of his ontology and epistemology[9] – but he claims not to have been 'significantly influenced by contemporary philosophy, on account of what it is . . . its uncritical point of departure'.[10]

[5] *cf* A Hägerström, 'Kelsen's Theory of Law and State' in K Olivecrona (ed), *Inquiries into the Nature of Law and Morals*, C Broad transl (Stockholm, Almqvist & Wiksell, 1953 [1928]) 261.

[6] A Hägerström, 'Is Positive Law an Expression of Will?' in K Olivecrona (ed), *Inquiries into the Nature of Law and Morals*, C Broad transl (Stockholm, Almqvist & Wiksell, 1953 [1916]) 17ff.

[7] Kelsen, *Hauptprobleme* (n 3) xii.

[8] *cf* H Kelsen, '"Foreword" to the Second Printing of *Main Problems in the Theory of Public Law*' in SL Paulson and BL Paulson (eds and transl), *Normativity and Norms. Critical Perspectives on Kelsenian Themes* (Oxford, Clarendon Press, 1998 [1923]) 13.

[9] *cf* A Hägerström, *Botanisten och filosofien. Om kunskapsfilosofiens nödvändighet* (Stockholm, Bonnier, 1910).

[10] See A Hägerström, 'A Summary of My Philosophy' in *Philosophy and Religion*, RT Sandin transl (London, George Allen & Unwin, 1964) 38. He mentions only his colleague Adolf Phalén (1884–1931), who was professor of theoretical philosophy at the University of Uppsala; and acknowledges the 'stimulation' (ibid 74) of his disciple AV Lundstedt (1882–1955), who was professor of civil law at the same University. It was thanks to Lundstedt's writings that Hägerström became known outside Sweden: see eg Lundstedt's *Die Unwissenschaftlichkeit der Rechtswissenschaft*, vol 1 (Berlin, W Rothschild, 1932); or his *Legal Thinking Revisited* (Stockholm, Almqvist & Wiksell, 1956). (In this latter work, at p 7, Lundstedt recounts having been 'impudently attacked' by Wedberg and Hedenius – whom in fact he does not name, referring to them instead as 'two brash youngsters' and 'two cocky boys' – who had accused him of 'misinterpreting Hägerström's thoughts on law'. Lundstedt translates part of Hägerström's own reply, 'where he proved that the criticism voiced was without foundation'. It is perhaps worth recalling that Wedberg was the trans-

There is no record of what Hägerström and Kelsen discussed at their meeting, nor does Kelsen mention it in his 1947 autobiography (the event was perhaps overshadowed by Kelsen's discharge from his Chair in Cologne by the Nazi government shortly after, on 12 April 1933).[11] It seems, however, that in Uppsala the debate was recalled as less than successful; Herbert Tingsten, a political scientist, described it as a curious encounter – for neither Kelsen nor Hägerström were able to understand each other.[12]

In what follows I shall try to act, retrospectively, as an intermediary of sorts, examining and contrasting Kelsen's and Hägerström's writings from the period.[13] The inquiry will reveal some common ground, and also that some points of dispute are, to a large extent, due to Hägerström's misunderstandings of Kelsen's views. The chapter is organised around four core topics. Section II is dedicated to Hägerström's and Kelsen's more general philosophical views; section III, to their (largely convergent) critiques of the 'will-theory' of law; section IV, to their (largely divergent) understanding of legal norms; and section V to their views on legal science.

II. PHILOSOPHICAL COMMITMENTS

There is common ground between Hägerström and Kelsen. Both endeavour to purify legal thinking of any 'foreign' elements. Both believe that it is the task of jurisprudence to address the epistemological and ontological questions that can be raised in connection with the law. Both agree that the object of a scientific study of the law is *positive* law – man-made law, law brought about by human action – to the exclusion of natural law or natural rights, whether based in the nature of things, reason, or God. And both accept a Kantian demarcation between 'is' ('*Sein*') and 'ought' ('*Sollen*'), endorsing the view that

> [t]he **ought** expresses a species of necessity and a connection with grounds which does not occur anywhere else in the whole of nature. In nature the understanding can cognize only **what exists**, or has been, or will be. It is impossible that something in it **ought to be** other than what, in all these time-relations, it in fact is; indeed, the **ought**, if one has merely the course of nature before one's eyes, has no significance whatsoever. We cannot ask at all what ought to happen in nature, any

lator into English of Kelsen's 1945 *General Theory of Law and State.*) For an overview of Hägerström's philosophy, with further references, see my essay 'The Philosophy of Scandinavian Legal Realism' (2005) 18 *Ratio Juris* 1ff; and P Mindus, *A Real Mind. The Life and Work of Axel Hägerström* (Dordrecht, Springer, 2009).

[11] *cf* H Kelsen, 'Autobiographie' in M Jestaedt (ed), *Hans Kelsen Werke. Volume 1* (Tübingen, Mohr Siebeck 2007 [1947]) 29ff.

[12] See Å Frändberg, 'Die skandinavische Reaktion auf Hans Kelsens *Reine Rechtslehre*' in *Der Einfluss der reinen Rechtslehre auf die Rectstheorie in verschiedenen Ländern*, vol 2 (Vienna, Manz, 1978) 69.

[13] I will concentrate therefore on Hägerström's and Kelsen's writings until 1935.

> more than we can ask what properties a circle ought to have; but we must rather ask what happens in nature, or what properties the circle has.[14]

How do these philosophical commitments manifest themselves in their works?

Kelsen maintains that there is a 'fundamental difference between thinking in terms of *is* and thinking in terms of *ought*';[15] he speaks of '*is*' and '*ought*' as two separate 'worlds'.[16] This ontological distinction identifies an unbridgeable gap. '*Is*'-questions can only be met with '*is*'-answers, '*ought*'-questions with '*ought*'-answers.

Because Kelsen also follows Kant in viewing scientific inquiry, not as a passive record of experience, but as constitutive of the very object of cognition – human beings being not mere spectators but active agents whose reason structures and orders experience – he holds that the ontological distinction between *is* and *ought* maps onto an epistemological distinction between two kinds of cognition, two kinds of science. The explanatory natural and social sciences, on the one hand, are concerned with the cognition and description of what there *is*; they purport to ascertain *causal* relations between events, and aim at formulating general causal laws to be used in explaining and predicting what happens. On the other hand we find the *normative* sciences, which are concerned with the cognition and description of *norms*, ie of what *ought* to happen, and which seek to ascertain *normative* relations between events – relations of 'imputation' ('*Zurechnung*'), as Kelsen calls them[17] – according to normative 'laws'.[18] Legal science, according to Kelsen, belongs to the latter group.[19] It is a normative science: a science of norms.[20]

In his account of German philosophy in 1911, Oscar Ewald describes Kelsen's *Hauptprobleme* as an attempt, 'with logical energy and strength, to introduce transcendentalism into jurisprudence', and notes that 'Kelsen's concept of will is remarkably similar to Herman Cohen's in his interpretation of Kant's philosophy and his *Ethik des reinen Willens*'.[21] Now, Cohen – the main figure in the so-called 'Marburg School' of Neo-Kantianism – had pressed the view that philosophical investigations into knowledge ought to proceed according to what he called the 'transcendental method', ie by inquiring into

[14] I Kant, *Critique of Pure Reason*, P Guyer and AW Wood transl (Cambridge, Cambridge University Press, 1998) 540 (A547/B575); Kant's emphasis.

[15] *Hauptprobleme* (n 3) 8.

[16] ibid 8, 10.

[17] ibid 72.

[18] See generally ibid 3ff, 57ff, and the '"Foreword" to the Second Printing of *Main Problems in the Theory of Public Law*' (n 8) 4ff, 7ff.

[19] see *Hauptprobleme* (n 3) 69f and 73 on '*legal* imputation, that is, imputation on the ground of legal norms' (Kelsen's emphasis).

[20] As we shall see in section V, this is a view with which Hägerström takes issue.

[21] *cf* O Ewald, 'Die deutsche Philosophie im Jahre 1911' (1912) 17 *Kantstudien* 397f.

the presuppositions involved in one's recognition of the fact of science.[22] But Cohen cannot have influenced Kelsen's early epistemological views. Rather, it was Ewald's piece that brought Cohen's work to Kelsen's attention.[23] As Kelsen writes in the 1923 'Foreword' to the second edition of the *Hauptprobleme*:

> It was by way of Hermann Cohen's interpretation of Kant, in particular Cohen's *Ethics of Pure Will* . . . that I arrived at the definitive epistemological point of view from which alone the correct employment of the concepts of law and state was possible. In 1912 in the *Kantstudien*, a review of *Main Problems* appeared in which my book was recognized as an attempt to apply the transcendental method to legal science, and this brought to my attention the wide-ranging parallels that existed between my concept of legal will and Cohen's views, which at that time were not known to me. I came to appreciate as the consequence of Cohen's basic epistemological position – according to which the epistemic orientation determines its object, and the epistemic object is generated logically from an origin (*Ursprung*) – that the state, in so far as it is the object of legal cognition, can only be law, for to recognize something legally or to understand something juridically means nothing other than to understand it as law.[24]

In turn, Kelsen does claim, in the Preface to his *Allgemeine Staatslehre*, to have been swayed by 'Kant's critique of reason'; he follows a method which

> is influenced – more or less consciously, more or less consistently – by Kant's critique of reason: Dualism of 'is' and 'ought'; substitution of transcendental categories as the conditions of experience for metaphysical postulates and hypostases; transformation of absolute (because qualitative and trans-systematic) antitheses within the same discipline into relative, quantitative, intra-systematic differences; passage from the subjective sphere of psychologism to the field of logical-objective validity: These are some important aspects of this method. They are the decisive guidelines for my theoretical work.[25]

It is in particular to Kant's account of theoretical reason, as put forth in the *Critique of Pure Reason* – and not to Kant's moral philosophy – that Kelsen appeals:

> Kant abandoned his method of transcendental logic . . . Kant, whose philosophy of transcendental logic was pre-eminently destined to provide the groundwork for a positivistic legal and political doctrine, stayed, as a legal philosopher, in the rut of the natural-law doctrine. Indeed, his *Groundwork of the Metaphysics of Morals* can be

[22] On Cohen (1848–1918), the 'transcendental method', and the so-called 'Marburg School' of Neo-Kantianism, see SL Paulson, 'The Great Puzzle: Kelsen's Basic Norm' in the present volume.

[23] On the topic of Kelsen's relation to Cohen, see G Edel, 'The *Hypothesis* of the Basic Norm: Hans Kelsen and Hermann Cohen' in BL Paulson and SL Pauslon (eds), *Normativity and Norms* (Oxford, Clarendon Press, 1998) 195ff.

[24] *cf* '"Foreword" to the Second Printing of *Main Problems in the Theory of Public Law*' (n 8) 15; see also Kelsen's autobiographical piece 'Selbstdarstellung' in M Jestaedt (ed), *Hans Kelsen Werke. Volume 1* (Tübingen, Mohr Siebeck 2007 [1927]) 21; and 'Autobiographie' (n 11) 36.

[25] H Kelsen, *Allgemeine Staatslehre* (n 4) vii.

> regarded as the most perfect expression of the classical doctrine of natural law as it evolved in the seventeenth and eighteenth centuries on the basis of Protestant Christianity.[26]

As for Hägerström, at the beginning of his philosophical career he, too, was influenced by Kant, as can be seen from his book on the relation between Kant's moral philosophy and his epistemology.[27] Hägerström proceeds on the assumption that philosophy is the science of sciences, concerned with providing an account of knowledge by reference to some ultimate principle that makes objective knowledge possible. But he takes contemporary Neo-Kantian philosophers to task for maintaining that Kant's inquiry into the transcendental conditions of knowledge is a *psychological* inquiry. This would imply the subordination of philosophy to psychology with regard to the foundations of the objectivity of knowledge. And such an endorsement of psychologism – with the resulting confusion of epistemological and psychological questions – is exemplified, thinks Hägerström, precisely in the work of Hermann Cohen.[28]

In Hägerström's own account, it was in the 'unity of the pure self-consciousness' that Kant had found the 'ultimate ground of the objectivity of knowledge':

> For if this consciousness – the thought, 'I think' – as present in every thought of reality, cannot itself be made an object of thought and consequently cannot be regarded as *one* consciousness among others but is rather the logical condition of the thought of a reality, then it is in and of itself universal and necessary.[29]

Yet this presupposes that 'consciousness itself is the only immediately given'; and such a presupposition – which, 'regarded as self-evident in the history of philosophy as well as in general', Hägerström himself had unquestioningly accepted in his early work[30] – is one which Hägerström eventually comes to regard as false:

[26] H Kelsen, 'Natural Law Doctrine and Legal Positivism', WH Kraus transl, published as an 'Appendix' to *General Theory of Law and State* (Cambridge, Mass., Harvard University Press, 1945) 445 (I modified the English translation of the title of Kant's *Groundwork*). In 'Die Rechtswissenschaft als Norm- oder als Kulturwissenschaft' in M Jestaedt (ed), *Hans Kelsen Werke. Volume 3* (Tübingen, Mohr Siebeck, 2010 [1916]) 590, Kelsen dismisses Kant's categorical imperative as an empty formula that only says that one ought to do what one ought to do.

[27] *cf* A Hägerström, *Kants Ethik im Verhältnis zu seinen erkenntnistheoretischen Grundgedanken systematisch dargestellt* (Uppsala, Almqvist & Wiksell, 1902); see also 'A Summary of My Philosophy' (n 10) 33ff.

[28] See ibid 2ff. The book opens with an 'Introduction to Kant's Ethics', and section 2, on pp 2–8, is dedicated to Cohen's reading of Kant. Arguably, Hägerström's charge is unjustified; Anderson has recently maintained that 'for Cohen's Kant, the transcendental forms that structure our experience are not psychological categories, but rather *epistemological conditions of the possibility of experience*': *cf* RL Anderson, 'Neo-Kantianism and the Roots of Anti-Psychologism' (2005) 13 *British Journal for the History of Philosophy* 300 (Anderson's italics, referring to Cohen's 1871 *Kants Theorie der Erfahrung*).

[29] 'A Summary of My Philosophy' (n 10) 33.

[30] see ibid.

> Every consciousness refers to something other than itself. The objectivity of knowledge cannot lie in its character of being a consciousness of its own inner objectivity of consciousness. The objectivity of knowledge must lie in the very nature of what is apprehended, in the very nature of the object.[31]

This leads him – in *Das Prinzip der Wissenschaft*,[32] which he judged his 'most important book'[33] – to advance the principle of reality as the new principle for the foundation of the objectivity of knowledge. Here Hägerström proposes his own 'Copernican revolution', which is meant as a reversal of Kant's. The latter concerned, as is well-known, the relation between the knowing subject and the known object:

> Up to now it has been assumed that all our cognition must conform to the objects; but all attempts to find out something about them *a priori* through concepts that would extend our cognition have, on this presupposition, come to nothing. Hence let us once try whether we do not get farther with the problems of metaphysics by assuming that the objects must conform to our cognition, which would agree better with the requested possibility of an *a priori* cognition of them, which is to establish something about objects before they are given to us. This would be just like the first thoughts of Copernicus, who, when he did not make good progress in the explanation of the celestial motions if he assumed that the entire celestial host revolves around the observer, tried to see if he might not have greater success if he made the observer revolve and left the stars at rest.[34]

Hägerström sees Kant's revolution as a version of epistemological idealism, or subjectivism.[35] His own counter-revolution is in turn a version of epistemological realism, or objectivism. It is a return to the pre-Kantian, medieval, scholastic view that there is an inherent conceptual structure to reality. There is for Hägerström but one world,[36] the world of objects in time and space, which is 'out there' to be known by experience. He rejects 'metaphysics', in the specific sense of the existence of any meta-physical, supernatural world over and above the physical or natural world.[37] But he is also committed to the view – which is a 'metaphysical' view, in the ordinary philosophical sense of the term – that 'sensible reality' has a 'completely logical character'.[38] Reality is intelligible; not (in terms of an idealistic metaphysics) as a spiritual reality (which he deems 'a *contradictio in adiecto*'),[39] but (in terms of a realistic

[31] ibid 36.

[32] *Das Prinzip der Wissenschaft. Eine logisch-erkenntnisstheoretische Untersuchung. I, Die Realität* (Uppsala, Almqvist & Wiksell, 1908). The title is interesting; in 1903 GE Moore had published his *Principia Ethica*, B Russell his *Principles of Mathematics*, and Frege the volume 2 of the *Grundgesetze der Arithmetik*.

[33] 'A Summary of My Philosophy' (n 10) 37.

[34] I Kant, *Critique of Pure Reason* (n 14) 110 (B xvi).

[35] *cf* 'A Summary of My Philosophy' (n 10) 38ff.

[36] ibid 54.

[37] ibid 60ff.

[38] ibid 37.

[39] ibid 55.

metaphysics) as a material reality consisting of causal relations between things and their properties which exist independently from the human mind, and indeed impact upon the human mind.[40] The knowing subject's position vis-à-vis the known object is passive rather than active.

The meta-ethical implications of these metaphysical and epistemological views are explored in 'On the Truth of Moral Ideas', Hägerström's 1911 inaugural lecture for the Chair of practical philosophy at the University of Uppsala.[41] The non-cognitivist conclusion of his inquiry as to whether there can be knowledge of what is good and bad, and right and wrong, is that – because no perceptible elements of values are present in things and actions – there are no value-concepts, and thus no value judgements that express truth-apt beliefs. This is a radical, sceptical view: a 'nihilist' view, in one sense of the term. Values are solely a matter of feelings and volitions expressed in exclamatory words for sensations of pain and pleasure:[42]

> [I]n the very conception of an obligation, of an action as valuable in the highest degree, there is present no conception of objectivity whatsoever . . . We recognize, in the midst of a manifold of other phenomena, a feeling of duty in connection with a judgment of value and a direct interest in a certain action. But all this yields nothing more than a certain kind of psychological event. That the action ought to be done is not at all a part of what we can discover. The keenest analysis of what is present reveals no such thing.[43]

Hägerström's understanding of objectivity *qua* mind-independence – for something to be objective is for it to be present outside the mind, and for it to come *to* the mind through sensation – again contrasts with Kant's. Hägerström denies that the will can be conceived as a faculty of knowledge, and rejects the idea of practical reason.[44]

[40] Hägerström's views were also at odds with CJ Böström's 'rational idealism', which was the prevailing idealist approach in Sweden (in lectures, Hägerström referred to his own approach as 'rational naturalism'). Böström (1797–1866) had occupied the Chair of practical philosophy at Uppsala University from 1842 to 1863, and enjoyed an enormous influence in Sweden; he had also been tutor to the royal princes between 1833 and 1837. Whereas Böström was hostile to empirical enquiries, Hägerström's rational naturalism is put forth as the foundation for a kind of naturalism as the only realistic approach to the scientific study of the world and the use of the method of induction to arrive at natural and social laws.

[41] My own translation of the title differs from the available English-language translation: see A Hägerström, 'On the Truth of Moral Propositions' in *Philosophy and Religion*, RT Sandin transl (London, George Allen & Unwin, 1964) 77ff.

[42] Hägerström's view is similar to Moore's in that it rejects that good is a natural property. It a moot question whether Hägerström was familiar with Moore's *Principia Ethica*; but he would certainly reject Moore's claim that good is a non-natural property that can be known by intuition. See GE Moore, *Principia Ethica* (Cambridge, Cambridge University Press, 1903) 40; and my article 'Ought and Reality. Hägerström's Inaugural Lecture Re-considered' (2000) 40 *Scandinavian Studies in Law* 11ff.

[43] Hägerström, 'On the Truth of Moral Propositions' (n 41) 88.

[44] 'A Summary of My Philosophy' (n 10) 68 ('in the area of so-called practical knowledge or knowledge of value and the alleged theoretical knowledge which is connected with it . . . every-

At one point, indeed, he objects to the Kantian principle of humanity – 'that one should treat himself and others as ends in themselves' – on the grounds that 'in this way any exploitation of man would be justified'.[45] This objection, self-contradictorily, seems itself grounded on a first-order moral judgement; moreover, and surprisingly, it appears completely to misunderstand Kant's moral philosophy. But in this regard the *political* context of those times – Hägerström refers to 'the present bitter strife between capital and labour'[46] – should be kept in mind. Hermann Cohen had declared Kant's practical philosophy to be 'the true and real originator of German socialism',[47] and to provide a programme for a new era and a new world order based on the principle of humanity. This view had met with criticism from the orthodox Marxist side; Kautsky had claimed that

> [t]he 'timeless moral law, that man ought to be an end, and at no time simply a means', has itself only an 'end' in a society in which men are used by other men simply as means to their ends. In a communist society, this possibility disappears and with that goes the necessity of the Kantian programme for the entire future world history.[48]

Though Hägerström does not mention this polemic, he was surely familiar with it, having written about Marxism himself.[49] His critique resembles Kautsky's. (He also follows the latter's view of Kant's moral philosophy as a defence of Protestantism, and objects to what he calls the 'religious element'[50] in 'popular morality',[51] which ultimately gives expression only to what he calls an 'apotheosis of man'.[52]) And – in contrast with the Kantian idea of autonomy, which he rejects – Hägerström claims that once the notion of an 'absolute authority' has been completely 'internalized and has become one with our own moral interest',

> it leads in fact to the disappearance of the moral authority . . . An actually autonomous morality is within us, determined *only* by direct regard for what we esteem most of all.[53]

thing *is* metaphysics, i.e. in reality there is for consciousness nothing but words, whose meaninglessness from a conceptual standpoint one does not see clearly').

45 'On the Truth of Moral Propositions' (n 41) 82.

46 ibid 78.

47 *cf* Cohen's introduction to FA Lange, *Geschichte des Materialismus und Kritik seiner Bedeutung in der Gegenwart*, vol 2, 7th edn (Leipzig, J Baedeker, 1902) 524.

48 *cf* K Kautsky, *Ethics and the Materialistic conception of History*, JB Askew transl, 3rd edn (Chicago, CH Kerr, 1909 [1906]) 57f.

49 A Hägerström, *Social Teleologi i Marxismen* [Social Teleology in Marxism] (Uppsala Universitets Årsskrift, 1909) 1–72.

50 'On the Truth of Moral Propositions' (n 41) 86.

51 ibid 94.

52 ibid 90.

53 ibid 93.

What we esteem most of all, what we long for 'more than anything else', he says, is 'happiness and the refinement of the race'.[54] These can be brought about by peaceful means if humans can be made to realise that their moral beliefs about what is right and wrong have no legitimate claim to absolute truth or correctness. 'As a matter of fact', he observes, 'the lack of restraint in the class-hatred of our day has its roots in the fact that popular morality makes its own values absolutely authoritative'[55]; after all, 'one fights better if one believes that one has right on one's side'.[56] But if the mind is thereby purified from the false belief that there are objective moral truths, and comes to realise that there is no possibility of being either *right* or *wrong* in such matters, then perhaps the way is paved for the dissolution of the conflict between social classes, which seems to be predicated upon just such a false belief.[57]

Although our moral vocabulary does not lend itself, according to Hägerström, to cognitivist interpretations, it can still be used either emotively, to express feelings and desires, or suggestively, to regulate and bring about human behaviour (eg with the imperative 'Thou shalt'). In effect Hägerström is adamant that his views do not lead to the 'dissolution of morality':

> Why should the universal, social feeling-reaction against the anti-social individual and anti-social behaviour, which in everyone is directed primarily against others and secondarily against himself, disappear just because one ceases to believe that the repulsiveness is a predicate of the person or of the behaviour? Should the 'Fie!' become impossible just because one knows that 'Fie' is not a property? When we understand what significance the matter has for the society in which we live and before which we simply cannot stand indifferent, why should we not wish to take part in the hammering together of a close association between the words, 'Thou shalt not!' and particular kinds of action, like theft, murder, and fraud, even if we do not assume that there is a practical law which declares what we 'must' do in an objectively valid manner?[58]

We are now in a position to draw more parallels with Kelsen's views, with regard to the two authors' general philosophical commitments. Like Hägerström, Kelsen held that 'science is unable, and therefore not entitled, to offer value judgments'.[59] Like Hägerström, Kelsen supported the Social Democratic Party, maintaining 'social and intellectual contacts with the lead-

[54] ibid 94.

[55] ibid.

[56] *cf* A Hägerström, 'General View. Introductory chapter to the work: *Der römische Obligationsbegriff im Lichte der allgemeinen römischen Rechtsanschauung. I.*' in K Olivecrona (ed), *Inquiries into the Nature of Law and Morals*, C Broad transl (Stockholm, Almqvist & Wiksell, 1953 [1927]) 5.

[57] See generally 'On the Truth of Moral Propositions' (n 41) 92–95.

[58] 'A Summary of My Philosophy' (n 10) 71f. The short answer, of course, would be that it is precisely because there can be no true moral beliefs that the use of the moral vocabulary is a sham; see TH Irwin, 'The Threefold Cord: Reconciling Strategies in Moral Theory' (2008) 108 *Proceedings of the Aristotelian Society* 123–24.

[59] Kelsen, 'Natural Law Doctrine and Legal Positivism' (n 26) 440.

ing theoreticians of the Austrian social democratic movement, including Karl Renner, Otto Bauer and Max Adler'.[60] Like Hägerström, he thought that Kant's account of natural law was rooted in Protestant Christianity, and that it ought to be discarded in favour of a 'frank and uncompromising confession of relativism, which is the inescapable consequence of any real elimination of metaphysics'.[61] And finally he believed, like Hägerström, that moral relativism leads to tolerance and peace.[62]

III. THE 'WILL-THEORY' OF LAW

'In nearly all modern jural and political discussion that styles itself scientific', writes Morris Cohen in a 1916 article, 'law is defined as the will of the sovereign'.[63] Cohen's article is a discussion of the division between idealists and realists. The former, in his account, 'are so impressed with the ideal order, which visible things only partly embody, that they are charged with neglecting the poor brute facts'. The latter 'are so impressed with the hard actual facts . . . that they are charged with neglecting the possibilities of change or improvement inherent in things'.[64] And both approaches are said to have representatives in the domain of jurisprudence:

> If . . . we look for the realistic and idealistic motives in legal thought, we find them in the conflicting views that law is reason or justice, and that law is force, the will of the sovereign, or the interest of the stronger or dominant class.[65]

One can safely classify both Kelsen and Hägerström as anti-idealistic in Cohen's sense. Both reject traditional theories of natural law or natural rights.[66] But this does not mean that they fall on the realistic side, at least not as Cohen defines it. Olivecrona, quoting Cohen, corrects the picture by pointing out that Hägerström was a prominent critic of the will-theory. In fact Olivecrona says more: he singles out Hägerström as 'the foremost among the critics of the will-theory'.[67] Yet this is too strong; it overlooks the influence of Kelsen's *Hauptprobleme* – where Kelsen 'emphatically reject[s] the received

[60] C Jabloner, 'Kelsen and his Circle: The Viennese Years' (1998) 9 *European Journal of International Law* 377.

[61] 'Natural Law Doctrine and Legal Positivism' (n 26) 444.

[62] This contention is of course debatable; see my essay 'Kelsen's Theory of Law and Philosophy of Justice' in R Tur and W Twining (eds), *Essays on Kelsen* (Oxford, Clarendon Press, 1986) 273ff.

[63] *cf* MR Cohen, '"Real" and "Ideal" Forces in Civil Law' (1916) 26 *International Journal of Ethics* 348.

[64] ibid 347.

[65] ibid 348.

[66] *cf Hauptprobleme* (n 3) 97; Hägerström, 'Is Positive Law an Expression of Will?' (n 6) 17f.

[67] *cf* K Olivecrona, *Rätten och Viljan. Två uppstser av Axel Hägerström* (Lund, Gleerup, 1961) 10.

opinion that the law is a collection of *imperatives*'[68] – on Hägerström's own views, and thus also (as Jansson points out) on the development of Scandinavian Legal Realism more generally.[69]

There are various points of similarity. In his essay 1916 'Is Positive Law an Expression of Will?' Hägerström departs from a familiar alternative:

> Law is sometimes regarded as being essentially an object of theoretical cognition, *i.e.* the kind of cognition which determines the nature of what actually exists. But it is also regarded as something which is in essence presented only to an evaluating consciousness, *i.e.*, an awareness of what ought to be regardless of the actual constitution of reality. In the first case it is assumed to be a certain actual existent, *e.g.*, a certain system of rules of conduct which are actually realized in practice, or as demands issuing from a certain will. In the second case it is regarded as being a certain system of valid principles which ought, either conditionally or unconditionally, to be obeyed.[70]

In taking the first route, as he does, Hägerström is of course in line with Kelsen. His concern is with emphasising 'the positive character of law . . . as against the theory of natural rights'.[71] Note, also, how he defines his specific object of inquiry:

> [My question] is obviously not a question of how law has *arisen* through human will. The question here is about positive law as such, no matter how it may have arisen. Is it, as it now exists and as jurisprudence analyses it, the content of a will in the sense suggested? To determine the conditions of its origin of course settles nothing about its essential nature. A machine comes into existence and is brought into action by a human will. But the investigation of the machine's structure and mode of operation is not, for that reason, an investigation of a certain human activity. It is concerned with a certain limited part of external nature, which works in a certain way in accordance with the laws of that nature.[72]

In maintaining that the origin of law is irrelevant Hägerström may have in mind Hegel's claim that 'the question of the form in which [legal and political

[68] *cf* '"Foreword" to the Second Printing of *Main Problems in the Theory of Public Law*' (n 8) 5 (Kelsen's italics). Kelsen's views on the will-theory of law would change at a later stage of his career; *cf* H Kelsen, 'Professor Stone and the Pure Theory of Law' (1965) 17 *Stanford Law Review* 1138f.

[69] *cf* eg Hägerström, 'Is Positive Law an Expression of Will?' (n 6) 19ff, 51f; 'On the Question of the Notion of Law. 1. The Will-Theory' in *Inquiries into the Nature of Law and Morals*, C Broad transl (Stockholm, Almqvist & Wiksell, 1953 [1916]); and see JM Jansson, *Hans Kelsens statsteori mot bakgrunden av hans rättsfilosofiska åskådning* (Helsinki, dissert. 1950) 89, 117.

[70] 'Is Positive Law an Expression of Will?' (n 6) 17.

[71] ibid.

[72] ibid 18. The implied analogy between law and a machine is hardly felicitous. There is a crucial difference between the mechanical accounts of the workings of machines according to causal laws which in no way depend upon human will, on the one hand, and jurisprudential accounts of the operations of positive legal systems, on the other.

institutions] arose or were introduced is irrelevant to a consideration of their rational basis'.[73] But then he might have been following Kelsen instead, who draws a similar distinction between 'genetic-material' questions regarding how legal norms may have come into existence – which is a purely 'social' issue – and questions about the nature of law, law in the 'objective' sense. It would be a methodological mistake, Kelsen holds, to infer, from the fact that positive laws have been intentionally enacted by state organs, that such laws are the product of the state's 'will'.[74] And, also like Kelsen, Hägerström grants, of course, that 'law is, at any rate to a large extent, an expression of interests'.[75] He does not deny that law is an 'expression of will' in the sense that law is intentionally posited by human acts. His point is, rather, that this does not settle the question whether the *content* of the law is itself to be regarded as an expression of will, which is what the imperative-theory holds.

Hägerström's general concern is to establish the claim that 'it is impossible to indicate any will such that rules of law could be held to be its commands or declarations'.[76] He summarises his results as follows:

> If the will-theory concerning positive law regards the latter as a system of imperatives or declarations on the part of the *legal* power, it is involved in a circle. If a '*general will*' is assumed, that will must be supposed to be either the will of all or a super-individual will. On the former alternative the theory comes into conflict with facts; on the latter it leads to absurdities. If the basis of the theory is alleged to be *the will of the holder or holders of de facto power* in a society, the difficulty arises that the law itself is the foundation and the limit of that *de facto* power. If, finally, the *power actually enforcing the law* (the 'state-will') is taken as starting-point, we are faced with the impossibility of assigning this to an actual will. But this exhausts the possible forms of the theory.[77]

In the process, he uses Kelsen's 'acute criticism'[78] of the 'will-theory' in his own assessment of attempts to conceptualise positive law as 'the content of a certain will, endowed with power and active in society'.[79] Thus he subscribes to Kelsen's view that

> the actual will of the sovereign can have no legal significance in regard to an act of the government; no more legal significance can be attributed to the actual intention of a member of parliament at the moment when he gives his vote, perhaps without having read the proposed enactment. . . . [T]he *permanence* of the validity of

[73] GWF Hegel, *Outlines of the Philosophy of Right*, TM Knox transl (Oxford, Oxford University Press, 2008) 208 (§219).

[74] *Hauptprobleme* (n 3) 98; see also 160, 183; and 'Is Positive Law an Expression of Will?' (n 6) 19.

[75] 'Is Positive Law an Expression of Will?' (n 6) 41.

[76] Hägerström, 'On the Question of the Notion of Law' (n 69) 250.

[77] 'Is Positive Law an Expression of Will?' (n 6) 55.

[78] 'Kelsen's Theory of Law and State' (n 5) 260.

[79] 'Is Positive Law an Expression of Will?' (n 6) 17.

> a law would be inconsistent with its being founded on the always contingent will of a certain person or persons.[80]

And he also agrees with Kelsen's contention, 'against the imperative-theory', that 'an imperative as such presupposes a recipient which is in some way influenced by it':

> If legal duties were constituted by imperatives, they would be conditioned by a social-psychological condition of obedience on the part of the subjects which would always be contingent. But such a notion of duties would not coincide with the juridical notion of duties, since the subjects are not in general acquainted with the legal prescripts, and moreover, are not always certainly influenced by them. The existence of a legal duty has always to be decided independently of such subjective conditions.[81]

This is not to say, of course, that there is no divergence. The very first argumentative step in Hägerström's inquiry is to criticise as 'circular' the theory – one of whose endorsers, he says, is Kelsen – according to which 'the will, whose content expressed in a certain way is to constitute law, [is] *itself determined by the law*'.[82]

In order to understand this charge we need to learn a bit more about Kelsen's own views. The gist of Kelsen's criticism of traditional will-theories is that such theories wrongly account for law by reference to an empirical, psychological concept of will. They unwarrantedly treat legal norms as identical with actual imperatives, ie with actual expressions of acts of will concerning the behaviour of another human being. Moreover, traditional theories are also wrong in supposing that the form of the inter-personal imperative aptly captures the normative content of a legal system. Legal norms have an 'objective' normative meaning; they cannot be conceptualised in terms of subjective acts of will such as commands or other imperative utterances.[83] Nor can their validity be accounted for by reference to the wilful acceptance on the part of their addressees: differently from morality, whose authority is autonomous – and thus will-based – the authority of the law is heteronomous, and the validity of legal norms independent of the will or opinion of legal subjects.[84]

For the traditional conception according to which legal validity is dependent upon its being willed, however, Kelsen substitutes his own view of the will of the state as a 'made up' ('*ersonnene*') fact – as a 'fiction' – that exists only

[80] 'Kelsen's Theory of Law and State' (n 5) 259 (referring to *Hauptprobleme* (n 3) 176, 487, 552f; Hägerström's emphasis).

[81] ibid 260. Hägeström also endorses Kelsen's objection, 'against the theory of moral natural law', that '[p]ositive legal duty can be distinguished from moral duty only through the fact that the former is connected with compulsion, and therefore can be constituted only through such legal prescripts': *cf* ibid (referring to *Hauptprobleme* (n 3) 340).

[82] 'Is Positive Law an Expression of Will?' (n 6) 18 (Hägerström's emphasis).

[83] *Hauptprobleme* (n 3) 228.

[84] ibid 204.

'in the ethical juridical point of view',[85] which is the point of view of legal science ('*Jurisprudenz*'). And this is the claim with which Hägerström takes issue. According to Kelsen, Hägerström points out, the reconstructed legal norms – the *Rechtssätze*[86] – present themselves as 'an expression of the will of the state'.[87] But at the same time Kelsen holds that the will of the state presents itself only from the 'ethical juridical point of view' – ie that 'the will of the state exists only in view of the reconstructed legal norms'.[88] Hence the charge of circularity, for

> in that case the position is that the notion of a reconstructed legal norm is defined in terms of the will of the state, whilst the latter is itself as juridical notion in the sense that it is essentially one that is applied in reconstructed legal norms. It cannot therefore be defined without the notion of a reconstructed legal norm.[89]

Does the charge stand? I do not think it does. Some pages ahead, Hägerström engages with John Austin's theory of law, and particularly with his well-known definition of a sovereign as a 'determinate human superior, not in the habit of obedience to a like superior', who receives 'habitual obedience from the bulk of a given society'.[90] And Hägerström agrees that in principle

> law can be defined *without circularity* as a system of imperatives or declarations of intention issuing from certain independently [de facto] authoritative persons or complexes of persons in a society, who are in a position to carry out the intentions thus expressed because the members of the society regularly obey them.[91]

His rejoinder to Austin's theory is, instead, that it implies that constitutional law can only be conceptualised as positive morality, and not as positive law: 'it implies that the constitution, *according to its own meaning*, cannot be applied to those in supreme authority'.[92] This, of course, is acknowledged by Austin; but

[85] ibid 179.

[86] 'Reconstructed legal norm' is Stanley Paulson's proposed translation for the specific sense in which in his earlier works – though not in later ones – Kelsen uses '*Rechtssatz*': see Paulson's 'Supplementary Notes' to his translation of H Kelsen, *Introduction to the Problems of Legal Theory* (n 1) 132ff.

[87] 'Is Positive Law an Expression of Will?' (n 6) 19.

[88] ibid 20. Here and in the excerpted passage that follows I modify CD Broad's translation, substituting 'reconstructed legal norm(s)' for Broad's 'rule(s) of law': see n 86.

[89] ibid.

[90] ibid 29. It is a comparative merit of Hägerström's approach that he engages with Austin's theory of law, which Kelsen had not addressed in the *Hauptprobleme*. Most likely Austin's works were unknown to Kelsen at the time. Alf Ross discusses and extols Austin's analytical approach in his *Theorie der Rechtsquellen. Ein Beitrag zur Theorie des positiven Rechts auf Grundlage dogmenhistorischer Untersuchungen* (Vienna, Franz Deuticke, 1929), and notes that Austin seems to be unknown on the Continent. Ross's book was dedicated to Kelsen, and published as vol 12 in the series *Wiener Staats- u. Rechtswissenschaftliche Studien*, which was edited by Kelsen. So it was most probably Ross who introduced Austin to Kelsen – who first discusses Austin's theory in 'The Pure Theory of Law and Analytical Jurisprudence' (1941) 55 *Harvard Law Review* 44ff.

[91] 'Is Positive Law an Expression of Will?' (n 6) 28f (my emphasis).

[92] ibid (Hägerström's emphasis).

by doing so, Hägerström objects, Austin is taking 'pure despotism' as a 'model' for his theory of law.[93] If on the other hand one were to agree that 'in constitutional states, the supreme authority must base itself on the established constitution' – if it is true, in other words, that a 'sovereign' can only be identified and defined *by reference to the law* – then any theory which, like Austin's, defines law in terms of the 'commands' of a sovereign *would* emerge as a 'gross logical circle'.[94]

This suggests, however, that Hägerström's charge of circularity supposes that those he criticises are indeed committed to the view that there *is* some unified 'will' of the state which must be (or assumed to be) in place if one is to be able to identify positive law to begin with. Yet this is not Kelsen's view. Kelsen's claims about the 'will of the state' *qua* juridical construction are simply a way of conveying the fact that we can only make sense of the notion that law is – as Hägerström would agree that it is – created by human actions if we are able to interpret such acts, not as mere 'subjective' acts of will performed by this or that individual, but indeed as acts 'of the state'. What this means, says Kelsen, is that such acts are *imputed* ('*zugerechnet*'), not to the individuals who have actually performed them, but to a different 'person' – viz. to the state – and thus that the 'will of the state' is the common point towards which all lines of imputation converge.[95] But of course not just *any* action by any individual will count as an action of the state: and if one asks what is the criterion according to which *some* acts of will by some individuals, but not others, can be imputed to the state as *its* actions, then the answer is evidently to be found, says Kelsen, *in the positive law itself.* It is the positive law that determines what facts – what '*Tatbestände*' – can be attributed, not to the individuals themselves, but to the state. And this is all that Kelsen means by the claim that the 'will' of the state is itself 'determined by the law', as Hägeström puts it:[96] that

> [i]f one says that the law (*Gesetz*) contains the will of the state, this means solely that the law determines what facts (*Tatbestände*) are to count as actions of the state, as actions 'willed' by the state, ie that such actions are to be attributed to the state and

[93] ibid 35; in 'Kelsen's Theory of Law and State' (n 5) 296–97 a similar objection is advanced against Kelsen (referring to the latter's *Allgemeine Staatslehre* (n 4) 334). It should be noted that both in 'Is Positive Law an Expression of Will?' (n 6) and in 'On the Question of the Notion of Law' (n 69) Hägerström refers to Sir Henry Maine's *Lectures on the Early History of Institutions*, 7th edn (London, Murray, 1905); and that at 349 Maine compares Austin's sovereign with a 'despot' with 'the power of compelling the other members of the community to do exactly as it pleases'. This seems to me to be a distortion of Austin's views: see my 'Sense and Nonsense About Austin's Jurisprudence from a Scandinavian Perspective' in M Freeman and P Mindus, *The Legacy of John Austin's Jurisprudence* (Dordrecht, Springer, 2013) 107ff.

[94] 'Is Positive Law an Expression of Will?' (n 6) 34.

[95] *Hauptprobleme* (n 3) 183.

[96] 'Is Positive Law an Expression of Will?' (n 6) 18.

> not to the physical agents (who for that reason are its 'organs'). It means solely that the rule according to which this imputation is to take place is found in the law.[97]

Thus Hägerström's charge of circularity fails. His concern, as we saw, is with establishing that in jurisprudence there is no actual fact that corresponds to the 'will' of the state, and – as Hägerström notes[98] – Kelsen would certainly agree. The point proves nothing against (or for, for that matter) Kelsen's own particular concern, which is with the conditions under which certain acts by certain individuals can count as acts of legal *norm*-creation.

IV. LEGAL NORMS

This brings us into the topic of legal norms. Here there seem to be quite a few more points of divergence between Hägerström and Kelsen – at least judging by the former's assessments of the latter's views. Kelsen is accused by Hägerström of misunderstanding 'the plain *meaning*' of positive legal rules.[99] On closer inspection, however, as we shall see, it emerges that it is Hägerström's who, for the most part, misunderstands Kelsen. I will focus on five points that illustrate this claim.

A. The Legal Duty

Kelsen characterises the legal norm as a hypothetical judgement[100] whose 'specific form'[101] – the form of legal 'imputation'[102] – is that under certain conditions (particularly certain human actions, which represent 'delicts'), the state ought to bring about certain other actions, which represent the consequences of those conditioning facts.[103] These consequences are coercive measures: penalties and executive acts.[104] A (simplified) example of a legal norm, then, would be 'If A steals, the state ought to punish A'. The act of stealing is

[97] *Hauptprobleme* (n 3) 183f (note the quotation marks, which are Kelsen's own); *cf* also ibid 294, 296, 521, 619f.

[98] 'Is Positive Law an Expression of Will?' (n 6) 19.

[99] 'Kelsen's Theory of Law and State' (n 5) 278.

[100] Let me once again stress that it is with Kelsen's early doctrine that I am presently concerned. At this stage Kelsen had not satisfactorily drawn the distinction between the (descriptive) legal proposition (the '*Rechtssatz*') and the (prescriptive) legal norm (the '*Rechtsnorm*'), which features in later works: see eg *General Theory of Law and State* (n 26) 45ff, or *The Pure Theory of Law*, 2nd edn, M Knight transl (Berkeley, University of California Press, 1967 [1960]) 71ff; and see also, on the topic, Kelsen's remarks in 'Professor Stone and the Pure Theory of Law' (n 68) 1132f.

[101] *Hauptprobleme* (n 3) 275.

[102] *cf* text to n 17.

[103] *Hauptprobleme* (n 3) 212.

[104] ibid 213.

not, therefore, a violation of the legal norm: it is, rather, says Kelsen, a *condition* for a given action of the state – is a condition of the attribution to the state, as *its* action, of a given act of punishment.[105]

This doctrine forms the basis of Kelsen's analyses of basic concepts such as the concept of a legal duty or that of a legal person.[106] We will come back to the latter issue in the following subsection. As for the former, Kelsen's view is that the reconstructed legal norm *implies* that legal subjects have the duty not to perform the action which conditions the sanction. In a passage that Hägerström quotes, Kelsen says that

> The judgment, which is justified on the ground of the legal order, that the state would will to punish or take executive action against a person if he were to behave in a certain way forces us to the judgment that this person is under a legal obligation to behave in a way which is the contradictory opposite to that which is the condition under which the state would so will.[107]

Hägerström takes issue with this analysis; it 'lands us', he says, 'in a curious situation'. According to Kelsen, he notes, 'the legal ought should as such mean a content willed by the state, and should therefore mark out a certain action as an act of the legal unity itself', ie as an act – which is the state's punishment or executive action – which is imputed the state.[108] But the 'duty' – for legal subjects – which Kelsen holds can be derived from the reconstructed legal norm is 'a legal ought which is not concerned with the state itself, and therefore cannot mean an action pertaining to the legal unity itself'.[109]

The implied accusation against Kelsen is not only one of inconsistency – it is one of anti-positivism: for Hägerström's explanation for this Kelsenian doctrine is that

> There can be no doubt that Kelsen has here allowed himself to be unconsciously influenced by the demands of the sense of justice. Punishment and executive action seem not to be *just* when no legal duty has been transgressed. So such a duty has to be assumed as the precondition of legal constraint. This of course conflicts with the positivist principle.[110]

But Hägerström misreads Kelsen. Kelsen is clear that in speaking of the legal subject's 'duty' he is not postulating any parallel strand of legal norms, or

[105] *cf* ibid 206f; *Allgemeine Staatslehre* (n 4) 51.

[106] For developments see my essay 'Hägerström's Critique of Kelsen's Pure Theory of Law' in O Weinberger and W Krawietz (eds), *Reine Rechtslehre im Spiegel ihrer Fortsetzer und Kritiker* (Vienna, Springer 1988) 38f.

[107] *Hauptprobleme* (n 3) 207. In this particular case I use Broad's translation in Hägerström, 'Kelsen's Theory of Law and State' (n 5) 266; but *cf* similar passages in *Hauptprobleme* 73 or 230; or in *Allgemeine Staatslehre* 51.

[108] Recall text to n 95.

[109] 'Kelsen's Theory of Law and State' (n 5) 266.

[110] ibid (Hägerström's emphasis).

committing himself to 'a legal ought which is not concerned with the state itself'. 'Objectively', the legal norm proper – which he refers to as the 'primary norm'[111] – is the norm in which the delict features as a condition of the state's sanction. It is only if one considers, 'subjectively', the social *purpose* of any such norm – which is to prevent legal subjects from performing certain acts – that one can speak of the 'obligation' imposed upon the subjects. The delict, says Kelsen, is a 'denial of the social purpose of the social order'.[112] This disposes of Hägerström's objection, which wrongly supposes that the secondary 'obligation' has the same meaning as the primary legal 'ought'.

Hägerström moreover protests – against Kelsen's claim, which he quotes, that 'to "infringe" a norm, or to "transgress" it, means simply and solely to behave in a way which is *opposed to the purpose* of a norm' – that 'the legal ought which can be transgressed, the ought which holds for men, reveals itself a curious hybrid of the juridical and the sociological points of view!'[113] But this again misses the point. Kelsen consistently acknowledges that a norm can be said to have a 'purpose' only if it is seen from a 'teleological' point of view – and he maintains that such investigations into social scope are not the concern of legal science, which occupies itself only with 'formal' analysis of the legal norm.[114] Purpose, he says, is 'alien to legal construction'.[115]

B. The Legal Person

The principle of imputation is related to Kelsen's concept of a legal person. This is a normative concept, to be distinguished from the biological and psychological concept of a man. A person, in Kelsen's analysis, is any subject of imputation: any subject (not necessarily a human being[116]) to whom an event can be imputed as their own action.[117] Thus personhood is an 'absolutely artificial' construct.[118] It is the product of a process of imputation which is itself based on the legal order:

> Although law is doubtlessly made by human beings and for human beings, and although the *scope* of a legal order is above all the human being, for the [specifically] legal consideration, which is essentially and solely *formal*, this scope is

[111] *Allgemeine Staatslehre* (n 4) 51.
[112] *cf Hauptprobleme* (n 3) 231, and also 311.
[113] 'Kelsen's Theory of Law and State' (n 5) 267.
[114] *Hauptprobleme* (n 3) 275.
[115] ibid 273.
[116] ibid 519.
[117] cp the Kantian formulation in *The Metaphysic of Morals* AK 6:233: 'person is a subject whose action can be *imputed* to him'; see I Kant, *Practical Philosophy*, MJ Gregor transl (Cambridge, Cambridge University Press, 1996) 378.
[118] *Hauptprobleme* (n 3) 518.

> immaterial; there is no essentially necessary connection between the concept of a man and that of a person.[119]

This means also that, from the formal, legal point of view, the state and the other legal subjects are, *qua* legal persons, on a par. Incidentally, this is something which, according to Kelsen, will-theories – defining law, as they do, in terms of a relation of superiority between the state (with its commands) and the legal subjects – fail to see.[120]

Hägerström does not mention this latter aspect in his critical assessment of Kelsen's views on the concept of a 'juridical person'. He finds the idea 'mystical' and 'other-wordly',[121] and inconsistent with claims – which Kelsen also makes – that *human beings* rather than persons 'have' rights and legal duties, and particularly that legal wrongs can be imputed to *human beings* rather than to juridical persons. Kelsen would have to concede, Hägerström suggests, that 'the "man" is relevant . . . only as an item in that state of affairs, viz. the wrong', which 'juridically is entirely referred' to the legal person. 'It is just a plain contradiction', he says, 'when Kelsen also speaks of the man as having legal rights and duties'.[122] Indeed, Hägerström asserts that Kelsen is committed to the view that 'the jurist as such must *deny* that there are men in the biological sense!'[123]

This criticism is unjustified. Hägerström fails to notice that Kelsen explicitly acknowledges that

> the legal system imposes obligations only on human beings. In this sense, only human beings 'have' rights or obligations, since it is precisely 'human' behaviour that is the content of legal norms. The 'person' – physical as well as legal – is nothing other than the personification of a complex of norms establishing human behaviour; specifically, the physical person is the personification of the legal norms imposing obligations on a particular human being. Thus, the person 'has' rights and obligations in an altogether different sense than does the human being. That the *human being* has legal obligations means that the behaviour of this human being is, in a specific way, the content of legal norms. That a *person* has obligations means that human behaviour established as a legal obligation is linked to the unity of a system of norms, is within the unity of a system alongside other reconstructed legal norms regulating human behaviour.[124]

Hägerström moreover remarks that Kelsen's attempt to 'purify the juridical notion of obligation' led him to approach 'primitive superstition and medieval scholasticism':

[119] ibid 518f (Kelsen's emphasis).
[120] ibid 233.
[121] 'Kelsen's Theory of Law and State' (n 5) 269.
[122] ibid 270.
[123] ibid 268; the exclamation mark is Hägerström's.
[124] '"Foreword" to the Second Printing of *Main Problems in the Theory of Public Law*' (n 8) 17.

> It is true that [Kelsen] holds that the mystical juridical person, elevated above the whole of nature, to whom wrong-doing is imputed, is only a juridical construct and therefore lacks the palpable reality of the ghosts of superstition. Nevertheless the jurist as such must surely *conceive* something as the subject of imputation for wrong-doing, when he uses his words person, partial system of norms, etc. In so far as he does so he approaches decidedly to the old animistic belief that the *innermost* part of a man – his *animus* or *anima* – is contaminated by his crime . . . Compare the statement of Kelsen that it is not the action or the failure to act 'which is praised or blamed, rewarded or punished, or held to be responsible, but the person.'[125]

Again, this seems to me to misunderstand Kelsen. In saying that a human being has an obligation or duty to φ one says *nothing* about this 'innermost part'. One says only (according to Kelsen) that the conduct of φ-ing is regulated by legal norms as a condition for the application of force by the state. Nor does Kelsen's view that only the juridical person, and not the biological man, can be the subject proper of responsibility and 'guilt', commit him to postulating some kind of supernatural 'inner essence of a man'.[126] Kelsen's emphasis, on the contrary, is that – differently from traditional theories, who view a man's (psychological) 'guilt' as a precondition of legal punishment – it is the fact that punishment is legally prescribed for a given action φ that grounds the attribution of (juridical) guilt, and that psychological guilt is legally irrelevant. In a passage that Hägerström also quotes, he clearly says that

> Only the man [ie the human being], and not the [legal] person, can 'will' or 'cognize' in the psychological sense; and, if the latter and not the former is the subject of 'guilt', then guilt cannot consist in any kind of willing or cognising.[127]

Again, this does not amount to any sort of *denial* that there 'is' such a thing as psychological guilt, a human being, or that 'one *should* act *morally*' (as Hägerström also complains[128]). It amounts only to the contention that it is not within the province of legal science to consider man from a biological perspective, or to consider a person from a moral perspective.

C. The Basic Norm and the Creation of Positive Law

Kelsen maintains (as Hägerström notes) that the 'ought' is 'an essentially different category' from the 'is'. It follows that 'the ought as such can . . . be deduced only from another ought'.[129]

[125] 'Kelsen's Theory of Law and State' (n 5) 271f.
[126] ibid 269.
[127] ibid 269 (referring to *Hauptprobleme* (n 3) 142f).
[128] ibid 268 (Hägerström's emphasis).
[129] ibid 262 (referring to *Hauptprobleme* (n 3) 6ff).

There are for Kelsen two different ways in which norms may be said to 'derive' – and thus 'obtain their validity' – from other norms.[130] The norms of a 'static' normative order may be 'directly' derived from other, 'higher' norms, in virtue of their content. For example, 'the basic norm of truth or truthfulness yields the norms: "you shall not defraud", "you shall keep your promise", etc': these norms 'follow from the basic norm *without requiring a special act of norm-making, and act of human will*'.[131] But this is not what typically happens with legal systems. A legal system is fundamentally a 'dynamic system'. Its basic norm 'empowers a specific human will to create norms', and thus 'no mere intellectual operation can derive a single special norm from it': a 'special act of norm-creation or law-making is needed'.[132] Thus the law 'regulates its own creation and application'[133] in a hierarchically structured system which takes the basic norm as its starting point. The basic norm authorises certain persons to create a constitution, which in turn regulates the creation by a legislature of 'lower'-level general norms; these are in turn applied by courts and administrative agents whose decisions create individual, concrete norms; and these norms may then – at the end-point of the legal process – be executed.[134]

As is well-known, the basic norm, according to Kelsen, is a necessary presupposition of legal thinking. It *grounds* ('*begründet*') the system of positive norms:

> [The basic norm is a hypothetical norm] which – qua hypothesis – has been introduced by legal cognition in order to understand, as elements of the same 'law'-system, both the material to be qualified as legal and the facts to be interpreted as legal acts.[135]

And Kelsen adds:

> the hypothesis and the material which is to be cognised in function of the hypothesis reciprocally determine one another. Theirs is a relation of correlation, analogous to the one that exists between fact and hypothesis in the domain of scientific-naturalist cognition.[136]

[130] *cf* 'Natural Law Doctrine and Legal Positivism' (n 26) 399.

[131] ibid 400 (my emphasis).

[132] ibid.

[133] *Allgemeine Staatslehre* (n 4) 250.

[134] See, generally, ibid 229ff. At 268 of his review of Kelsen's *Allgemeine Staatslehre* Hägerström quotes Kelsen's assertion, in the *Hauptprobleme* (n 3) 411, that 'That which takes place in the act of legislation is the great *mystery* of law and of the state'. Hägerström exclaims, ironically, that 'one is inevitably reminded of a medieval thinker who discusses the great mystery of the *God-man*!' (Hägerström's emphasis). This is uncharitable; what Kelsen offers in the *Hauptprobleme* is a *static* account of law: the procedure of law-making is not part of his scope. It is only in later works – including the *Allgemeine Staatslehre* – that he presents and develops his doctrine of the basic norm to account for the creation and application of legal norms.

[135] *cf Allgemeine Staatslehre* (n 4) 104.

[136] ibid (my emphasis).

Hägerström seeks to dismiss Kelsen's basic norm as having 'a strong affinity with primitive positivism'[137] – in the sense that it regards the act of legislation 'as directly creating, in a mystical magical way, the connection between legal fact and legal consequence':[138]

> [i]t is curious that, although the basic norm, in accordance with which a certain authority is *supreme*, cannot be a *positive* law . . . It is said to 'establish' a supreme authority, just as the authority so constituted establishes others subordinate to it. But . . . this judgment . . . merely hovers in the air. It does not exist in the soul of any individual man, nor does it exist by means of a certain proposition referable to an authority. Really Kelsen ought to have reduced the mystical basic norm to words possessed of power, which nevertheless have not acquired that property on any particular occasion but exist from all eternity![139]

Kelsen's theory of the basic norm – and in his theory of legal norms more generally – is committed, says Hägerström, to rules of a 'supernatural character' that 'stand above nature but which yet are held to be valid for nature'.[140] Kelsen's legal norm has a 'non-natural kind of existence'[141]; it concerns 'a supernatural existent, which nevertheless . . . must be completely realized in the world of nature'.[142] Hägerström finds this 'an absurd idea':

> The supernatural juridical system cannot be thought of as even existing alongside of the natural order. For no knowledge of any reality is possible except through relating its object to a systematically interconnected whole. But the supernatural and the natural systems, as being different in kind, cannot be co-ordinated in a *single* system. Therefore, so far as I contemplate the one, the other does not exist for me.[143]

Therefore, he continues,

> if the jurist as such must abstract from the natural order, it is to be feared that the legal prescripts which he sets forth will be far too empty. He cannot, e.g., talk of legal transactions as juridical facts, for that becomes altogether meaningless if one may not assume any natural causal nexus. Again, he cannot speak intelligibly of punishment, since a 'punishment' which led to no consequences by way of natural causal connections could not be called a punishment. He must simply be left gasping for air![144]

And because Kelsen holds, says Hägerström, that 'from the juridical standpoint law and nothing but law exists', thereby excluding 'other systems of

[137] 'Kelsen's Theory of Law and State' (n 5) 272.
[138] ibid 274.
[139] ibid 276f (Hägerström's emphasis).
[140] ibid 265.
[141] ibid 266.
[142] ibid 267.
[143] ibid.
[144] ibid.

norms',[145] then what Kelsen presents as '*the* specifically juridical question' – 'What are the rules which ought to be applied by the organs of the state and observed by its subjects?' – is really but 'a question of natural law',[146] to be dismissed as unscientific and meaningless.

But Hägerström's criticism is based on two related misunderstandings of Kelsen's doctrine. The basic norm, presupposed in legal thought, accounts for the validity of some actual, *efficacious* constitution that authorises human beings to act as legal authorities. It provides, as Kelsen would later make clearer, the scheme according to which *certain* acts of will by certain agents can be interpreted as creating valid norms without reference to moral evaluations. For legal positivism, says Kelsen, 'declines to regard positive law as a mere complex of empirical facts, and the State as but an aggregate of *factual* power relationships'.[147] Positive law, according to Kelsen, is an institutionalised, coercive *normative* order – but one created (mostly intentionally) by human beings. Kelsen's claim, then, is not that the 'natural' and the 'legal' systems are to be 'co-ordinated' in a 'single system', as Hägerström puts it. Kelsen's claim, rather, is that there is a specifically *legal* interpretation – which is a normative rather than causal perspective – from which certain facts can be described and explained.

Second, Hägerström's criticism appears to suppose that Kelsen equates legal validity with moral justification. But that is also not the case. Even though Kelsen thinks that to say that a legal norm is valid does imply that it *ought* to be complied with, he is clear that legal validity implies nothing about the moral merits of any given legal system. In his view, legal positivism, just as it resists the reduction of law to purely empirical, de facto power relations, also 'discards the attempt to deduce' law 'from nature or reason'.[148] True, Kelsen does maintain that 'the basic norm, in a certain sense, means the transformation of power into law'.[149] And he grants that – in so far as the function of the basic norm is 'not only to recognize a historically given material as law', but also 'to comprehend it as a meaningful whole' – the basic norm involves, 'with the postulate of a meaningful, that is, non-contradictory order', overstepping the 'boundaries of pure positivism':

> The basic norm has here been described as the essential presupposition of any positivistic legal cognition. If one wishes to regard it as an element of a natural-law doctrine despite its renunciation of any element of material justice, very little objection can be raised; just as little, in fact, as against calling the categories of Kant's

[145] ibid 268.

[146] 'Is Positive Law an Expression of Will?' (n 6) 52 (referring to *Hauptprobleme* (n 3) 353).

[147] 'Natural Law Doctrine and Legal Positivism' (n 26) 436; and see also eg *Introduction to the Problems of Legal Theory* (n 1) 59ff; *General Theory of Law and State* (n 26) 122; or *The Pure Theory of Law* (n 100) 211ff.

[148] 'Natural Law Doctrine and Legal Positivism' (n 26) 436.

[149] ibid 437.

> transcendental philosophy metaphysics because they are not data of experience, but conditions of experience. What is involved is simply the minimum, there of metaphysics, here of natural law, without which neither a cognition of nature nor of law is possible.[150]

But Kelsen is clear that there is an 'enormous difference' between the basic norm, 'which merely makes possible the cognition of positive law as a meaningful order', and 'a natural-law doctrine which proposes to establish a just order beyond, and independent of, all positive law'.[151] Therefore his theory can escape both of Hägerström's charges: the charge of 'emptiness'; and that of collapsing into natural-law theory.

D. Legal Rights and the Equivalence of Judicial and Administrative Decisions

In Kelsen's hierarchical structure, there is no relevant difference between a judicial decision and an administrative act ordaining (non-punitive) compulsion. Both kinds of act are placed at the same hierarchical level; both amount, simultaneously, to the application of higher, general norms, and to the creation of individual norms.[152]

Hägerström objects to this equation. He says that Kelsen is fighting

> against the living ideas of law which manifest themselves in the statutes. According to these ideas, a judicial decision in civil and criminal cases is from time immemorial a protection of already existing legal rights; in the civil law of rights individualized through an object, in the penal case of general legal interests. These rights . . . are completely independent of the formal rules of legal processes, which are secondary in relation to the substantive law. In the procedural rules the state makes use of its *imperium* in order to regulate the mode of exercising the coercive powers which are involved in the right themselves. . . . [T]he judge has to establish the actual legal states of affairs which existed before the case was tried, and therefore he is necessarily regarded as completely bound. The case is quite otherwise with administration. According to the living view of law, the state does not here use its *imperium* to uphold already existing rights. It uses it for the purpose of the general welfare, and therefore the administrative authority is free to decide each case, within the limits laid down for it, from the point of view of utility. . . [I]n administrative coercion the state is obviously determined only by its own interests.[153]

Yet this again misses the point. Kelsen's claim is precisely that the received view, which depicts the two kinds of decision as being different, conceals what,

[150] ibid.
[151] ibid 437f.
[152] *cf Allgemeine Staatslehre* (n 4) 238.
[153] 'Kelsen's Theory of Law and State' (n 5) 290f.

from the point of view of the science of law, emerges as a formal and logical equivalence. So Hägeström's reply – which is but a restatement that according to the received view (and to the 'living ideas of the law which manifest themselves in the statutes') the two kinds of decision are indeed seen as being different – is neither here nor there.

What the quote above reveals is, again, Hägerström's resistance to Kelsen's analysis of the legal norm and the notion of a legal obligation, an analysis which Hägerström thinks fails completely to take into account the 'meaning' of positive laws as seen by legislators themselves. Hence his reference to 'the view of law which is alive in legislation': 'no legislator before Kelsen's time', he says, has 'ever dreamed' of a notion of obligation like Kelsen's, which has a very

> different sense from that in which the prescript itself does. The civil and penal laws, according to their own meaning, impose obligations in such a way that they establish certain rights (rights in the proper sense of the word and general legal interests) with powers of coercion attaching to them. It is in respect of these rights that the obligation exists, and the function of the [judicial] judgment is to make the concrete – pre-existing legal relationship indubitable.[154]

Yet again this is but a restatement of the traditional approach – which Kelsen dismisses as the product of an ideology at the service of a distinctive economic, social and political view – that sees positive law as the protection of rights that exist independently of it. Hägerström fails to show – as he would have to in order for his objection to succeed – that legal rights are *not* dependent upon the positive law as the mere reflex of duties or obligations (which Kelsen holds are the relatively primary notions, and which in turn he analyses by reference to the sanction-stipulating legal norm).

And in effect Hägerström would not be able to do this – for he maintains that legal rights and obligations do not qualify as legal concepts, and that the corresponding terms are but words for 'magical' forces. Indeed, Hägerström's account of legal vocabulary is the result of an inquiry into ancient Roman law – where, he shows, notions of a legal obligation or a legal right do not correspond to any facts at all. Such ideas are not concepts proper expressing thoughts, but words employed to express feelings. The very same holds, he thinks, of modern uses of such terms. For Hägerström, our legal vocabulary is not a cognitive vocabulary, used to express thoughts in terms of judgements. It is instead an emotive vocabulary of feelings expressed in imperative words. Legal rules are commands, issued by superiors to inferiors without reference to the latter's values; and the imperative form – 'thou shalt' – is used to bring about 'a feeling of conative impulse associated with the idea of a certain action

[154] ibid 292.

on the part of the recipient of the order'.[155] If 'pushed on by the demand which is made on modern science', jurisprudence 'tries to exhibit the facts which correspond to its characteristic notions of rights and legal duties', then

> [o]n the one hand, it can discover nothing which corresponds to those notions as they are actually used; on the other hand, it has recourse to something which is only apparently an object of experience. Thus it is shown that the notions in question cannot be reduced to anything in reality. The reason is that, in point of fact, they have their roots in traditional ideas of mystical forces and bonds.[156]

His legal 'nihilism' – the denial that there are any legal rights and duties – is but the juridical counterpart of his moral 'nihilism', which we considered above in section II.[157] Hägerström accuses Kelsen of misunderstanding the meaning of legal rules. It seems to me that it is Hägerström who misunderstands our legal vocabulary. But this is not the place to mount a criticism of his views.

E. Sovereignty and the Relation between National and International Law

Hägerström's criticism of Kelsen's basic norm extends to the latter's account of the relation between national and international law. He summarises Kelsen's view as follows:

> According to him [Kelsen], the state is a system of legal norms. If the state is regarded as sovereign, this must mean . . . that the legal order of the state has independent validity, so that the basic norm, which must always be presupposed, expresses the validity of the special constitution of the state. Because of the necessary unity of the law, it is then impossible to recognize anything as law except what is either included in the constitution of the sovereign state in question or is made into law by it.[158]

This means that for Kelsen either (a) international law is to be construed as subordinate to one's state (in which case 'every breach of international law on the part of a state which recognises that law is to be regarded as an unconstitutional enactment');[159] or, conversely, (b) the 'validity of the legal orders of the several states' is to be derived 'from a general norm which would determine the condition of statehood in reference to international law'.[160] In the

[155] 'On the Question of the Notion of Law' (n 69) 124.
[156] Hägerström, 'General View. Introductory chapter to the work: *Der römische Obligationsbegriff im Lichte der allgemeinen römischen Rechtsanschauung. I.*' (n 56) 16.
[157] *cf* text preceding n 42.
[158] 'Kelsen's Theory of Law and State' (n 5) 285.
[159] ibid.
[160] ibid 286.

first case, it is to the state's legal system that 'primacy' is attributed. In the second case, it is to the system of international law. No other possibility exists.[161]

From the point of view of a theory of positive law, says Kelsen, the two constructions are 'equivalent';[162] the choice between them is a choice between a 'subjectivist' and an 'objectivist' theory of knowledge, respectively. An objectivist theory of knowledge starts from the world as a whole in order to reach the subject: it presupposes an objective reason inherent in the world, and views that knowing and willing individuals are manifestations of the objective reason. The doctrine of the primacy of the national law is based, by contrast, upon a subjectivist theory of knowledge, which takes the natural world as the subject's own creation, and values as a product of the subject's will.[163]

As Hägerström notes, Kelsen seems to express a preference for the objectivist approach, and thus for the doctrine of the primacy of international law: 'a subjectivist theory of knowledge', Kelsen says, 'would lead "in the last resort to a complete negation of law"'.[164] Thereby Kelsen again departs, in Hägerström's assessment, from 'the actual living conception of law', lacking 'all basis in reality'.[165] Not that Hägerström would subscribe to a subjectivist theory of knowledge. His point is rather that no 'constitution of international law' – which would have to be in place as the direct reference-point of the corresponding basic norm – can be identified which is not 'just pure natural law'; and 'the de facto recognition of this natural law in the practice of states is a merely social-psychological fact which can in no way affect the question of legal validity':[166]

> Because of the right of self-determination of the states, the special constitutions independently determine the state-organs and the legal validity of certain acts within the state. But at the same time the individual states are responsible before international law, which is valid according to this same 'constitution', for their acts, which are always valid within their own territory. That is to say, it is involved in its very content that law lacks a unifying principle.[167]

Equally doomed, in Hägerström's view, is the attempt to interpret war as a special means of coercion characteristic of international law. Kelsen holds, as Hägerström notes, that, even though war is permissible 'only as a reaction, *i.e.* only under quite definite conditions laid down by international law', he also

[161] *cf Allgemeine Staatslehre* (n 4) 119ff.
[162] ibid 128.
[163] ibid 131.
[164] 'Kelsen's Theory of Law and State' (n 5) 286 (referring to *Allgemeine Staatslehre* (n 4) 132).
[165] ibid 287.
[166] Hägerström is here considering Verdross's account: but he thinks that 'the difference between Kelsen and Verdross is not essential': *cf* ibid 287.
[167] ibid.

concludes from the fact that 'the law of nations does not posit any objective court of appeal, which would decide who is in the wrong, and therefore on which side the war is a legal act', that 'both coercion and resistance to coercion are counted equally as war by the law of nations, and therefore as legal acts'.[168] This view, says Hägerström,

> must goad nations who feel themselves injured in their 'rights' to bloody wars . . . One drapes oneself in one's own egoism with the cloak of an 'organ of international law' . . . No doubt the law of nations contains highly natural rules for that co-operation which is useful to all states, and these must be respected if a state is to take part in the general intercourse and is not to meet with universal distrust. But the cloak of natural law is nowadays an obvious cultural danger.[169]

Hägerström's argument here seems to be that it is the doctrine of primacy of international law that may *lead* to war, and therefore that that doctrine must be rejected. This is evidently not a valid objection. As Hume says,

> [t]here is no method of reasoning more common, and yet none more blameable, than, in philosophical disputes, to endeavour the refutation of any hypothesis, by a pretence of its dangerous consequences to religion and morality. When any opinion leads to absurdities, it is certainly false; but it is not certain that an opinion is false, because it is of dangerous consequence. Such topics, therefore, ought entirely to be forborne; as serving nothing to the discovery of truth, but only to make the person of an antagonist odious.[170]

V. LEGAL SCIENCE

We have already seen that Kelsen views legal science as a *normative* science – a science of norms – concerned with the cognition of law according to the principle of imputation.[171] As such, it is fundamentally distinct from the empirical sciences, which are based on the methodological principle of causality. But we have also seen that Kelsen – in the early works which we have been considering – characterises legal norms as hypothetical *judgements*. This means that he draws no clear distinction between legal norms (as the products of law-making activity of legal authorities), on the one hand, and propositions of law (as the product of the descriptive endeavour of legal scientists), on the other.[172] As Hägerström remarks,

[168] ibid 288 (referring to *Allgemeine Staatslehre* (n 4) 213, 248).

[169] ibid 288f; he credits Lundstedt with having pressed the same point in *Superstition or Rationality in Action for Peace? Arguments Against Founding a World Peace on the Common Sense of Justice* (London, Longmans Green, 1925) 161ff.

[170] *cf* D Hume, *An Enquiry Concerning Human Understanding*, TL Beauchamp ed (Oxford, Clarendon Press, 2000 [1748]) 73.

[171] *cf* text preceding n 19.

[172] Recall n 86 and n 100.

> according to Kelsen, a norm is essentially a *legal proposition* and therefore a true *judgment* about the connection between legal fact and legal consequence, so that the object of legal science is the law's own judgments. It follows from this that the true judgment, in which a certain legal connexion is thought of as existing, makes its own content real. A norm, which is a true judgment about a legal relationship, itself creates this relationship, either because it concerns the way in which norms are created or because it signifies the connexion between the 'wrong' and the appropriate punishment or executive action.[173]

Hägerström then objects (quite naturally) that

> it is possible that this absurd view, which makes knowledge *of* the existence of a legal relationship to be creative of its existence, is influenced by Kant's critical subjectivism.[174]

As we also saw, Hägerström rejects Kant's subjectivism. He believes that the pursuit of knowledge is restricted to the natural and social sciences:[175]

> In general, all that is called *Geisteswissenschaft* [ie normative science] – whether it concerns the I, society, the state, morality, or religion – is only an intellectual play with expressions of feeling, as if something real were designated thereby.[176]

Naturally, then, Hägerström's and Kelsen's contrasting epistemological views reflect themselves in their different accounts of legal 'science'. But quite apart from this there seems to be another point on the character of legal science or jurisprudence – a science, says Hägerström, 'which touches our most important interests':[177]

> [I]n point of fact jurisprudence as such has a definite practical aim, *viz.* to help in carrying out the existing law. Those who practise jurisprudence come therefore to feel that, just because they investigate law, they are its servants. It is therefore natural for them to 'recognize' the legal imperatives which are presented to them as valid assertions of what ought to happen.[178]

In Kelsen's account, however, says Hägerström,

> the task of jurisprudence is narrowed down into a systematization of the laws according to merely formal principles, without any regard to the requirements of social life or to the 'ethico-political' postulates which are in fact present in the community.[179]

[173] 'Kelsen's Theory of Law and State' (n 5) 275 (referring to *Allgemeine Staatslehre* (n 4) 54; Hägerström's emphasis).

[174] ibid.

[175] *cf* text to n 44.

[176] 'A Summary of My Philosophy' (n 10) 74. Hägerström's 'motto' is '*Praeterea censeo metaphysicam esse delendam*' ('Moreover I propose that metaphysics must be destroyed'): *cf* ibid.

[177] 'Kelsen's Theory of Law and State' (n 5) 262.

[178] 'On the Question of the Notion of Law' (n 69) 205.

[179] 'Kelsen's Theory of Law and State' (n 5) 274.

'Kelsen makes no incorrect statements about social facts', Hägeström observes: 'but one finds also that he avoids all risk of doing so because he does not allow jurisprudence to have anything to do with actual social existence!'[180]

What should we make of this charge? Two rejoinders come to mind. One is that by 'jurisprudence' or 'legal science' Hägerström probably has in mind a different activity than Kelsen. For Kelsen legal science is indeed a formal science, concerned with the structure of legal norms and with the construction of legal concepts, free – 'purified' – from psychological and sociological elements, on the one hand, and from reference to the social 'purpose' of the law, on the other hand.[181] It is simply not within the scope of this discipline, thus understood, to provide solutions to particular legal questions: which is not to say, of course, that Kelsen believes that to provide solutions to particular legal questions is unnecessary, unimportant or impossible; simply that it is not the province of legal science.

Second, is it Hägerström's contention that legal science has the 'practical' aim to offer legal solutions (in terms, presumably, of value-judgements concerning what one ought to do according to the law), solutions that are not inconsistent with either his moral scepticism, or with his 'nihilist'[182] view that value-judgements are not really judgements proper, but, rather, the expression of conative attitudes? Indeed, Hägerström seems to be committed to the view that there can be no cognition of the law in terms of rights and duties. He is forced, in other words, to acknowledge either that so-called legal science is not 'scientific' at all – or that it must restrict itself to the pursuit of sociological and psychological inquiries.

He takes the latter view. In a 1935 essay he writes that

> jurisprudence has become one of the special sciences. Like physics and chemistry, *e.g.*, its function is merely to establish the facts within a certain region, to reach general principles by induction, and to make deductive inferences from the inductively established results.[183]

Thus the only way in which jurisprudence can carry out its 'definite practical aim' must be by offering empirical information about the facts of the law in terms of causal regularities. But plainly this kind of information, though not unimportant, cannot assist legal practitioners in 'carrying out the existing law'; to maintain otherwise would be to confuse 'is' and 'ought'.

Kelsen would dispute this view that jurists cannot *meaningfully* talk about the law in terms of juridical facts. He would agree, of course, that one's overall

[180] ibid 267.
[181] *Hauptprobleme* (n 3) v, 58ff, 184f, 468.
[182] *cf* text to n 42.
[183] A Hägerström, 'The Conception of a Declaration of Intention in the Sphere of Private Law' in K Olivecrona (ed), *Inquiries into the Nature of Law and Morals*, C Broad transl (Stockholm, Almqvist & Wiksell, 1953 [1935]) 299.

philosophical commitments – including one's ontology and epistemology – will reflect itself on one's choice of jurisprudential theories.[184] And he says in the 'Foreword' to the first edition of the *Hauptprobleme* that the jurist

> cannot conceptually link the world of the is with the world of the ought and he must therefore *decide* whether he wants to explain as a sociologist or psychologist factual occurrences, the behaviour of human beings, or whether he wants to understand legal norms, whether he wants to abstract his concepts from one world or from the other.[185]

Kelsen's own choice is to adopt the normative perspective according to which legal science is concerned with the positive law as a system of *norms*. But he also makes room for a naturalistic perspective, which will concern itself with the impact of legal norms, as causes, upon the behaviour of human beings. Hägerström, by contrast, rejects the very possibility of the normative point of view. He would thus side with the sociologist or the psychologist, and see no further task for a science of law (though he offers no detailed account of how this is to be carried out). So though Kelsen's and Hägerström's metatheoretical views may be at odds, their actual positive accounts of law are not strictly speaking incompatible: for they are, after all, addressing law from two different perspectives.[186]

[184] *cf* 'Natural Law Doctrine and Legal Positivism' (n 26) 445f.

[185] *Hauptprobleme* (n 3) viii (my emphasis).

[186] Unsurprisingly, Hägerström's critiques of Kelsen were largely adopted by other Scandinavian Realists, such as Lundstedt or Olivecrona. Thus Lundstedt dismisses Kelsen's basic norm as 'pure metaphysics', and rejects Kelsen's view of legal science as ignoring the realities of social life; *cf Die Unwissenschaftlichkeit der Rechtswissenschaft* (n 10) 211f, 252; and see also my essay 'Scepticism and Scandinavian Legal Realists' in T Endicott, J Getzler and E Peel (eds), *Properties of Law. Essays in Honour of Jim Harris* (Oxford, Oxford University Press, 2006) 52ff. Lundstedt's own view is that 'there are no legal norms at all' – which nicely illustrates Kelsen's own point that unless the basic norm is presupposed there are no legal norms. Olivecrona believes that Kelsen's phrase 'the great mystery' (recall n 134) is a fitting description of Kelsen's own views: if law has a place among other facts in the world of time and space, then it cannot, contra Kelsen, belong to another world of 'ought'; *cf* K Olivecrona, *Law as Fact* (London, Oxford University Press, 1939) 21 (referring to Kelsen's *Hauptprobleme* (n 3) 411). As for Alf Ross, he thought of himself as a pupil of Kelsen's, and regarded Kelsen's *Hauptprobleme* as a turning point in jurisprudential thought: *cf* A Ross, *Theorie der Rechtsquellen* (n 90) 191. Ross would later change his allegiance to Hägerström, and then to Rudolf Carnap and logical positivism; but he pays his respects to Kelsen in *On Law and Justice*, M Dutton transl (London, Stevens & Sons, 1958 [1953]) 8. For a more detailed account, see my essay 'Alf Ross' in R Walter, C Jabloner and K Zeleny (eds), *Der Kreis um Hans Kelsen. Die Anfangsjahre der reinen Rechtslehre* (Vienna, Manz, 2008) 409ff.

9

A 'Realistic' Theory of Law and the Pure Theory of Law: Remarks on Alf Ross's On Law and Justice*

HANS KELSEN

IN THE FOLLOWING discussion I do not mean to offer an exhaustive 1
assessment of the important body of work that Alf Ross, a leading legal theorist, has recently published. I confine myself to a critical discussion of certain tenets of Ross's theory of positive law: tenets by virtue of which his theory not only differs from, but openly contradicts, the Pure Theory of Law, which I myself endorse. It goes without saying that my criticism by no means detracts from the esteem in which I hold Alf Ross, as both an outstanding scholar and an amiable person.

I

The core respect in which Ross's theory of positive law differs – in his view[1] – from the Pure Theory of Law is that his is a 'realistic' theory of law. By 'realistic' he means an 'empiricist' theory. In the 'Preface' to *On Law and Justice*, his most recent publication, he speaks of 'a realistic interpretation of law, that is, an interpretation in accordance with the principles of an empirical philosophy'. 'The leading idea of this work', he says, 'is to carry, in the field of law, the empirical principles to their ultimate conclusions'.[2]

* H Kelsen, 'Eine "Realistische" und die Reine Rechtslehre. Bemerkungen zu Alf Ross: On Law and Justice' (1959/60) 10 *Österreichische Zeitschrift für Öffentlich Recht* 1–25. (The paper appeared in 1959.) Translated by Luís Duarte d'Almeida (with thanks to Kevin Toh, Leslie Green, Uta Bindreiter and especially Stanley L Paulson for many helpful suggestions). Page numbers of the original text are shown in the margins.

[1] A view already stated by him in *Towards a Realistic Jurisprudence. A Criticism of the Dualism in Law*, AI Fausbøll transl (Copenhagen, Einar Munksgaard, 1946).

[2] *On Law and Justice* (London, Stevens & Sons, 1958) ix.

According to Ross, empirical cognition is characterised by two features: one negative, the other positive. The negative feature is the rejection of metaphysical speculation. The positive feature, its focus on *is*-facts (*Seinstatsachen*). Pointedly diverging from the Pure Theory, Ross affirms that

> [t]he underlying thought in jurisprudential realism is the desire to understand the cognition of law in conformity with the ideas of the nature, problems and method of science as worked out by modern, empiricist philosophy. Several philosophical trends – logical empiricism, the Uppsala philosophy, the Cambridge school, and
> 2 others – find common ground in the rejection of metaphysics, speculative cognition based on *a priori* apprehension by reason. There is only one world and one cognition. All science is ultimately concerned with the same body of facts . . .[3]

Ross concludes that 'the fundamental legal notions must be interpreted as conceptions of social reality, the behaviour of man in society, and as nothing else'.[4]

Now it is true that a science, if understood as empirical cognition, can have as its object only material facts. It is also true that the object of what we call 'legal science' is law. But law, as the Pure Theory holds, is a norm, or a system of norms. There can thus be no empirical legal science, no empirical cognition of law itself. For a norm is an *ought*-prescription, not an *is*-fact. A norm is the meaning (*Sinn*) of an *is*-fact: it is the meaning of an intentional act directed to the behaviour of someone. The meaning of such an act is that someone *ought* to behave in some given way, and so the norm, *qua* meaning of that *is*-fact, must be distinguished from the *is*-fact itself. The act – the command – whose meaning is a norm (or, to put it figuratively: the act by which a norm is created) is an Is (*ein Sein*). The norm, which is the meaning of that fact, is an imperative, an Ought (*ein Sollen*). Cognition can be directed either to the act or to its normative meaning. It can thus be directed to two different objects: one real, the other ideal. When directed at the law *qua* norm, cognition is directed at a normative meaning.

If there is to be an 'empirical' science of law in the specific sense in which Ross employs the notion, then law must be understood as an *is*-fact, and legal norms as *is*-rules (*Seinsregeln*). Legal rules must be understood, that is, as rules that assert or describe how people in fact behave, rather than as rules that prescribe how people are to behave. Whether such a theory captures the essence of law – whether it captures the specific way in which law addresses those whose behaviour it regulates – remains to be seen. There *is* in any case such a doctrine: the doctrine that law consists of nothing more than certain regularities of human behaviour, and that the notion of a legal Ought is a mystifying ideology.

[3] ibid 67.
[4] ibid ix.

But what is law according to Ross's realistic theory? In keeping with his programmatic statement, quoted above, that 'the fundamental legal notions must be interpreted as conceptions of social reality', it would seem that law can be understood only as a fact, not as a norm. And likewise in his book *Towards a Realistic Jurisprudence*, published 12 years before *On Law and Justice*, Ross holds – in direct opposition to the Pure Theory of Law – that law is to be understood as an *is*-fact, resolutely rejecting the theory that law is a norm or a system of norms.[5] In this latest book of his, however, and in spite of that pro-
grammatic statement, he appears – on this issue – to drift closer to the Pure 3
Theory. For Ross now characterises law, as does the Pure Theory, as a norm or system of norms that determine that people *ought* to behave in a certain way. He speaks of law as a 'legal norm'.[6] He distinguishes between law as a complex of rules ('law itself as the legal rules'), and legal science as 'knowledge about law as propositions about legal rules'[7] – the difference being, he says, that law *qua* norm 'prescribes', while legal science 'describes'.[8]

In his 1944 essay 'Imperatives and Logic' Ross had already adopted this familiar contrast between the descriptive statement and the prescriptive imperative: '"Imperative", as used here, means a sentence, the object of which is to express an immediate demand for action, but not to describe a fact'.[9] He now says in *On Law and Justice*, similarly, that 'the radical diversity between legal norms (that is, the legal rules contained in statutes or derived from precedents or other sources of law) and doctrinal propositions of text-books' is owing to the fact that '[t]he former are (alogical) directives' whereas 'the latter are (logical) assertions (to the effect that certain directives are valid law)'.[10] He characterises 'norms' as 'directives'.[11] He affirms that '"Danish law" is the name of an individual set of norms', and uses the expressions 'set of norms' and 'system of norms' synonymously.[12] He says that 'the norms of law . . . prescribe a certain course of action'[13], that 'the real content of a norm of conduct is a directive to the judge'[14], and finally that 'a national law system is an integrated body of rules, determining the conditions under which physical force *shall* be exercised against a person'.[15]

[5] *Towards a Realistic Jurisprudence* (n 1) 78, 93 ('According to the current view . . . [the law] consist[s] . . . of the norms (rules) as the meaning of the law-creating acts. . . . [T]his [current] view is untenable').

[6] *On Law and Justice* (n 2) 1.

[7] ibid 10.

[8] ibid 9.

[9] 'Imperatives and Logic' (1944) 11 *Philosophy of Science* 31.

[10] *On Law and Justice* (n 2) 9f, fn 4.

[11] ibid 10.

[12] ibid 30.

[13] ibid 32.

[14] ibid 33.

[15] ibid 34 (my italics).

This means that Ross's realistic theory – fully in line with the Pure Theory – characterises law as a system of coercion-stipulating *ought*-norms: norms that prescribe that certain organs *ought*, in certain circumstances, to direct certain coercive acts against certain individuals. The object of a realistic legal science, therefore, is an Ought – not an Is.

In *Towards a Realistic Jurisprudence*, however, Ross firmly rejects the definition of law as a norm. But he also criticises some theories of law which, calling themselves 'realistic', offer an account of 'law as fact' by trying 'to separate all
4 normative points of view from the concept of law and determine the law as purely a fact, a part of social behaviour of men'.[16] Here is what Ross has to say about such theories:

> [I]t would seem that these theories which propose to spirit away entirely all normative points of view, all notions of validity [note that 'validity' is here identified with normativity], are in a strange way doomed to failure. Broadly speaking, for the following reason: If the law is defined as a certain actual behaviour, dualism [of 'validity' and 'reality'] is indeed avoided to begin with. Statements about the law will be purely theoretical statements about what happens or what will happen. But this results in a complete disruption of the concept of law . . . Our object in determining the concept of law is not to spirit away the normative ideas, but to put a different interpretation on them . . .[17]

And further:

> [O]ne cannot arrive at a true realistic doctrine of law merely by spiriting away all notions of validity [which are 'normative ideas'] from the concept of law.[18]

Ross says that this 'spiriting away' of 'normative ideas' would amount to an elimination of the 'specifically legal' element of the concept of law.[19] And to say this is to hold – as the Pure Theory of Law also holds – that law cannot be understood solely as a fact ('as purely a fact', as Ross puts it). It must be understood as a norm. And yet this criticism of certain 'realistic' theories of law is completely at odds with the hostile stance adopted by Ross, in the very same book, towards a normative concept of law. We shall return to this point.

Now if the object of legal science is law (as no one would seriously deny); if law is a system of norms (a system, that is, of *ought*-prescriptions); and if 'normative ideas' are the 'specifically legal' element of the concept of law (which means that law cannot be understood 'as purely a fact') – then how can legal science *qua* 'empirical' science (in the sense in which Ross employs the adjective) be directed to *is*-facts? If the attempt of some 'realistic' theories to characterise law as pure fact – to define law as 'a certain actual behaviour' –

[16] *Towards a Realistic Jurisprudence* (n 1) 49.
[17] ibid.
[18] ibid 145.
[19] ibid.

leads, in Ross's own words, to a 'disruption of the concept of law', how, then, can Ross contend, in the name of a 'realistic' legal science, that 'the fundamental legal notions must be interpreted as conceptions of social reality, the behaviour of man in society, and as nothing else'?[20] If Ross rejects those 'realistic' theories on the grounds that they regard legal statements as statements 'about what happens or what will happen', as he puts it – then how can Ross himself maintain that 'statements concerning valid law at the present time must be understood as referring to hypothetical future decisions' (even if the qualification 'under certain conditions' is added)[21]?

We have here a blatant contradiction. It is not possible to understand law as a norm (in the sense of an *ought*-prescription) and simultaneously to characterise legal science as a science descriptive of *is*-facts (and in this sense as an 'empirico-realistic' science). We shall later see how Ross deceives himself into 5
ignoring this contradiction. For the moment, let us merely remark that this is a contradiction that he is in no position to avoid. For although he wishes to characterise legal science as an 'empirical' science, his concept of an empirical science is too narrow. If it is to be 'empirical', legal science must not undertake the impossible task of describing *ought*-norms (*Soll-Normen*) in *is*-propositions. Yet a science is 'empirical' – as opposed to 'metaphysical' – not only when it describes facts occurring in time and space, but also when it describes the *meaning* of certain human acts. A theory of law remains empirical if it confines itself to the description of norms that are the meaning of empirical human acts occurring in space and time, and if it does not concern itself with norms arising from supra-human instances such as God or a god-created Nature. Provided that the Ought of the norms it describes is not the Ought of some sort of metaphysical justice, a theory of law remains empirical. The Pure Theory of Law meets these conditions. With the utmost emphasis – and like hardly any other theory of law – the Pure Theory eliminates from its scope all metaphysical elements. It can therefore claim to be regarded as no less empirical, and in this sense as no less 'realistic', than Ross's 'realistic' theory.

II

It is one of the Pure Theory of Law's core theses that there is a distinction between the legal norm, issued by the legal authority, and the legal proposition, formulated by legal science. The legal norm is a prescription. It prescribes that people ought to behave in a certain way. The legal proposition is a description. It is the description of a legal norm; it states that, according to a norm belonging to a certain legal system, people ought to behave in a certain way. A

[20] *On Law and Justice* (n 2) ix.
[21] ibid 41.

norm prescribing a certain course of conduct is neither true nor false; rather, it is either valid or invalid. The proposition that describes it, in turn, is a judgement; it can be true or false. Of course, the legislator may occasionally use, when issuing a norm, the linguistic form of a judgement, and even the linguistic form of a judgement about *is*-facts. For example, a statutory provision might read 'Theft is punished by imprisonment'. What is thereby meant, however, is a prescription; it means that theft *ought* to be punished by imprisonment.

The proposition that describes the legal norm must convey the specific meaning with which law addresses those whose behaviour it regulates. In other words, it must convey the meaning that the legal norm has – or rather, to be precise, the meaning that the legal norm *is*. That proposition, the legal proposition, must therefore be a normative one. For the statements of legal science are not statements about how people actually behave. They are statements about how people ought to behave according to a certain national or international legal system. Thus, whilst in the legal norm the 'ought' has a prescriptive (imperative) meaning, the 'ought' in the legal proposition has a descriptive (indicative) meaning.

6 Since legal propositions describing legal norms can be either true or false, the principles of logic – viz. the principle of contradiction and the usual rules of inference – are applicable to them. Such principles of logic are therefore also applicable – if only indirectly – to legal norms, even though norms can be neither true nor false. Two norms that can only be described in a pair of contradictory legal propositions may be said to 'contradict' each other: they cannot be simultaneously regarded as valid. Likewise the validity of a legal norm can be logically derived from the validity of another legal norm if the legal propositions describing each norm can occur in a logical syllogism.

Traditional legal theory, conflating legal norm and legal proposition, fails to draw a clear distinction between law and legal science, between the function of law-creation and the function of law-application. Ross avoids this mistake. He emphatically distinguishes law from legal science. 'The law', he says, 'is not written in order to impart theoretical truths, but to direct people – judges and private citizens alike – to act in a certain desired manner'.[22] In turn, legal propositions – such as those that might occur, for example, in a textbook on the criminal law of a certain jurisdiction – are not 'directives'; they are not legal norms. On the difference between legal norms and the propositions in a legal textbook, Ross says the following:

> Despite the similarity there must, however, be a difference in the logical meaning of the same sentences in the two settings. There can be no doubt that the propositions in a textbook, at any rate to a certain extent, intend to describe, not to prescribe.[23]

[22] ibid 8.
[23] ibid 9.

He stresses, as we saw, 'the radical diversity between legal norms (that is, the legal rules contained in statutes or derived from precedents or other sources of law) and doctrinal propositions of textbooks',[24] pointing out that

> [t]he proposition of a textbook which prima facie has the character of a directive D [seemingly because it is formulated as a normative proposition] must therefore, in order to be understood as a proposition not *of* the law but *about* the law, be rewritten thus: 'D [an individual norm prescribing a certain course of action] is valid (Illinois, California, common, etc.) law.'[25]

Yet such a proposition is, according to Ross, an *is*-proposition, an statement about an *is*-fact. He rejects the idea that propositions describing legal norms are normative propositions. He is thus at odds with the Pure Theory of Law:

> I reject the idea that legal cognition constitutes a specific normative cognition, expressed in *ought*-propositions, and interpret legal thinking formally in terms of the same logic as that on which other empirical sciences are based (*is*-propositions).[26]

But let us consider, for example, a proposition, in a textbook on the criminal law of California, describing the norm that prescribes imprisonment for theft
with the following words: 'The norm *Theft ought to be punished by imprisonment* is 7
valid California law'. What does this proposition state?

Is it a proposition about the existence of a certain fact, viz. the norm-issuing act? Surely not. For the norm, about which the textbook proposition states something, is different from the fact of its issuance by a human act. This difference is familiar to any lawyer as the difference between, on the one hand, the legislative process, and, on the other, the statute, which is its product. To be sure, the legislative process – or, to put it more generally, the creation of law – is also a proper object of law-describing legal science. For it is a feature of law that it regulates its own creation. The creation of law, that is to say, is an object of legal science, not as a factual event in natural-causal connections, but as an event regulated by norms – as the content of legal norms. And in this regard, too, it is norms, not facts, that legal science describes.

Does that proposition – the textbook proposition describing the California criminal law on theft – state that theft in California is *in fact* punished by imprisonment? If it did state this, then such a statement would be false. There are numerous cases in which theft in California is in fact not punished, for example if the thief cannot be arrested. The proposition also does not state that theft is (in fact) *generally* punished. This statement may well be true; but it is not a description of the legal norm in question. It is, rather, a description of behaviour that corresponds – generally – to the norm. But the norm is no less valid in those cases in which theft is not punished, that is, in cases in which

[24] ibid 9 fn 4.
[25] ibid 9.
[26] ibid x.

people's behaviour does not correspond to the norm. Behaviour that *corresponds to* the law is not itself *the law* – any more than behaviour that fails to correspond to the law is the law. The law is a different thing from the behaviour that either corresponds or fails to correspond to it. 'Correspondence' denotes a relation between two elements, and precisely because they stand in a relation to one another, these two elements cannot be identical.

The law in California is not that theft is generally punished by imprisonment. The law in California is that theft *ought* to be punished, always and without exception, even if in fact it is not always punished. Theft *ought to be punished*: therein, not in theft actually *being punished*, lies in the law. It can thus only be described in normative propositions.

Now this is indeed what Ross himself does in his realistic theory. In describing the law he says, as we have seen, 'A national law system is an integrated body of rules determining the conditions under which physical force shall be exercised against a person',[27] rather than 'A national law system is an integrated body of rules determining the conditions under which physical force is in fact exercised against a person'.

Ross claims that the propositions of descriptive legal science must be *is*-propositions, because he wishes to establish legal science as an empirical science. He proceeds from the erroneous belief that a science can only be
8 empirical if it describes *is*-facts, and that only *is*-judgements can be true or false. Thus he fails to see that the term 'ought' can have a *de*scriptive as well as a *pre*scriptive character, and that the 'ought' in legal propositions – in contradistinction to the 'ought' in legal norms – is descriptive in character. He fails to see that, logically, legal propositions are judgements and – differently from norms – can therefore be true or false. I refer in this regard to the writings of Christian Sigwart, a leading logician. Sigwart differentiates between imperatives – which purport to be complied with rather than true – and judgements, which, *qua* statements or assertions, do purport to be true, and can therefore be true or false. Among the latter, Sigwart stresses, we find statements about imperatives. He says:

> The imperative . . . does not call for belief but obedience. . . . No essential difference occurs in this primary and usual meaning of the imperative as the expression of a particular individual will when it takes the form of a general law. When the legislator addresses an imperative to the citizens of the state or members of the religious community his relation to them is that of one individual to another. His purpose in speaking is not to communicate a truth which they are to believe, but to announce a command which they are to obey. It makes no difference whether the source of the command be an actual individual or a collective body, whether the assumed motive of obedience be submission to personal authority or an

[27] ibid 34.

> impersonal constitution – the import of what is said is not the communication of a truth but the summons to do this, to leave that undone.
>
> The form 'Thou shalt' again, which appears in laws such as those of the Decalogue, has originally no other significance. Shall is the correlative of will. . . . But this form does now contain a twofold meaning not to be found in the simple imperative. 'Shall' (*sollen* = shall + ought) may also have the force of a proper predicate in a statement meant to be true; it signifies duty, obligation, and is thus a modal predicate expressing the relation between the subjective individual will and an authoritative power, or an objective law. The original imperative here passes over into the significance of a predicate . . .; and if we assume a legal or moral constitution, the statement that I am under an obligation [that is, that I ought to behave in a certain way] may be true or false. . . .
>
> Finally the same ambiguity extends to propositions which bear the grammatical form of a simple [assertoric] statement. That portion of the penal code which says that whoever acts in a certain way will incur a certain penalty, is not meant, like the formulae of a natural law, as a communication of what actually happens, it conveys a command. But when the law is depicted as taking effect, the same proposition contains an actual statement; it states what regularly happens within a given state.[28]

Following traditional legal theory, Sigwart identifies validity with efficacy.
Since legal science describes the validity of a legal system, it does not state 9
what regularly happens, but what ought to happen in a given legal system. But what matters is that, according to Sigwart, these normative propositions are judgements, which can be true or false. A norm stipulating that one ought to behave in a certain way, and which can be neither true nor false (but only valid or invalid), is therefore to be contrasted with two kinds of judgement that can be true or false, namely with an *is*-judgement (descriptive of a factual conduct) and with a normative judgement (descriptive of a norm).

III

The crucial problem for Ross's realistic theory of law – the problem in response to which his theory seeks to distance itself substantially from the Pure Theory of Law – is the relation between the validity and the efficacy of law.

This is indeed one of the most important and difficult problems that a positivist theory of law must address. It is but a special case of the relation between the Ought of law and the Is of natural reality. For although efficacy – that is, the fact that people's conduct corresponds, to some extent, to the norms that prescribe that they behave in certain ways – is an *is*-fact, so, too, are the acts by which legal norms are posited. To say that a legal system is a 'positive' system means that its norms are created, posited, by human acts, and that

[28] Christoph Sigwart, *Logic*, 2nd edn, H Dendy transl (London, Swan Sonnenschein, 1895) 17f fn 1.

they are by and large efficacious. But the law – that is, legal norms – must not be confused either with such acts of norm-creation, or with the factual behaviour that corresponds to what is prescribed.

A positivist theory of law faces the task of steering a middle course between two theoretically untenable extremes. One extreme is the thesis that there is no relation whatsoever between validity, which is an Ought, and efficacy, which is an Is: the thesis that validity and efficacy are completely independent. The other extreme is the thesis that the validity of law is identical with its efficacy: the thesis that by saying that a norm is valid one is saying only that the norm is in fact complied with and applied. An idealistic theory will tend toward the former thesis; a realistic theory, toward the latter.

That first thesis is wrong, since it cannot be denied that a legal system as a whole, and likewise an individual legal norm, is no longer considered valid – that is, that they lose their validity – if they cease to be efficacious. Nor can it be denied that a relation does exist between the Ought of law – that is, its validity, which is its specific existence – and the Is, the existence, of natural reality. Indeed, a legal norm, in order to become valid, must be posited by an *is*-act (even though the existence of the legal norm – its validity, which is therefore an Ought – is different from, and should not be confused with, the existence of the norm-positing act, which is an Is). The second solution is also wrong, because it also cannot be denied that there are numerous cases in which legal norms are considered valid even though they are neither complied with nor applied, and thus not efficacious.

A legal norm – a norm, that is, prescribing that under certain conditions, especially under the condition that a person behave in a certain way, a coercive act ought to be directed, as a sanction, against that person (or against someone else standing in a certain relation to that person) – is efficacious if it is complied with (that is, if the sanction-avoiding conduct is in fact adopted by the legal subjects); or, when the conduct does occur which is the condition of the sanction, if the norm is applied (that is, if the sanction prescribed by the legal norm is in fact ordered and carried out by the competent legal organs). But a legal norm is valid, which means that it ought to be applied, also when, and indeed precisely when, it is not complied with (and is not, in *this* sense, efficacious); and indeed a legal norm is valid – which means, to repeat, that it ought to be applied – even when it is not applied, because, for example, the delinquent has in fact managed to avoid the execution of the sanction.

If one assumes that the aim of law is to prevent illegal conduct (conduct, in other words, which is the condition of a sanction) then the ideal case of legal validity is the case in which the sanction prescribed by the legal norm is not applied at all – and valid law is not, in *this* sense, efficacious – because individuals, motivated by the representation of the sanction to be executed, avoid the conduct which is the condition of that sanction. The general norms in a statute become valid before they become efficacious in either sense; a judge applying the statute for the first time, immediately after it has become valid and thus before it has had any prospect of becoming efficacious, applies valid law. And a legal system can be valid as a whole even if not all of its norms are always and fully complied with and, if not complied with, always and fully applied. (A legal system will not, however, be considered valid if it ceases, by and large, to be efficacious.)

Therefore – and this is the Pure Theory of Law's thesis – law's validity cannot be identical with its efficacy. The efficacy of legal norms, just like its creation by human acts, is a condition of their validity. But efficacy is itself not validity, nor is it the basis of validity. The basis of the validity of a legal system is a presupposed basic norm stipulating that one ought to behave in accordance with an actually established constitution that is by and large efficacious, and thus in accordance with the norms issued in accordance with this constitution, and which are by and large efficacious as well. The basic norm thus makes both the issuance of norms by human actions and the efficacy of such norms a condition of their validity. *Efficacy is a condition of validity in the sense that efficacy must follow norm-issuance if the legal system as a whole, as well as an individual legal norm, is not to lose its validity.* In order to live, one must be born, and then other conditions must obtain if one is to stay alive (one must be fed, for example). If such conditions are not satisfied, one will lose one's life. But life is identical neither with being born nor with being fed.

It is against this distinction between legal validity as an Ought and legal 11
efficacy as an Is – a distinction that the Pure Theory of Law emphatically stresses – that Ross's realistic theory places itself. This distinction is simply the unavoidable consequence of the fact that law *qua* norm – that is, legal validity, law's specific existence – is an Ought and not an Is, and that efficacy, understood as the fact that that people's conduct corresponds to the legal norm, implies a relation between law and this factual conduct (for a relation can obtain only between two non-identical elements). Against this distinction – and also against the dualism of 'validity' and 'reality' – Ross's realistic theory is essentially based on the identification of validity with efficacy.

In *Towards a Realistic Jurisprudence* Ross presents as the 'starting point' of his realistic account the view that 'the dualism of *reality* and *validity*' is a 'fundamental source of error'.[29] 'Validity' is nothing more than 'certain subjective experiences of impulse'[30] toward a certain course of action. These 'impulses to action'[31] are 'rationalised'[32] in the concept of an objective *ought*-validity

[29] *Towards a Realistic Jurisprudence* (n 1) 11.
[30] ibid 12.
[31] ibid 81.
[32] ibid 12.

(*Soll-Geltung*), but 'erroneously'[33] so, according to Ross, who speaks of the 'epistemological impossibility'[34] of such a 'meaningless'[35] rationalisation. This leads Ross to dismiss the concept of normative legal validity as a concept of something that is not real. He says:

> Validity in the sense of a category or sphere of existence coordinated with reality is nonsense in the literal meaning of the word: validity (value or duty) is nothing objective or conceivable whatsoever, it has no meaning, is a mere word.[36]

If 'validity', when used to refer to something different from 'reality', is a meaningless term, then a realistic theory should certainly refrain from using it. Yet this is not the case with Ross's theory. He does employ the concept of 'validity'. Indeed, from the passages that we have already quoted from his work it emerges that the idea of normative validity is essential to the concept of law. Ross refuses to eliminate the idea of the normative.[37]

He believes, however, that he can give 'validity' a different sense than it has in the Pure Theory of Law. 'Validity' would not be normative validity: that would be the erroneous rationalisation of a psychological fact. Rather, 'valid-
12 ity' would be a fact, viz. an impulse to a certain action. Ross calls this impulse a 'behaviour attitude': he speaks of a 'disinterested behaviour attitude having the stamp of validity'.[38] Together with the 'interested behaviour attitude' – which is the fear of the execution of the legally prescribed sanction, an 'impulse of fear of compulsion'[39] – it constitutes the motive for lawful conduct: the motive, in other words, of the efficacy of law.

The 'interested behaviour attitude having the stamp of validity' consists in the fact that those individuals who create and apply the legal sanction-stipulating norms are regarded by legal subjects as being 'competent' to create and apply the law:

> The authorities who enforce the law . . . must be regarded as authorities, . . . [that is, as possessing] *legal competence* to establish the law and exercise compulsion.[40]

To hold the 'opinion' or 'belief' that such individuals are 'competent' to establish and apply the law is to 'respect' them as authorities. This 'belief in competence or authority'[41] enables the law-creating individuals to bring legal subjects to comply with the law ('to induce men to act in accordance with

[33] ibid 80.
[34] ibid 91.
[35] ibid 95.
[36] ibid 77.
[37] See ibid 49, 145; and *cf* the text following n 5 above.
[38] ibid 78.
[39] ibid.
[40] ibid 80.
[41] ibid.

their commands',[42] as Ross puts it). These two psychological factors – respect for the authorities regarded as competent, and fear of sanctions – are thus causes of lawful behaviour, and thus of law's efficacy:

> Obedience to the law will follow, not merely by virtue of an original behaviour attitude of compliance with and respect for the authoritative system (disinterested attitude), but if necessary also for fear of punishment (interested attitude).
>
> In reality . . . there is an intimate fusion and real inductive interaction between the two factors, compulsion and authority, interested and disinterested compliance.[43]

If by 'validity' one means this 'disinterested' impulse to action – the psychological fact of a certain 'opinion' or 'belief' that is a motive of lawful conduct – then the dualism of validity and efficacy will indeed be abolished. 'It is obvious', Ross says,

> that if the element of validity is determined in the manner here indicated, all dualism in the legal phenomenon will disappear: *'validity' itself becomes a phenomenon of reality*.[44]

The dualism disappears because, if legal 'validity' is a fact of reality, it is no longer a 'normative idea'. But this 'normative idea' is the very idea that, Ross insists (in passages quoted above), cannot be eliminated from the concept of law. Here, too, he manifestly contradicts himself.

Despite his claims, Ross did not simply 'interpret' the concept of validity 13
differently from the Pure Theory. He has eliminated the concept of validity as a normative idea. Indeed, 'to put a different interpretation' on 'the normative ideas' does not amount, in spite of what he says, to 'reading them for what they are, [namely] the expression of certain peculiar psycho-physical experiences which are a fundamental element in the legal phenomenon'.[45] Normative ideas cannot be *interpreted* as psycho-physical facts; an Ought cannot be *interpreted* as an Is. What Ross calls an 'interpretation' – or a 'reinterpretation'[46] – of 'normative ideas' (and of the concept of 'validity') amounts, in effect, to their complete elimination.

Ross continues by saying that

> spiriting away all notions of validity from the concept of law . . . would mean the unavoidable spiriting away of the specifically legal, the very element which is the decisive criterion of that part of human behaviour which is made the subject of study in jurisprudence.[47]

[42] ibid.
[43] ibid 82.
[44] ibid 90 (my italics).
[45] ibid 49.
[46] ibid 145.
[47] ibid.

If law, the object of jurisprudence, is indeed 'human behaviour' – if it is an *is*-fact – then the normative idea of validity cannot be the criterion of law. An *is*-fact cannot be valid. It can only be or not be. Only a norm, an Ought, can be valid. We saw that Ross rejects certain 'realistic' theories on the grounds that they 'separate all normative points of view from the concept of law', that they 'determine the law as purely a fact, a part of the social behaviour of men', and that they 'propose to spirit away entirely all normative points of view, all notions of validity'.[48] Yet his 'reinterpretation' of normative ideas – his 'reinterpretation' of the concept of validity, as Ross presents it – leads precisely to the same result. Ross begins, he explains, 'from the supposition that the science of law is a branch of the doctrine of human behaviour'.[49] And this means that law, as the object of legal science, must be defined exclusively as factual human behaviour: 'as purely a fact, a part of the social behaviour of men', as maintained by those 'realistic' theories that Ross rejects. The consequence of Ross's account of legal science as a 'doctrine of human behaviour' is that 'the legal phenomenon must be found within the field of psycho-physical phenomena constituting the domain of psychology and sociology'.[50] This means that legal science is a branch of psychology and sociology, and that law cannot be understood as a norm.

14 In *Towards a Realistic Jurisprudence*, then, Ross rejects the view that 'the law consists of norms' – 'this view', he says, is 'untenable'[51] – and offers the above-quoted definition of law as a 'psycho-physical' phenomenon. Now, this is also precisely what is claimed by those 'realistic' theories that Ross rejects. It is telling, however, that Ross's reason for rejecting these theories is that they eliminate 'normative ideas' from the concept of law. Ross himself seeks to avoid this result. Indeed, he thinks he has managed to retain 'normative ideas' in the concept of law by maintaining that an essential element of the legal phenomenon is that legal subjects believe in the 'competence' or the 'authority' of the law-creating individuals. This 'belief in validity'[52] on the part of legal subjects is what he characterises, as we have seen, as a 'disinterested behaviour attitude'; it is the belief that one ought to act in accordance with what the law-creating individuals prescribe. So according to Ross, this 'disinterested behaviour attitude' – which he also characterises in terms of 'notions of validity of a specifically legal nature induced by the social suggestive power of custom'[53] – is one of the factors of the legal phenomenon.

Yet to hold that people's belief that they ought to behave in a certain way is an element of the phenomenon called 'law' is not the same as retaining

[48] ibid 49.
[49] ibid 78.
[50] ibid.
[51] ibid 93.
[52] ibid 147.
[53] ibid 88f.

'normative ideas' in the concept of law. For the belief that one ought to behave in a certain way is a fact, not a norm. It is a belief which has an Ought as its content; but this belief is itself an Is.

The fact that Ross insists on maintaining, as we have seen, that such a belief is 'erroneous' – that is, that people who believe that they ought to behave in a certain way are erroneously 'rationalising' their feelings of being bound – goes to show how far his theory really is from retaining 'normative ideas' in the concept of law. That an individual A is 'competent' to establish law with regard to an individual B, means only, according to Ross, that there is a 'spontaneous feeling or behaviour attitude (on the part of B) toward A, erroneously rationalised in the idea of an object, a notion'.[54] This 'notional objectivation of a subjective impulse' is, he says, 'characteristic of the practical idea of validity'.[55] But such an 'objectivation' (which consists in the belief that one ought to act in a certain way), such a 'rationalisation' of a 'subjective impulse' to action, is – as Ross seems never to grow tired of saying – 'erroneous', 'impossible', 'nonsense'. In rejecting this 'rationalisation', then, Ross's realistic theory repudiates the normative idea of the Ought. It is only because – contradicting his own rejoinders to some 'realistic' theories – Ross himself also rejects such 'normative ideas' that he is in a position to define the phenomenon of law as a psychological fact, and to characterise legal science as a part of psychology and sociology, thus arriving at the very conclusion arrived at by those 'realistic' theories that he criticises. When he claims that his attempt to debunk the concept of validity as a falsely rationalised psychological fact is a mere 'reinterpretation', Ross – in order to go on using the notion of 'validity' – deceives himself into ignoring this contradiction.

Ross's contradiction is also apparent in the fact that, on the one hand, he agrees with the Pure Theory of Law's thesis that legal statements – if indeed they are to describe the specific sense in which law addresses individuals when prescribing that they ought to behave in a certain way – must be *ought*-statements and cannot therefore be *is*-statements, especially not statements about actual behaviour in the future:

> Kelsen . . . remarked that if all meaning is to be denied to the norm or '*Sollen*', and statements about the law are to be reinterpreted to mean statements about certain probable actual courses of conduct, this will conflict decisively with the special meaning immediately inherent in the law . . . Kelsen is undoubtedly right in this.[56]

On the other hand, however, Ross claims that the normative meaning of law is merely a 'pretended meaning', and he rejects 'the normative conception of the nature of law':

[54] ibid 80.
[55] ibid 81.
[56] ibid 106.

> But the question is whether this pretended meaning really is a meaning, and can be recognized without criticism as the jurisprudential form of cognition. In my opinion these questions must be answered in the negative.[57]

He adds, nevertheless, the following:

> By this, however, I do not mean to say that the legal proposition – as some have believed – can be reinterpreted as a statement in the indicative mood as to what will (probably) happen in the future. This would, in fact, be to overlook the tendency of the legal proposition towards 'what is valid'.[58]

Note that by a 'legal proposition' Ross seems to mean, in this passage, the utterance of the legal *authority*. Such an utterance is to be interpreted, he maintains, not as a 'statement in the indicative mood', but rather as an utterance in the imperative mood. It is to be interpreted, in other words, as an Ought, as a norm. But then the conclusion to draw should be that the normative meaning of law is not a 'pretended meaning'; it is, rather, the true meaning of law. The authority's utterance, accordingly, is a norm – even though this is something that is denied by Ross in this very work, as we have seen. For if the 'legal proposition' – if we understand it as the utterance of the legal authority – must be an utterance in the imperative mood rather than a 'statement in the indicative mood'; and if the 'indicative mood' is incompatible with the 'tendency of the legal proposition towards "what is valid"', then 'validity' must be understood as an Ought, as normative validity. It cannot be, despite Ross's insistence to the contrary, an *is*-fact – for otherwise there would be no reason to object to an interpretation of the 'legal proposition' as a 'statement in the indicative mood'.

The same holds if by 'legal proposition' Ross means instead a statement *about* the law, a proposition describing the law. (This hypothesis cannot be excluded, since in the passages quoted above Ross is addressing himself to the Pure Theory of Law's thesis that statements *about* law must be normative propositions.) If Ross grants that statements about law are not statements about factual events, and especially that they are not statements about future
16 factual events, then he must also grant that they can only be normative propositions.

We have already seen, however, that in his latest work, *On Law and Justice*, Ross sets forth the following programmatic statement:

> I reject the idea that legal cognition constitutes a specific normative cognition, expressed in *ought*-propositions, and interpret legal thinking formally in terms of the same logic as that on which other empirical sciences are based (*is*-propositions).[59]

[57] ibid.
[58] ibid.
[59] *On Law and Justice* (n 2) x.

This means that 'legal propositions' – understood as statements about law – must be 'statements in the indicative mood'. And Ross does now indeed claim – as we have also seen, but it must now be pointed out again – that 'statements concerning valid law at the present time must be understood as reference to hypothetical future decisions', and that the statement that a rule is valid means only that 'the rule will be applied by the courts'.[60] In *On Law and Justice*, in other words, a statement about valid law (that is, a statement describing the law) is nothing more than a 'statement in the indicative mood as to what will (probably) happen in the future'.

Ross rejects certain 'realistic' theories of law that define law as factual behaviour, because they eliminate normative validity from the concept of law. He thus perceives, in a way, that the concept of law cannot be defined without resorting to the concept of normative validity. For some reason, however, he represses this insight; he never seems to be aware of the contradiction in which he entangles himself.

IV

In *On Law and Justice* Ross presents the relation between validity and efficacy differently than in his book *Towards a Realistic Jurisprudence*.

In the latter work, he distinguishes between two psychological factors as causes of lawful action: an 'interested' impulse to action, which is the fear of sanctions; and a 'disinterested' impulse, which is the feeling of being bound by the law, the belief in the competence or the authority of the law-creating organs. According to Ross, the only fact that can be regarded as 'validity' from the point of view of a realistic theory of law is such an 'uninterested' impulse to action. He rejects, as we saw, the concept of an objective, normative validity, which is, in his view, simply an 'erroneous' rationalisation of that impulse. Thus 'validity', in Ross's realistic theory, is a certain motive for the kind of factual conduct that constitutes the 'efficacy' of law. This means that in order to determine the efficacy of law one is to take into consideration, not only the application of law on the part of legal organs, but also the observance of law on the part of legal subjects. Indeed, fear of sanctions, which Ross presents as a possible motive for lawful conduct, can only refer – as a possible cause of the efficacy of law – to the observance of law on the part of legal subjects.

In *On Law and Justice*, in turn – a work in which Ross, by contrast with his
views in *Towards a Realistic Jurisprudence*, characterises law as a system of norms 17
– the concept of efficacy is restricted to the application of law by legal organs. He says:

[60] ibid 41.

> The effectiveness which conditions the validity of the norms can . . . be sought solely in the judicial application of the law, and not in the law in action among private individuals. If, for example, criminal abortion is prohibited, the true content of the law consists in a directive to the judge that he shall under certain conditions impose a penalty for criminal abortion. The decisive factor determining that the prohibition is valid law is solely the fact that it is effectively upheld by the courts where breaches of the law are brought to light and prosecuted.[61]

Ross thus refuses to regard the legal norm in question as efficacious, as 'effective', if legal subjects, fearing the sanction, refrain from committing the criminal offence of abortion.

It is only if one conceptualises legal norms as norms that prescribe sanctions – as does Ross, in agreement with the Pure Theory of Law – that one is able to distinguish between the application of legal norms (on the part of the organs in charge of applying and executing those sanctions) and their observance (on the part of the legal subjects who adopt the behaviour that avoids the sanction). One is therefore able to recognise that the efficacy of law lies not merely in the fact that law is applied, but likewise in the fact that law is observed. Ross's refusal to include the observance of legal norms in the concept of efficacy is hardly justifiable, especially from the perspective of a psychologico-sociological account like the one his realistic theory propounds – for the aim of sanction-prescribing legal norms is precisely to prevent the occurrence of those actions that are the conditions of the legally prescribed sanctions.

Having now restricted the concept of efficacy, Ross correspondingly modifies his account of legal validity. That a legal norm is 'valid' now means only that the norm will be felt by the judge as binding, and accordingly applied:

> A national law system, considered as a valid system of norms, can . . . be defined as the norms which actually are operative in the mind of the judge, because they are felt by him to be socially binding and therefore obeyed.[62]

The validity of law, then, amounts to its efficacy. It is the fact that legal norms are actually applied by the courts (or, to put it more generally, by the organs in charge of applying the law), and applied, indeed, because these organs feel bound by such norms. With respect to the meaning of the phrase 'a system of norms is "valid"', Ross now says that

> this capacity within the system is based on the fact that the norms are effectively complied with, because they are felt to be socially binding.[63]

[61] ibid 35.
[62] ibid.
[63] ibid 34.

There are therefore two factors in the concept of validity: an external, physical factor, which is the efficacy of law (that is, the fact that the law is actually observed), and an internal, psychological, factor, which is the feeling of being bound by the law. As Ross puts it:

> In the concept of validity two points are involved: partially the outward observable 18
> and regular compliance with a pattern of action, and partly the experience of this pattern of action as being a socially binding norm.[64]

But it is in the external factor – in efficacy – that the emphasis lies. 'Jurisprudence', says Ross,

> must have as its task the interpretation of the 'validity' of the law in terms of social effectivity, that is, a certain correspondence between a normative idea content and social phenomena.[65]

In *Towards a Realistic Jurisprudence*, by contrast, Ross's account of validity emphasised the psychological factor. Validity was there the 'disinterested behaviour attitude', the 'disinterested impulse to action': validity was, in other words, the *cause* of efficacy.

Now, if validity is defined as efficacy, and if one takes into consideration the social reality of the facts of human behaviour, then it is a mistake to think that there is any necessary connection between the factual conduct – the lawful conduct – that represents efficacy and a particular motive (viz. the feeling of being bound by legal norms). For it is undeniable that there can be many different motives as to why people – legal subjects as well as legal organs – choose to behave according to the law. People will often refrain from an offence simply because they have no motive for committing it, or because they feel bound, not by the *legal* norm that proscribes the offence (a norm of which they might not even be aware), but by the representation of some norm of morality or religion proscribing that course of conduct. It is not because they fear foreclosure of their assets that most debtors pay their debts; it is because they wish to avoid losing their credit (which is a consequence, but not a *legal* consequence, of non-payment).

The same holds if one chooses (as does Ross in *On Law and Justice*) to ignore the actions of legal subjects and to take into account in one's definition of efficacy only the behaviour of judges. For it is likewise undeniable that judges may in many cases behave according to the law, applying the legal norms that ought to be applied, not because they feel bound by such norms (or, more precisely, by their representation of such norms), but because they are convinced that their decision is just, or that it is politically desirable, or because they wish to avoid having their decision annulled by a higher court. What

[64] ibid 37.
[65] ibid 68.

actually happens is that very often that a judge will first – for whatever reason – reach a decision on the case at hand, and only afterwards seek to justify it on specifically legal grounds.

Ross does stress, as we have seen, that the key aspect of the validity of a
19 legal norm is 'solely the fact that it is effectively upheld by the courts'.[66] This amounts to the thesis that a legal norm is valid only if it is applied by courts. The validity of law, in other words, is identified with its efficacy, and efficacy is tantamount to application by courts. Yet Ross seems dissatisfied with this identification, for he affirms:

> [I]t is often said that a rule is valid law when it is applied in the practice of the courts. But this is a clumsy and vague statement, needing more precise analysis in several respects.[67]

He then considers the case of a norm that is valid even before it is applied by a judge, and observes that

> a rule may be considered valid law although it has as yet not been applied in the courts – for example, if it is a recently promulgated law.[68]

If this is correct – as it most certainly is – then the validity of a legal norm cannot consist in the fact that it is applied by courts. In other words, validity cannot be the same as efficacy; it must be something else. If a norm can be valid before it is applied, then its 'validity' can only mean that it *ought* to be applied: for that is all that can be said before the norm is actually applied. Ross retorts, however, that a norm

> is considered to be valid if on some basis other than previous practice of the courts there is reason to assume that the rule will be applied in any future legal decision; . . . [S]tatements concerning valid law at the present time must be understood as referring to hypothetical future decisions under certain conditions: if an action should be brought on which the particular rule of law has bearing, and if in the meantime there has been no alteration in the state of the law (that is to say, in the circumstances which condition our assertion that the rule is valid law), the rule will be applied by the courts.[69]

A legal norm is valid before it is efficacious, in other words, if it can be predicted that it *will* be applied. Now, this is something that cannot be predicted with certainty even if the norm has been applied in a previous case, let alone if it has never been applied at all. Ross grants the point: 'Even after one or more legal decisions have been given which verify A', he says (where A is the statement that some given legal norm is valid, that is, that it will be applied), A

[66] ibid 35.
[67] ibid 40.
[68] ibid.
[69] ibid 40f.

'continues to be in principle an uncertain prediction'.[70] Why is this prediction uncertain? Because the possibility exists that a norm which is regarded as valid – and which must indeed be regarded as valid – fails to become efficacious, remaining either not applied at all, or not applied in certain particular cases.

But if a legal norm can be valid before it becomes efficacious – and even in spite of the possibility that it will never be efficacious – then legal validity must, as an *ought*, be distinguished from the *is*-fact of efficacy. Of a law already enacted but which has not yet been applied, one can say that it is valid, and that it will probably also become efficacious. If validity were identical with efficacy, however, one would be able to say only that such a law *will* probably *become valid*, but is *not* valid *yet*. And Ross grants (as indeed he must) that a law that has just been enacted, but is not yet efficacious, is already 'valid'.

The only thing that can aptly be said of such a law is that if the prediction that the law *will* be applied – that is, that the law will become efficacious – turns out to be false, then such a law will no longer be regarded as valid; it will lose its validity. Efficacy, then, is *in this sense* a condition of validity. But it is itself not the same as validity. This account of the relation between validity and efficacy is the one that the Pure Theory of Law proposes. And Ross seems occasionally to avail himself of it, for example in this previously quoted passage:

> The effectiveness which *conditions* the validity of the norms can therefore be sought only in the judicial application of the law.[71]

We have also already quoted the normative proposition that comes after this sentence. It is the proposition by which Ross – contradicting his own programmatic statement that the propositions of a realistic theory of law can only be *is*-propositions – describes a norm: 'the judge . . . *shall* under certain conditions impose a penalty for criminal abortion'.[72]

If the efficacy of a legal norm is to be seen only in its application by the courts, then the ideal case of the validity of a legal norm is the case in which it is not efficacious at all – the case in which it is not applied at all – because it has fulfilled its aim of preventing the behaviour that constitutes the condition of its application. Moreover, if the statement that a legal norm is valid is but a prediction that it will be applied by courts – and if this is something that cannot be predicted with certainty, but only with some higher or lower degree of probability – then statements about the 'validity' of legal norms can only claim to have a higher or lower degree of probability. Ross explicitly affirms that such statements 'can never claim absolute certainty, but can only be

[70] ibid 42.
[71] ibid 35 (my italics).
[72] ibid (my italics).

maintained with a greater or lesser degree of probability'.[73] But Ross grants that a law that has not yet been applied can already be valid and that the judge who applies such a law is applying a valid law. Moreover, he cannot deny that courts must apply only valid laws. Given this, however, it follows that it is merely the statement about the future *efficacy* of a legal norm – and not the statement about its *validity* – that claims to have certain degree of probability. It is efficacy that is merely probable rather than certain – not validity. The reason why the statement about the future efficacy of a legal norm is merely
21 probable rather than certain is that the possibility always remains that some court or other, in some particular case, will in fact fail to apply the norm that it ought to apply. There can thus be higher or lower degrees of efficacy. A legal norm is efficacious in the highest degree if it is in fact applied in all cases in which it ought to be applied. It is efficacious to a lower degree if there are some cases in which it is not applied, even though it ought to be applied.

Because Ross identifies validity with efficacy, he claims that there can be 'degrees' of validity, and assumes that a norm's degree of validity corresponds to the degree of probability with which efficacy can be predicted. He says that

> a rule can be valid law to a greater or lesser degree varying with the degree of probability with which it can be predicted that the rule will be applied . . . The probability is high, and the rule possesses a correspondingly high degree of validity, if the prediction is based on a well-established doctrine sustained by a continual series of undisputed precedents; or if it is based on a statutory provision whose interpretation has been established in long and continuous practice. On the other hand, the probability is low, and the rule has a correspondingly low degree of validity, if the prediction is based on a single and dubious precedent or even on 'principles' or 'reason'.[74]

The efficacy of a legal norm, if understood as the fact that courts actually apply it, can indeed have different degrees. The degree of probability with which the efficacy of a legal norm can be predicted, however, does not necessarily correspond to the norm's degree of efficacy. It may well happen that the degree of probability with which one is able, at any given moment, to predict the efficacy of a legal norm is very low, but that that norm later turns out to be highly efficacious; or vice versa. Moreover – and more importantly – the legal norm must be considered valid even in those cases in which it is not applied (though it ought to be applied), and thus in those cases in which it has not been efficacious, for in such cases the norm must already be regarded as 'existing', and the 'existence' of the norm cannot, therefore, be the fact of its application – it can only be its validity. If one agrees that a legal norm can be valid even in a case in which it is not applied – and that for it to remain valid it is

[73] ibid 44f.
[74] ibid 45.

necessary only that it be applied in a sufficient number of cases – then one cannot identify validity with efficacy: one must distinguish between normative validity and factual efficacy.

V

Ross's reason for rejecting the dualism of Ought and Is – of normative validity and factual efficacy – is that he finds it 'metaphysical' in character. 'It leads consistently', he says, 'to a metaphysical assertion that existence itself in its innermost being is valid (Hegel)'.[75]

The 'metaphysical' view that Ross has here in mind, however, is by no 22
means dualistic. On the contrary: it is monistic. It admits of no dualism between Is and Ought, between reality and value. For it sees the Ought *in* the Is; it situates value squarely in the domain of reality. It is the metaphysics of value-immanence: a view that is 'metaphysical' only in the sense that it is logically committed to the claim that the will of some supra-empirical, transcendent authority (such as the will of God, or of some comparable instance) manifests itself in reality. Indeed, the dualism of Is and Ought – of which the dualism of efficacy and validity is an expression – arises precisely from the wish to avoid such a metaphysical monism.

Ross asserts that

> [l]ike most metaphysical constructions, the construction of the *immanent validity of positive law* rests on a misinterpretation of certain experiences, in this case the experience that the law is not merely a factual customary order, but an order which is experienced as being socially binding.[76]

From the way in which Ross presents the dualistic view that he seeks to oppose, one might be led to think that what a dualistic theory of law maintains is – like Hegel, who held that value (the Ought) is immanent in reality (the Is) – that the normative validity (an Ought) of positive law is immanent in the reality of law (an Is, according to Ross). Yet the exact opposite is the case. The Pure Theory of Law does not maintain that the normative validity is 'immanent' in the *is*-reality of law. What the Pure Theory of Law maintains is that law *qua* norm – that is, law understood as the meaning of a norm-creating act – is just as different from that act as the validity of the norm is different from its efficacy. The Pure Theory of Law – deliberately rejecting the 'metaphysical' view that value is immanent in reality – denies that validity is immanent in reality, that 'ought' is immanent in Is. Validity and reality, Is and Ought, are, the Pure Theory holds, essentially separated.

[75] ibid 38.
[76] ibid (my italics).

In another passage, Ross maintains – once more against the Pure Theory – that 'ideas of validity', in the sense of normative validity, 'are metaphysical constructions built on a false interpretation of the "binding force" experienced in the moral consciousness'.[77] I find it completely impossible to understand this claim. There is nothing at all 'metaphysical' in the assertion that the meaning of a certain norm-creating human act is that people ought to behave in a certain way, and that the validity of the legal norm lies in this Ought. And in fact Ross himself, as we have repeatedly seen, describes the legal norm in a normative proposition.

Ross does grant that 'validity' in the Pure Theory of Law is a merely 'formal category of thought without any claim in respect of the content of the material which is apprehended in this categorical form'.[78] He distinguishes, rather aptly, between validity as a 'formal category', and validity 'in terms of a material a priori idea of justice'.[79] This latter construction, which the Pure Theory rejects, can indeed be called 'metaphysical'. The former, however,
23 cannot. The claim that the validity of a legal norm means that it *ought* to be complied with and applied (and not that it *is* complied with and applied) is simply the consequence of the fact that the legal norm, being a prescription, is therefore an Ought rather than an Is. There is nothing 'metaphysical' about this claim. And Ross's own realistic theory agrees, as we have seen, that the legal norm is a prescription, and that, as such, it can only be understood as an Ought.

Having characterised normative validity as a 'metaphysical' construction, Ross then defines the efficacy of law (which his realistic theory identifies with 'validity') as 'a certain correspondence between a normative idea content and social phenomena'.[80] Yet what can possibly be understood by a 'normative idea content' – if not the idea of an Ought? This 'normative idea content' is nothing other than the normative validity asserted by the Pure Theory of Law. It is the idea that one ought to behave in a certain way. It is also, however, the idea that Ross denounces again and again as 'erroneous', and likewise (in the pages from which we have just quoted) as a 'misinterpretation'[81] or a 'false interpretation'[82].

Ross says in *Towards a Realistic Interpretation* that 'validity' is not 'something objectively given'.[83] With this, however, he is saying nothing that the Pure Theory of Law – precisely from the perspective of its focus on the legal Ought – does not also maintain. For the Pure Theory strongly emphasises that the

[77] ibid 68.
[78] ibid 66.
[79] ibid 68.
[80] ibid.
[81] ibid 38.
[82] ibid 68.
[83] *Towards a Realistic Jurisprudence* (n 1) 77.

statement that the subjective meaning of the law-creating act is also its objective meaning – the statement, that is, that law has objective validity – is only a possible interpretation of that act, not a necessary one. One does not have to attribute to the law-creating act such an objective meaning; one may, for example, regard it from a sociological rather than from the legal point of view. This is no reason, however, to disqualify the concept of law's objective validity as an 'erroneous rationalisation' of the belief in the authority of the law-creating organs; it is no reason to characterise the concept of 'validity' as the 'feeling' of being bound by legal norms. The concept of normative validity is not a rationalisation of these psychological facts (which are certainly not present, at any rate, in many cases in which the 'legal phenomenon' exists – to use a 'realistic' phrase). The concept of normative validity is, rather, an interpretation; it is an interpretation made possible only by the presupposition of a basic norm. To say that such an interpretation is 'erroneous' can only mean that it is unfounded. But such an interpretation is indeed founded, as the Pure Theory of Law explains, *if* one presupposes the norm – the basic norm – that legitimises the law-creating act, the norm in virtue of which the subjective meaning of this act becomes also its objective meaning. What Ross calls an 'erroneous rationalisation' is thus nothing other than the objective validity of law, which is conditioned, as the Pure Theory claims, by the presupposition of the basic norm.

Ross rejects the doctrine of the basic norm. In *Towards a Realistic Jurisprudence* he claims that the doctrine of the basic norm, based as it is on the dualism of
'validity' and 'reality', gives rise to an antinomy.[84] The antinomy is this. On 24
the one hand, the normative validity of law is determined by reference to the historical act by which the constitution was established and to the efficacy of this constitution. This means that the normative validity of law is determined by reference to *is*-facts. Such facts, however, are in turn themselves determined by reference to the normative validity of law.

Austin's theory of law reflects, according to Ross, a similar antinomy: the constitution is valid because it has been authoritatively enacted by the sovereign; but the sovereign's authority rests upon the constitution; and this, says Ross, is a 'circle'.[85]

With regard to Austin's theory, Ross is indeed correct. In the Pure Theory of Law, however, the authority of those who enact the constitution does not itself rest on the positive constitution that has been enacted by human acts. Their authority rests, rather, on a presupposed basic norm. Indeed, it is precisely in order to avoid the circle mentioned by Ross that the Pure Theory makes reference to a presupposed basic norm. The basic norm, far from being

[84] ibid 57ff.
[85] ibid 58.

arbitrarily determined, refers directly to some actually established constitution that is by and large effective.

Ross does grant that the Pure Theory avoids the specified antinomy; but it avoids it, he claims, only 'formally',

> for even if the 'choice' of a fundamental norm [that is, a *Grundnorm*, a basic norm] is free, it is not arbitrary. If the system is not to be the expression of a mere figment, the fundamental norm must be chosen in such a way that it will 'accord' with the legal system actually functioning. This again lands us in the antithesis.[86]

This conclusion is false. What the Pure Theory holds is simply that the meaning of the constitution-issuing act can be interpreted as an objectively valid norm *only if* one presupposes the basic norm; *only if*, in other words, one presupposes that one ought to behave according to the established, efficacious constitution. With this the Pure Theory avoids, not merely 'formally', but completely, the antinomy that Ross detects in Austin's theory.

In *On Law and Justice*, in turn, Ross tries to show that the doctrine of the basic norm does not really provide the foundation of the normative validity of law. Instead, the doctrine of the basic norm confirms – so he claims – Ross's own definition of law as an *is*-fact. This would again follow from the fact that the basic norm, rather than being arbitrarily chosen, directly refers to an actual positive constitution that is by and large efficacious, and thus to a coercive order established in accordance to that constitution, and by and large efficacious. He argues as follows:

> If the system is to make sense, it is clear that the initial hypothesis cannot be chosen arbitrarily. Kelsen himself says that it must be chosen in such a way that it covers the system which is actually in effect. But it is then clear that, in reality, effectivity is the criterion for positive law; and that the initial hypothesis, once we know what is positive law, in reality only has the function of investing it with the 'validity' which is demanded by the metaphysical interpretation of legal consciousness, though no one knows what it is.[87]

We have already seen that there is no trace of 'metaphysical' speculation in the claim that it is only by presupposing the basic norm that it is possible to interpret the constitution-issuing act – as well as any further norm-creating acts performed in accordance with the constitution – as having the meaning of objectively valid norms. Indeed, the Pure Theory explicitly stresses the hypothetical character of objective validity. The charge of 'metaphysical' speculation is therefore particularly unjustified.

Yet if from the doctrine of the basic norm Ross can derive nothing other than the conclusion that 'effectivity is the criterion for positive law', then he has simply stated something that the Pure Theory of Law by no means denies.

[86] ibid 59.
[87] *On Law and Justice* (n 1) 70.

After all, the Pure Theory also holds that the positivity of law lies in its creation by human acts and in its efficacy.

But the positivity of law is not its validity. To say that positive law is 'valid' is to say that its norms ought to be complied with and applied; and positive law is 'valid' only if such norms are (a) posited by human acts (rather than by super-human entities such as God or a god-created Nature) and (b) by and large efficacious (that is, actually complied with and applied). And this is precisely what the basic norm stipulates. Efficacy is, together with the creation of legal norms by human acts, a condition of normative validity. Efficacy is thus itself not validity. It is, rather, one of the elements stipulated in the basic norm as a condition of the validity of a constitution and of the norms created in accordance with it.

Still with regard to the doctrine of the basic norm, Ross also claims that

> [i]t might be possible to pass this over as a superfluous but harmless construction were it not that it results in shutting the eyes to a closer analysis of the criterion of effectivity. By making validity an internormative relation (deriving the validity of one norm from validity of another). Kelsen has at the outset precluded himself from dealing with the heart of the problem of the validity of the law – the relation between the normative idea content and social reality.[88]

I take note, with gratitude, of this half admission of Ross's that the doctrine of the basic norm is 'harmless'. Regarding the charge of superfluity: the doctrine of the basic norm, far from purporting simplistically to set aside as 'erroneous' the millenary view of law as a system of objectively valid norms, is an attempt to show *how* – that is, under what *epistemological condition* – such an interpretation is possible. This seems to me to be no more superfluous than Kant's attempt to determine the logico-transcendental conditions of experience, even if it is not as important.

As for the accusation that I 'shut my eyes' to the problem of the relation between validity *qua* 'normative (!) idea content' and efficacy *qua* 'social reality', I believe I can, in good conscience, dismiss the allegation. No other theory of law has ever dealt with this problem as intensively as the Pure Theory of Law.

[88] ibid.

Part III

Legal Norms and Legal Science

10

Kelsen on the Completeness and Consistency of Law

EUGENIO BULYGIN*

I. TWO DUBIOUS THESES IN KELSEN'S THEORY OF LAW

MY AIM IN this essay is to discuss two prominent theses of Kelsen's which I find rather dubious. One is the thesis of the necessary completeness of law. This thesis states that every legal system is necessarily complete in the sense that there is no legal question for which it provides no answer, no legal problem for which it has no solution. As Kelsen puts it: 'The legal order cannot have any gaps'.[1] The second is the thesis of the necessary consistency of law. This thesis states that no two legal norms that belong to the same system can ever contradict each other: in other words, no two contradictory norms can be simultaneously valid. 'It is not possible', Kelsen writes, 'to describe a normative order by asserting the validity of the norm "*a* ought to be" and at the same time "*a* ought not to be"'.[2] Together, these theses state that, whatever its content, any given set of legal norms belonging to the same system is necessarily complete and consistent.

Both theses are to be understood as referring to positive (ie man-made) law. Perhaps to anyone who believes that there is a 'natural' law the two theses would seem fairly reasonable, especially if natural law is believed to be God-made. But Kelsen's only concern is positive law. It seems strange, however, that a human artefact like positive law should necessarily possess those two properties. It seems, moreover, that neither thesis is true. It appears to be trivially true that legal systems can be inconsistent. A system is inconsistent if

* For many useful comments and helpful suggestions, which greatly improved this chapter, I am grateful to Cristina Redondo, Hernán Bouvier, Jorge L Rodríguez, Pablo Navarro, Paolo Comanducci and Stanley L Paulson; and to two anonymous reviewers, whose remarks allowed me to avoid several mistakes.

[1] H Kelsen, *General Theory of Law and State*, A Wedberg transl (Cambridge, Mass., Harvard University Press, 1945) 147.

[2] H Kelsen, *The Pure Theory of Law*, 2nd edn, M Knight transl (Berkeley, University of California Press, 1967 [1960]) 328.

it contains at least two norms, one of which prohibits, and the other permits, the performance of some given action; and as every lawyer knows, examples of such situations abound. The case of completeness is perhaps less obvious, though many jurists would maintain that a legal system has 'gaps', ie that there are situations which the law does not regulate at all. In *Normative Systems*, Carlos Alchourrón and I have argued that the completeness thesis is indeed also false.[3] It is the product of a failure to draw two crucial distinctions. One is the distinction between *norms*, which are prescriptive, and therefore neither true nor false, and *norm-propositions*, which are truth-apt descriptions of (the existence of) norms. The other is the distinction between *negative* (or 'weak') and *positive* (or 'strong') *permissions*. In this essay I shall again take up these distinctions. I will also try to answer a more puzzling question: Why would anyone think that positive law is always and necessarily complete and consistent? Why would Kelsen, in particular, endorse such strange and seemingly false theses?

I have just mentioned that our proposed refutation of the completeness thesis was in part based on the distinction between norms and norm-propositions. Though Kelsen does not use this terminology – which was introduced by von Wright[4] – he does draw a seemingly analogous contrast between the '*Rechtsnorm*' (the legal norm) and the '*Rechtssatz*' (the legal sentence or proposition). But are the two distinctions really analogous? This is by no means clear. I propose to begin by taking a closer look at these two Kelsenian notions, and by trying to determine what he may have meant by them.

II. KELSEN'S DISTINCTION BETWEEN '*RECHTSNORM*' AND '*RECHTSSATZ*' AND HIS CONSISTENCY THESIS

Although the *terminological* distinction between '*Rechtsnorm*' and '*Rechtssatz*' is one that to some extent Kelsen has always drawn, the fact is that the *meaning* of these terms undergoes important changes throughout his body of work, reflecting a radical modification in his conceptions of the law and the role of legal science.

During the first 'period' of his work (until 1940[5]), indeed, the terms were used more or less interchangeably to refer to *legal norms* rather than to sentences or propositions. This was consistent with contemporary usage. In 'traditional German jurisprudence', as Kelsen remarks elsewhere, '*Rechtssatz*' and

[3] CE Alchourrón and E Bulygin, *Normative Systems* (Vienna-New York, Springer, 1971) 116ff.

[4] GH von Wright, *Norm and Action. A Logical Inquiry* (London, Routledge and Kegan Paul, 1963) 106; von Wright's terminology has been widely used in the literature ever since.

[5] On the periodisation of Kelsen's Works, see SL Paulson, 'Four Phases in Hans Kelsen's Legal Theory?' (1998) 18 *Oxford Journal of Legal Studies* 153–66; and SL Paulson, 'Arriving at a Defensible Periodization of Hans Kelsen's Legal Theory' (1999) 19 *Oxford Journal of Legal Studies* 311–14.

'*Rechtsnorm*' were employed as synonymous terms.[6] Thus in his first major work (1911) Kelsen uses, almost exclusively, the term '*Rechtssatz*';[7] in the 1925 *Allgemeine Staatslehre* he indistinctly speaks of 'objective law constituted by legal norms (*Rechtsnormen*) or legal propositions (*Rechtssätze*);'[8] and in the first edition of *Reine Rechtslehre* (1934) the term '*Rechtssatz*' stands for the 'reconstructed legal norm'.[9]

The differentiated use of '*Rechtsnorm*' and '*Rechtssatz*' to refer to two distinct entities occurs for the first time in 1941,[10] and features prominently in his 1945 *General Theory of Law and State*. In both cases, however, the distinction is obscured by an unfortunate translation: though '*Rechtsnorm*' is correctly translated into English as 'legal norm', '*Rechtssatz*' is confusingly rendered as 'rule of law'.[11] A similar thing happened with *Théorie Pure du Droit* (1953) – a revised version, in French, of the first edition of the *Reine Rechtslehre* – in which we find '*normes juridiques*' contrasted with '*règles de droit*'.[12] But what does the term '*Rechtssatz*' now mean for Kelsen?

We need to keep in mind that in this second, 'Kantian' stage of Kelsen's development – which runs until 1960 – a legal norm is not simply a norm issued by legal authorities such as legislatures or judges; it is a product of the reformulation or reconstruction of legal science. Prohibitions and commands issued by legal authorities by means of statutes or judicial decisions constitute only the 'raw material' out of which legal science constructs legal norms.

This idea of a science that 'creates' its own object was repeatedly formulated by Kelsen in many of his works. Here is a quotation from the 1953 *Théorie Pure*:

> We can thus state simultaneously that the rules of law (*règles de droit*) are judgments formulated by legal science and that the object of such science is constituted by legal norms. Here there is no contradiction. Without a doubt, one can consider

[6] Kelsen makes the remark in a footnote to the second edition of the *Pure Theory of Law*, a footnote not included in the English translation: but see the original *Reine Rechtslehre*, 2nd edn (Vienna, Franz Deuticke, 1960) 74 fn. On that note Kelsen goes on to add that even Adolf Merkel, whom he characterises as 'perhaps the most remarkable representative of [traditional] general jurisprudence' (my translation), explicitly identified the concepts of '*Rechtsnorm*' and '*Rechtssatz*'.

[7] Already in the title of the book – which can be translated as *Main Problems in the Theory of Public Law Developed From the Doctrine of the Legal Norm* – the term turns up: see H Kelsen, *Hauptprobleme der Staatsrechtslehre entwickelt aus der Lehre vom Rechtssatze* (Tübingen, Mohr, 1911).

[8] H Kelsen, *Allgemeine Staatslehre* (Berlin, Julius Springer, 1925) 47.

[9] H Kelsen, *Reine Rechtslehre. Einleitung in die rechtswissenschaftliche Problematik* (Vienna, Franz Deuticke, 1934); translated into English as *Introduction to the Problems of Legal Theory*, BL Paulson and SL Paulson transl (Oxford, Clarendon Press, 1992 [1934]); see at 23 and the translators' supplementary note 5 at 132ff in the English-language edition.

[10] Stanley Paulson drew my attention to this. See H Kelsen, 'The Pure Theory of Law and Analytical Jurisprudence' (1941) 55 *Harvard Law Review* 44–70.

[11] See Kelsen, *General Theory of Law and State* (n 1) eg at 45; and *cf* also 'The Pure Theory of Law and Analytical Jurisprudence' (n 10) 51.

[12] H Kelsen, *Théorie Pure du Droit* (Boudry-Neuchâtel, Éditions de la Baconnière, 1953).

> that the norms created and applied within the framework of a legal system have the character of legal norms only if it is ascribed to them by legal science. It is the role of this science to attribute to certain acts the objective meaning of legal norms. But this does not prevent us from stating that legal norms form the object of legal science or, what is the same, that law is a system of norms. This definition is in full accord with Kant's theory according to which knowledge constitutes or creates its object, for what is in question here is an epistemological creation and not something created by man's work in the sense in which the law-maker creates a law. In the same way, natural phenomena which are the objects of causal science are only created by it in a purely epistemological sense.[13]

This forms the basis of Kelsen's views, during this period, on the normativity of legal science: legal science is normative not merely in the sense that it is concerned with norms, but also, and above all, because its propositions are normative; its propositions are *norms*.[14]

An echo of the same idea can be found even in the second edition of his *Reine Rechtslehre* (1960):

> Just as the chaos of sensual perceptions becomes a cosmos, that is, 'nature' as a unified system, through the cognition of natural science, so the multitude of general and individual legal norms, created by the legal organs, becomes a unitary legal system, a legal 'order', through the science of law. But this 'creation' has a purely epistemological character.[15]

Here, however, it is in connection with the legal 'order' as a unitary and consistent system – and not with the reconstruction of legal norms – that Kelsen speaks of 'epistemological creation'; it is the legal order *qua* unitary and consistent system that is produced by legal science.

Now, the idea that a legal system *should* be complete and consistent stems from the doctrines of popular sovereignty and separation of powers; it can be traced back to the Enlightenment, and particularly to Montesquieu. The strict divide between, on the one hand, the *legislative* power as the political power *par excellence*, to be exercised by a parliament composed of representatives of the people and tasked with enacting general norms and thus of creating 'the law'; and, on the other hand, a purely technical *judicial* power, to be exercised by professional judges whose role is that of strictly applying general law to particular cases, yields the requirement that for every legal problem there be one and only one legal solution. The law must, in other words, be both complete and consistent – for otherwise judges would not be able to perform their task.

[13] ibid 45 (English translation by Anne Collins).

[14] The thesis of the normativity of legal science played an important role in the development of Kelsen's thought. It enabled him to draw a distinction between causal (factual) and normative social sciences: between sociology and jurisprudence. According to Kelsen, the difference lies in the kind of proposition used by these sciences for the description of their objects. See eg *General Theory of Law and State* (n 1) 163ff.

[15] Kelsen, *The Pure Theory of Law* (n 2) 72.

Of course, one should not mistake this *ideal* of a complete and consistent legislation – an aspiration which to this day, rightly or wrongly, many jurists would share – for a description of how things actually are. French commentators of Napoleon's 1804 *Code Civil* – the first serious attempt to implement the doctrine of separation of powers – were well aware of this gap. 'In reality, there is no doubt', writes Demolombe, one of the most important commentators of the *Code*, that 'laws can by no means encompass all the various, numerous hypotheses which emerge in practice on a daily basis'.[16] They thus acknowledged the possibility of non-regulated actions or states of affairs: of 'gaps' in the law.

This insight, however, was progressively lost. Particularly among German jurists – and even though the German Civil Code came to be enacted only in 1900 – the idea of a complete and consistent codification did not lose steam. And the specific idea that legal science 'epistemologically' creates law was partly rooted in the fact that it then fell to jurists – ie to legal science – to construe and adapt legislation to those requirements of completeness and consistency. Legal norms are understood as being 'created' by legal science in the sense that only the latter can confer 'objective' normative meaning to prescriptive acts performed by legal authorities (viz. the acts of issuing commands and prohibitions); for such acts themselves are seen as having only the 'subjective' meaning of legal norms.[17] Buttressed by Neo-Kantian epistemology, this idea became characteristic of Kelsen's second, 'Kantian' period.

It is this idea of an epistemological 'creation' of legal norms that explains why Kelsen regarded legal systems as being necessarily consistent. If legal norms are 'created' or at any rate 'reconstructed' by legal science, then it is hardly surprising that they should be consistent: for it would be unusual, to say the least, if a science were to formulate contradictory sentences. 'The unity of the object of enquiry', Kelsen wrote in 1934, is an 'epistemological postulate', and 'the negative criterion of this unity is non-contradiction, a logical principle that also applies to cognition in the realm of norms';[18] 'normative cognition tolerates no contradiction between two norms of the same system'.[19] One finds passages to the same effect in the *General Theory of Law and State*. For example:

> All quest for scientific knowledge is motivated by an endeavour to find unity in the apparent multiplicity of phenomena. Thus, it becomes the task of science to describe its object in a system of consistent statements, that is, statements not

[16] 'En réalité, sans doute, les lois ne peuvent pas embrasser toute les hypothèses si variées, si nombreuses, que chaque jour la pratique soulève': *cf* C Demolombe, *Cours de Code Napoléon*, vol 1 (Paris, Lahure, 1880) 136.

[17] See eg Kelsen, *Introduction to the Problems of Legal Theory* (n 9) 9.

[18] ibid 111f.

[19] ibid 75.

> contradicting each other. That is true also for the sciences of law and morality, sciences whose objects are norms. Contradictions are also banned within the sphere of these sciences. Just as it is logically impossible to assert both 'A is' and 'A is not', so it is logically impossible to assert both 'A ought to be' and 'A ought not to be' . . . It is one of the main tasks of the jurist to give a consistent presentation of the material with which he deals. Since the material is presented in linguistic expressions, it is *a priori* possible that it may contain contradictions. The specific function of juristic interpretation is to eliminate these contradictions by showing that they are merely sham contradictions. It is by juristic interpretation that the legal material is transformed into a legal system.[20]

And once again the idea subsists even in the second edition of *Reine Rechtslehre*:

> To be sure, it is undeniable that legal organs may create conflicting norms – that they perform acts whose subjective meaning is an 'ought' and which may be in conflict with each other if their subjective meaning is interpreted as their objective meaning . . . But since the cognition of law, like any cognition, seeks to understand its subject as a meaningful whole and to describe it in noncontradictory statements, it starts from the assumption that conflicts of norms within the normative order which is the object of this cognition can and must be solved by interpretation.[21]

Yet during this very same period in his work, Kelsen simultaneously – and self-contradictorily – insists that the *Rechtssätze* are not to be confused with the legal norms produced by legal authorities, and indeed that the 'functions' of legal science and legal authority are quite distinct; the former is 'descriptive', the latter 'prescriptive'. In the *General Theory of Law and State*, for example, he already writes that:

> It is the task of the science of law to represent the law of a community, i.e. the material produced by the legal authority in the law-making procedure, in the form of statements to the effect that 'if such and such conditions are fulfilled, then such and such a sanction shall follow.' These statements, by means of which the science of law represents law, must not be confused with the norms created by the law making authorities. It is preferable not to call these statements norms, but legal rules [*Rechtssätze*]. The legal norms enacted by the law-creating authorities are prescriptive; the rules of law formulated by the science of law are descriptive. It is of importance that the term 'legal rule' or 'rule of law' be employed here in a descriptive sense.[22]

It is true that at this stage – 1945 – there are still vacillations. Having previously insisted that legal norms are 'hypothetical judgments' rather than imperatives,[23] in the *General Theory of Law and State* Kelsen still resists the

[20] *General Theory of Law and State* (n 1) 374f.
[21] *The Pure Theory of Law* (n 2) 205f; see also ibid 328ff.
[22] *General Theory of Law and State* (n 1) 45.
[23] See eg Kelsen, *Introduction to the Problems of Legal Theory* (n 9) 23.

characterisation of legal norms as imperatives or commands.[24] But in the second edition of *Reine Rechtslehre* – even though, as already noted, there are still echoes, in this book, of the Kantian idea that legal science epistemologically 'creates' its object[25] – the view is much more explicitly stated that the judgements of legal science, *Rechtssätze*, are *not* to be confused with legal norms issued by legal authorities:

> The differentiation between the 'rule of law' (in German: Rechts-*Satz*) and 'legal norm' (in German Rechts-*Norm*) expresses the difference between the function of legal cognition and the entirely different function of legal authority represented by the organs of the legal community. The science of law has to know the law – as it were from the outside – and to describe it. The legal organs, as legal authorities, have to create the law so that afterward it may be known and described by the science of law.[26]

This step cannot but lead Kelsen to reject his earlier theses that legal norms are judgements and not imperatives, and that norms are epistemologically 'created' by legal science:

> The science of law describes the legal norms created by acts of human behaviour and to be applied and obeyed by such acts; and thereby describes the norm-constituted relations between the facts determined by the norms. The sentences by which the science of law describes these norms and relationships must be distinguished as 'rules of law' from the legal *norms* that are created by the legal authorities. . . . Rules of law (in a descriptive sense) . . . are hypothetical judgments stating that according to a national or international legal order, under the conditions determined by this order, certain consequences determined by the order ought to take place. Legal *norms* are not judgments, that is, they are not statements about an object of cognition.[27]

In spite of the odd Kantian passage, then, we can say that with the publication of the second edition of *Reine Rechtslehre* Kelsen rejects his earlier thesis that legal *norms* are the epistemological 'creation' of legal science. Indeed, he comes to recognise that 'the science of law is just as incompetent to solve by interpretation existing conflicts between norms, or better, to repeal the validity of positive norms, as it is incompetent to issue legal norms'.[28] He should therefore have also expressly rejected the normativity of propositions of legal science. For he now assigns to legal propositions – to *Rechtssätze* – a much more modest role: *Rechtssätze* are descriptive of norms created by legal authorities. Kelsen does not explicitly acknowledge the change, and proceeds without

24 *General Theory of Law and State* (n 1) 35.

25 See passage quoted to n 15.

26 *The Pure Theory of Law* (n 2) 72.

27 ibid 71.

28 H Kelsen, 'Derogation' in RA Newman (ed), *Essays in Jurisprudence in Honor of Roscoe Pound* (Indianapolis, Bobbs-Merrill 1962) 155.

modifying his terminology.[29] But it is very clear that after 1960 he no longer takes legal norms to be created by legal science, and that he takes legal science and its propositions to be strictly descriptive. Not to abandon his earlier doctrine that the propositions of legal science are normative would therefore have been self-contradictory. If *Rechtssätze* are descriptive, then they are not normative; if they are normative, then they are not descriptive. (Incidentally, this explains Hart's perplexities when he tries to find a coherent interpretation of Kelsen's theory in view of Kelsen's insistence that legal propositions are 'normative'. Hart failed to realise that this claim of Kelsen's rises and falls with the idea of the epistemological creation of norms, and that this was an idea that Kelsen had tacitly given up by 1960.[30])

In fact, the Kantian trend in Kelsen's work – the trend to which the thesis of the normativity of legal science belongs – is radically incompatible with its positivistic trend – the trend which includes the theses that all law is man-made and that there is a sharp distinction between description and prescription, between cognition of law and creation of law. Elsewhere I have explored this antinomy, which lies at the core of the Pure Theory of Law.[31] I have also argued that Kelsen's development of this positivistic trend is the most important one. For our present purposes, however, what matters is that we were able to bring out how Kelsen's views on the necessary consistency of law stem from his Kantian doctrine of the normativity of legal science. And this is a doctrine which I believe Kelsen was right eventually to reject. His early analogy between the 'chaos of sensual perceptions' and the products of the legislative organs' activities[32] is extremely weak, as is his analogy[33] between laws of nature – a product of observation and description of certain regularities by the natural sciences – and positive laws – created by human actions.[34]

[29] Some years later, curiously, admitting that in his works there was no clear terminological distinction between the concepts of '*Rechtsnorm*' and '*Rechtssatz*', Kelsen nonetheless claims *always* to have had in his mind the difference between the creative function of legal authorities and the cognitive function of legal science. (H Kelsen, 'Professor Stone and the Pure Theory of Law' (1965) 17 *Stanford Law Review* 1132ff and 1136f.) This claim seems not to be warranted.

[30] See HLA Hart, 'Kelsen Visited' in his *Essays in Jurisprudence and Philosophy* (Oxford, Clarendon Press, 1983 [1963]) 286ff. Kelsen's attempt to preserve something of his original doctrine by introducing a distinction between prescriptive and descriptive 'Sollen' – a distinction he borrows from Christoph Sigwart, a second-rate 19th-century German logician – only added to the confusion. Again the relevant footnote is omitted from the English-language translation; but see *Reine Rechtslehre* (n 6) 77f, as well as C Sigwart, *Logic*, H Dendy transl, vol 1 (London, Swan Sonnenschein, 1895) 17 fn 1.

[31] See my essay 'An Antinomy in Kelsen's Pure Theory of Law' (1990) 3 *Ratio Juris* 29–45, reproduced with minor revisions in SL Paulson and BL Paulson (eds), *Normativity and Norms. Critical Perspectives on Kelsenian Themes* (Oxford, Clarendon Press, 1998).

[32] See passage quoted to n 15.

[33] See eg *Introduction to the Problems of Legal Theory* (n 9) 24f.

[34] For detailed criticism, see my essay 'Kant y la Filosofía del Derecho Contemporánea' in CE Alchourrón and E Bulygin, *Análisis Lógico y Derecho* (Madrid, Centro de Estudios Constitucionales, 1991 [1980]) 371ff.

Thus deprived of its original theoretical framework, moreover, the thesis that law is necessarily consistent is clearly to be rejected. The idea, which at one point Kelsen explicitly endorses,[35] that if there were contradictions between legal norms then the corresponding legal propositions would be contradictory, too, is an extravagant one: consistent descriptions can surely be given of inconsistent states of affairs.

III. THE PRINCIPLE OF PROHIBITION AND KELSEN'S COMPLETENESS THESIS

Having granted, as Kelsen does from 1960 onwards, that *Rechtssätze* are descriptions of legal norms – having admitted, in other words, the distinction between norms and norm-propositions – we are now in a position to assess Kelsen's equally unwarranted views on the completeness of law.

The thesis that all legal systems are necessarily complete is one which Kelsen firmly holds throughout his works, even after 1960. He bases this idea on the putative principle that everything that is not legally prohibited is legally permitted. We can refer to this, for short, as the 'Principle of Prohibition'. Let us examine his argument.

'Genuine gaps', Kelsen writes in 1934, 'do not exist':

> A genuine gap would mean that a legal dispute could not be settled in accordance with prevailing norms because the statute – as one says – lacks a provision addressing the case, and therefore cannot be applied. Every legal dispute consists in one party making a claim against another party, and the decision granting or rejecting the claim depends on whether or not the statute – that is, a valid norm to be applied in the concrete case – establishes the claimed legal obligation. Since there is no third possibility, a decision can always be made, and, indeed, can always be made on the basis of the statute, that is, by applying the statute. Even a decision rejecting the claim is made by appeal to the prevailing legal system. By imposing obligations on human beings to behave in particular ways, the legal system guarantees them liberty outside those obligations.[36]

There are similar passages, for example, in *General Theory of Law and State*,[37] in the second edition of the *Reine Rechtslehre*,[38] and even in the posthumously published *Allgemeine Theorie der Normen*.[39] Here is Kelsen in 1960:

> [A] positive legal order can always be applied by a court to a concrete case, even when the legal order does not contain, according to the court's view, a general

[35] See *The Pure Theory of Law* (n 2) 74.

[36] Kelsen, *Introduction to the Problems of Legal Theory* (n 9) 84.

[37] *General Theory of Law and State* (n 1) 146ff.

[38] *The Pure Theory of Law* (n 2) 245ff.

[39] *General Theory of Norms*, M Hartney transl (Oxford, Clarendon Press, 1991 [1979]) 131, 227.

> norm positively regulating the behaviour of the defendant or accused . . . For in this case his behaviour is regulated negatively, that is, legally not prohibited, and in this sense permitted.[40]

The popular idea that law has gaps is, according to Kelsen, but a 'fiction' made up by jurists and judges – and also by legislators – in order not to apply norms which they regard as unjust:

> The intention obviously is that the judge has to assume the role of legislator if there is no general legal norm stipulating the obligation of the defendant asserted by the plaintiff and if the judge considers the lack of such a norm unsatisfactory, unjust, inequitable. The condition under which the judge is authorized to decide a given dispute as legislator is not – as the theory of gaps pretends – the fact that the application of the actually valid law is logically impossible, but the fact that the application of the actually valid law is – according to the opinion of the judge – legally-politically inadequate.[41]

It is relatively easy, however – now that we are equipped with the distinction between norms and norm-propositions – to prove that the Principle of Prohibition cannot fulfil the function that Kelsen expects it to fulfil, viz. to make it the case that all legal systems are necessarily complete.

Kelsen argues that law prohibits some actions; in virtue of the Principle of Prohibition, then, all other actions are therefore permitted. The conclusion is that all actions are attributed a normative status – either prohibited or permitted – by any given legal system, whatever its content. There is therefore no conduct which law does not regulate.

But the argument is fallacious. Let us consider what the terms 'prohibited' and 'permitted' mean in this context. An action φ is prohibited by a given set of norms – call this set 'α' – if α contains a norm prohibiting φ. But to say that an action or state of affairs φ is permitted may mean one of two different things. It may mean that there is in α a norm permitting φ; ie that φ is positively (or 'strongly') permitted. Alternatively, it may mean that there is in α no norm prohibiting φ; ie that φ is negatively (or 'weakly') permitted. We can thus distinguish between two concepts of permission as they may occur *in a norm-proposition*. These two *descriptive* concepts are both relative to a given action or state of affairs φ and a given set of norms or system α. In contrast, the concept of permission as found *in norms* is a genuinely *prescriptive* concept, used to permit or authorise some given action under certain circumstances, and which is not relative to a system.

With this in mind, we can now turn our attention to Kelsen's Principle of Prohibition – 'everything that is not legally prohibited is legally permitted'. It can be understood in one of two ways. It can be understood either as a norm

[40] *The Pure Theory of Law* (n 2) 246–47.
[41] *General Theory of Law and State* (n 1) 147–48.

– as a *positive* norm, for Kelsen admits of no other kind – or as a normative proposition. If conceived of as a positive norm, however, then the Principle of Prohibition must be contingent rather than necessary. It will exist only if and when it has either been issued by a legal authority, or customarily created. Therefore it cannot *necessarily* belong to all possible normative systems. If, on the other hand, the Principle of Prohibition is conceived of as a normative proposition, then, as we saw, we need to establish whether, within it, the term 'permitted' occurs in its negative, weak sense, or, rather, in its positive, strong sense. If it is used in the negative sense, then 'permitted' means 'not prohibited'. Consequently, what the Principle says is that *what is not prohibited is not prohibited*, which is analytically true but completely trivial, as well as perfectly compatible with the existence of non-regulated actions (ie with 'gaps' in the law). If, on the other hand, 'permitted' is taken in its strong sense, then the Principle says that *what is not prohibited is positively permitted*. But this is surely false; from the mere absence of a prohibition we cannot infer the existence of a positive permissive norm. Whether or not such a positive permission exists in some given system is a purely contingent matter. (The Principle of Prohibition holds true only in one very special case: when the system happens to contain a general closure rule permitting all actions not prohibited by the system; the *nullum crimen sine lege* principle, which is characteristic of modern criminal law, would be an example of such a rule. But again: whether or not any such rule exists is a contingent matter.)[42]

Now, Kelsen seems in his early works to have adopted the *strong* reading of the Principle of Prohibition, ie to use 'permitted' in the sense of 'positively permitted'. In the first *Reine Rechtslehre*, for example, he states that

> [b]y imposing obligations on human beings to behave in particular ways, the legal system guarantees them liberty outside those obligations. . . . The legal system embraces not only the principle that one is obligated to behave in a certain way (in so far as behaving in the opposite way is set as condition for the specific consequence of an unlawful act), but also the principle that where one is not obligated to do or to forbear from doing, then one is free. It is this negative norm that is applied in a decision rejecting a claim directed to behaviour not established as obligatory.[43]

This presupposes the truth of the Principle of Prohibition in its strong version; but as we saw, in its strong version the Principle is false. At a later stage, in the second edition of the *Reine Rechtslehre*, Kelsen seems to change his approach. He no longer claims that every legal system contains a norm permitting all actions which are not prohibited; he now seems to adopt the *weak* version of

[42] For a fuller development of these arguments, see *Normative Systems* (n 3) ch VII; and on the general theme of gaps in the law *cf* also the exchanges collected in F Atria, E Bulygin, JJ Moreso, PE Navarro, JL Rodríguez and J Ruiz Manero, *Lagunas en Derecho* (Madrid, Marcial Pons, 2005).

[43] See Kelsen, *Introduction to the Problems of Legal Theory* (n 9) 85.

the Principle.[44] But this version, as we saw, is perfectly compatible with the existence of 'gaps' in the law.

In short: *qua* norm, the Principle of Prohibition is contingent; *qua* norm-proposition, it is either vacuous, or false. In no case can it support Kelsen's thesis that legal systems are necessarily complete.

IV. ARE THE CONSISTENCY AND COMPLETENESS THESES REALLY THAT STRANGE?

Oddly enough, many important legal philosophers have endorsed versions of the completeness thesis, as well as, in some cases, the consistency thesis. This includes not only such legal positivists as Kelsen or Joseph Raz, but also anti-positivist authors like Ronald Dworkin. The common problem with their views is that they do not always clearly distinguish between norms and norm-propositions – a distinction which lies, as we have seen, at the core of both issues. Not for nothing did Georg Henrik von Wright once remark, alluding to this distinction: 'It has taken me nearly thirty years to see its full significance. And not all logicians and philosophers have seen it even now'.[45]

A. Raz and the Silence of the Law

Raz's case is particularly interesting. In his well-known paper 'Legal Reasons, Sources, and Gaps',[46] Raz defends the Principle of Prohibition by means of exactly the same argument as Kelsen. He simply uses different terminology, which gives the impression of novelty. Instead of norms, Raz speaks of 'reasons for action'. He also employs several rather unusual and cumbersome formulas;[47] but I think we can well dispense with these, and translate his arguments into plain English.

Raz distinguishes between two types of legal gaps. Gaps of the first type are due to the indeterminacy of the law. They stem either from the vagueness of the relevant concepts ('where the law speaks with an uncertain voice') or from unresolved conflicts between reasons for action ('where [the law] speaks with many voices').[48] Such gaps, according to Raz, are unavoidable. Gaps of the

[44] See eg *The Pure Theory of Law* (n 2) 42ff, 243f.

[45] GH von Wright, 'Value, Norm and Action in My Philosophical Writings' in G Meggle (ed), *Actions, Norms, Values. Discussions with Georg Henrik von Wright* (Berlin, de Gruyter, 1999) 20.

[46] J Raz, 'Legal Reasons, Sources, and Gaps' in *The Authority of Law*, 2nd edn (Oxford, Oxford University Press, 2009 [1979]).

[47] The formula '$LR_c\, x, \varphi$' means the same as 'Legally (or according to law), there is a conclusive reason for *x* to φ', where *x* is a person and φ an action. '$LPer_c\, x, \sim \varphi$' means: 'Legally, there is a conclusive permission for *x* not to φ'. See ibid 71.

[48] ibid 77.

second type stem from the silence of the law, and Raz emphatically denies that such gaps can exist. This means that Raz accepts, at least in this restricted form, the completeness thesis as we have discussed it so far.

It is Raz's argument against the possibility of legal gaps of this second kind – gaps deriving from the silence of the law – that can be shown to be precisely the same as Kelsen's.

Raz's proof of the impossibility of legal gaps of the second kind is relatively simple. His starting point is that such gaps can exist only if it is simultaneously possible that (a) it is not the case that, legally, there is conclusive reason for *x* to φ; and (b) it is not the case that, legally, there is a conclusive permission for *x* not to φ.[49] A 'conclusive permission' to φ is defined as the absence of a reason to omit φ-ing.[50] Thus a gap of the second kind can exist only if it can simultaneously *not* be the case that legally, there is a conclusive reason for φ-ing, *and* that, legally, there is no conclusive reason for φ-ing. But to say that *it is not the case that, legally, there is a reason to* φ is the same, according to Raz, as saying that *legally, there is no reason to* φ. It follows that a gap of the second kind is possible only when the two following statements are both true: 'Legally, there is no reason for *x* to φ' and 'It is not the case that, legally, there is no reason for *x* to φ'. But this is a contradiction; one statement affirms, and the other denies, that legally, there is no reason for *x* to φ. Hence the condition can never be satisfied. Therefore, there can be no gaps of the second kind. Moreover, says Raz, the statement 'It is not the case that, legally, there is a conclusive reason for *x* to φ' is logically equivalent to 'Legally, there is a conclusive permission for *x* not to φ': this, he writes, is 'the familiar closure rule that whatever is not legally prohibited is legally permitted and vice versa'.[51] His conclusion:

> Contrary to much popular imagining, there are no gaps when the law is silent. In such cases closure rules, which are analytic truths rather than positive legal rules, come into operation and prevent the occurrence of gaps.[52]

It can easily be shown, however, that Raz is wrong; gaps of this kind are perfectly possible.[53]

Raz's 'familiar closure rule that whatever is not legally prohibited is legally permitted' is what, in the previous section, I have called the 'Principle of Prohibition'. For Raz – as in Kelsen's second stage – it is the *weak* version of this principle that is in issue, not the strong one. For here 'permitted' means only 'not prohibited': it means only that there is no reason not to φ. Raz's

[49] ibid 76.
[50] ibid 64.
[51] ibid 76.
[52] ibid 77.
[53] In what follows I resume some arguments first presented in my essays 'El Silencio del Derecho' (2002) 22 *Análisis Filosófico* 103–14; and 'On Legal Gaps' (2003) *Analisi e Diritto* 21–28.

'conclusive permission', in other words, is the mere absence of a prohibition – it is a negative or 'weak' permission. Indeed, a 'conclusive permission' is defined as the absence of a reason for omitting to do an action: and the mere absence of a reason is not a reason. Raz admits this when he writes that '[i]ntuitively, the negation of a legal reason is nothing more than the absence of a legal reason', and that though 'explicit permissions are always source-based, conclusive permissions never are'.[54] If conclusive permissions have no sources, then they are not reasons; not *legal* reasons, at any rate. Raz's conclusive permissions are weak permissions, which do not regulate actions. It is hard to fathom what is 'conclusive' about them.

Therefore Raz's argument against gaps due to the silence of law is exactly the same as Kelsen's; it is based on the weak version of the Principle of Prohibition. And, as we have already seen, the weak version of the Principle of Prohibition merely states that what is not prohibited is not prohibited. This is a rather trivial tautology. It tells us just as much about legal gaps as the sentence 'it is false that it is raining if and only if it is not raining' tells us about the weather. That his closure rule amounts to a tautology is something that Raz explicitly acknowledges in the passage just quoted; he calls it an 'analytic truth'. It is far from clear, however, how analytic truths can prevent the law from having gaps.

Indeed, rather than showing that the law cannot have gaps of that second kind, Raz is *defining* such gaps out of existence. For according to him, as we saw, a gap due to the silence of the law is *possible* only when it is simultaneously true that (a) legally, there is no reason for x to φ, and that (b) it is not the case that, legally, there is no reason for x to φ.[55] But *precisely* because this is a contradiction, the very condition postulated by Raz for the existence of gaps can, by definition, never be met. This seems to be a case of what Hart once called a 'definitional stop'.[56] It is hardly surprising that Raz claims that such gaps cannot exist; but that would be too easy a way of getting rid of them.

Raz's core mistake lies, I think, in his characterisation of these second-type gaps. On the one hand, he writes that

> A legal system is legally complete if there is a complete answer to all the legal questions over which the courts have jurisdiction. It contains a gap if some legal questions subject to jurisdiction have no complete answer.[57]

A 'complete answer is provided', he says, 'by pointing to a decision which the law requires'.[58] So far one could agree. But soon after Raz adds that regarding

[54] Raz, 'Legal Reasons, Sources, and Gaps' (n 46) 67. Also, 'x has explicit permission to φ' is defined as 'there is a fact with some force to cancel reasons for not φ-ing': see ibid 64.

[55] ibid 75f: 'Gaps of the second kind can exist only if it is possible that $(\sim LR_c, x, \varphi)$ & $(\sim LPer_c, x, \sim\varphi)$'.

[56] HLA Hart, 'Prolegomenon to the Principles of Punishment' in *Punishment and Responsibility. Essays in the Philosophy of Law*, 2nd edn (Oxford, Oxford University Press 2008 [1959]) 5.

[57] 'Legal Reasons, Sources, and Gaps' (n 46) 70.

[58] ibid 71.

the question of 'whether or not a person ought (conclusively) to perform a certain action [φ], there are two possible complete answers': (1) that the law conclusively requires the performance of φ; and (2) that the law conclusively permits the omission of φ.[59] Now, (1) means that there is a norm requiring the performance of φ, and (2) means that there is no norm requiring the performance of φ. In other words, differently from what Raz suggests, the two answers are not independent; (2) is but the negation of (1), and thus if (1) is true (2) is false and vice versa.[60] Hence the disjunction of (1) and (2) is analytic, and the conjunction of the respective negations a contradiction.[61] It follows that there is always a complete answer for every legal question, and that all systems are complete – only of course something is seriously wrong if one supposes one can prove by purely logical means that all legal systems are complete.

The problem lies in (2), ie in the second answer, and in Raz's notion of a 'conclusive permission'. In fact, a conclusive permission to omit φ-ing, as Raz defines it, is *not* a complete answer, if by a 'complete answer' one means a proposition stating that the action at stake is legally regulated in some way. For the mere fact that an action is not prohibited does not imply that it is legally regulated; it is legally regulated if the law *positively*, ie strongly permits it. And note that, even though in the essay that I have been discussing Raz maintains that analytic closure rules can eliminate legal gaps by regulating (by weakly permitting) those cases which are not explicitly regulated by the law, he affirms elsewhere – in an essay included in the same book – that

> [a] normative system does not . . . regulate behaviour which is merely weakly permitted by it. An act is weakly permitted if the system contains no norm prohibiting it. It is strongly permitted if the system contains a norm permitting it.[62]

This is a contradiction, not in the law, but in Raz's thought.

Contrary to Raz's opinion, in summary, gaps stemming from the silence of law are perfectly possible, and, as a matter of fact, occur rather frequently in

[59] ibid.

[60] For the possibility of working with von Wright's T-Logics, in which there are propositions which are neither true nor false (a possibility that Raz admits *expressis verbis*), see JJ Moreso, PE Navarro and MC Redondo, 'Legal Gaps and Conclusive Reasons' (2002) 68 *Theoria. A Swedish Journal of Philosophy* 52–66, and 'Sobre la Lógica de las Lagunas en el Derecho' (2001) 33 *Crítica. Revista Latinoamericana de Filosofia* 47–73.

[61] This is precisely how Raz defines his second-type gaps: '"($\sim LR_c$, x, φ) & ($\sim LPer_c$, x,$\sim$φ)" is true'; see 'Legal Reasons, Sources, and Gaps' (n 46) 71.

[62] J Raz, 'The Institutional Nature of Law' in *The Authority of Law*, 2nd edn (Oxford, Oxford University Press, 2009 [1975]) 117 fn 4. cp also J Raz, *Practical Reason and Norms*, 2nd edn (Oxford, Clarendon Press, 1990 [1975]) 150: 'A normative system regulates all the acts regulated by its norms. This means that a normative system regulates all the acts permitted by norms of the system which grant exclusionary permissions. But a system does not regulate acts which are merely weakly permitted by it, that is acts permitted merely because of the absence of a norm requiring their omission'.

legal practice. The problem of completeness of law is a contingent matter, depending on the content of each legal system.

B. Dworkin, 'Right' Answers and True Answers

Surprisingly, Kelsen's and Raz's views on the completeness of law bear a striking resemblance to some of the consequences emanating from Dworkin's idea of law as an interpretive concept.[63] If, as Dworkin maintains, interpretation consists in showing the law in its best moral light, then it seems to follow that the law must be complete and consistent; that, as Dworkin would have it, there is always one right answer to every legal problem.

But what, exactly, does 'right answer' mean?[64] We can say that a legal system provides answers to legal questions. The form of a typical legal question is 'Is action φ obligatory (prohibited, permitted) in circumstance *q* according to legal system *L*?'. Now, answers to such questions are of two kinds: *positive* and *negative* answers. An example of a positive answer would be 'According to *L*, φ is obligatory (prohibited, permissible) in circumstance *q*'; I call it a 'positive' answer because, if the answer is true, the law *determines* the normative status of φ in *q*. But an answer can also be negative. This is the case if the law *does not determine* the status of φ. Negative answers, in turn, are themselves of two (sub) kinds. If there is a normative gap in *L* regarding φ in *q*, the answer is that φ is *not regulated* by *L*; in other words, φ is neither prohibited, nor obligatory, nor permissible. If, on the other hand, the system is inconsistent, the answer is also negative in the sense that it does not *univocally* determine the deontic status of φ: eg 'φ is obligatory and prohibited' (or: 'φ is prohibited, but not-φ is permissible').[65]

Let me also introduce another distinction, between two different (though related) issues. One is whether there can be true statements about the law; this we can call the issue of legal 'objectivity'. A legal system is objective in so far as it provides a *true* answer to a legal question. The answer can be either positive or negative: this is something that turns on the content of each system. In other words, an incomplete or contradictory system is just as 'objective' as a complete and consistent one. The second issue is whether the deontic status of any given action φ is legally determinate; this is the 'determinacy' issue. These two issues are obviously independent. That some legal system *L* does *not* deter-

[63] R Dworkin, *Law's Empire* (Oxford, Hart Publishing, 1998 [1986]) esp chs 2 and 11.

[64] In what follows I recuperate some lines of argument first presented in my essay 'Objectivity of Law in the View of Legal Positivism' (2004) *Analisi e Diritto* 219ff.

[65] Strictly speaking, it is only in the former case – ie the case of a normative gap – that the status of φ can be said to be *un*determined; in the latter case – the case of inconsistency – φ is rather *over*determined. But the practical outcome is similar in both cases: the law does not univocally determine the status of φ.

mine the normative status of some action φ does certainly not mean that there is no *true* answer to the question 'Is action φ obligatory (prohibited, permitted) according to legal system *L*?'. On the contrary, one of the two possible negative answers will be true: that 'neither φ nor its negation is obligatory *or* permitted according to *L*'; or that 'φ is both obligatory and permitted according to *L*'.

In contemporary debates, however, authors refer to '*right* answers' rather than to *true* ones. The difference, I suspect, is the product of some confusion between *describing* and *evaluating* the law. A 'right' answer is not merely a true answer. It is a satisfactory or good answer. And in order for an answer to a legal question to be a good one, it must, it seems, inform us of the obligations and rights that we have according to the law. *Negative* answers, such as 'the legal system *L* says nothing about this situation', even if true, would not count as 'good' answers to legal questions, at least in the sense in which the phrase is commonly used. Moreover, the 'objectivity' of law is often defined in terms of whether or not there are *right* answers to legal questions. But this confuses the two issues that I have distinguished in the previous paragraph. It may be objectively true that the law is incomplete or inconsistent, and thus that it does not (not at all, or not univocally) determine the normative status of some given action. In such cases there may be no 'right' answer; but there is certainly a *true* answer to the corresponding question about the legal status of that action.

The motivation behind the conception of legal objectivity in terms of *right* rather than *true* answers is probably that negative answers to legal questions cannot be used to justify judicial decisions. If the legal system contains a gap or a contradiction, then it does not determine a positive answer, and the judge won't be able to justify her decision by appealing to the norms of that system. And here we face the following alternative: we must either accept that our legal systems may actually be defective, and thus that there may be cases in which judges are unable to justify their decisions on the grounds of *legal* norms (in which case they will have to make use of other, non-legal criteria); or we can simply deny – as does Dworkin – that the system can be defective in such a way. In the latter case, however, in order to ensure that the law is complete and coherent we would have to inject moral principles into the law, and suppose that such principles will remedy all defects, doing away with all gaps and contradictions. Quite apart from its other flaws, then, Dworkin's conception unwarrantedly assumes that a system containing both legal and moral rules would be complete and consistent.[66]

[66] Others have expressed this doubt. Thus JL Mackie thinks (because of his meta-ethical views) that resorting to moral norms would amount to 'automatically inject[ing] . . . subjectivity into statements about what the law is', given that judgements about what is 'morally best' have an 'irreducibly subjective element': *cf* J Mackie, 'The Third Theory of Law' in M Cohen (ed), *Ronald Dworkin & Contemporary Jurisprudence* (London, Duckworth, 1984 [1977]) 165; Brian Leiter remarks that 'If . . . one thinks that adjudication is "objective", in the sense that there are objectively right

V. CONCLUSION

Comparing the ideas of these three outstanding philosophers with regard to the completeness and the consistency of law yields the following picture.

Kelsen always maintained that there can be no gaps in the law, and thus that all legal systems are necessarily complete. For a long period he also maintained that legal systems are necessarily consistent. He came, however, to abandon the latter claim; it was rooted in the Kantian trend (mentioned above in section II) which, though present in much of his work, is nonetheless incompatible with the other, positivist trend which is also a trademark of the Pure Theory of Law and which became more and more dominant in the course of his many active years.[67] Kelsen's evolution, in fact, should also have led him to abandon the completeness thesis. He was on the right path, but did not take the last step. In the end, this is the only charge that can be made against Kelsen. And taking into account that he was already in his 80s by the time his 'late' period began, the omission is quite understandable.

Raz grants the possibility of inconsistency, but emphatically denies the possibility of legal gaps stemming from the silence of the law. His position is considerably more questionable. Though Raz accepts both the distinction between norms and norm-propositions, and the distinction between strong and weak permissions, he treats the Principle of Prohibition ('All that is not legally prohibited is legally permitted') as an analytic truth (with 'permitted' meaning simply 'not prohibited'). This is clearly insufficient for doing away with gaps; what Raz calls the 'familiar closure rule'[68] does in fact not close the system. A closure rule must provide a solution to cases that are not regulated (ie to *normative* gaps), and that is something no trivial tautology can achieve.[69] So the charge that can be made against Raz is that he fails to follow through on the implications of his own premises.

Dworkin's case is different. He regards law as necessarily complete and consistent, but this tenet is a direct consequence of his conception of law. For Dworkin there is no sharp distinction to be drawn between law as it is and law as it ought to be. Moreover, law as it ought to be determines (at least partially)

answers to legal disputes, then it might seem a bad idea to make right answers in law depend on moral considerations as Dworkin does': *cf* B Leiter, 'Objectivity, Morality, and Adjudication' in *Naturalizing Jurisprudence. Essays on American Legal Realism and Naturalism in Legal Philosophy* (Oxford, Oxford University Press, 2007 [2001]) 225; and Russ Schafer-Landau has convincingly argued that it is by no means clear that ethical theory can be construed as the project of developing 'a coherent set of rules from which one can infer all determinate moral verdicts': R Schafer-Landau, 'Moral Rules' (1997) 107 *Ethics* 584.

[67] See text to n 31.

[68] See text to n 51.

[69] For a detailed analysis of the concept of closure and of closure rules, see *Normative Systems* (n 3) ch VII.

the law as it is. But whereas the idea of a complete and consistent legal order is acceptable as a rational *ideal*, it is certainly wrong as a description of what happens in actual legal systems.[70] To use Raz's metaphor, then, we can say that for Dworkin the law is never silent, and that it always speaks with a single voice. The law's voice is always there. One must only look for it (if with Herculean energy).

The outcome of our discussion, then, is that Kelsen, Raz and Dworkin all endorse some version of the thesis that the law is necessarily complete, even if they do so for different reasons. That the greatest philosophers sometimes make mistakes is nothing new. But that these three very different and prominent legal philosophers happen to have made the same mistake is rather curious.

[70] In addition, there is no room in Dworkin's theory for the distinction between norms and normative propositions. His 'propositions of law' – see eg R Dworkin, *A Matter of Principle* (Oxford, Clarendon Press, 1985) 146ff – are neither norms nor normative propositions proper, for they are normative *and* descriptive at the same time. For criticism of this aspect of Dworkin's theory see my essay 'Norms, Normative Propositions and Legal Statements' in G Floistad (ed), *Contemporary Philosophy. A New Survey*, vol 3 (The Hague, Nijhoff, 1982) 127ff.

11

The Alternative Character of the Legal Norm: Kelsen as a Defeasibilist?

RICHARD HS TUR

I. INTRODUCTION

AMONG KELSEN'S MANY maddening and beguiling notions, one of the most perplexing and paradoxical is the 'alternative character' of the legal norm. In this chapter I shall first offer an interpretation and appreciation of that doctrine in the context of Kelsen's theoretical approach to the law making-and-applying enterprise. I shall then seek to deploy that analysis in assessing the extent to which Kelsen's account of what he calls 'the dynamic aspect of law' is consistent with what I take to be a defeasibilist conception of law. This is a small part of my continuing intellectual endeavour to take defeasibilism beyond methodology or pragmatism and ground it as a general theoretical truth about law.

Defeasibilism – to give a summary characterisation – is first and primarily the methodological view that law is best represented, understood and theorised as a body of defeasible, open-ended normative conditional propositions of the form 'If A is, then B ought to be, unless. . .'.[1] 'A', the antecedent clause, contains only legally determined facts. The 'B' clause stipulates the consequence that, according to law, ought to follow in the event that the facts in 'A' have occurred. The 'unless' clause contains circumstances which defeat the imputation of B to A: it falls to be filled, depending on which area of law is under consideration, by equity, policy, mercy and similar considerations; and although it will include already known and hitherto established circumstances, the full list of defeating considerations is not and cannot be determined in advance.

[1] For developments, see my essays 'Subjectivism and Objectivism: Towards Synthesis' in S Shute, J Gardner and J Horder (eds), *Action and Value in Criminal Law* (Oxford, Oxford University Press, 1993), esp 241ff; 'Defeasibilism' (2001) 21 *Oxford Journal of Legal Studies* 355ff; '*Res Judicata* and Theories of Law' (2001) 1 *Oxford University Commonwealth Law Journal* esp 129ff; 'Two Theories of Criminal Law' (2003) 56 *SMU Law Review* 797; and 'Defeasibility and Adjudication' in J Ferrer and G Ratti (eds), *The Logic of Legal Requirements. Essays on Legal Defeasibility* (Oxford, Oxford University Press, 2012).

A significant feature of this reconceptualisation is that it addresses the descriptive shortcomings of understanding law in terms of wholly closed, all-or-nothing conditionals of the form 'If A is, then B ought to be, full stop'. This 'canonical' formulation of the legal norm is unable to represent or explain a cluster of salient features of many, perhaps all, legal systems which impact negatively upon the normal attribution of a legally determined consequence B to legally defined conditions A. It is true that in a well-structured legal system many legal rules will not be substantially out of line with requirements of justice as to call conditions of defeasance into play. But occasionally one does come upon circumstances in which the application of the rule would lead to great absurdity or gross injustice – and courts may then be empowered to disapply, nullify or override the rule in a particular case on grounds such as mercy, justice, equity, purpose, policy or rights. This is by no means an uncharacteristic, purely accidental feature of law. It is, rather, how legal systems typically seek to accommodate justice, and like notions, without jettisoning to an unacceptable degree the certainty and communication that comes with the availability of general rules. It is, indeed, a common enough feature of legal systems for it to be counted as an outstanding aspect which any descriptively sound account of law must be able to represent and theorise – which is possible only if the 'canonical' understanding of legal norms is, as defeasibilism proposes, abandoned.[2] Thus defeasibilism claims, secondly, a significant degree of descriptive accuracy arguably not met by other legal theories (such as exclusive legal positivism).

Thirdly, and more controversially, defeasibilism aspires to the status of legal theory and not mere methodology and pragmatism. The approach seeks to go beyond descriptive accuracy and normative appeal to establish the universal and timeless truth about law that all legal norms, however they are expressed by the law-maker, are susceptible of and subject to defeat at the point of application under conditions which are incapable of exhaustive statement. This truth, if accepted as such, impacts on the concept of law.

Now, if there is a degree of 'fit' between Kelsen's 'dynamic aspect' on a 'realist' reading, and defeasibilism's core claim – that no legal norm is immune from overriding – then it may be possible to move defeasibilism forward a little from methodology and pragmatism to legal theory.

Seeking to enlist Kelsen's aid in the cause of defeasibilism may seem odd, even perverse, given how firmly mainstream jurisprudence seems to have placed him in what appears to me the barren soil of 'hard' or 'exclusive' legal

[2] Although it rejects the reduction of law to the traditional logic of closure, defeasibilism is also able to avoid the evident shortcomings of conceptualising law in terms of absolute discretion. The way in which the law works fits neither the absolute formalist's picture of a system of all-or-nothing, fixed rules, not the similarly extreme picture of wholly unstructured discretion.

positivism. In this, mainstream jurisprudence may have been rather too one-eyed. Kelsen himself observed that

> the Pure Theory of Law is not at all opposed to the so-called Free Law School . . . rather it is true that the Pure Theory of Law, with its deeper insight into the structure of the law, has given a theoretical foundation to one of the main theses of the Free Law School, that the so-called application of statutes by courts and administration is true *law-making.*[3]

William Ebenstein expressly draws out a similarity between aspects of the Pure Theory of Law and American Legal Realism, in some ways a like movement in law and legal thought in America to the Free Law School in mainland Europe:

> Both emphasize the unpredictability, the indeterminacy, of the legal process. This is a product of the volitional character of the lawmaking function; if it were merely a cognitive function, the jurist could predict for every individual case. This alogical, irrational element is recognized by the Pure Theory of Law as inhering in every stage of the law.[4]

II. HIERARCHICAL OR 'STEPS AND STAIRS'[5] THEORY OF LAW

'At the end – or in the beginning, according to the point of view – is the word or the deed'.[6] The basic norm is pure law-making with no element of law-application and the ultimate implementation of the legal consequence is pure law-application with no element of law-making. All else in between is both law-applying and law-making:

> Creation of law is always application of law. These two concepts are by no means, as the traditional theory presumes, absolute opposites. It is not quite correct to classify legal acts as law-creating and law-applying acts; for, setting aside [the] two borderline cases [ie the basic norm and the ultimate implementation of the legal consequence] . . . every act is, normally, at the same time a law-creating and a law-applying act.[7]

For Kelsen, a peculiarity of law is that it regulates its own creation:

[3] H Kelsen, 'Juristischer Formalismus und Reine Rechtslehre', as cited by W Ebenstein, *The Pure Theory of Law* (New York, Rothman Reprints, 1969 [1945]) 201f. A more recent translation of this 1929 essay – 'Legal Formalism and the Pure Theory of Law' – can be found in AJ Jacobson and B Schlink (eds), *Weimar: A Jurisprudence of Crisis* (University of California Press 2000) 76–83.

[4] Ebenstein, *The Pure Theory of Law* (n 3) 204.

[5] See ibid 157ff.

[6] H Kelsen, *Allgemeine Staatslehre* (Berlin, Julius Springer, 1925) 250.

[7] H Kelsen, *General Theory of Law and State*, A Wedberg transl (Cambridge, Mass., Harvard University Press, 1945) 133. On the point see also *The Pure Theory of Law* (n 3) 158f.

> The legal order is a system of general and individual norms connected with each other according to the principle that law regulates its own creation. Each norm is created according to the provisions of another [higher] norm . . . A norm belongs to this legal order only because it has been created in conformity with the stipulations of another [higher] norm of the order.
>
> [T]he creation of a legal norm can be determined in two different directions: the higher norm may determine: (1) the organ and the procedure by which the lower norm is to be created, and (2) the contents of the lower norm.[8]

From this perspective, the judicial decision creates an individual norm, the content of which is very often partly determined by the higher norm, though not necessarily so:

> the decision of the court represents an individual norm, which is created on the basis of a general norm of statutory or customary law in the same way as this general norm is created on the basis of the constitution. The creation of the individual legal norm by the law-applying organ, especially by the court, must always be determined by one or more pre-existent general norms.

This determination may have, Kelsen says, 'different degrees'. 'Normally, courts are bound by general norms determining the procedure as well as the contents of their decisions'. 'It is possible', however,

> that the legislator is content with institutionalizing courts, and that these courts are authorized by the legal order to decide the concrete cases at their own discretion.[9]

This is even more obviously so with administrative agencies. Even in such circumstances, Kelsen insists that this is law-application: 'Even in this case', he says, 'the courts are not only law-creating but also law-applying organs'.[10]

Kelsen goes further, and claims that the general norm of adjective law which authorises this and only this individual or institution to decide is to be understood in the alternative. The judge is 'to decide the concrete case at his own discretion or according to a general norm of substantive law'.[11]

This may make a degree of sense to some only if the 'or' is strongly disjunctive. If there is no substantive norm to apply, the judge, obviously, has strong discretion. But where there is a substantive norm, some might take the view that the judge is bound to apply it according to its meaning and not to override or disregard it. However, Kelsen's position appears to be supported by a weaker conjunctive sense of 'or' such that even when there is an identifiable valid substantive norm, the judge may trump it with strong discretion. This is what I shall refer to in the sequel as 'discretion to disobey'.

[8] Kelsen, *General Theory of Law and State* (n 7) 132f.
[9] ibid 144.
[10] ibid.
[11] ibid.

Kelsen wishes us to understand that the 'determination' of the lower norm by the higher norm

> can never be complete. The higher norm cannot bind in every direction the act by which it is applied. There must always be more or less room for discretion, so that the higher norm in relation to the lower one can only have the character of a frame to be filled by this act.[12]

This entails that several different interpretations of the substantive norm are possible, and that 'every act is legal that stays within the frame'.[13] For Kelsen, 'every law-applying act is only partly determined by law'.[14] It is also partly determined by 'an act of will by which the law-applying organ chooses between the possibilities shown by cognitive interpretation'.[15] Unless it is the eventual execution of a coercive act, this act of will is law-creating: it creates a 'lower-level norm'.[16] The judge thus enjoys, as Holmes apparently put it, the 'sovereign prerogative of choice'.[17]

This entails that there is no law in the individual case until the judge decides, and that, in the words of Adolf Merkl, '[i]f legal science wants to be able to say what the law is for the individual case, then it must ask the judge'.[18] The judge's is the only 'authentic interpretation'. Anything else is legally irrelevant opinion.

III. THE ALTERNATIVE CHARACTER OF THE NORM

So far this is perhaps tolerably orthodox. 'One right answer' theses, such as Ronald Dworkin's, have attracted few friends. Perhaps 'we are all Legal Realists now' – having long recognised that judges are not mere 'subsumption automatons', and that law-application is 'irreducibly dispositive', rather than a matter of watertight logical deduction.

But then comes this remarkable twist:

> By way of authentic interpretation (that is, interpretation by the law-applying organ) not only one of the possibilities may be realized that have been shown by

[12] H Kelsen, *The Pure Theory of Law*, 2nd edn, M Knight transl (Berkeley, University of California Press, 1967 [1960]) 349.

[13] ibid 351.

[14] ibid 349.

[15] ibid 354.

[16] ibid.

[17] Attributed in ES Corwin, *The Twilight of the Supreme Court. A History of Our Constitutional Theory* (Hamden, Conn., Archon Books, 1970) 115.

[18] As cited in Ebenstein, *The Pure Theory of Law* (n 3) 202; Merkl's essay, 'Das Recht im Lichte seiner Anwendung', is reprinted in H Klecatsky, R Marcic and H Schambeck, *Die Wiener Rechtstheoretische Schule* (Vienna, Europa Verlag, 1968 [1917]) 1167ff.

> the cognitive interpretation of the norm to be applied; but also a norm may be created which lies entirely outside the frame of the norm to be applied.[19]

At first this is surprising. It entails that the judge, authorised by an adjective norm to apply a substantive norm, always has the choice: 'Apply the substantive norm, or not!'

But there can be little room for doubt that this is exactly what Kelsen meant by the 'alternative character' of the norm.[20] We can accept that the legislator is perhaps less bound by the constitution than the judge is by a statute, and that administrative authorities may be less bound by administrative statutes than are the courts by substantive civil and criminal statutes.[21] Nonetheless, Kelsen's overall approach is that any such differences are relative:

> Just as the courts may be authorized, under certain circumstances, not to apply the existing statutory or customary law but to act as legislator and to create new law, so the ordinary legislator may be authorized, under certain circumstances, to act as constitutional legislator. If a statute enacted by the legislative organ is considered to be valid although it has been created in another way or has another content than prescribed by the constitution, we must assume that the prescriptions of the constitution concerning legislation have an alternative character. The legislator is entitled by the constitution either to apply the norms laid down directly in the constitution or to apply other norms which he himself may decide upon. Otherwise, a statute whose creation or contents did not conform with the prescriptions directly laid down in the constitution could not be regarded as valid.[22]

But such a deviant statute is valid if it is part of a by and large effective legal order, is made by an authorised institution, and becomes by and large effective itself.

Kelsen also deploys *res judicata* to support his notion of the alternative character of the norm. He takes the view that any judicial decision, however 'erroneous' or 'deviant', is valid if not annulled by and through an authorised process. It follows that an 'incorrect' decision is and remains law if not set aside in a further judicial process (for example, appeal or judicial review):

> [T]he law also prescribes that a judicial decision which does not conform to the direct stipulations shall remain in force until it has been abolished by a decision of another court . . . If this procedure is exhausted, or if no such procedure has been provided, then there is *res judicata*. In relation to the higher norm, the lower norm possesses the force of law. Thus the determination of the lower norm by the higher norm has . . . the character of an alternative prescription.[23]

[19] Kelsen, *The Pure Theory of Law* (n 12) 354.
[20] *cf* ibid 273, as well as *General Theory of Law and State* (n 7) 156, 159.
[21] *General Theory of Law and State* (n 7) 130.
[22] ibid 156.
[23] ibid 159.

Kelsen applies like reasoning to the relationship between international and national law:

> If the contents of norms of a national legal order are determined by international law, it is in an alternative sense only. The possibility of norms with contents other than those prescribed is not excluded.[24]

For Kelsen, of course, the 'alternative character' of the norm is an integral part of his whole theory, because it ensures that there is 'no contradiction between an inferior and a superior norm'.[25] It is important, too, to his thesis about 'the unity of a normative order'.[26] For Kelsen, 'a "norm contrary to a norm" . . . is a self-contradiction'.[27] And in addition to such internal coherence, justification for the 'alternative character of the norm' may also be found in the core elements of legal positivism.

IV. THE CORE ELEMENTS OF LEGAL POSITIVISM

As is well-known, Kelsen's is a radical 'pedigree' theory:

> The norm system that presents itself as a legal order has essentially a dynamic character. A legal norm is not valid because it has a certain content, that is, because its content is logically deducible from a presupposed basic norm, but because it is created in a certain way . . . Therefore any kind of content might be law.[28]

To this standard element of legal positivism, Kelsen adds a further criterion: 'A minimum of effectiveness is a condition of validity'.[29] Indeed, for Kelsen,

> the correct determination of this relationship [between validity and effectiveness] is one of the most important and at the same time most difficult problems of a positivistic legal theory.[30]

Taking these two points together means that

> even if a general norm, to be applied by the court, is valid, which predetermines the content of the individual norm to be created by the court, an individual norm, created by the court of last instance can become valid whose content does not conform to this general norm'.[31]

[24] ibid 372.
[25] *cf* ibid 161ff.
[26] *cf* ibid 110ff.
[27] *The Pure Theory of Law* (n 12) 267.
[28] ibid 198.
[29] ibid 11.
[30] ibid 211.
[31] ibid 269.

In short, the principle of 'subsumption' is subordinated to the principle of 'delegation'; pedigree always trumps content. But this entails that any valid legal norm is always subject to defeat.

V. DEFEASIBILISM

Accordingly, Kelsen appears to be saying that it is a necessary feature of his conception of a legal order that a court can choose not to apply a general norm and make new law outside the 'frame'. But that looks very like asserting a power to disregard, disapply or defeat a valid norm, and to substitute a different norm of the court's own devising.

Kelsen takes the general view that 'the legal order cannot have any gaps'.[32] The law is binary: either it provides the remedy that the plaintiff seeks or it does not. Faced with that, the court has only two options. First, it may dismiss the plaintiff's claim, on the basis that the general norms provide no remedy. The alternative is that where the court finds the lack of such a general norm 'unsatisfactory, unjust or inequitable'[33] it may

> create for the concrete case the norm of substantive law it considers satisfactory, just or equitable. The court then functions as a legislator.[34]

In fact, Kelsen qualifies this last point, observing that in such cases the court need not be creating general norms, as under a system of precedent, but creates only 'an individual norm, valid for the single, present case'.[35] I agree. That looks a lot like defeasibilism, in its strongest incarnation.

As an example of the first option, consider *Paton v British Pregnancy Advisory Service Trustees*, in which the plaintiff husband was refused an injunction to restrain the first defendant from causing an abortion to be carried out on his wife, the second defendant, without his consent. No previous claim of this sort had been litigated in the British courts. At the start of his judgment, Sir George Baker P said:

> In the discussion of human affairs and especially of abortion, controversy can rage over the moral rights, duties, interests, standards and religious views of the parties. Moral values are in issue. I am, in fact, concerned with none of these matters. I am concerned, and concerned only, with the law of England as it applies to this claim.[36]

As an example of the second option, consider *Henningsen v Bloomfield Motors*. Mr Henningsen had bought a car (for his wife) under a contract which

[32] *General Theory of Law and State* (n 7) 147.
[33] ibid 145.
[34] ibid.
[35] *The Pure Theory of Law* (n 12) 244.
[36] [1979] QB 276.

included a term limiting the manufacturer's liability exclusively to repairing defective parts. The court, however, agreed with his argument that the manufacturer should not be protected by the term, and should meet the medical and other expenses of those injured in a crash, even though there was no statute or common law rule in support. The court relied on the following ringing dictum from an earlier case:

> Is there any principle which is more familiar or more firmly embedded in the history of Anglo-American law than the basic doctrine that the courts will not permit themselves to be used as instruments of inequity and injustice?[37]

Interestingly, Kelsen notes that

> [t]he fact that a legal order lacks a legal norm that stipulates punishment for the theft of electricity may be regarded as inequitable or unjust as much as the fact that a legal order contains a legal norm applicable to murder with robbery in the same way as to a case in which a son kills his incurably ill father upon the latter's request.[38]

In England, the Larceny Act 1916 made special provision for the stealing of electricity because it was not subject to (the old common law requirement of) 'asportation', that is taking and carrying away. The novel conception of 'appropriation' (somewhat akin to *contrectatio* in Roman law), introduced in the Theft Act 1968, might have been wide enough to include abstraction of electricity, but the legislator, in the event wisely, enacted in section 13 a specific offence of 'abstracting electricity'; wisely, because it was duly held that electricity is not 'property' within section 4, and switching on the current is not 'appropriation'.[39]

Kelsen's second example takes us straight to the heart of a recent and continuing controversy in law and morals in Britain, namely assisted suicide.[40] In common with other prosecutors, the Director of Public Prosecutions has discretion, and no prosecution can be brought in England for assisted suicide under the Suicide Act 1961 without his consent. Those whose relatives are in tragic circumstances and travel from the UK to Switzerland for 'death with dignity' naturally would have liked to know in advance if they were likely to be prosecuted, but at the original time of writing the Director of Public Prosecutions had neither given any assurance in advance in individual cases, nor had he published any statement of policy. Since then the controversy has

[37] 32 NJ 358, 161 A.2d 69 (1960). Another very well-known example is *Riggs v Palmer* 115 NY506, 22 NE188 (1889). Examples can be multiplied: see further my essays 'Defeasibilism' (n 1) and 'Defeasibility and Adjudication' (n 1).

[38] *The Pure Theory of Law* (n 12) 246f.

[39] *Low v Blease* [1975] Crim LR 513; it would be interesting to explore how criminal codes in mainland Europe have dealt with this issue and how judges have responded.

[40] *R (on the application of Pretty) v DPP* [2002] 1 AC 800; [2002] HRLR 10 and *R (on the application of Purdy) v DPP* [2008] EWHC 2565 (Admin); [2009] EWCA Civ 92.

moved on and (for good or ill) guidelines on policy have been published. Nonetheless, and as to the generality of the point, aptly has it been written that

> when legal officials have either delegated or deviational discretion to determine the classes of cases covered by peremptory rules they may or may not enforce, the citizen is left with a puzzle. The law forbids a form of conduct under circumstances A, B, and C. But officials charged with the enforcement of the law enforce it only, or for the most part, under circumstances A, and B . . . What then are the citizens to make of their obligations towards the peremptory rule under circumstance C?[41]

Kelsen cites the following provision of Swiss Civil Code (as it was at the time of his writing) as a typical illustration of the untenable 'gap theory':

> The law is applicable to all legal problems for which it contains a rule explicitly or by interpretation. If no prescription is contained in the law, the judge shall decide according to custom and, where this too is lacking, according to the rule he would establish were he a legislator.[42]

Kelsen comments that

> a legal order is always applicable and is actually applied even when the court must dismiss the action on the grounds that the legal order does not contain a general rule imposing . . . the obligation asserted.[43]

It follows for Kelsen (and I agree) that the theory of gaps is a 'fiction', falsely assuming the impossibility of applying the norms of the legal order.[44] Kelsen suggests that the 'moral-political' point of this fiction is to encourage what he calls 'legal security', at the expense of 'flexibility'[45] and what I refer to as the twin *desiderata* of certainty and justice, both of which cannot be realised fully by any legal order.

Defeasibilism has seemed to some of its critics, whatever merits they may otherwise acknowledge, to be potentially anarchical, licensing any and every departure from general legal norms. Although not a fully paid-up, card-carrying, self-styled 'defeasibilist', Kelsen offers a telling answer to that charge:

> A status where everybody is authorized to declare every norm, that is to say everything that presents itself as norm, as null, is almost a state of anarchy. . . Modern national law . . . reserves the competence to declare a norm as null, that is to annul a norm, for special organs. What is practically possible within a national legal order is, at most, that everybody is authorized to consider a legal norm as null, but at the risk that his conduct, if contrary to the norm, might be considered by the compe-

[41] MR Kadish and S Kadish, *Discretion to Disobey: A Study of Lawful Departures from Legal Rules* (Stanford, Cal., Stanford University Press, 1973) 189.
[42] *The Pure Theory of Law* (n 12) 247.
[43] ibid.
[44] ibid.
[45] ibid 250ff.

> tent organ to be a delict, provided that the competent organ does not confirm the subject's opinion as to the invalidity of the norm.[46]

That 'a norm may be created only by the competent organ'[47] entails also that only the competent organ can create a norm annulling another norm:

> If the legal order were to permit everybody to decide this question, a judicial decision binding the parties would hardly come to pass. Hence, according to positive national law, this question can only be decided by the court itself or a higher court.[48]

VI. DISCRETION TO DISOBEY[49]

Kadish and Kadish distinguish 'deviational' and 'delegated' discretion. The first involves 'the exercise of authority in ways or on the basis of considerations either unauthorised or prohibited by rules of competence'.[50] An example might be the refusal of the Court of Appeal in England to follow the rules of precedent in two recent cases, one civil, and one criminal.[51] This entails

> not only an official's deciding the substantive issue without the guidance of legal rules, but also his disregarding the answer provided by law in favour of his own judgment on the merits[52]

The second involves delegated discretionary powers expressly provided for in norms of competence, including wide discretionary authority vested in governmental departments, agencies and emanations of the state. As Unger recognised, even delegated discretion raises serious issues for any rule of law approach.[53] Obviously, deviational discretion raises such issues even more acutely, so much so that Kadish and Kadish boldly argue that 'the rule-of-law model is not necessarily the ideal model for the functioning of legal systems'.[54]

The need for delegated discretion is widely recognised and accepted nowadays. No modern system of law and government can exist without delegating discretionary powers. So the modern issue as to delegated discretion is the scope and reach of judicial review and the requirement of public bodies to conduct themselves in accordance with the provision of such texts as the

[46] *General Theory of Law and State* (n 7) 160.
[47] *The Pure Theory of Law* (n 12) 276.
[48] ibid 268.
[49] Kadish and Kadish, *Discretion to Disobey* (n 41).
[50] *Discretion to Disobey* (n 41) 42.
[51] *Great Peace Shipping Ltd v Tsavliris Salvage International Ltd* [2003] QB 679 and *R v James and Karimi* [2006] QB 588; see further my essay 'Defeasibility and Adjudication' (n 1).
[52] *Discretion to Disobey* (n 41) 42f.
[53] RM Unger, *Law in Modern Society* (New York, The Free Press, 1976).
[54] *Discretion to Disobey* (n 41) 44f.

European Convention on Human Rights.[55] It is therefore deviational discretion that poses the greater challenge for law and legal theory. Roscoe Pound suggested long ago that '[a]lmost all of the problems of jurisprudence come down to a fundamental one of rule and discretion'.[56] Whereas that may be an overstatement, 'discretion' is a central issue in legal theory. As is well-known, Ronald Dworkin offered a tripartite account of discretion, distinguishing between two weak senses and one strong sense.

First, and very weak, is the notion 'that for some reason the standards an official must apply cannot be applied mechanically but demand the use of judgment'.[57] There is nothing of great significance or novelty in this: 'the successful functioning of a legal system depends upon repeated acts of human judgment at every level of the system'.[58]

Secondly, in 'a different weak sense', 'some official has final authority and cannot be reviewed and reversed by any other official'.[59] Dworkin turns to baseball to illustrate this point, but association football is perhaps more familiar to Europeans. At the time of original writing, Mr Darren Fletcher, a Manchester United player, had just been sent off by the referee in a UEFA semi-final with the consequence that he automatically had to miss the final, a match of huge significance in the career of a player for whom, conceivably, it might be the only chance. Many commentators considered, and I agreed, that no foul was committed and that the referee manifestly erred. In England, where I used to sit on FA Regulatory Commissions, we have the power to rescind a red card either on grounds of mistaken identity or where the referee has made an obvious error. UEFA only allows appeals on mistaken identity. In England we consider our approach fairer and we believe that it is desperately unjust to deny an innocent player a special career opportunity because of an obvious error by an official. But the decision of a referee under UEFA jurisdiction is final, in the sense that there is no forum of appeal or review; therefore that decision, irrespective of how erroneous, is instantly *res judicata*, as Kelsen might put it. However, as Kelsen actually does put it, 'the opinion that an innocent individual was sentenced is legally excluded', because all other than the duly authorised official are 'individuals legally not competent [ie authorised] to ascertain this'.[60] Given that the referee's decision is final within the system, opinions of managers, players and fans, however sound in footballing terms, are not 'authentic' interpretations and are irrelevant. Rule One is 'The referee is always right'. Rule Two is 'When the Referee is wrong, Rule One applies'!

[55] Human Rights Act 1998, s 6.
[56] R Pound, *An Introduction to the Philosophy of Law* (New Haven, Yale University Press, 1922) 111.
[57] R Dworkin, *Taking Rights Seriously* (London, Duckworth, 1977) 31.
[58] LL Fuller, *Anatomy of the Law* (New York, Frederick A Prager, 1968) 59.
[59] Dworkin, *Taking Rights Seriously* (n 57) 32.
[60] *The Pure Theory of Law* (n 12) 240.

Thirdly, and in a strong sense, according to Dworkin, 'discretion' connotes 'that on some issue he [the official] is simply not bound by standards set by the authority in question'.[61] In Kelsenian terms, this is an instance of the norm of competence determining the institutional but not the material element, such that the official is wholly unconstrained by any material general norm. This is what Kadish and Kadish refer to as 'delegated' discretion, and (without offering examples) it is nowadays a very familiar feature of modern legal systems.

Significantly missing from Dworkin's account, however, is anything remotely akin to 'deviational' discretion, which is discretion in a stronger sense still, being 'discretion to disobey':

> The question for an addressee of the rule is not so much about the rule's existence or content but whether one is free to act on one's own judgment. The issue is the degree to which, if at all, a legal rule is binding upon individual conscience or is a reason for action in all the circumstances of the case.[62]

A final question, then, is whether Kelsen's notion of discretion is 'delegated' or 'deviational'. Is it a de jure or de facto power to disregard, disapply or defeat an applicable substantive general norm?

Much of what Kelsen actually writes is consistent with delegated discretion, and modern legal systems reveal many instances. An example is the Forfeiture Act 1982, which provides in section 2:

> (1) Where a court determines that the forfeiture rule has precluded a person (in this section referred to as 'the offender') who has unlawfully killed another from acquiring any interest in property mentioned in subsection (4) below, the court may make an order under this section modifying the effect of that rule.

Subsection 2(2) adds:

> (2) The court shall not make an order under this section modifying the effect of the forfeiture rule in any case unless it is satisfied that, having regard to the conduct of the offender and of the deceased and to such other circumstances as appear to the court to be material, the justice of the case requires the effect of the rule to be so modified in that case.

Here the legislature has delegated to the judiciary discretion to do justice, though quite why legislative authorisation should be thought necessary is unclear (given a plausible view that 'doing justice' is an inherent power and duty of all courts). Perhaps that is merely a result of the eccentricities of the British Constitution?

Be that as it may, the whole thrust of Kelsen's theory is consistent only with deviational discretion, because the alternative character of the norm involves disregarding, disapplying or defeating an applicable general norm, going

[61] *Taking Rights Seriously* (n 57) 32.
[62] *Discretion to Disobey* (n 41) 190–94

outside the 'frame' and creating new law, not least in an individual case. This, for Kelsen, involves a degree of legislative decentralisation.

He says:

> The law-creating function of the courts becomes particularly visible when a court is authorized to create a general norm by establishing a precedent. To give such an authorization to a court, especially a court of last resort, is particularly commendable[63] when the court is authorized to decide a case under certain circumstances not by applying a general norm, but according to its own discretion; in other words, if the court is authorized to create an individual norm whose content is not predetermined by a general norm of positive law. To bestow the character of a precedent on such a decision is only a consistent enlargement of the court's law-creating function.[64]

This passage reveals much, not least that Kelsen himself is not perhaps all that clear on whether his notion of discretion is delegated or deviational. But there is a sense in which that distinction may be unimportant in Kelsenian exegesis. Although he deploys the language of authorisation and delegation, Kelsen embraces a very strong form of discretion which permits the court to disregard, disapply or defeat an applicable general norm, and, again, to substitute a new individual or general norm of its own devising, not least in an individual case. That seems essentially defeasibilist – not merely as a matter of description or methodology but as an incontestable truth of legal theory.

VII. CONCLUSION

In this chapter I have sought to address the issue left hanging at the conclusion of my paper on 'Defeasibility and Adjudication':[65] the possibility of moving from adjudication to legal theory. I have tried to deploy an understanding of Kelsenian legal theory to that end.

If Kelsen may be 'captured' for a defeasibilist conception of law or legal order, then perhaps I have moved the debate on defeasibilism – as a legal theory rather than methodology or pragmatism – forward a little.

[63] *Sic* – but this surely means 'commentable' or noteworthy, rather than deserving praise and approbation. The original reads: 'Einem Gericht, insbesondere einem Gericht letzter Instanz, diese Ermächtigung zu erteilen, liegt dann besonders nahe wenn . . .' ('The attribution of such a power to a court, especially a court of last resort, is especially evident when . . .'); *cf* H Kelsen, *Reine Rechtslehre*, 2nd edn (Vienna, Franz Deuticke, 1960) 256.

[64] *The Pure Theory of Law* (n 12) 251.

[65] See n 1.

12

In Canonical Form: Kelsen's Doctrine of the 'Complete' Legal Norm

LUÍS DUARTE D'ALMEIDA*

I. INTRODUCTION

A. Legal Propositions

IN ORDER PROPERLY to define my subject, let me begin by inviting your attention to the following quotation from the second edition (1960) of Kelsen's *Pure Theory of Law*:

> [A legal order] may be described in sentences pronouncing that under specific conditions (that is, under conditions determined by the legal order) specific coercive acts ought to be performed. All legally relevant material contained in a legal order fits in this scheme of the legal proposition formulated by legal science – the *legal proposition* which is to be distinguished from the *legal norm* established by the legal authority.[1]

The background to this claim lies in Kelsen's understanding of legal science as one of the 'normative' sciences, and thus as 'essentially different' from the

* For helpful comments and discussion I am grateful to Eugenio Bulygin, Fábio Shecaira, Hugo Zuleta, John Gardner, José António Veloso, José de Sousa e Brito, Pedro Múrias and Stanley L Paulson; and to audiences in Buenos Aires, Genoa, Krakow, Lisbon, Mar del Plata and Oxford.

[1] H Kelsen, *The Pure Theory of Law*, M Knight transl (Berkeley, University of California Press, 1967 [1960]) 58. I modify Knight's translation, substituting 'legal proposition' for 'rule of law'; on this terminology *cf* n 20. Even apart from this point, it should be noted that Knight's translation of this passage (as of others) is not quite faithful to the original, whose second sentence begins instead (in my translation) 'All the material given in the norms of a legal order . . .': *cf Reine Rechtslehre*, 2nd edn (Vienna, Franz Deuticke, 1960) 59. But Knight notes in his 'Translator's Preface' (at vi) that his version was 'carefully checked' by Kelsen; and whether or not that was indeed the case, in this passage, at least, I do find his English-language rendition to convey (what seems to me to be) Kelsen's actual view more accurately than the autograph text: compare eg Kelsen's remarks on 'legally irrelevant contents' at 52f of *The Pure Theory of Law* or in *General Theory of Law and State* (Cambridge, Mass., Harvard University Press, 1945) 123, 131.

natural sciences.[2] The natural sciences describe their objects according to the principle (the '*Ordnungsprinzip*'[3]) of causality, which connects two elements as cause and effect, and whose 'fundamental form' is 'if *A* is, *B* is'.[4] But in so far as a *normative* science – a science of norms, a science of what ought to be – is at all possible, says Kelsen, it 'must describe its object according to a principle different from causality'.[5] A normative science must describe its object according to a principle connecting two elements, not as cause and effect, but according to an essentially normative copula. Kelsen calls this principle 'imputation' ('*Zurechnung*'). Its form – the form, or scheme, of the propositions with which a normative science describes its object – is 'If *A* is, *B* ought to be'.[6]

Such propositions, Kelsen maintains, are truth-apt. They are descriptions of what ought to be the case according to some given normative system. Hence they are true if, and only if, the corresponding norm 'exists' in that system: if, and only if, that is to say, it is a 'valid' norm of the system.[7] That is why these propositions are called 'normative' propositions (Kelsen's term is '*Sollsätze*'[8]). They are propositions *about* norms. Thus in submitting that, according to some normative system *S*, some state of affairs *B* 'ought' to be the case if some state of affairs *A* is the case, one is not prescribing anything. One is not thereby issuing a norm. One is merely describing the contents of *S*. The 'ought' has here, Kelsen says, 'only a descriptive character'.[9] Of course, a linguistic formulation with that very same form – 'if *A* is, *B* ought to be' – might be used prescriptively rather than descriptively. It could naturally be uttered, for example, by someone in a position of practical authority who intends to make a requirement or issue a command. In that case the authoritative speaker is not describing anything. She is instead requiring or commanding that *B whenever A is the case*. If she does indeed enjoy the necessary authority,

[2] Natural sciences such as 'physics, biology, or physiology' are not 'essentially different' from social sciences such as 'psychology, ethnology, history, [or] sociology'. The latter, says Kelsen, are *causal* social sciences: they, too, seek to 'interpret the mutual behaviour of men according to the principle of causality'. Legal science, in turn is one of the *normative* social sciences: *cf The Pure Theory of Law* (n 1) 75, 85–86; and see also H Kelsen, *Introduction to the Problems of Legal Theory*, BL Paulson and SL Paulson transl (Oxford, Clarendon Press, 1991 [1934]) 13f.

[3] *Reine Rechtslehre* (n 1) 79.

[4] *cf The Pure Theory of Law* (n 1) 76f.

[5] ibid 75.

[6] ibid 76f; *Reine Rechtslehre* (n 1) 79f; and see also H Kelsen, *Allgemeine Staatslehre* (Berlin, Julius Springer, 1925) 47f; *Introduction to the Problems of Legal Theory* (n 2) 23f; *General Theory of Law and State* (n 1) 46f, 164; and *General Theory of Norms*, M Hartney transl (Oxford, Clarendon Press, 1991 [1979]) 290f.

[7] *cf The Pure Theory of Law* (n 1) 10: 'By the word "validity" we designate the specific existence of a norm'; see also *Introduction to the Problems of Legal Theory* (n 2) 12; *General Theory of Law and State* (n 1) 30; *General Theory of Norms* (n 6) 28.

[8] *cf Reine Rechtslehre* (n 1) 77.

[9] *The Pure Theory of Law* (n 1) 79; see also *General Theory of Law and State* (n 1) 163: 'ought-statements . . . have a merely descriptive import; they, as it were, descriptively reproduce the "ought" of the norms'.

she will be issuing a norm. This means that the difference between the norm and the normative proposition may not be apparent at the linguistic level of the formulations employed by a speaker to express one or the other. But it is 'logically' rather than linguistically, says Kelsen, that the difference between the norm and the normative proposition is to be drawn.[10]

Legal science, however, does not describe its object merely *as a norm*. Legal science comprehends and describes its object 'legally' – 'from the viewpoint of the law'.[11] It comprehends its object, not merely as a norm, but 'as a *legal* norm'.[12] What does Kelsen mean by this? Consider, first, that according to Kelsen legal norms must be reconstructed from the variety of legal source-'materials' that are the 'products of the law-making procedure':

> The different elements of a norm may be contained in very different products of the law-making procedure, and they may be linguistically expressed in very different ways. When the legislator forbids theft, he may, for instance, first define the concept of theft in a number of sentences which form an article of a statute, and then stipulate the sanction in another sentence, which may be part of another article of the same statute or even part of an entirely different statute.[13]

It is 'the task of the science of law', says Kelsen, to reconstruct the content of the law in the form of normative propositions – to 'represent' the law as a system of norms.[14] Yet not just any set of normative propositions, even if it were completely and truthfully to describe the contents of some given legal system, would succeed in presenting that system as a system of *legal* norms. This is because the scheme of imputation – 'If *A* is, *B* ought to be' – is not a specifically legal scheme. It is, rather, a *common* scheme to the domain of the normative sciences, a domain that includes (according to Kelsen), apart from legal science, the 'science of morals' (or, as he also calls it, 'ethics').[15] But if there is, within this general frame of the normative sciences, an autonomous science of legal norms, then there must be, thinks Kelsen, a specifically legal

[10] *The Pure Theory of Law* (n 1) 73; though in connection with a different issue, Kelsen remarks in *Hauptprobleme der Staatsrechtslehre*, 2nd edn (Tübingen, JCB Mohr, 1923 [1911]) 271 that 'there is no discipline in which reliance on ordinary linguistic usage is more dangerous than in jurisprudence' (my translation).

[11] *The Pure Theory of Law* (n 1) 70.

[12] ibid, my emphasis.

[13] *General Theory of Law and State* (n 1) 45; see also *Hauptprobleme der Staatsrechtslehre* (n 10) 237.

[14] *General Theory of Law and State* (n 1) 45.

[15] *cf The Pure Theory of Law* (n 1) 86; see also at 90 for examples of (non-legal) normative propositions describing positive 'moral' norms such as those 'enacted by a religious leader or created by custom': 'If someone has rendered to you a good service, you ought to show gratitude; if someone has sacrificed his life for his country, his memory ought to be honoured; if someone has sinned, he ought to do penance'. In other works Kelsen also mentions logic, aesthetics and even grammar as further examples of non-legal normative sciences: see eg *Hauptprobleme der Staatsrechtslehre* (n 10) 4, 6.

way of representing legal norms.[16] A formulation that applies 'only to legal norms', he says, will have to include 'the essential element which distinguishes a legal norm from other norms'.[17] This element, in Kelsen's view, is coercion: 'the legal norm is a coercive norm (a norm providing for coercion), and . . . precisely thereby the legal norm is distinguished from other norms'.[18] Accordingly, the form of the legal normative proposition – the form, in short, of the 'legal proposition': Kelsen's term is '*Rechtssatz*' – corresponds to a partial interpretation of the general form of imputation 'If *A* is, *B* ought to be'.[19] In the legal proposition, '*B*' is to be interpreted as standing for a legally determined 'act of coercion':

> If the law is conceived as a coercive order, that is, as an order stipulating coercive acts as sanctions, then the law-describing legal proposition appears as the statement that under certain conditions, determined by the legal order, a certain coercive act, likewise determined by that order, ought to be performed.[20]

[16] In 'J.W. Harris's Kelsen' in T Endicott, J Gezler and E Peel (eds), *Properties of Law. Essays in Honour of Jim Harris* (Oxford, Oxford University Press, 2006) 17ff, Stanley L Paulson proposes to understand Kelsen's views on this matter in terms of the idea – which Paulson traces back to the work of Baden Neo-Kantian philosopher Heinrich Rickert – that it is the hallmark of an autonomous scientific discipline that it has own 'methodological form'. See also SL Paulson, 'A "Justified Normativity" Thesis in Hans Kelsen's Pure Theory of Law? Rejoinders to Robert Alexy and Joseph Raz' in M Klatt (ed), *Institutionalized Reason. The Jurisprudence of Robert Alexy* (Oxford, Oxford University Press, 2012) 109ff.

[17] *General Theory of Norms* (n 6) 272.

[18] *Introduction to the Problems of Legal Theory* (n 2) 26; see also *Hauptprobleme der Staatsrechtslehre* (n 10) 212; and *The Pure Theory of Law* (n 1) 56, 145.

[19] The form of the legal proposition (the '*Rechtssatz*') may thus be characterised as a *species* of the form of the normative proposition (the '*Soll-satz*'); the 'methodological form' of legal science (see n 16), in other words, is a species of the general form of imputation. In 'J.W. Harris's Kelsen' (n 16) 18, Stanley Paulson maintains that Kelsen views imputation as *the* characteristic methodological form of legal science. My suggestion is instead that – just like causality, which, as Paulson rightly remarks (*cf* ibid 17), 'has to be taken as the *genus* of the methodological forms in the natural sciences generally, for it has application to all of them' (which is to say that each of the natural sciences will have its own specific methodological form) – Kelsen's imputation has to be taken, analogously (and to use the same words), as the *genus* of the methodological forms in the normative sciences generally, for it has application in all of them. Compare, indeed, Kelsen's own contention (which I quote in Bonnie and Stanley Paulson's own translation) that 'the formal category of the norm – the category designated by 'ought' – yields only the genus, not the *differentia specifica*, of the law', in *Introduction to the Problems of Legal Theory* (n 2) 26.

[20] *The Pure Theory of Law* (n 1) 108. Again I substitute 'legal proposition' for the translator's 'rule of law' – an unfortunate choice of terminology which has brought about a great deal of confusion among those who have read Kelsen in English (see eg HLA Hart, 'Kelsen Visited' in his *Essays in Jurisprudence and Philosophy* (Oxford, Clarendon Press, 1983 [1963]) 286ff). In fact, 'rule of law', in this sense, occurs already in the *General Theory of Law and State* (n 1) eg at 45f, although elsewhere in the same work (eg on the opening pages of ch I, or on p 29) the expression seems also to be used as a synonym for 'general legal norm'. With 'rule of law', I presume, the translators were attempting to convey Kelsen's point that, by analogy to the '*Naturgesetz*' – a term which translates straightforwardly as 'law of nature' – the proposition of law (ie the '*Rechtssatz*') could also be *called* '*Rechtsgesetz*': *cf* the exposition in *General Theory of Law and State* (n 1) 46, and see also *The Pure Theory of Law* (n 1) 77 and 79f. Yet the two nouns from which the compound term '*Rechtsgesetz*' is formed – '*Recht*' and '*Gesetz*' – both translate into English as 'law'. (Not so in other languages: '*Recht*' translates into

These introductory exegetical remarks are meant to put into context the quotation with which I opened the chapter. But Kelsen's general point should be fairly familiar. It was highlighted by HLA Hart, who in *The Concept of Law* and in other works discussed what he characterised as Kelsen's view that there is a

> canonical form for the representation of law . . .: statements that if such and such conditions are fulfilled then such and such a sanction will follow. These are the statements by which the normative science of law is said by Kelsen to describe or represent law.[21]

B. Kelsen's 'Complete' Legal Norm

Let us now pay closer attention to an example of a legal proposition. Consider, first, the following hypothetical situation, again excerpted from Kelsen's *Pure Theory*:

> Suppose that the legal order of a state prohibits theft by attaching to it in a statute the penalty of imprisonment. *The condition of the punishment is not merely the fact that a man has stolen.* The theft has to be ascertained by a court authorized by the legal order in a procedure determined by the norms of the legal order; the court has to pronounce a punishment, determined by statute or custom; and this punishment has to be executed by a different organ. The court is authorized to impose, in a certain procedure, a punishment upon the thief, only if in a constitutional procedure a general norm is created that attaches to theft a certain punishment. The norm of the constitution, which authorizes the creation of this general norm, determines a condition to which the sanction is attached.[22]

French as '*droit*', into Italian as '*diritto*', into Spanish as '*derecho*', into Portuguese as '*direito*'; and '*Gesetz*', respectively, as '*loi*', '*legge*', '*ley*' and '*lei*'). Kelsen's '*Rechtsgesetz*' would therefore literally translate into English, confusingly, as 'the law of law'. (The idea could perhaps be slightly less opaquely rendered as the 'law of Law', the 'legal law', perhaps also as the 'juridical law'). It is this 'law' ('*Gesetz*') of Law ('*Recht*') that – just like the 'law' ('*Gesetz*') of nature ('*Natur*') – is said by Kelsen to be a 'law' in a purely 'descriptive sense': a thought which, though reasonably clear in German, does not come across in English at all if 'rule' is used instead of 'law' (and '*Rechtsgesetz*' translated as 'rule of law'). In later writings Kelsen himself no longer uses the equivocal 'rule of law' to translate '*Rechtssatz*', which he now renders as 'proposition of law': see eg 'Professor Stone and the Pure Theory of Law' (1965) 17 *Stanford Law Review* 1132ff.

[21] Hart, 'Kelsen Visited' (n 20) 298; see also his 'Analytical Jurisprudence in Mid-Twentieth Century: A Reply to Professor Bodenheimer' (1957) 105 *University of Pennsylvannia Law Review* 959; 'Positivism and the Separation of Law and Morals' in his *Essays in Jurisprudence and Philosophy* (Oxford, Clarendon Press, 1983 [1958]) 61; 'Prolegomenon to the Principles of Punishment' in *Punishment and Responsibility. Essays in the Philosophy of Law*, 2nd edn (Oxford, Oxford University Press, 2008 [1959]) 7; and *The Concept of Law*, 3rd edn (Oxford, Oxford University Press, 2012 [1961]) 35ff.

[22] *The Pure Theory of Law* (n 1) 56 (my emphasis); a similar example is given in *General Theory of Law and State* (n 1) 143f.

The topic at stake is the description of the law on theft in a given legal order. It might at first blush seem that a proposition stating that 'whoever steals ought to be punished [by some court *C*, with a certain sanction *S*]' would aptly discharge that task. But note the italicised sentence. Kelsen observes here that the legal consequence – viz. that the punishment ought to be brought about – depends on the verification of a complex set of conditions. Thus 'the legal proposition that describes this situation' will read, according to Kelsen, as follows:

> 'If the individuals authorized to legislate have issued a general norm according to which a thief is to be punished in a certain way; and if the court authorized by the Code of Criminal Proceedings in a procedure prescribed by this code has ascertained that an individual has committed theft; and if that court has ordered the legally determined punishment; then a certain organ ought to execute the punishment.'[23]

Kelsen's point, then, is that the 'independent' ('*selbständige*') or 'complete' ('*vollständige*')[24] formulation of the legal proposition requires that in its antecedent all the conditions on which the consequent depends – which conditions encompass, for example (and besides the fact of theft itself), the enactment, by an authorised organ, of the corresponding criminal statute – be included and spelled out. This again illustrates the point, highlighted above,[25] that the variety of provisions that are the result of law-making activities (and to the contents of which lawyers will naturally refer as 'norms') are to be represented as 'elements', as 'parts', of 'complete' legal propositions (and thus also of 'complete' norms). Constitutional law is a case in point. Those constitutional norms which empower legislators and regulate the organisation and procedure of legislation are viewed by Kelsen as adding to the 'conditions' under which the sanction is to be applied,[26] and thus as 'intrinsic parts of all the legal norms' – that is, the 'complete' legal norms – 'which the courts and other organs have to apply'.[27]

This, too, is a familiar doctrine. It was discussed by HLA Hart as the 'extreme' version of the argument that 'what are loosely or in popular modes of expression referred to as complete rules of law, are really incomplete fragments of coercive rules which are the only "genuine" rules of law':[28]

> On this view, what is ordinarily thought of as the content of law, designed to guide the conduct of ordinary citizens, is merely the antecedent or 'if-clause' in a rule

[23] *The Pure Theory of Law* (n 1) 57.

[24] For these adjectives *cf* eg *General Theory of Law and State* (n 1) 53, 143; *The Pure Theory of Law* (n 1) 57, 238; and for the original text see *Reine Rechtslehre* (n 1) 58, 244.

[25] *cf* text to n 13.

[26] *The Pure Theory of Law* (n 1) 57.

[27] *General Theory of Law and State* (n 1) 143f.

[28] Hart, *The Concept of Law* (n 21) 35.

> which is directed not to them but to officials, and orders them to apply certain sanctions if certain conditions are satisfied. All genuine laws, on this view, are conditional orders to officials to apply sanctions . . . Thus, the theory bids us disentangle the substance from the obscuring forms; then we shall see that constitutional forms such as 'what the Queen in Parliament enacts is law', or the provisions of the American constitution as to the law-making power of Congress, merely specify the general conditions under which courts are to apply sanctions. These forms are essentially 'if-clauses', not complete rules: 'If the Queen in Parliament has so enacted . . .' or 'if Congress within the limits specified in the Constitution has so enacted . . .' are forms of conditions common to a vast number of directions to courts to apply sanctions or punish certain types of conduct. This is a formidable and interesting theory, purporting to disclose the true, uniform nature of law latent beneath a variety of common forms and expressions which obscure it.[29]

Such a theory, Hart objected, distorts the 'different social functions which different types of legal rules perform'.[30] I am not convinced by Hart's rejoinder, which seems to me beside the point. But I do agree, for different reasons, that Kelsen's views on norm-completeness are questionable. Such views are also fully autonomous from his views on the specific form of the *legal* norm and its distinctively *legal* consequent. (Neither set of views, incidentally, amounts to a doctrine of norm-'individuation'. Instead, they both concern the structure of legal norms and propositions, and tell us nothing about the criterion by which to determine whether any given true legal proposition describes exactly *one* norm. In fact, and in spite of what is sometimes claimed, Kelsen has no doctrine of individuation at all.[31]) Kelsen's criterion of completeness, in effect, concerns the relation between the antecedent and the consequent of a norm or normative proposition, irrespective of their peculiarly legal character. The

[29] ibid 36f.

[30] ibid 38f, and *cf* also Hart's essay 'Legal Powers' in his *Essays on Bentham. Studies in Jurisprudence and Political Theory* (Oxford, Clarendon Press, 1982) 219.

[31] See J Raz, *The Concept of a Legal System*, 2nd edn (Oxford, Clarendon Press, 1980) 73f (for the contrast between questions of structure and questions of individuation proper) and 77ff and 109ff (for a conjectural reconstruction of what Raz unassumingly refers to as Kelsen's 'implicit' doctrine of individuation). Raz does sometimes frame the issue of individuation as that of determining which statements describe 'one *complete* norm' (or, in a slightly different formulation, which statements '*completely*' describe 'exactly one' norm): *cf* eg ibid 49f, 73f, 113 fn 2, 219ff (my emphases). But the adjective 'complete' has here a different meaning than it does in Kelsen's works. Consider the statement '*Every person* ought to inform the Home Office of his address within a fortnight of the passing of this Act, and thereafter within a fortnight of changing his address'. If this statement describes one complete law, then the otherwise identical statement beginning '*All adult males* ought to inform the Home Office' is said, in Raz's terminology, not to describe a 'complete' norm but only 'part of the content of a norm' (and thus 'less' than a complete norm): *cf* ibid 73 (my emphases). (By the same token, the conjunction of at least two true statements describing complete laws would itself be a statement describing 'more' than one complete law.) Given that those two statements are identical in structure, Raz's idea of a 'complete' norm, as well as his corresponding idea of a 'part' of a norm, is at least partly a structure-independent idea. In Kelsen, in turn, the labels refer to purely structural notions.

two issues can thus be taken separately for discussion and criticism. In this chapter I deal only with the first; I offer a critique of Kelsen's account of 'complete' legal norms.

II. THREE NOTIONS OF NORM-COMPLETENESS

As Hart notes in the passage just quoted, we do often (if 'loosely') refer to the prescriptive contents of discrete legal provisions – such as a section or article in a statute – as 'norms'. Think of some legislative provision stipulating, say, that whoever performs an action of some given type 'shall be punished' in some given manner: we would naturally speak of *the* corresponding 'sanction norm'. Consider, then (to work with Kelsen's theft example), the following formulation:

> (T) Whoever dishonestly appropriates property belonging to another with the intention of permanently depriving the other of it ought to be punished [with sanction *S*].

In effect, Kelsen, too, would employ the term 'norm' to refer to the contents of such provisions, or indeed to refer to the content of constitutional provisions such as those empowering certain agents as legislators and laying down law-making procedures. So his point is not that the term 'norm' is not aptly used in connection with such provisions.[32] His point seems rather to be that no such legislative or constitutional norms – and thus no norm like (T) – would count as a 'complete' norm, in a particular reading of the adjective.

But what reading is that? There is clearly more than one sense in which a formulation like (T) may be said to be 'complete' or 'incomplete'. There is, for one, an elementary sense in which (T) is complete: it is a well-formed, autonomous unit of meaning. As we saw, however, Kelsen's complete norm purports to be 'complete' in a different sense. Kelsen's 'complete' norm is the norm whose antecedent includes the *total set* of elements (or at any rate *one* such total set, if there happens to be more than one set of elements whose ascertainment suffices to trigger the consequence) on which the normative consequent depends. And it is surely true that in order for a judge correctly to convict and sentence someone for theft it is not sufficient that the actual theft has been committed. Other conditions must obtain: that no justificatory or exculpatory circumstances emerge, for example; that the act-type of theft has in fact been validly defined by law as a criminal offence; that the particular

[32] In several of the passages quoted above, in fact, Kelsen uses the term 'norm' in this very sense: he refers eg to the '*norm* of the constitution' which 'determines a condition to which the sanction is attached' (*cf* the passage quoted to n 22, now with my emphasis) or to the 'general *norm*', issued by the legislature, 'according to which a thief is to be punished in a certain way' (*cf* the passage quoted to n 23, now with my emphasis).

court has jurisdiction to try the case; and so on. I wish to suggest, however, that to frame the issue of norm-completeness in this way is to propitiate confusion. Let me introduce the following distinction.

Keeping with Kelsen's theft example, formulation (T), which, to repeat, I am taking as a reconstruction of a corresponding section or article in some statute or criminal code (and which is at any rate 'complete' in the first, elementary sense mentioned in the previous paragraph) can usefully be said to be *in*complete in (at least) two (other) relevant senses. At this preliminary stage of the discussion I offer only semi-ostensive characterisations.[33] Thus: (a) in a certain sense of the 'complete'/'incomplete' distinction, the formulation in (T) is incomplete because there are cases in which someone who steals ought *not* to be punished: for example when the agent has a valid justification or excuse; and (b) in another sense of the adjectives, the formulation in (T) is incomplete because for someone to be convicted of, and punished for, theft it is also necessary, for example, that the statutory provision criminalising theft has been validly issued by a legally authorised law-making organ. More precisely, then:

(*A*) In sense *A*, (T) is incomplete because it fails to incorporate (as either positive or negative conditions[34]) the circumstances under which whoever steals *ought not* to be punished (circumstances which *in our example* would mainly be the available defences).

(*B*) In sense *B*, (T) is incomplete because it fails to incorporate the circumstances that regard the valid production (eg issuance by the authorised organ) of the legal source-material (which would *in our example* be the statutory provision or article making theft a criminal offence) whose content is reconstructed in (T).

Kelsen's notion of norm-completeness assumes that this distinction tracks no relevant difference. And in fact it was only with reference to a given norm-formulation – it was only with reference to formulation (T) – that I was able to distinguish between senses (*A*) and (*B*). Kelsen, in contrast, frames the issue relative to a given normative *consequence* (which is, in his example, the criminal conviction for theft). He therefore treats as equivalent all the 'conditions' on which that consequent can be said to depend, and accepts as 'complete' only the antecedent in which all such conditions are incorporated. What I will now argue is that there is indeed a fundamental difference between (*A*) and (*B*), and moreover that the notion of completeness-(*B*) is devoid of theoretical usefulness.

[33] More rigorous definitions will be given in section V.

[34] I now gloss over the debate about how, exactly, the absence of defences (and of exceptions more generally) is to be represented in our formulations of conditional legal norms. On this issue see my 'A Proof-Based Account of Exceptions' (2013) 33 *Oxford Journal of Legal Studies* 133.

III. NORM-'LEVELS' AND THE DESCRIPTION OF LAW

In our theft example – and it is important to stress that my discussion will be carried out in view of this example – the problem of completeness-(*B*) concerns the possibility of incorporating into the antecedent of (T), as further conditions, the circumstances of the valid issuance of those provisions on whose contents (T)'s consequent can be said (in some sense) to 'depend'. The problem thus regards, more generally, the relation between power-conferring norms (or 'norms of competence', as they are also sometimes called) and the norms, particularly the duty-imposing norms of conduct, issued by the competent authorities.[35]

It is not fully clear what claim or claims should be attributed to Kelsen on this classic jurisprudential topic. On this matter there seems to be no single, unitary thesis consistently endorsed by him at any given point of his career, let alone across time. But let me continue to focus on the second edition of the *Pure Theory*, where it is safe to say that the notion of 'competence' (or 'authorisation'), in what Kelsen calls the 'narrowest' sense of the term,[36] is very closely connected to the notion of a duty. This is not a specifically legal connection. Kelsen illustrates what he dubs the 'dynamic type' of normative system – the type of system, that is, the validity of whose norms ultimately depends on 'nothing but . . . the authorization of a norm-creating authority'[37] – with the following example:

> A father orders his child to go to school. The child answers: Why? The reply may be: Because the father has so ordered and the child ought to obey the father. If the child continues to ask: Why ought I to obey the father, the answer may be: Because God has commanded 'Obey Your Parents', and one ought to obey the commands of God.[38]

Similar examples are given for the case of law. They are meant to illustrate the thesis that a legal norm is valid not 'because it has a certain content', but 'because it is created in a certain way': because it has been created, 'posited', by an authorised law-making agent.[39] Kelsen also maintains (because of his much-criticised conflation of two notions of 'validity': systemic membership and binding force) that to say that a norm is valid 'means that it is binding –

[35] Here, again, the term 'norm' is employed in its ordinary sense, not in the sense of Kelsen's 'complete' norm: recall n 32.

[36] In its 'strict sense', the term 'competence' designates the power to create legal norms; in a wider sense it also encompasses powers to perform acts other than acts of norm-creation: *cf* eg *The Pure Theory of Law* (n 1) 57, 147, 149. There are finer distinctions to be drawn, but they need not detain us here: see E Bulygin 'On Norms of Competence' (1992) 11 *Law and Philosophy* 202f.

[37] *The Pure Theory of Law* (n 1) 196.

[38] ibid.

[39] see ibid 198ff.

that an individual ought to behave in the manner determined by the norm'.[40] It seems, then, that Kelsen would have endorsed one particular version of the claim that power-conferring norms can be 'reduced' to duty-imposing norms: the version according to which the attribution of norm-creating power to an organ *A* is tantamount to a prescription, addressed at subject *B*, to do as *A* requires.[41] In the simplest case – the case in which norm-creating power is attributed to *A* with no restriction as to the possible content of the norms that *A* may choose to issue – the prescriptive norm of conduct to which the attribution of power is (according to this view) reducible can be formulated as:

(1) One ought to do as *A* requires.

In order for it to be the case that someone ought, on the grounds of (1), to perform some given action, it is necessary that *A*, the power-holder, does happen to exercise her power by issuing (by 'positing', as Kelsen would put it) some determinate prescription. In this regard, (1) is an indeterminate prescription, and *A* might be said to hold the power to determine its content – and thereby to bring about changes to the legal positions of those to whom (1) may happen to be addressed.[42] Let us then assume that *A* prescribes that everyone pay 40 per cent tax on professional income. In that case, the norm

(2) One ought to pay 40 per cent tax on professional income

is 'valid', in Kelsen's sense, for it was issued by an authorised (a 'competent') agent. But (1) and (2) are two different norms. If (1) is valid, then the corresponding normative proposition – the proposition that *one ought to do as A*

[40] ibid 193. For discussion, see A Ross, 'Validity and the Conflict Between Legal Positivism and Natural Law' (1961) *Revista Jurídica de Buenos Aires* 46ff; MP Golding, 'Kelsen and the Concept of "Legal System"' (1961) 47 *Archiv für Rechts- und Sozialphilosophie* 368ff; CS Nino, 'Some Confusions Around Kelsen's Concept of Validity' (1978) 64 *Archiv für Rechts- und Sozialphilosophie* 357ff; E Bulygin, 'An Antinomy in Kelsen's Pure Theory of Law' (1990) 3 *Ratio Juris* 29ff. Ross's, part of Nino's, and Bulygin's articles are reproduced, with minor revisions, in SL Paulson and BL Paulson (eds), *Normativity and Norms. Critical Perspectives on Kelsenian Themes* (Oxford, Clarendon Press, 1998) at 147ff, 253ff and 297ff, respectively.

[41] See Bulygin, 'On Norms of Competence' (n 36) 204; and J Ferrer Beltrán, *Las Normas de Competencia. Un Aspecto de la Dinámica Jurídica* (Madrid, Centro de Estudios Políticos y Constitucionales, 2000) 29ff. The ascription of this particular reductionist view to Kelsen is further supported by the fact that the basic norm, whose function is to authorise (ie to empower) the creators of the historically first constitution (see *The Pure Theory of Law* (n 1) eg at 197, 202ff), can also be formulated, according to Kelsen, as 'One ought to behave as the [historically first] constitution prescribes' (ibid eg at 8, 46, 201). Compare in any case Kelsen's very clear assertion, in a 1963 essay on the self-determination of law, that 'in empowering an individual to issue norms commanding other individuals to behave in certain ways, law commands these individuals to comply with the norms issued by the empowered individual': H Kelsen, 'Die Selbsbestimmung des Rechts' in H Klecatsky, R Marcic and H Schambeck, *Die Wiener Rechtstheoretische Schule* (Vienna, Europa Verlag, 1968 [1963]) 1446 (my translation); and also *General Theory of Norms* (n 6) 103f.

[42] See L Lindahl, *Position and Change. A Study in Law and Logic* (Dordrecht, Reidel, 1977) 193ff; T Spaak, *The Concept of Legal Competence. An Essay in Conceptual Analysis* (Aldershot, Dartmouth, 1994) 102ff, 171ff.

requires – is true whether or not *A* has in fact ever exercised her competence. But the proposition that *one ought to pay 40 per cent tax on professional income* is true (in our example) only if and when the power-holder has indeed issued the norm indicated as (2).

Kelsen would say here that *A*'s act of prescribing that everyone pay 40 per cent tax on professional income is a norm-'creating' act – it 'creates' the norm in (2) – and thus that (1) is a 'higher' norm than (2).[43] We may express this point in a different way. Always assuming that *A*'s norm-creating power is not substantively restricted, (1) entails, say, that

> (3) If *A* requires everyone to pay 40 per cent tax on professional income, then one ought to pay 40 per cent tax on professional income.

But (3) is but an instance of the following conditional reformulation of (1):

> (1′) If *A* requires *X* to φ, then *X* ought to φ,

in which 'φ' is a placeholder for any type of action (be it the payment of the mentioned 40 per cent tax, or any other type of action whatsoever), and '*X*' stands for the addressee(s) of *A*'s prescriptions. So we can derive (3) from (1) with no need for further premises. In fact we can immediately derive from (1) an infinite number of formulations like (3). But the same is not true of (2), which does not straightforwardly follow from (1). In order to get (2) it is also necessary that *A* does in fact prescribe the payment of 40 per cent tax on professional income (rather than some other action). For the 'existence' of the norm in (2) – in the sense in which Kelsen speaks of a norm's 'existence'[44] – is dependent on the exercise by *A* of her norm-creating power. Only then will the normative proposition that *one ought to pay 40 per cent tax on professional income* be true. But (1) remains a valid norm; and even after (2) has been validly created, the normative proposition will of course remain true that *one ought to do as A requires.*[45]

[43] *The Pure Theory of Law* (n 1) 221: 'The relationship between the norm that regulates the creation of another norm and the norm created in conformity with the former can be metaphorically presented as a relationship of super- and subordination. The norm which regulates the creation of another norm is the higher, the norm created in conformity with the former is the lower one'.

[44] See n 7.

[45] In our example, the exercise by *A* of her norm-creating power simultaneously amounts, as I noted (*cf* text to n 42), to a determination of the content of her subjects' duty. But there is a distinction to be drawn between levels of norm-creation and degrees of content-determinacy. If, modifying the example, we now suppose that instead of prescribing the payment of 40% tax on professional income, *A* prescribes (thereby 'delegating' her power) that one does as *C* requires, then the norm

> (2′) One ought to do as *C* requires

will also be 'valid', because, again, it will have been issued by an authorised agent. Thus everything said in the text with regard to (2) would also hold true of (2′). (2′) is 'created' by *A* in the same sense in which, in our first example, (2) had been; and (1) is a 'higher' norm than (2′) in the same sense in which it was a 'higher' norm than (2). In what concerns the determination of

With these examples in mind, we may now return to the notion of completeness-(*B*) introduced in the previous section. For clarity, let us adapt our formulations to Kelsen's theft example. We shall thus have, say, as an example of the same type as (1),

> (1K) One ought to do as Parliament requires,

which is to be taken – as was (1), mutatis mutandis – as the formulation of a partially indeterminate norm of conduct equivalent to the attribution of norm-creating power to Parliament. Assuming, then, that Parliament validly issues a provision stipulating that 'Whoever dishonestly appropriates property belonging to another with the intention of permanently depriving the other of it shall be imprisoned for up to three years', the corresponding norm – paralleling (2) – might be formulated as

> (2K) Whoever dishonestly appropriates property belonging to another with the intention of permanently depriving the other of it ought to be imprisoned for up to three years,

or, in a more explicitly conditional rendition, as

> (2K′) If someone dishonestly appropriates property belonging to another with the intention of permanently depriving the other of it, he or she ought to be imprisoned for up to three years.

Kelsen's claim here would be, as we have seen, that a formulation like (2K) is not 'complete' because it omits any reference to the exercise by Parliament of the corresponding norm-creating power. The complete formulation, according to Kelsen, would read instead as follows:

> (3K) If Parliament prescribes that whoever dishonestly appropriates property belonging to another with the intention of permanently depriving the other of it shall be imprisoned for up to three years, then whoever dishonestly appropriates property belonging to another with the intention of permanently depriving the other of it ought to be imprisoned for up to three years.

We also saw that Kelsen holds that legal propositions – truth-apt descriptions of the law – are true just in case the corresponding norms 'exist'. Yet the truth of (3K) depends only on the truth of (1K), for (3K) and (1K) are related in precisely the same way as (3) and (1). It would be possible to substitute any other contents whatsoever for the references in (3K) to the action of theft and to the consequence of imprisonment for up to three years. Thus (3K) would *not* amount to a description of the law on theft in any given legal system. (3K) would be true even if (2K) were false: even if, that is, Parliament had *not* made

the types of action which anyone ought to perform on the grounds of (1), however, (2′) is – differently from (2) – just as indeterminate as (1). A difference in 'level' does not necessarily map onto a difference in content-determinacy.

theft a punishable criminal offence, and the corresponding norm had never come to be valid.

To be clear, propositions (1K) or (3K) *are* truth-apt legal propositions in Kelsen's sense. Their truth, relative to some given legal system *S*, depends on its being the case that Parliament – rather than some other agent, or indeed none at all – is indeed the organ authorised, in *S*, to legislate on criminal subjects (which is a contingent matter of positive law). And (2K), too, is a truth-apt legal proposition; its truth depends on its being the case that Parliament has indeed issued the corresponding norm making theft a criminal offence. So it may well be that (3K) and (2K) are *both* true relative to the same legal system. But they are set at different 'levels', and both are needed in a complete description of the corresponding legal system.

Interestingly, Kelsen seems to have had an inkling of this problem. He states at one point that his 'complete' propositions of law are meant to describe only what he calls 'general' norms. But 'individual' norms, as created by judicial decisions or administrative acts, cannot, he tells us, be similarly described:

> The proposition of law ('*Rechtssatz*') that presents itself as a legal law ('*Rechtsgesetz*'[46]) has a general character, like the law of nature ('*Naturgesetz*'), which means that the legal law *describes the general norms* of the legal order and the relationships constituted by these norms. The individual legal norms, created by judicial decision or administrative acts, are described by the science of law as a concrete experiment is described by natural science referring to the law of nature that manifests itself in the experiment. A textbook in physics might, for example, contain the words: 'Since, according to a law of nature, a metallic body expands when heated, the metallic sphere that physicist *X* dropped before heating through a wooden ring, did not pass through it after heating'. Or a text on German criminal law might say: 'According to a legal law to be formulated with reference to German law, an individual who committed theft ought to be punished by a court by imprisonment; therefore the Court *X* in *Y*, having determined that *A* committed theft, has decided that *A* ought to be forcibly confined in prison *Z* for one year'. By saying that '*A* having committed a certain theft ought to be forcibly confined in prison *Z* for one year' the individual norm is described which Court *X* in *Y* has enacted.[47]

Though the example is slightly misconstrued, the passage reads clearly enough as an application of Kelsen's 'dynamic' account of the 'foundation of the validity of a positive norm' in terms of a syllogism in which both the major premise and the conclusion are normative propositions, and the minor premise is a non-normative proposition asserting the instantiation of the antecedent of the major premise:

> [t]he major premise is the assertion about a norm regarded as objectively valid, according to which one ought to obey the commands of a certain person, that is,

[46] See n 20.

[47] *The Pure Theory of Law* (n 1) 80 (my emphasis).

> one ought to behave according to the subjective meaning of these commands; the minor premise is the assertion of the fact that this person has commanded to behave in a certain way; and the conclusion is the assertion of the validity of the norm: one ought to behave in this particular way.[48]

We already know that Kelsen 'figuratively' refers to the norm described in the major premise as 'higher' than the one asserted in the conclusion.[49] A legal system, he says, 'is not a system of coordinated norms of equal level, but a hierarchy of different levels of legal norms'.[50] A change in 'level' is therefore dependent on the verification of certain facts – which are said (also figuratively) to 'create' the lower-level norms. Evidently 'the major premise and the minor premise are both conditions of the conclusion'; but Kelsen stresses that the '*is*-statement' in the syllogism's minor premise is indeed an 'essential link'.[51] Without the corresponding fact or facts, the respective lower-level norms are not created, not 'posited' – they do not come into 'existence' – and cannot therefore be truthfully 'described' in normative propositions. And *this* is what Kelsen appears to be acknowledging in the lengthy passage quoted above:[52] that given that the 'existence' of the individual norm is dependent on the verification of the fact that instantiates the antecedent of the general norm, that individual norm can be described only (for it comes into existence only) if and when such a fact can be said to have occurred. For what the proposition describing the individual norm asserts is not that thieves (in general) ought to be punished in a given way. What the proposition describing the individual norm asserts is that *some individual agent* ought to be punished in a given way. The individual norm is 'lower' than the general one, and the proposition describing the former cannot be incorporated in the proposition describing the latter; for the 'higher' proposition is true independently of the verification of any individual theft.

But then it is also the case (is it not?) that this differentiation of 'levels' of normative propositions does not yield only *these* two strands (the 'general' and the 'individual'). In effect, the norms that Kelsen calls 'general' do not all belong to the same 'level'. They are rather distributed by many 'levels': by as many levels, indeed, as those into which any given legal system may be plausibly divided (which is again, of course, a contingent feature of the particular legal system in question). Kelsen identifies three main strata in what he calls the 'normal situation'[53] of a legal system: (a) the constitution (in the 'material sense'), understood as the 'positive norm or norms which regulate the creation

[48] ibid 202.
[49] *cf* ibid 193, and see n 43.
[50] ibid 221.
[51] ibid 194.
[52] To n 47.
[53] ibid 224.

of general legal norms';[54] (b) the 'next step down in the hierarchy', integrated by the 'general norms created by legislation or custom'[55] which have the complex function of determining the 'content' of individual norms, the organs authorised to create them and 'the procedure to be observed by them';[56] and (c) the level of the individual norms produced by judicial or administrative organs.[57]

Stated in this order, these levels are progressively less 'abstract'; the process of law-creation, Kelsen says, 'is a process of increasing individualization and concretization':

> Contemplated from the point of view of the dynamics of the law, the creation of individual norms by the courts represents a transitional stage of the process that begins with the establishment of the constitution, continues via legislation or custom to the judicial decision, and leads to the execution of the sanction. This process, in which the law keeps renewing itself, as it were, proceeds from the general (abstract) to the individual (concrete); it is a process of increasing individualization and concretization.[58]

In this case, however, it is also not possible to describe the norms placed at *each* of the supra-'individual' levels except in the very same way by which, according to Kelsen, individual judicial norms are to be described. If there are different levels of norms, there are different levels of normative propositions; and there must be, for each level of norms, the corresponding level of propositions.

Therefore, though Kelsen rightly notices (if I read him correctly) that no single legal proposition can simultaneously take up material from the 'general' and from the 'individual' levels, he fails to see that this very argument has application within the very domain of 'general' law. For this domain is itself divided into more than one 'level' of norms. Differently from what Kelsen claims in the quotation with which this chapter began, then, it is not possible to describe the *whole* of general law by means of his supposedly 'complete' propositions, which are meant to incorporate 'material' from at least two norm-levels (the constitution, and ordinary legislation). The point is not that it is not possible to reconstruct *true* 'complete' Kelsenian legal propositions[59] from the legal materials of any given legal system. It is. (Many such propositions, if not all, will be made true, as Joseph Raz remarks, on the grounds of

[54] ibid 222.
[55] ibid 224.
[56] ibid 230.
[57] ibid 233ff; further specificities are irrelevant for our present purposes.
[58] ibid 237.
[59] Like the one in the passage quoted to n 23.

constitutional law alone.[60]) The point is rather that it is not possible to describe the *whole* of positive law with just those propositions.

IV. MISUNDERSTANDING MERKL?

As an aside, and although my goals in this chapter are not primarily exegetical, I would like to put forth a tentative conjecture regarding the origin of this flaw in Kelsen's theory.

It was only in the 1920s that Kelsen became concerned with legal 'dynamics', that is, with theorising the process by which law is created and applied. His programme in the 1911 *Hauptprobleme* was restricted, as he acknowledged 12 years later, to the issue of '*static* legal cognition'.[61] Kelsen's 'dynamic turn', as Stanley Paulson has called it,[62] was incited by the work of Adolf Julius Merkl – the ground-breaking theorist to whom the '*Stufenbau*' doctrine, the doctrine of the hierarchical structure of the legal system, is entirely owed. Kelsen himself explicitly notes that

> it is Adolf Julius Merkl who deserves the credit for recognizing and then characterizing the legal system as a *genetic* system of legal norms that proceed from one level of concretization to another, from the constitution to the statute to the administrative regulation and to other intermediate levels, right down to the individual act of enforcement. In a number of writings, Merkl energetically put forward this *theory of hierarchical levels of the law* qua theory of *legal dynamics*, combatting the prejudice – still

[60] *cf* Raz, *The Concept of a Legal System* (n 31) 118; see also Robert Walter's criticism in *Der Aufbau der Rechtsordnung. Eine rechtstheoretische Untersuchung auf Grundlage der Reinen Rechtslehre*, 2nd edn (Vienna, Manz, 1974 [1964]) 26f; and J Ferrer Beltrán, *Las Normas de Competencia* (n 41) 24ff. In *La Teoria del Diritto di Hans Kelsen. Una Introduzione Critica* (Bologna, Il Mulino, 1999) 359ff, Bruno Celano offers a different reading of Kelsen's proposal to recast power-conferring norms as 'fragments' of complete norms. In our theft example, the antecedent of the complete norm, in Celano's reconstruction, would embed not only the proposition that Parliament *has* prescribed that thieves be sentenced for up to three years, but also the proposition asserting that Parliament is indeed authorised to do so; the antecedent of the complete norm, in other words, would embed, as a clause, the proposition describing the very norm attributing norm-creating power to Parliament. Thus the Kelsenian norm in its 'canonical form' should be formulated, Celano would suggest, along the following lines: 'If ((if Parliament requires *X* to φ, then *X* ought to φ) & (Parliament requires courts to sentence whoever commits theft to up to 3 years' imprisonment) & *P* has committed theft), then courts ought to sentence *P* to up to 3 years' imprisonment'. But this reading (irrespective of whether it aptly reconstructs Kelsen's views, which I doubt) not only does not avoid the problem discussed in the present chapter, but indeed exacerbates it – for the corresponding legal proposition would now *always* be true: it would be true, that is, relative to any legal system whatsoever, and whatever the content of the law might be.

[61] *cf* Kelsen, '"Foreword" to the Second Printing of *Main Problems in the Theory of Public Law*', SL Paulson and BL Paulson transl, in *Normativity and Norms* (n 40) 11, my emphasis. For an account of Kelsen's 'constructivist' programme in the *Hauptprobleme* and up to 1920, see SL Paulson 'Hans Kelsen's Earliest Legal Theory: Critical Constructivism' (1996) 59 *Modern Law Review* 797ff.

[62] *cf* SL Paulson, 'On the Implications of Kelsen's Doctrine of Hierarchical Structure' (1996) 18 *The Liverpool Law Review* 50ff.

> firmly held in my *Main Problems* – that the law is found only in the general statute. . . . Drawing support from the work of Merkl . . . I took up the theory of hierarchical levels in my own later writings, adopting it as an essential component in the system of the Pure Theory of Law.[63]

Paulson says that Merkl's doctrine of hierarchical structure was adopted by Kelsen 'lock, stock, and barrel'.[64] I am not so sure. As Paulson observes, it is in Merkl's work that we find the first occurrences of what came to be called the 'complete' legal norm in the sense in which Kelsen, as we have seen, uses the term. Here is how Merkl articulates what Paulson calls 'the best approximation of a so-called complete legal norm'[65] (even though 'complete legal norm' is not a term that Merkl uses in connection with this example); I quote Paulson's own translation:

> [a] If an organ, authorized by federal constitutional statute to initiate legislation, has introduced a bill in the National Assembly (*Nationalrat*) to the effect that the seller of certain wares is to pay a tax on sales amounting to a certain percentage of the proceeds from the sale, and, further, [b] if the National Assembly, first in committee and then in plenary session, in the procedure specifically prescribed by parliamentary rules of order, has passed a bill to this effect, and, further, [c] if this legislation has been submitted to the Federal Assembly (*Bundesrat*), which either raised no objection within a period of eight weeks or decided before this deadline to raise no objection, and, further, [d] if the Federal President has signed this legislation, and the Federal Chancellor as well as the Federal Minister for Finance have countersigned the presidential signature, and, further, [e] if the Federal Chancellor has published the signed and countersigned legislation in the Federal Statute Book, and, further, [f] if, after the effective date of this legislation, the tax official designated in the statute, [following] a certain procedure, has [determined the tax] of a particular individual and prescribed its payment, and, finally, [g] if this particular individual does not pay the prescribed amount within the prescribed time, then the penalty for tax offence ought to be imposed on him.[66]

This complex formulation – which regards the goods sales tax in Austrian law at the time – is meant to display the way in which different acts by various organs relate to one another in a 'chain-like series'.[67] It does look similar in

[63] *cf* '"Foreword" to the Second Printing of *Main Problems in the Theory of Public Law*' (n 40) 13f.

[64] See eg SL Paulson, 'On the Implications of Kelsen's Doctrine of Hierarchical Structure' (n 62) 49; 'Four Phases in Hans Kelsen's Legal Theory? Reflections on a Periodization' (1998) 18 *Oxford Journal of Legal Studies* 164; or his 'Introduction' to *Normativity and Norms* (n 40) xxv.

[65] See eg Paulson, 'On the Implications of Kelsen's Doctrine of Hierarchical Structure' (n 62) 56 fn 26.

[66] ibid 59; the original passage is in AJ Merkl, 'Prolegomena einer Theorie des rechtlichen Stufenbaus' (1931) in *Die Wiener Rechtstheoretische Schule* (n 41) 1337; the letters within square brackets are Paulson's own interpolations.

[67] Merkl speaks of a '*kettenförmige Aktreihe*': see 'Prolegomena einer Theorie des rechtlichen Stufenbaus' (n 66) 1337.

structure to Kelsen's own examples of 'complete' legal norms,[68] only more carefully phrased. But Merkl makes a series of important remarks in connection with this series of acts. He stresses, first, that only *some* of the links in the 'chain' – viz. only those acts that require some given action under the threat of legal punishment – can be interpreted as 'legal norms'.[69] These 'normative acts' find themselves included in a series of other acts which, though they cannot be similarly interpreted, are nonetheless necessary links in the multi-staged process by which law is created and applied.

Note that in denying that all the acts in the series have the meaning of legal norms, Merkl is simply using – as he informs us[70] – *Kelsen's* notion of a legal norm *qua* 'hypothetical judgement' about the state's will with respect to a punitive legal consequence. This is Kelsen's early articulation of the notion, as developed in the *Hauptprobleme*. It is therefore a 'static' notion, not a 'dynamic' one. But then if one wishes to refer to Merkl's 'chain-like series' of acts by calling it a 'complete norm', one will be using 'norm' in a different sense. Merkl's series does not purport to represent the structure of whatever 'static' legal norms may be reconstructed, from any given set of validly produced legal materials, at any given moment. Merkl's series purports instead to reconstruct and model the dynamic process of law-production and law-application. Indeed, Merkl explicitly remarks that if one is concerned with the (static) reconstruction of the law as a system of norms rather than with the (dynamic) process by which the law is created, then the *only* links in the chain that are to be considered are those that can be understood as legal norms:

> For the dynamic consideration, the introduction of the bill in the *legislative* collegial body, for example, is just as important as the publication of the legislation in the Statute Book; the opening of the judicial proceeding by calling the parties and the witnesses is an essentially complete act as much as the publication of the judicial decision; all these partial acts are equivalent. The static consideration, on the contrary, introduces a break in the continuous course of the legal process, brings one partial act to the fore, and converts all the preceding procedural links into similarly ordered pre-requisites of this act.[71]

This sounds exactly right. If one wishes to know, say, what the law on theft is in a given legal system at some given moment, one will not be at all concerned with the *structure* of the legal process – one will be concerned with the *results* of this process.[72] The 'static' inquiry is an inquiry into the normative contents of validly created materials, not an inquiry into the process by which such materials came to be validly created.

[68] Like the one in the passage quoted to n 23.

[69] Merkl, 'Prolegomena einer Theorie des rechtlichen Stufenbaus' (n 66) 1337.

[70] ibid 1325.

[71] ibid 1338 (my translation; Merkl's italics).

[72] Merkl's expression is '*Verfahrensergebnisse*': the 'results of the process'; see ibid 1338.

Now, the view that all the 'legally relevant' results of the legal process can be reconstructed (as parts of either the antecedent or the consequent) in the form of sanction-stipulating norms is a claim about the 'static' reconstruction of law.[73] The set of materials which forms the basis of such reconstructions will be the result of validly performed acts of law-creation. It follows that any reference *to* the occurrence of those facts of law-creation *in* the antecedents of the reconstructed legal norms is quite simply out of place.[74] And this, as we have learned in section III, was the very point that Kelsen got wrong. If I understand him correctly, though, Merkl not only avoids this mistake, but anticipates and explicitly denounces it. It amounts to a misconstruction of the doctrine of hierarchical structure and of the difference between the 'dynamic' and the 'static' points of view.

We have here, then, an important aspect of Merkl's doctrine that Kelsen seems either to overlook or plainly to misunderstand. Whereas Merkl's 'complete' chain-like series of law-creating acts – the 'complete' model of the legal process, from top to bottom – is clearly presented as a matter of legal dynamics, Kelsen seems to want to graft his idea of a 'complete' norm onto legal statics.

It is true that there are some passages in Kelsen's works in which he seems to be in line with Merkl. Thus he rightly affirms that

> [i]f we adopt a static point of view, that is, if we consider the legal order only in its completed form or in a state of rest, then we notice only the norms by which the legal acts are determined. If, on the other hand, we adopt a dynamic outlook, if we consider the process through which the legal order is created and executed, then we see only the law-creating and law-executing acts.[75]

Kelsen also appears to acknowledge that his views on the possibility of reconstructing the entire content of the law in the form of coercive norms are views that he is putting forth as a matter of legal 'statics':

> If one looks upon the legal order from the dynamic point of view . . . it seems possible to define the concept of law in a way quite different from that in which we have tried to define it in this theory. It seems especially possible to ignore the element of coercion in defining the concept of law. . . . According to this [dynamic] concept, law is anything that has come about in the way the constitution prescribes

[73] Recall the remarks on Kelsen's reference to 'all legally relevant material' in the passage quoted to n 1; we find the same idea in Merkl's 'Prolegomena einer Theorie des rechtlichen Stufenbaus' (n 66) 1330.

[74] Not that there is no room to ask what would count as a *complete* 'static' norm. After all Merkl explicitly observes (as does Kelsen, as we have seen: *cf* eg the passage quoted to n 13) that we will often have to articulate the contents of different provisions in order properly to reconstruct legal norms. And in fact Merkl does literally speak of 'complete' (*'vollständige'*) norms *in this sense*: see ibid 1333. But these are not Kelsen's 'complete' norms. Merkl's static 'complete norms' are not meant to incorporate, as elements or conditions in their antecedents, the higher-level facts of law-creation.

[75] *General Theory of Law and State* (n 1) 39.

> for the creation of law. This dynamic concept differs from the concept of law defined as a coercive norm. According to the dynamic concept, law is something created by a certain process, and everything created in this way is law. This dynamic concept, however, is only apparently a concept of law. It contains no answer to the question of what is the essence of law, what is the criterion by which law can be distinguished from other social norms. This dynamic concept furnishes an answer only to the question whether or not and why a certain norm belongs to a system of valid legal norms, forms part of a certain legal order.[76]

Yet he simultaneously (and, to my mind, inconsistently) says the following. Having pointed out (correctly) that 'the court has to answer not only the *quaestio facti* but also the *quaestio juris*', and that it has 'in particular to examine whether the general norm it intends to apply is really valid', that is, 'whether it has been created in the way prescribed by the constitution',[77] Kelsen goes on to assert that

> [t]he norms of the constitution *which regulate the creation of the general norms to be applied by the courts are* . . . not independent complete norms. They are *intrinsic parts of all the norms which the courts and other organs have to apply*. . . . What, from a dynamic point of view, is the creation of a general norm determined by a higher norm, the constitution, becomes in a static presentation of law one of the conditions to which the sanction is attached as a consequence in the general norm (which, from the dynamic point of view, is the lower norm in relation to the constitution). In a static presentation of law, the higher norms of the constitution are, as it were, projected as parts into the lower norms.[78]

This passage encapsulates Kelsen's mistake. The italicised sentences alone illustrate his inconsistency. It is precisely because constitutional norms regulate the *creation* of the general norms to be applied by the courts that *these* norms cannot have *those* norms as their 'parts'.[79]

V. RESULTS

Let me now generalise the point made in section III. My remarks so far have been made with Kelsen's (and Merkl's) own 'hierarchical structure' in mind. But we are certainly not bound to reconstruct norms according to the specific normative levels described in the *Pure Theory of Law*. It is perfectly possible (and

[76] ibid 122.
[77] ibid 143.
[78] ibid 143f (my emphasis).
[79] See also R Walter's *Der Aufbau der Rechtsordnung* (n 60) for a very useful discussion of the ambiguity of the term 'norm' as used by Kelsen throughout his works. Walter distinguishes (among others) a 'dynamic' and a 'static' sense of a norm (ibid 16ff), and points out that the only consistent way of reconstructing Kelsen's idea of the 'complete' legal norm is to understand it as a 'dynamic' rather than a 'static' norm (18, 26f). See, in this regard, n 32.

by no means unusual), for example, that in order to identify the law on any given matter and reconstruct the corresponding legal norm (or norms) one has to read together several different provisions variously issued by authorities placed at different levels in the Kelsenian structure. Yet any such legal norm – as well as the corresponding legal proposition – will also itself define a 'level', in the exact same sense in which, in Kelsen's structure, a 'legislative' norm defines a distinct 'level' from the constitutional or the judicial ones.

Any conditional norm *N*, to put it more precisely, defines (a) a level 'higher' than that of the norm *N-minus-1* which is (or would be) created by the verification of any one of the facts that feature as elements in the antecedent of *N*; and (b) a level 'lower' than that of the norm *N-plus-1* which may be reconstructed by incorporating, as conditions of *its* antecedent, the set of facts on whose verification the 'existence' of *N* depends.

The facts in either group – the facts 'above' and the facts 'below' any given norm *N*, to keep with Kelsen's metaphor – may be facts of any sort. They may be intentional acts by which some authorised agent or organ issues or posits some provision or section of the legal materials. But they may also be facts of any other kind which happen to instantiate any one of the elements featured in the antecedent of any given conditional norm. Seen from this perspective, in other words, the acts of norm-issuance performed by the competent authorities are equivalent to any other acts, and even to any other events more generally. All are equally well-placed to 'create' or 'posit' norms.

Kelsen does propose to expand the notion of authorisation – understood, he says, 'in the broadest sense' – to include an individual's 'capacity of committing a delict'. He refuses, however, to extend the notion even further, so as to encompass events other than facts of 'human behaviour'.[80] I do not mean to question the linguistic propriety of this restriction. Nor do I mean to suggest, more generally, that there is no good reason, in many contexts, jurisprudential as well as practical, to emphasise the usual division between, on the one hand, the facts whose occurrence gives rise to an expansion and/or a contraction of the set of valid legal materials (and thus to a change in the so-called 'general' law), and, on the other hand, the facts of the 'cases' to which general law is said to 'apply'. My point is merely that from the point of view of the role of facts in the norm-creation process there is no reason to draw such a line. And of course in contexts in which one's concern is with the reconstruction of such 'general' norms, then while one may simply assume that the relevant facts of the first kind (those facts, whatever they may happen to be, on which the valid production of the legal materials depends) have duly occurred, the successful reconstruction of any given norm will have to specify, in the antecedent, *all* the facts of the 'case' to which the consequent is attached. This

[80] *cf The Pure Theory of Law* (n 1) 146.

is the only relevant sense in which the norm can be said to be 'complete': the antecedent specifies a sufficient condition of the consequent.

We may now return to the example, introduced in section II, with which our discussion began: the example of a candidate 'sanction norm' (T), corresponding to a statutory provision making theft a punishable offence. Here it is again:

> (T) Whoever dishonestly appropriates property belonging to another with the intention of permanently depriving the other of it ought to be punished [with sanction *S*].

If indeed we are concerned, as Kelsen says, with accurately reconstructing and stating the general law on theft on the basis of the set of valid legal 'materials' at any given moment, then it is true that (T) may (and typically would) be *incomplete* in the sense just mentioned. For there may be other facts or circumstances – that is, facts other than the actual commission of a theft – that pertain to the relevant 'case'. As mentioned in section II, these facts may conceivably include, for example, the absence of justificatory or exculpatory circumstances, which, if present, would mandate an acquittal.[81] As for the other facts on which the consequence in some sense 'depends' – the facts, that is, on which the valid production of the respective legal 'material' depends – they are presupposed, in the sense that they are deemed to have occurred, and could in principle be discriminately pointed out (in conjunction with further normative premises) if someone were to call into question the legal 'validity' of the reconstructed norm. But there is simply no conceptual room for embedding them as further, lower-'level' elements, in the reconstructed norm's antecedent.

More precise definitions can now be given of the two notions of completeness – completeness-(*A*) and completeness-(*B*) – introduced in section II. The distinction does not essentially concern, as I hope I have made clear, the contrast between conditions concerning norm-creating power, on the one hand, and conditions concerning the 'case'. This was merely what happened to be the case in our (or rather, Kelsen's) theft example. The distinction concerns instead the contrast between two different 'levels' of facts on which any given normative consequence may be said in some sense to 'depend'. Here, then, are the relevant definitions:

(*A*) For any norm-formulation *NF*, *NF* is *complete in sense* (*A*) if, and only if, its antecedent incorporates all the conditions on whose verification the normative consequent actually depends (as a matter of law, in some given legal system).

[81] See text to n 34.

(*B*) For any norm *N*, *N* is *complete in sense* (*B*) if, and only if, the conditions on which the (validity) of *N* depends are satisfied.

The notion of completeness-(*A*) is the notion just identified as the only relevant one. The notion of completeness-(*B*) concerns the facts on which the validity of any given norm *N* depends, and these facts are 'conditions' of the consequent of *N* only in the oblique and trivial sense that in a deductive argument the premises are 'conditions' of the conclusion. The notion of completeness-(*B*) does not speak to the question of whether the *formulation* of any given norm (or of the corresponding normative proposition) is in fact 'complete' or 'incomplete'. As a theoretical notion of normative completeness, it is useless; and, what is more, to employ these adjectives in sense (*B*) is, at best, to risk confusing the problem of normative completeness with the problem of a norm's validity conditions. So the notion of completeness-(*B*) may now be abandoned. As for completeness-(*A*), it is but the expression of the elementary idea that the joint verification of the elements represented in the antecedent of a conditional legal norm should allow the consequent to follow.

Index